AN
OPPOSING
MAN

Ernst Fischer

AN
OPPOSING
MAN

Translated by Peter and Betty Ross

With an introduction by John Berger

LIVERIGHT New York

The translators wish to thank Herr Robert Rauscher of
the Austrian Institute in London for his invaluable
assistance and advice.

This book is dedicated to Lou
as I myself am

Contents

III MOSCOW

Plates between pages 204 and 205

Introduction

A Philosopher and Death

It was the last day of his life. Of course we did not know it then – not until almost ten o'clock in the evening. Three of us spent the day with him: Lou (his wife), Anya and myself. I can write now only of my own experience of that day. If I tried to write about theirs – much as I was conscious of it at the time and later – I would nevertheless run the risk of writing fiction.

Ernst Fischer was in the habit of spending the summer in a small village in Styria. He and Lou stayed in the house of three sisters who were old friends and who had been Austrian Communists with Ernst and his two brothers in the 1930s. The youngest of the three sisters, who now runs the house, was imprisoned by the Nazis for hiding and aiding political refugees. The man with whom she was then in love was beheaded for a similar political offence.

It is necessary to describe this in order not to give a false impression of the garden which surrounds their house. The garden is full of flowers, large trees, grass banks and a lawn. A stream flows through it, conducted through a wooden pipe the diameter of an immense barrel. It runs the length of the garden, then across fields to a small dynamo which belongs to a neighbour. Everywhere in the garden there is the sound of water, gentle but persistent. There are two small fountains: tiny pin-like jets of water force their way hissing through holes in the wooden barrel-line: water flows into and empties continually from a nineteenth-century swimming pool (built by the grandfather of the three sisters): in this pool, now surrounded by tall grass, and itself green, trout swim and occasionally jump splashing to the surface.

It often rains in Styria, and if you are in this house you sometimes have the impression that it is still raining after it has stopped on account of the sound of water in the garden. Yet the garden is not damp and many colours of many flowers break up its greenness. The garden is a kind of sanctuary. But to grasp its full meaning one must, as I said, remember that in its outhouses men and women were hiding for their lives thirty years ago and were protected by the three sisters who now arrange vases of flowers and let rooms to a few old friends in the summer in order to make ends meet.

When I arrived in the morning Ernst was walking in the garden. He was thin and upright. And he trod very lightly, as though his weight, such as it was, was never fully planted on the ground. He wore a wide-brimmed white and grey hat which Lou had recently bought for him. He wore the hat like he wore all his clothes, lightly, elegantly, but without concern. He was fastidious – not about details of dress, but about the nature of appearances.

The gate to the garden was difficult to open and shut, but he had mastered it and so, as usual, he fastened it behind me. The previous day Lou had felt somewhat unwell. I inquired how she was. 'She is better,' he said, 'you have only to look at her!' He said this with youthful, unrestricted pleasure. He was seventy-three years old and when he was dying the doctor, who did not know him, said he looked older, but he had none of the muted expressions of the old. He took present pleasures at their full face-value and his capacity to do this was in no way diminished by political disappointment or by the bad news which since 1968 had persistently arrived from so many places. He was a man without a trace, without a line on his face, of bitterness. Some, I suppose, might therefore call him an innocent. They would be wrong. He was a man who refused to jettison or diminish his very high quotient of belief. Instead he readjusted its objects and their relative order. Recently he *believed* in scepticism. He even believed in the necessity of apocalyptic visions in the hope that they would act as warnings.

It is the surety and strength of his convictions which now make it seem that he died so suddenly. His health had been frail since childhood. He was often ill. Recently his eyesight had begun to fail and he could read only with a powerful magnifying glass – more often Lou read to him. Yet despite this it was quite impossible for anyone who knew him to suppose that he was dying slowly, that every year he belonged a little less vehemently to life. He was fully alive because he was fully convinced.

What was he convinced of? His books, his political interventions, his speeches are there on record to answer the question. Or do they not answer it fully enough? He was convinced that capitalism would eventually destroy man – or be overthrown. He had no illusions about the ruthlessness of the ruling class everywhere. He recognized that we lacked a model for Socialism. He was impressed by and highly interested in what is happening in China, but he did not believe in a Chinese model. What is so hard, he said, is that we are forced back to offering visions.

We walked towards the end of the garden, where there is a small lawn surrounded by bushes and a willow tree. He used to lie there talking with animated gestures, fingers plucking, hands turning out and drawing in – as though literally winding the wool from off his listeners' eyes. As he talked, his shoulders bent forward to follow his hands; as he listened, his head inclined forward to follow the speaker's words. (He knew the exact angle at which to adjust the back of his deckchair.)

Now the same lawn, the deckchairs piled in the outhouse, appears oppressively, flagrantly empty. It is far harder to walk across it without a shiver than it was to turn down the sheet and look again and again at his face. The Russian believers say that the spirits of the departed stay in their familiar surroundings for forty days. Perhaps this is based on a fairly accurate observation of the stages of mourning. At any rate it is hard for me to believe that if a total stranger wandered into the garden now, he would not notice that the end under the willow tree surrounded by bushes was flagrantly empty, like a deserted house on the point of becoming a ruin. Its emptiness is palpable. And yet it is not.

★

It had already begun to rain and so we went to sit in his room for a while before going out to lunch. We used to sit, the four of us, round a small round table, talking. Sometimes I faced the window and looked out at the trees and the forests on the hills. That morning I pointed out that when the frame with the mosquito net was fitted over the window, everything looked more or less two-dimensional and so composed itself. We give too much weight to space, I went on – there's perhaps more of nature in a Persian carpet than in most landscape paintings. 'We'll take the hills down, push the trees aside and hang up carpets for you,' said Ernst. 'Your other trousers,' remarked Lou, 'why don't you put them on as we're going out?' Whilst he changed we went on talking. 'There,' he said, smiling ironically at the task he had just performed, 'is that better now?' 'They are very elegant, but they are the same pair!' I said. He laughed, delighted at this remark. Delighted because it emphasized that he had changed his trousers only to satisfy Lou's whim, and that that was reason enough for him: delighted because an insignificant difference was treated as though it didn't exist: delighted because, encapsulated in a tiny joke, there was a tiny conspiracy against the existent.

*

The Etruscans buried their dead in chambers under the ground and on the walls they painted scenes of pleasure and everyday life such as the dead had known. To have the light to see what they were painting they made a small hole in the ground above and then used mirrors to reflect the sunlight onto the particular image on which they were working. With words I try to decorate, as though it were a tomb, the last day of his life.

We were going to have lunch in a *pension* high up in the forests and hills. The idea was to look and see whether it would be suitable for Ernst to work there during September or October. Earlier in the year Lou had written to dozens of small hotels and boarding houses and this was the only one which was cheap and sounded promising. They wanted to take advantage of my having a car to go and have a look.

There are no scandals to make. But there is a contrast to draw. Two days after his death there was a long article about him in *Le Monde*. 'Little by little,' it wrote, 'Ernst Fischer has established himself as one of the most original and rewarding thinkers of "heretical" Marxism . . .' He had influenced an entire generation of the left in Austria. During the last four years he was continually denounced in Eastern Europe for the significant influence he had had on the thinking of the Czechs who had created the Prague Spring. His books were translated into most languages. But the conditions of his life during the last five years were cramped and harsh. The

Fischers had little money, were always subject to financial worries, and lived in a small, noisy workers' flat in Vienna. Why not? I hear his opponents ask. Was he better than the workers? No, but he needed professional working conditions. In any case he himself did not complain. But with the unceasing noise of families and radios in the flats above and on each side he found it impossible to work as concentratedly in Vienna as he wished to do and was capable of doing. Hence the annual search for quiet, cheap places in the country – where three months might represent so many chapters completed. The three sisters' house was not available after August.

We drove up a steep dust road through the forest. Once I asked a child the way in my terrible German and the child did not understand and simply stuffed her fist into her mouth in amazement. The others laughed at me. It was raining lightly: the trees were absolutely still. And I remember thinking as I drove round the hairpin bends that if I could define or realize the nature of the submission of the trees, I would learn something about the human body too – at least about the human body when loved. The rain ran down the trees. A leaf is so easily moved. A breath of wind is sufficient. And yet not a leaf moved.

We found the *pension*. The young woman and her husband were expecting us and they showed us to a long table where some other guests were already eating. The room was large with a bare wooden floor and big windows from which you looked over the shoulders of some near-by steep fields across the forest to the plain below. It was not unlike a canteen in a youth hostel, except that there were cushions on the benches and flowers on the tables. The food was simple but good. After the meal we were to be shown the rooms. The husband came over with an architect's plan in his hands. 'By next year everything will be different,' he explained, 'the owners want to make more money and so they're going to convert the rooms and put bathrooms in and put up their prices. But this autumn you can still have the two rooms on the top floor as they are, and there'll be nobody else up there, you'll be quiet.'

We climbed to the rooms. They were identical, side by side, with the lavatory on the same landing opposite them. Each room was narrow, with a bed against the wall, a wash-basin and an austere cupboard, and at the end of it a window with a view of miles and miles of landscape. 'You can put a table in front of the window and work here.' 'Yes, yes,' he said. 'You'll finish the book.' 'Perhaps not all of it, but I could get much done.' 'You must take it,' I said. I visualized him sitting at the table in front of the window, looking down at the still trees. The book was the second volume of his autobiography. It covered the period 1945-55 – when he had been very active in Austrian and international politics – and it was to deal principally with the development and consequences of the Cold War which he saw, I think, as the counter-revolutionary reaction, on both sides of what was to become the Iron Curtain, to the popular victories of 1945. I visualized his magnifying glass on the small table, his note-pad, the pile of current reference books, the chair pushed away when, stiffly but light on his feet, he had gone downstairs to take his regular walk before lunch. 'You must take it,' I said again.

We went for a walk together, the walk into the forest he would take each morning. I asked him why in the first volume of his memoirs he wrote in several distinctly different styles.

'Each style belongs to a different person.'

'To a different aspect of yourself?'

'No, rather it belongs to a different self.'

'Do these different selves co-exist, or, when one is predominant, are the others absent?'

'They are present together at the same time. None can disappear. The two strongest are my violent, hot, extremist, romantic self and the other my distant, sceptical self.'

'Do they discourse together in your head?'

'No.' (He had a special way of saying No. As if he had long ago considered the question at length and after much patient investigation had arrived at the answer.)

'They watch each other,' he continued. 'The sculptor Hrdlicka has done a head of me in marble. It makes me look much younger than I am. But you can see these two predominant selves in me – each corresponding to a side of my face. One is perhaps a little like Danton, the other a little like Voltaire.'

As we walked along the forest path, I changed sides so as to examine his face, first from the right and then from the left. Each eye was different and was confirmed in its difference by the corner of the mouth on each side of his face. The right side was tender and wild. He had mentioned Danton. I thought rather of an animal:

perhaps a kind of goat, light on its feet, a chamois maybe. The left side was sceptical but harsher: it made judgements but kept them to itself, it appealed to reason with an unswerving certainty. The left side would have been inflexible had it not been compelled to live with the right. I changed sides again to check my observations.

'And have their relative strengths always been the same?' I asked.

'The sceptical self has become stronger.' he said. 'But there are other selves too.' He smiled at me and took my arm and added, as though to reassure me: 'Its hegemony is not complete!'

He said this a little breathlessly and in a slightly deeper voice than usual – in the voice in which he spoke when moved, for example when embracing a person he loved.

His walk was very characteristic. His hips moved stiffly, but otherwise he walked like a young man, quickly, lightly, to the rhythm of his own reflections. 'The present book,' he said, 'is written in a consistent style – detached, reasoning, cool.'

'Because it comes later?'

'No, because it is not really about myself. It is about an historical period. The first volume is also about myself and I could not have told the truth if I had written it all in the same voice. There was no self which was above the struggle of the others and could have told the story evenly. The categories we make between different aspects of experience – so that, for instance, some people say I should not have spoken about love *and* about the Comintern in the same book – these categories are mostly there for the convenience of liars.'

'Does one self hide its decisions from the others?'

Maybe he didn't hear the question. Maybe he wanted to say what he said whatever the question.

'My first decision,' he said, 'was not to die. I decided when I was a child, in a sick-bed, with death at hand, that I wanted to live.'

★

From the *pension* we drove down to Graz. Lou and Anya needed to do some shopping; Ernst and I installed ourselves in the lounge of an old hotel by the river. It was in this hotel that I had come to see Ernst on my way to Prague in the summer of '68. He had given me addresses, advice, information, and summarized for me the historical background to the new events taking place. Our interpretation of these events was not exactly the same, but it seems pointless now to try to define our small differences. Not because Ernst is dead, but because those events were buried alive and we see only their large contours heaped beneath the earth. Our specific points of difference no longer exist because the choices to which they applied no longer exist. Nor will they ever exist again in quite the same way. Opportunities can be irretrievably lost and then their loss is like a death. When the Russian tanks entered Prague in August 1968 Ernst was absolutely lucid about that death.

In the lounge of the hotel I remembered the occasion of four years before. He had already been worried. Unlike many Czechs, he considered it quite likely that Brezhnev would order the Red Army to move in. But he still hoped. And this hope still carried within it all the other hopes which had been born in Prague that spring.

After 1968 Ernst began to concentrate his thoughts on the past. But he remained incorrigibly orientated towards the future. His view of the past was for the benefit of the future – for the benefit of the great or terrible transformations it held in store. But after '68 he recognized that the path towards any revolutionary transformation was bound to be long and tortuous and that Socialism in Europe would be deferred beyond his life-span. Hence the best use of his remaining time was to bear witness to the past.

We did not talk about this in the hotel, for there was nothing new to decide. The important thing was to finish the second volume of his memoirs and that very morning we had found a way of making this happen more quickly. Instead, we talked of love: or, more exactly, about the state of being in love. Our talk followed roughly these lines.

The capacity to fall in love is now thought of as natural and universal – and as a passive capacity. (Love strikes. Love-struck.) Yet there have been whole periods when the possibility of falling in love did not exist. Being in love in fact depends upon the possibility of free active choice – or anyway an apparent possibility. What does the lover choose? He chooses to stake the world (the whole of his life) against the beloved. The beloved concentrates all the possibilities of the world within her and thus offers the realization of all his own potentialities. The beloved for the lover empties the world of hope (the world that does not include her). Strictly speaking, being in love is a mood in so far as it is infinitely extensive – it reaches beyond the stars; but it cannot develop without changing its nature, and so it cannot endure.

The equivalence between the beloved and the world is confirmed by sex. To make love with the beloved is, subjectively, to possess and be possessed by the world. Ideally, what remains outside the experience is – nothing. Death of course is within it.

This provokes the imagination to its very depths. One wants to use the world in the act of love. One wants to make love with fish, with fruit, with hills, with forests, in the sea.

And those, said Ernst, 'are the metamorphoses! It is nearly always that way round in Ovid. The beloved becomes a tree, a stream, a hill. Ovid's *Metamorphoses* are not poetic conceits, they are really about the relation between the world and the poet in love.'

I looked into his eyes. They were pale. (Invariably they were moist with the strain of seeing.) They were pale like some blue flower bleached to a whitish grey by the sun. Yet despite their moisture and their paleness, the light which had bleached them was still reflected in them.

'The passion of my life,' he said, 'was Lou. I had many love affairs. Some of them, when I was a student here in Graz, in this hotel. I was married. With all the other women I loved there was a debate, a discourse about our different interests. With Lou there is no discourse because our interests are the same. I don't mean we never argue. She argued for Trotsky when I was still a Stalinist. But our interest – below all our interests – is singular. When I first met her, I said No. I remember the evening very well. I knew immediately I saw her, and I said No to myself. I knew that if I had a love affair with her, everything would stop. I would never love another woman. I would live monogamously. I thought I would not be able to work. We would do nothing except make love over and over again. The world would never be the same. She knew too. Before going home to Berlin she asked me very calmly: "Do you want me to stay?" "No," I said.'

Lou came back from the shops with some cheeses and yoghourts she had bought.

'Today we have talked for hours about me,' said Ernst, 'you don't talk about yourself. Tomorrow we shall talk about you.'

On the way out of Graz I stopped at a bookshop to find Ernst a copy of some poems by the Serbian poet, Miodrag Pavlovic. Ernst had said some time during the afternoon that he no longer wrote poems and no longer saw the purpose of poetry. 'It may be,' he added, 'that my idea of poetry is outdated.' I wanted him to read Pavlovic's poems. I gave him the book in the car. 'I already have it,' he said. But he put his hand on my shoulders. For the last time without suffering.

★

We were going to have supper in the café in the village. On the stairs outside his room, Ernst, who was behind me, suddenly but softly cried out. I turned round immediately. He had both his hands pressed to the small of his back. 'Sit down,' I said, 'lie down.' He took no notice. He was looking past me into the distance. His attention was there, not here. At the time I thought this was because the pain was bad. But it seemed to pass quite quickly. He descended the stairs – no more slowly than usual. The three sisters were waiting at the front door to wish us good night. We stopped a moment to talk. Ernst explained that his rheumatism had jabbed him in the back.

There was a curious distance about him. Either he consciously suspected what had happened, or else the chamois in him, the animal that was so strong in him, had already left to look for a secluded place in which to die. I question whether I am now using hindsight. I am not. He was already distant.

We walked, chatting, through the garden past the sounds of water. Ernst opened the gate and fastened it because it was difficult, for the last time.

We sat at our usual table in the public bar of the café. Some people were having their evening drink. They went out. The landlord, a man only interested in stalking and shooting deer, switched off two of the lights and went out to fetch our soup. Lou was furious and shouted after him. He didn't hear. She got up, went behind the bar and switched on the two lights again. 'I would have done the same,' I said. Ernst smiled at Lou and then at Anya and me. 'If you and Lou lived together,' he said, 'it would be explosive.'

When the next course came Ernst was unable to eat it. The landlord came up to inquire whether it was not good. 'It is excellently prepared,' said Ernst, holding up the untouched plate of food in front of him, 'and excellently cooked, but I am afraid that I cannot eat it.'

He looked pale and he said he had pains in the lower part of his stomach.

'Let us go back,' I said. Again he appeared – in response to the suggestion – to look into the distance. 'Not yet,' he said, 'in a little while.'

We finished eating. He was unsteady on his feet but he insisted on standing alone. On the way to the door he placed his hand on my shoulder – as he had in the car. But it expressed something very different. And the touch of his hand was now even lighter.

After we had driven a few hundred metres he said: 'I think I may be going to faint.' I stopped and put my arm round him. His head fell on my shoulder. He was breathing in short gasps. With his left, sceptical eye he looked hard up into my face. A sceptical, questioning, unswerving look. Then his look became unseeing. The light which had bleached his eyes was no longer in them. He was breathing heavily.

Anya flagged down a passing car and went back to the village to fetch help. She came back in another car. When she opened the door of our car, Ernst tried to move his feet out. It was his last instinctive movement – to be ordered, willed, neat.

When we reached the house, the news had preceded us and the gates, which were difficult, were already open so that we could drive up to the front door. The young man who had brought Anya from the village carried Ernst indoors and upstairs over his shoulders. I walked behind to stop his head banging against the door-jambs. We laid him down on his bed. We did helpless things to occupy ourselves whilst waiting for the doctor. But even waiting for the doctor was a pretext. There was nothing to do. We massaged his feet, we fetched a hot-water bottle, we felt his pulse. I stroked his cold head. His brown hands on the white sheet, curled up but not grasping, looked quite separate from the rest of his body. They appeared cut off by his cuffs. Like the forefeet cut off from an animal found dead in the forest.

The doctor arrived. A man of fifty. Tired, pale-faced, sweating. He wore a peasant's suit without a tie. He was like a veterinary surgeon. 'Hold his arm,' he said, 'whilst I give this injection.' He inserted the needle finely in the vein so that the liquid should flow along it like the water along the barrel-pipe in the garden. At this moment we were alone in the room together. The doctor shook his head. 'How old is he?' 'Seventy-three.' 'He looks older,' he said.

'He looked younger when he was alive,' I said.

'Has he had an infarctus before?'
'Yes.'
'He has no chance this time,' he said.

★

Lou, Anya, the three sisters and I stood around his bed. He had gone.

★

Besides painting scenes from everyday life on the walls of their tombs, the Etruscans carved on the lids of their sarcophagi full-length figures representing the dead. Usually these figures are half-reclining, raised on one elbow, feet and legs relaxed as though on a couch, but head and neck alert as they gaze into the distance. Many thousands of such carvings were executed quickly and more or less according to a formula. But however stereotyped the rest of these figures, their alertness as they look into the distance is striking. Given the context, the distance is surely a temporal rather than a spatial one: the distance is the future the dead projected when alive. They look into that distance as though they could stretch out a hand and touch it.

I can make no sarcophagus carving. But there are pages written by Ernst Fischer where it seems to me that the writer wrote adopting an equivalent stance, achieving a similar quality of expectation.

John Berger
August 1972

AN
OPPOSING
MAN

Was that Me?

Here, for the record, are the confessions of a man who was weak but who endeavoured to live beyond his strength, one whose poor constitution demanded restraint but whose insatiable imagination urged him on to extravagance, one whose gift was for dreaming, not for shaping reality, but whom reality compelled to become what his nature rejected – a politician.

But here a word of warning is necessary. What I am offering the reader is not in fact a record. For that, even today, I do not have the required detachment from myself, from the succession of figures that pursue me, imperiously demanding to be recognized as 'I', a whole swarm of 'Is', all entitled to ascribe to me, as I am today, the responsibility for everything I have been, everything I have done and omitted to do. And in asking 'Was that me?' I am not trying to shrug off responsibility. Indeed, I am quite prepared to conduct the case against myself, despite the difficulty of apportioning the roles between prosecutor, defence counsel and judge in the best interests of truth and so as to exclude from the proceedings all vanity, whether in the usual form of self-embellishment or in the even worse one of self-laceration, and despite the added difficulty of distinguishing conscientiously between the irrelevant, however alluring, and the pertinent, however turbid.

By far the greatest difficulty, however, is that though I have a vivid memory, my capacity to recall events in ordered sequence is poor, so that situations emerge like islands bathed in light, conversations distinct as when they first took place, with all the flavour and atmosphere of the moment, but between those islands impenetrable mists have drifted, confusing chronology and blurring contexts. And since the painstaking work of reconstructing those contexts bores me – not being an historian, I do not intend to write the hundred or so volumes the history of my times would demand – I am leaving the gaps empty or else filling them in with a minimum of facts. Hence this book will not provide material for historians, the less so in that I am averse to what are known as 'revelations' and, having no intention of exposing anybody – apart from my various selves – however deserving of exposure, I shall say no more than is necessary to make myself understood. Moreover it must be realized that memory is a trickster and that what is remembered is hardly ever a situation as a whole but rather my own experience of it or, more precisely, the experience as it has been arranged and moulded into permanent form by repeated reproduction.

Why then am I writing down these recollections and reflections? Because I enjoy doing so? Only sometimes. Am I already so old that the past is fetching me back out of the present and the future, back into the immutable out of a world that is undergoing such violent change? Only the future is interesting, the fullness of what is possible, not the strait-jacket of what has already been, with its attempt to impose on us the illusion that, because things were thus and not otherwise, they belong to the realm of necessity. The rebellious younger generation is closer to me than the septuagenarian that I am; but to them I represent the past, risible pathos, threadbare romanticism. Nevertheless the most attractive of these young people are themselves romantics, if harder, more cool-headed, more articulate than we were. How incongruous the process of ageing! Fifty years ago there were situations in which I felt like a centenarian and today I sometimes feel so young I could burst, which is nonsensical since my constitution sardonically calls me to order, the idiotic order of nature, of mortality. Yet in spite of that I turn to the young, those who cover venerable walls with insolent posters and obscene drawings, who totally disrupt the mechanisms of routine and who, in a world of institutions, organizations and manipulations, proclaim the victory of the imagination. As I write this I would like to be among them. For always I have wanted too much and hence achieved too little, always the flame has leapt too high for the fuel that fed it, always reality has been consumed by imagination. But does not such a life become in this way the reflection of an age of unrealized possibilities, when the life in question is that of a man whose achievements were not commensurate with his abilities, whose talent demanded the maximum concentration of insufficient powers if it was not to remain stuck in mediocrity? And is not an account of that life, or an attempt to recount it, justified after all?

It would seem so, more especially since that life began with a negation of the world which gave it birth, of everything comprised today in the term 'Establishment'. The word was then unknown, but the thing itself, so pitiful, so crabbed and coffined in provincial Austria, oppressed me with its uniforms, barracks, conventions, brutalities, obscurantism and hypocrisy. But at that time even the students in the provincial town where I grew up belonged, with an arrogance that repelled, to the Establishment, and from childhood onwards I loathed it all, the philistine meannesses, the fustiness of the marriage bed, the nightmare pressure of the hierarchy, command and obedience, authority and subjection. Very early on I began to dream of a world of freedom that did not reek of poverty, of cooking and cloaca, of dust and sweat, but instead was pervaded by the fragrance of women and lilac, the breath of a warmer world. It was a paradise of anarchy, *eros* and fraternal sentiment that I used to dream about; but then came the war and with it, fourteen years post-dated, the beginning of the twentieth century, the century of wars, crises, revolutions and counter-revolutions, of great expectations and even greater disappointments – the world in a permanent state of convulsion.

I was not really moulded by the front; to say so would be rhetorical over-simplification. I only reached the front line in the spring of 1918, a few months before the collapse of the army. It had been at my own request. The Medical Officer who examined my thin, not very robust body was a friend of my grandfather the retired general. With a kindly twinkle in his eye he declared: 'Graded C!' which meant clerical duties behind the lines. To his amazement I demanded: 'Grade me A!' which meant service at the front. From the very first day I had abominated the war, but since it was happening I wanted to be in it. There wouldn't, I thought in the innocence of my ignorance, be another world war and this was a unique experience which ought not to be missed. It was not so much the front as the perpetual state of emergency that drew me, the desire for self-destruction under the guise of self-preservation. To that extent I, the lone wolf, was representative of a generation, of an age that was new not only as each in turn has always been new, but extravagant in its novelty, the era which began in 1914 and whose end is not yet in sight.

Those who are twenty years old today, whose spontaneity goes hand in hand with technological expertise, whose violent activities aspire towards a world devoid of violence, whose disgust with the Establishment has called forth an insatiable hunger for freedom, these are my contemporaries, the contemporaries of a septuagenarian. I feel the need to communicate to them the experiences and mistakes, the fortunes and disappointments, the decisions and the miscalculations of one who, though intellectually a lone wolf, a stubborn individualist, had made up his mind to belong to a politically militant community. That lone wolf began by becoming a Social Democrat. After 15 July 1927 and the burning of the Palace of Justice in Vienna when defenceless men and women were mown down by the power of the state, he began to despair of parliamentary democracy. In the face of encroaching Fascism and of democracy's self-emasculation he became an anti-democrat, convinced that only the dictatorship of the proletariat was capable of forestalling or breaking a Fascist dictatorship. After the battles of February 1934, as an *émigré* in Prague deprived of Austrian citizenship, he decided to join the Communist Party. His hatred of Hitler and his concentration on the struggle against Nazi Germany led him to silence all his doubts and to conform to the Communist discipline. The Seventh World Congress of the Communist International, whose underlying concept he still holds to be right, made it easier for him to accept Communism, even in its Stalinist distortion. He went to Moscow and, like millions of other Communists, believed in Stalin's genius and importance in world history. Although he did not regard himself as such, he was in fact a Stalinist.

And today?

The break with Stalinism was followed by the laborious process of overcoming it. In 1948 I was still convinced that Tito's courageous revolt against Stalin's attempt to degrade Yugoslavia to the status of a Russian satellite was a betrayal of Socialism. I, who was already turning away from Stalinism, again became a Stalinist, defending the monstrous idea of the monolithic power bloc and writing an atrocious play attacking Tito. Unfortunately I did not listen to Lou, then not yet my wife, the only person who begged me to abandon the play.

What, then, had happened to me? I am neither bad, mad, nor ambitious, no one had requested me to write anything of the kind and it was not in the least my intention to put myself into the lime-light. I was afraid that a third world war was inevitable and therefore believed that any break with Moscow was a betrayal. But to under-stand the motive is not to exonerate the deed.

From out of the depths of my memory, from out of the sorrow for all that went to waste, for what I was and no longer am and never will be again, an unknown self calls out to me, a stranger asking: 'What, then, had happened to you?' I do not know whether I can find the answer, one that to me would seem real and convincing. But it is something to do with the dichotomy that besets the intel-lectual whenever he finds himself in a collective that he has chosen and recognized of his own free will. For he is forever calling himself to heel in the name of the collective to which he belongs and yet, in his critical self-assertion, does not belong to fully. His consciousness tells him that he is imperfectly aligned and his conscience reproaches him for it, a conscience that has not been forced upon him but was born of his own free decision, and the more refractory the rebellion of the primary, anarchic self, this irrepressible *no* of the consenting intellectual, the more vehement, out of his self-imposed conformity, will be his defence of discipline – that to him so antipathetic discipline – against insubordination, against the heretic that is himself.

In 1952 two trials took place, the first, that of the Rosenberg couple in the U.S.A., the second, that of Slansky and other leading Com-munists in Czechoslovakia.

The Rosenbergs were sentenced to death and executed on an unproven charge of spying for Soviet Russia. In the Prague trial Slansky and many of the other accused were sentenced to death and executed – on the grounds of an unproven and non-existent Zionist–Titoist–imperialist conspiracy.

There had been many such trials before, but this was the first time that I did not believe a word of the monstrous charges, of the extorted confessions. Yet I made no public protest. I refused to defend the judicial murder, but I remained silent – in the name of a misconceived idea of discipline that amounted to complicity. The pretext that it would have helped no one had I spoken is without substance. My silence was inexcusable.

The Twentieth Congress of the C.P.S.U. shook the Stalin myth to its foundations but did not, alas, destroy it. Khrushchev was over-thrown by the apparatus. The contempt for all Socialist, democratic, humane principles increasingly manifested by the lesser men who followed Stalin – further arrests, further trials, further measures to suppress the faintest breath of freedom – compelled us to ask: is this still Socialism? Has alienation diminished? Have relationships between human beings become kindlier? Are people freer, more self-respecting, happier than elsewhere? Is there in fact such a thing as Socialism?

Yes, came the answer. And it came from Prague, from Bratislava, from Czechoslovakia. What happened there provided justification for our existence as Communists, whatever the mistakes, aberrations and failures we may have to reproach ourselves with.

Czechoslovakia had given proof that European Socialism was possible; 21 August 1968 was to prove the contrary. Within the briefest possible span we saw Socialism as a possibility and yet as an impossibility – so long as the fate of nations continues to be decided by power politics. Such is the paradox that calls us in question as Communists. Hence the dead weight of sorrow and anger that makes it so difficult to speak calmly about it.

'Speak calmly!' Lou admonishes, 'exaggeration has always been a weakness of yours!'

She is right. I do exaggerate. No, it is reality that exaggerates. Reality cannot retract a single word. Yet I am to speak calmly! About what?

The sun was setting as I walked downhill. Far below, on the hairpin bend, someone was coming towards me, a shadow, tall and thin. It was climbing. That, too, was me. Shall we two meet before the sun goes down?

Am I exaggerating? Socialism, growing into a reality in that small country, Czechoslovakia, presaged the union, at the bend of the road, between the wanderer and his shadow, the self and its pro-jection into the world.

To hold to the dream of Socialism had become harder year by year. Was it not fear of the truth, of the immensity of dark and cold, of the loss of the cosy integument, which prevented us from realizing how thin the dream had already worn? Being old – hitherto no more than the echo of an axe in the dwindling wood, the rasp of the saw, a momentary perplexity, the protest of the flesh too quickly tired by the demands made upon it – had now become a listening deep down within, inside this hollowed-out self, in the cavern of time, late time, final time, inexorably, senselessly running out, with nothing effective to hold on to any more and nothing but nothingness. Was not Czechoslovakia 1968 the last chance for one whose time was nearing its end? The great chance for European Socialism? The synthesis of freedom and Communism? The human face?

In the laborious and paradoxical process of world revolution which is the content of this century, Vietnam and Cuba and China are all essential factors, yet it would be foolish to look to them for a prototype for Europe or to regard the latter as obsolete, as a continent with a past but without a future. Czechoslovakia could have been such a prototype. No more. Foolish phrase. But what are we to do?

Resign ourselves?

Should not a man of my age, all passion spent and armed with the cynicism born of experience, recognize the vanity of all our striving – recognize it without bitterness or despair but rather with the tranquillity of one who hobnobs with death?

I am not resigned.

That it is possible to overthrow a country by superior force of arms has been known for thousands of years. That it was possible for a small country to achieve Socialism with a human face, fleeting though this may have been, is of greater significance than the far from surprising victory achieved by force of arms. This victory was predictable. What was unpredictable was the prolonged failure of the powerful victor to find collaborators. Again and again it is man who proves to be the unpredictable factor in all the calculations of *Realpolitik.*

Thus it is no folly to be hopeful.

I am addressing my thirty-year-old and twenty-year-old contemporaries – a no longer lost or pragmatic, but militant younger generation. Heterogeneous it may be: Socialists, Communists, Maoists, anarchists, Trotskyists, atheists and Christians, left-wing democrats and fanatical anti-democrats, mystical advocates of violence and those who preach non-violence; yet, or so it seems to me, they all have one common denominator – the longing for a phantom now become almost a mockery – *freedom.*

I am aware of the wealth of meaning and undertone this almost undefinable term comprises, a term that lends itself all too often and too easily to phrase-making, tending to lose itself in generalities, so that only the most unswerving optimist can fail to despair of it. But the very word – not in the innocuous form of ritual rhetoric but uttered as a demand – is enough to stir up the official bile of every established order. For officials of whatever camp, when confronted with the demand for freedom, will have recourse to the same phraseology: revolutionaries, extremists, provocateurs, and then proceed to inform us that there can be no such thing as absolute freedom, only what is permitted being admissible as such. 'If I may make so free!' is what a subordinate says in Austria when he accepts a cigarette from his superior. 'So they want to be free, eh? Back to school with 'em! Freedom? All they think of is playing truant and it's we who have to foot the bill! Chaos, that's what it is, chaos! A Communist plot!' Conversely, I once heard a Communist official say: 'Whenever somebody mentions freedom of opinion, I know that he's succumbed to bourgeois ideology. Of course I myself advocate freedom of opinion in the capitalist world because it's a bad world and hence deserving of criticism. But in the Socialist world, which is a good world, freedom of opinion can only help to foster counter-revolution.' But we should not allow all this to discourage us. That the universities, in my time hotbeds of reaction, have become dynamic centres of revolt, that rebellious self-consciousness is on the increase in intellectual circles, that the educated can no longer be implicitly relied upon to support their rulers – all this is symptomatic of revolutionary development. When, during a public discussion, a Social Democrat assured us that it was high time we abandoned the ill-starred concept of revolution, not only did a Catholic priest reply that the hungry and downtrodden peoples of Asia and Latin America had an incontestable right to revolt, but a woman, a Catholic university teacher, cried: 'We have only just discovered revolution. We won't let anyone put us off!'

Such is the here and now by which I am surrounded, voices from Prague and Paris, from Vienna and Cuba filter through to me as I write, and voices from Moscow. How many friends are there, courageously striving for a synthesis of Socialism and freedom, steadfastly and with intelligence, in a world of twilight and agonizing contradiction: Lenin's tomb and the Revolution, once the great dynamic force and now all too often an impediment. Yet without Moscow there can be no freedom for Vietnam! And no hope of peace. Socialism has been buried alive by imperialist power politics, but this is not to admit the widely held belief that there is no longer any difference between the Soviet Union and the U.S.A. True, the Soviet Union is governed, not by the people, but by an apparatus whose power is unlimited, and to speak of 'the leading role of the working class' is either cynicism or cant. Yet this is no capitalist economy based on profit; the elementary economic pre-conditions for Socialism do exist. And even though every step forward may be hampered by a leaden-footed bureaucracy so that there can be no immediate prospect of any socialist impulse from the Soviet Union, the Socialism that has been buried alive may well prove to be the explosive charge of renewal. In such a context recollection acquires the incandescence of the future I anticipate, a future to which, despite every doubt, failure and defeat, I have perhaps contributed – and hope I may continue to contribute – some small part. That this future will be different from what we are now dreaming and planning and preparing, that every contradiction we resolve contains in it the seeds of another, that no liberation is possible without some infringement of liberty – none of this is cause for despair. For, after all, freedom is more than the negation of the unfreedom it displaces. Freedom is present whenever imagination prevails, in every act of creation, in every transcendence of the self. And this is why – and once again I apologize for the digression – I have returned to myself as I was when I set out, when I first began to strive for freedom and free community. To one who looks back it may seem as though everything was inevitable and that, confronted with the same situations again, he would react as before because he *had to react* in that way. The past is fossilized; it stares at us with the stony face of necessity. Freedom is the future.

That it need not have been thus, that there were alternatives is evident to me when I remember, or allow myself to remember. I am free to force myself to write, to acknowledge my responsibility without appeal to necessity.

Of that freedom I make full use.

2

Race against Death

'What is improbable,' my visitor was saying, 'is the fact that you are alive. According to the law of probability you're dead, you *must* be dead.'

The man sitting opposite me was Professor Walter Laqueur, head of London's Wiener Library, an institution where anti-Fascist records are housed. He had previously telephoned me, saying that he very much wanted to make my acquaintance. For some time, he went on, he had wished to tell me something of interest to myself and now that he was in Vienna our meeting need no longer be postponed.

'I learned about you from a secret report. It was discovered in 1945 in the Ministry of Foreign Affairs in Berlin. The microfilm is now in the archives of our Institute. It's a document of about eighty pages.'

'N.S.D.A.P.?'

'No, not the N.S.D.A.P. The report is written in Russian, bad Russian, no doubt by a German. Who, I don't know, there's no name attached. A double agent, perhaps, for both the Gestapo and the N.K.V.D. Or he may have changed sides or been taken prisoner. I don't know. The only evidence is this document he wrote. He had been ordered to keep an eye on you in Moscow. From 1936 onwards. His report is thorough, a pedantic, purposive accumulation of detail. According to this report, you're a dead man, a ghost. The man who wrote it concluded that, after Palmiro Togliatti, you were the most dangerous foreign intellectual in the Soviet Union.'

So that was how it was.*

---

*It is difficult to follow up one's own traces.

In May 1967, when I began writing my memoirs, I wrote to Walter Laqueur,

As Laqueur went on talking about that deadly document that had not after all spelt death – death against which I was running a race – I became lost in memories of the distant past: voices in the next room, doctors' voices, they can do nothing more to save you, a child, dying, ten years old, the journey across Germany in 1936, the S.S. waking you, taking your passport, two men, where were you born, and your memory failing, the Czech town you had committed to memory, you knew so well, you can't remember it, and the journalist at the café table, something important to tell you, change the number of your car, they're going to stage an accident, who? The man is evasive, works for at least one secret service, probably two, in occupied Vienna in 1945, and the little revolver Anny gave you, dainty, mother-of-pearl and silver, a toy, in your mouth, pressed against your temple, and that curious conversation with Togliatti in Moscow in 1937, and before that the sinister Moskvin, we shall make a thorough investigation into your activities in Paris, and Laqueur telling you about this secret report, and everything dissolves, becomes fluid, I am carried away, engulfed, I see myself, the other that I once was, we shall make a thorough investigation, diagnosis, we can do nothing to save him, and yet I am alive, against

---

requesting him to send me a copy of the microfilm or at least to let me have the essential part of the document. On 31 May 1967 he wrote saying that unfortunately he could not help me just then since to search through dozens of microfilms in order to find the one that concerned me would be too time-consuming. But if one of my friends in London was prepared 'to spend a few days looking through this material, we would, of course, be pleased to give him access to these films'. A London publisher, Wolfgang Foges, with whom, in the thirties, I had planned to bring out a newspaper, agreed to do this. But his search was unsuccessful and, on 9 May 1968, he wrote: 'As Mr Laqueur was not very helpful, I am enclosing a copy of a memorandum about finding the Ernst Fischer report, and you will see from this memorandum that the material in question was returned to the Germans and the suggestion is that you should write direct to Dr Sasse in Bonn . . .' I applied to Dr Sasse, head of the political archives section of the Ministry of Foreign Affairs in Bonn. On 21 May 1968 Dr Sasse replied that he had to inform me with much regret that 'in spite of an intensive search among all the relevant files, no document such as the one you describe can be found among those in the political archives of the Ministry of Foreign Affairs . . . Might it not be possible to obtain further details from Professor Laqueur?' Further details not being forthcoming, I abandoned the search for the traces I had left behind in the files.

all the laws of probability. But then life of any kind is improbable in this apocalyptic world.

As soon as I entered the room I saw the letter lying on my desk. The previous day, before leaving my office in the Comintern, I had locked away all the books and papers into the drawer. Every night the offices were inspected to make sure that the desks had been properly cleared and all the drawers locked. The drawers were locked. The top of the desk was clear. Right in the middle of that empty space lay the letter.

It was addressed to me. Written on the envelope in Russian script: 'To Tovarich Ernst Fischer', not Peter Wieden, as I was known in Moscow.

I opened it without haste, circumspectly. It was as though, in this unreal silence, in this bare room, I were somehow being covertly observed. It was nonsense, of course, but vaguely I sensed the presence of an eye, the eye of a camera. The letter was from Gustl Deutsch, who had been arrested months before. I had intervened with Dimitrov on his behalf, but in vain.

In an almost illegible scrawl, Gustl D. wrote that an unexpected opportunity had enabled him to send me this letter from prison; it would be brought to me by a reliable friend. He begged me to forgive him and to appreciate the position he was in. After repeated refusals he had finally signed a confession to the effect that he had worked with me as a spy, that I was acting as contact with Trotsky's wife and son in Paris, that I had been to the Gestapo and had come to Moscow to pass on instructions to deviationists in the Soviet Union. He had not had the strength to hold out, but had signed the confession and thus confirmed slanderous allegations which might put my life in danger. It was, he wrote, some slight alleviation to his conscience that he had at least been able to inform me of what had happened and to warn me in good time, thus perhaps enabling me to find some way of escaping the same fate as his own, if not something worse.

So that was how it was!

It was not until I had re-read the letter for the second and third time that my brain really began to take it in, to establish some connection between myself and its contents. At first I felt no fear of any kind, but merely wondered what means had been used to extort such a crackpot statement from so lovable, sincere and gentle a person as Deutsch. What, I asked myself, could be done to help him? Then suddenly another question flashed across my mind. How did that letter get onto my desk? What friend, irrespective of his reliability, would have had the chance, not only to smuggle it out of the prison or camp, but actually to see that it found its way to my desk in this carefully guarded building? I could think of no one except a member of the N.K.V.D. – the political police. It therefore seemed probable that Gustl D. had written the letter under duress and, even if he hadn't, in no circumstances could the bearer have been a 'reliable friend'. Or could he? In that opaque situation might there not even be men in the N.K.V.D. capable of disregarding its inhuman methods and regulations? But who, I asked myself, who? . . .

After Stalin's death, when Agnes J., Gustl D.'s wife, returned from fifteen years' imprisonment, I told her about this letter. She said: 'I'm glad that he had strength enough left to write and warn you . . .' She had been confronted with him and ordered to sign the same confession but had steadfastly refused, in spite of all the mal-treatment meted out to her. She told me, however, that her husband had been hardly recognizable, to such an extent had their beat-ings succeeded in driving out all semblance of his real self and reducing him to a complete wreck. It had been her last meeting with him, and by then he had been barely alive. He never came back . . .

Who has passed on this letter to me? Shall I tear it up . . . ? But isn't that precisely what I am intended to do, in accordance with a carefully laid plan – destroy the letter and behave as though it had never been . . . ? Where's that letter? We saw it on your desk. And you mean to say you didn't even see it, read it? If I destroy the letter, then they will destroy me, they, the men at the top, the apparatus in the separate wing to which no one can gain access without special authorization . . . The men at the top don't care for you, Klara S. had told me one day, to them you're the 'Social Democrat'. That's what they call you when they talk about you . . . Well, then, ought I to discuss the letter with my party officials . . . ? An absurd idea. It would make them mistrust me, or at any rate shun me as one who is stigmatized . . .

Having read the letter yet again, I drafted a note to the N.K.V.D. 'Herewith a letter found this morning on my desk. I request to be taken at once and confronted with D. so that I can have the opportunity of repudiating the calumny.'

Then I went to see Dimitrov.

He read the letter without comment, re-read it and then, avoiding my eyes, said: 'That's bad, very bad! What do you propose to do?'

I gave him the draft of my letter to the N.K.V.D. 'I'd be grateful if you could pass on both letters to the N.K.V.D. and, if at all possible, speak to Stalin. There can be no doubt of Gustl D.'s innocence. I can vouch for him.'

'It's you we're concerned with now, not him . . . I think you've made the right decision. I will pass on the letters personally. But you mustn't tell anyone – d'you hear? *No one at all* . . . We can only hope . . .'

He shook my hand and looked at me as though this were a leave-taking, his expression friendly and concerned.

Two days later he told me: 'I've intervened on your behalf.'

The matter was never mentioned again. No questions were asked, no answers given; no one summoned me. Somewhere the facts of the case had been recorded and filed away. How heavy those files may have been I cannot say, but they did not crush me. And that is all I know.

It was probably Dimitrov who saved me, but here again I cannot say . . .

And the secret report mentioned by Laqueur – I would never have heard of it had Nazi Germany not collapsed and the microfilm been found in the Ministry of Foreign Affairs in Berlin.

We live in a world of secret reports. We are taken care of and preserved somewhere in the archives of this opaque world; some time or other it may happen that a file emerges into the light of day, and someone leafs through it. Indeed, one's own memory is crammed with secret reports of this nature, reports drawn up by one's doppelgänger, often in a code decipherable only in dreams, or a name may evoke a tangled skein of complex associations. My memory does not associate like a filing system, nor does it conform to any calendar, not knowing *when* but most vividly *how* something happened, even down to the tone of a voice, the twitching of a lip. Out of this indeterminate flux, this nebulous stream, rolling along now at speed, now at a snail's pace – out of this something we call time, orderly and chronological to the historian, alarming and chaotic to one in search of his past self – situations emerge, sharply defined as though caught by searchlights, Calypso's islands where the storm-driven Odysseus keeps himself company.

In the secret report under discussion Palmiro Togliatti's name occurs, and in my memory the letter on my desk becomes confused with a conversation that took place in the Comintern – whether before or after that episode I cannot say.

An agent of the N.K.V.D. whom we called Moskvin (I have forgotten his real name) had been put in charge of the Comintern's apparatus. He was a small man with pinched, indeterminate features from which his eyes looked out, cold and watchful.

After the Comintern's Seventh World Congress, and at Dimitrov's and Manuilsky's request, I had been appointed representative of the Austrian Communist Party in Moscow, a post I accepted only on condition that I should be allowed to spend part of my time in Prague and thus maintain direct contact with Austria. If memory serves me aright it was in the summer of 1937 that I was preparing to leave for Prague, having already settled the day of my departure, when I was sent for by Dimitrov. Moskvin was with him.

'I'm sorry,' Dimitrov began, 'but you can't go. Something's happened . . . Comrade Moskvin will explain.'

'Somebody or other has informed the police,' said Moskvin. 'They're waiting for you. And on your arrival . . .'

'What police?'

'What police?' said Moskvin, grinning. 'You know very well what police!'

'My journey's absolutely legal. I'm travelling with a passport under my own name, Ernst Fischer. I've never meddled in Czechoslovakian politics and my registration's* in order. What possible interest can the police have in me?'

'But they *are* showing interest in you – quite considerable interest. You can't go.'

'It's utterly incomprehensible,' I said and, turning to Dimitrov, continued: 'Please will you give instructions for me to be allowed to travel.'

'We must leave all questions of security to Comrade Moskvin. Doubtless he has good reason to believe that you are in danger. You'll be able to go when the situation changes.'

* With the police.

As we were leaving the room, Moskvin hissed in my ear: 'We shall make a thorough investigation into your activities in Paris!'

Some time later, one evening after office hours, I had a conversation with Togliatti, who, under the pseudonym 'Ercoli', was head of the Central European Secretariat of the Comintern. I cannot remember the subject of our discussion but, as I was about to leave, Togliatti said: 'Have you a moment to spare?'

Getting up from his desk, he went over to the door and first opened, then circumspectly closed it again, before offering me a chair in the corner of the room farthest from the desk and himself sitting down next to me.

'What do you think of this man Comrade Moskvin?'

The question was totally unexpected, but I knew I could trust Togliatti implicitly.

'He's either a fool or a knave.'

'He's no fool!' was Togliatti's rejoinder.

There was a short silence. Then he asked:

'Upon what do you base that opinion?'

'Nothing definite,' I said, 'but there's something distinctly suspect going on and it's worrying, to say the least. We send comrades into Austria equipped with radio sets and false passports and in next to no time they've been picked up – every single one of them. The whole thing's utterly irresponsible. Most suspect. And what's going on all around us? These arrests, these hopeless attempts at intervention, all this frightful uncertainty? What's it all about?'

'What's your own opinion?'

'Enemies have found their way into the apparatus. It's quite clear that they've gained a foothold somewhere very near the top. But who are they working for? They can't all be agents of the Gestapo. Who is fighting whom? What's going on?'

The whole thing, Togliatti explained, had become so impenetrable a web that no one could trust themselves to find their way about. Doubtless some of them were enemies of Stalin, Trotskyists, agents of foreign powers, but that alone was not enough to explain everything; there must be other factors at work, long-standing rivalries, irresponsible place-hunting, persecution mania whether genuine or feigned; or again, the lure might be a house or a decoration. And so the machine had got out of control, had become a machine that crushed those beneath it.

'But why don't you speak to Stalin?' I cried, for it was generally believed that Stalin thought very highly of Togliatti.

'Stalin is a very suspicious man,' replied Togliatti after a moment's hesitation. Then he changed both his tone and the subject of conversation. His reason for asking me about Moskvin, he said, was that the man was no friend of mine; but his real intention in engaging me in the present conversation had been to prevent me from falling into the error of believing that the ghastly caricature with which we were now confronted was the true face of Communism. In fact, a concatenation of circumstances had led to a tragic interlude during which all that we were fighting for had become temporarily obscured. I must not, he said, jump to false conclusions, but rather learn a lesson for the future: 'If ever we return to our own countries, there is one thing we will have to recognize from the start: the struggle for Socialism means the struggle for more democracy. If we Communists fail to be the most consistent of democrats, history will pass us by.' This, he went on, was the kind of development I must bear in mind and, for the time being, I must be careful not to talk too much – always bearing in mind that Moskvin was no friend of mine, but that Dimitrov was.

Then one day Moskvin was no longer there. Why he had been arrested I do not know. Still less do I know why I should have survived the witches' sabbath.

Life itself is improbable enough; survival in this age of iron stretches improbability to its limits.

I was ten years old when I made the decision not to die.

Coming round after a prolonged spell of unconsciousness, I heard voices in the next room.

'He'll die within the next hour or two,' said one doctor.

'Perhaps not quite as soon as that,' said another doctor.

'He might live,' said a third doctor, 'but it would be with an incurable heart condition.'

'In my opinion, he cannot live,' said the first doctor.

At that moment I came to the decision that I would neither die nor pine away the rest of my days with an incurable heart condition.

I felt very calm. At first it had all been a joke. Once again I was ill – when wasn't I ill as a child? There was a bowl of water between my thighs and my mother was washing me. Suddenly my thighs began to twitch. 'What are you up to now?' exclaimed my mother. 'I can't help it!' I said, laughing at her surprise, for the fact that I couldn't help it seemed to me very funny. Here was a part of my body, acting quite independently and getting up to all sorts of tricks and I, my own self, watching it impotently – amused at first, then anxious, then protesting against the nonsense and finally succumbing to convulsions . . .

Now it had returned to me, that impotent but persistent self.

My mother was looking at me.

'Don't be afraid,' I said cheerfully. 'I'm not going to die. Not a bit of it!'

The cat-and-mouse game with death had begun when I was six years old; my sister was born while death was making its first onslaught on my heart, and my mother, whose womb had produced an as yet unknown being at a time when one she knew was threatened with extinction, appeared at my bedside with the baby. It was a hideous black-haired object and I didn't like it – this creature whom, in all her luminous beauty, I was later to love so much.

Childhood: an open window. Outside, children's voices, barking dogs, cheerful noise. And I, lying in bed, forbidden to move, with pounding heart. Every day the doctor with his indelible pencil drew the outline of that heart on my narrow chest. It was much too large, pericarditis and myocarditis. A bird wildly flapping its wings, it was attempting to break out of the cage of my ribs and escape into nothingness.

To be ill meant to be privileged. I was given special food, dainty and light. At four years old, my sister approached me and my food ingratiatingly. 'Dear, darling, wonderful Ernst, my only Ernst – may I . . . ?' It was pleasant to be addressed thus, to contemplate the beautiful little creature, so blonde, so sweet. To my brothers, slightly younger than myself, I was an ailing tyrant. I would threaten them, saying that any excitement might be the death of me and then they would be murderers. It was the egoism of the weakling, presuming on the rights conferred by his weakness. Being privileged, I had death for my bodyguard.

I longed to be outside with the others, underneath my window. But does not he who is set apart belong to the elect? Is not the invalid divinely endowed? My body is of small account, a fragile instrument – therefore it is my mind that will put you to shame. *Mens sana in corpore sano?* Isn't mind contrary to nature, a disease that raises man above the animal kingdom? I will be a cardinal or a poet or ... anyone, in fact, whose frail hands are more powerful than the muscles of the robust, whose voice rises above the din, that alluring, detestable din underneath my window. That insolent enviable healthiness, so sure of itself, football and fisticuffs, feel my biceps, hard as iron.

The ice-pack on my chest, for weeks a bulwark against death, was at the same time its silent, constant presence. When the former was removed, the latter also withdrew. Absent during the daytime, it took possession of my sleep, weaving the web of my dreams and lurking somewhere among its strands to pounce upon me, the rescued one, and suck me dry.

But I was still very far from being rescued. The beating of my damaged heart was irregular. The rhythm was upset by extra systoles: a constantly recurring feeling of syncope. Recuperating slowly – the tremulous joy of recovery – I would dream of death.

Then came the dream of the sea, all-engulfing. I had known the sea only from books and pictures and suddenly, there it was – the 'oceanic feeling', the breath of eternity. Its inexorable rhythm was more powerful than the irregular beat of my heart, which adapted itself to its gentle insistence. Borne up by that motion, over the deep abyss, a 'child gently rocked', my hands clasped beneath my head, and above me the sky, azure and light, my sick body cast off and free as air and blissful renewal, I woke up and said to my mother: 'I want to go to the seaside.'

'And why do you want to do that?'

'I'd get well there.'

'Do you really believe it?'

'I know it.'

'Then we'll go.'

The doctor advised against it. It was the air of the forests I needed, not that of the sea. It might be the death of me and certainly would not cure me.

My mother decided in favour of my dream rather than of the doctor's opinion.

My father said that he was not rich enough to pander to such whims. The doctor's orders must be obeyed. Dreams were mere phantasmagoria. Science must be given its due.

My grandfather gave my mother money for the journey. We
went to a children's holiday home beside Capodistria Bay. Apart
from myself there was only one boy there who could speak German.
He appeared to be proud of this fact. I didn't like him. The children
I preferred were the '*Čičen*', who were part Slav, part Italian.

Best of all I liked the darkly beautiful Lucia, a fifteen-year-old
girl with mischievous eyes and pointed breasts. Twelve-year-old
Anka was prettier than she, more impetuous and original. She ran
after me, kissed me wildly, bit my lips. But I was enamoured of
Lucia. Anka was the land, Lucia was the sea. To sink down into
her must be that unimaginable thing called love.

Though the boys and girls were segregated when bathing, they
were allowed to go and visit each other. My mother had sent me
some sweets with which I went over to the girls. I offered all
of them sweets except for Lucia. '*Ed io?*' she exclaimed, in a tone
that betrayed derision as well as hurt feelings. Throwing the bag into
her face, I ran away, followed by shrill peals of heartless laughter.

I didn't know how to swim. Once I fell from the jetty into the
sea and paddled ludicrously, like a dog. However carefully I observed others swimming, the knack and rhythm of it eluded me. One
night I dreamt about swimming, dreamt that I was able to swim
effortlessly. In the silver-grey of the dawn, when everyone else was
still in bed, I ran down to the beach and into the water. I could
swim!

But even this was not enough to win Lucia's heart. She would
smile coquettishly whenever she saw me and sometimes kiss her
hand to me, but she spent her time with Mario, the sturdy, sixteen-
year-old Italian boy whose chest was done up in plaster.

I was lying in a heap of dry seaweed whose sharp tang I adored.
I had snuggled down into the heap and was watching the sun set:
the shimmering peacock sea, the unearthly glow gradually fading,
the horizon towered with gold and, on the slopes of the hills, the
purple twilight.

Strolling along the beach came Lucia and Mario with the plaster
round his chest. Up in the house the bell was ringing for supper.
Darkness was falling. In a hollow between two rocks Mario drew
Lucia down onto the sand. He pulled her skirt up above her thighs,
which he parted with his hands as though they were flowering shrubs;
she made no attempt to stop him. She offered him her lips, her breasts,

arching herself towards him. Their bodies rose and fell with the rhythm of the sea. It was as though a wave had left the sea to disport itself here among the rocks. The gurgle and murmur of the water mingled with the panting, with the little cries uttered by the lovers. Then all grew dark and still.

At supper there were three late-comers. Mario was sitting opposite me. In spite of the satiated look on his face he ate with enormous appetite. As, with evident relish, he swallowed a piece of meat, I flung a knife at him. It bounced back off his plaster. There was a frightful row.

A few days later Mario left. Sister Vittoria, sentimental, would stroke me at bedtime with hands that were all too soft. Lucia gazed at me meditatively, without hint of rebuff; it was almost a challenge. Anka, who had seen through the whole thing, wept with rage and shouted that Lucia was a silly fool, heartless, vulgar, man-mad. She'll give herself to anyone. Why not take her if you want her?

Absent-mindedly I kissed Anka. From Lucia I kept my distance. Much though I desired her, there was something about her that frightened me. I had identified her with the sea. But was she not rather related to death? Was not the voluptuous flesh she proffered the bait of putrefaction? Vittoria bored me. Anka was too childishly aggressive. Lucia made my heart contract as though it were her mission to crush it.

At the end of three months my mother came to collect me. I was brown, I was strong, I could swim, and the children had acknowledged me as their leader. Life was no longer a noise beneath my window. I was part and parcel of that noise.

The report after my medical examination was hard to credit. I was healthy. No heart condition. A few necrotic areas that would disappear with time. An account of my case appeared in a medical journal.

Why, on that occasion, I won the race against death I do not know.

In the final analysis, one is bound to lose the cat-and-mouse game. But when the game with death begins so early the mouse learns to take adroit evasive action, to outwit the cat and to enjoy watching its near misses. What I acquired at that time was a relationship with death that was both unemotional and ambiguously intimate: though death repelled me, I also saw it as the by-blow of freedom. The fact of having to die is the negation of all that we call freedom, reason and human dignity; but the possibility of taking one's own life augurs a freedom not altogether devoid of pleasure.

Why was Lucia's opulent flesh an intimation of death to the skinny boy I then was? Because I wasn't muscular, like Mario? Because I desired her destruction so that, having destroyed her, I could first possess and then revert with her to chaos? Because my ascetic body was in such strong antithesis to my insatiable appetite? Because I was nearly always afraid of fulfilment?

I should like to be immortal, and yet nothingness beckons; on the one hand the wish that sometime in the unattainable future I may attain myself, be the person I am; on the other, the tendency to eliminate all trace of my existence, to lose manuscripts, not to preserve what is past and done with, to evade the equation of self and identity, to go on living my later life as though I were still only ten years old, outwitting death in the opening moves, having no thought for the end-game, always and only metamorphosis, never permanence or stability.

Yet in this age of tremendous striving, survival is little short of guilt, for so many of those who died were superior to us, the survivors.

Is it really true that confrontation with a corpse evokes first surprise ('He was once alive!'), then fear ('And now he's dead!'), and finally joy ('He's dead and I'm still alive!')? After rigorous self-analysis I can say that I have never felt like that. I am very egoistical, and death has frequently left me indifferent. But when my sister died, all else paled beside this question – why her and not me? Since childhood my life had been held on lien, wrested from death by stealth; now it was as though she were paying the price, had discharged the bond on behalf of myself, the debtor. She was beautiful, strong, lovable – why her? Why not me?

Such questions are as meaningless as the whole game of procreation, birth and death, the disproportionate expenditure of passion, hope, fear, travail and torment that is invested in the nurture of the fertilized ovum through all the stages of becoming and departing, through the growth and mutilation of an individuality, until its extinction in nothingness, its reduction to dust. Job's words continue to ring in our ears:

For there is hope of a tree, if it be cut down, that it will sprout again, and that a tender branch thereof will not cease. Though the root thereof wax old in the earth, and stock thereof die in the ground; yet through a scent of water it will bud, and bring forth boughs like a plant. But man dieth and wasteth away; yea, man giveth up the ghost, and where is he?

Why, then, this account of a race against death, and a highly insignificant one at that, when millions of my contemporaries lost that race in so ghastly a fashion, when millions won it against far greater odds and when, indeed, it would better behove one who has never been imprisoned in a concentration camp, never been tortured, never fought as a partisan or guerrilla, to remain silent in a world whose continents are but a single scream from out of the hell of systems, orders and structures?

I derive courage from the conviction that every one of us, however insignificant, is yet of some importance, that the individual race against death has now become a collective one and that humanity, even if medical pundits have predicted its decline and its mutilation, must not be allowed to lose that race.

Clov: Something is taking its course.
   [*Pause.*]
Hamm: Clov!
Clov [*impatiently*]: What is it?
Hamm: We're not beginning to ... to ... mean something?
Clov: Mean something! You and I, mean something! [*Brief laugh.*] Ah that's a good one!
Hamm: I wonder. [*Pause.*] Imagine if a rational being came back to earth, wouldn't he be liable to get ideas into his head if he observed us long enough ... And without going so far as that, we ourselves ... [*with emotion*] ... we ourselves ... at certain moments ... [*Vehemently*]: To think perhaps it won't all have been for nothing!*

Anyone who means nothing is responsible for nothing, hence the fear felt by Hamm, who was always 'absent', that he might come to mean something. 'To think perhaps it won't all have been for nothing ...' confronts us with the question of meaning; we are asked what we have done towards extracting meaning from 'meaninglessness'. If you *ask* about meaning, you *presuppose* it.

*Samuel Beckett, *Endgame*.

If any being of any kind is able to conceive of something like 'meaning', then he has constituted it.

Man is the author of his own becoming. The master craftsman has to answer for his work. What he does is meaningful *in relation to his work*. Having, in his design, to choose one out of many possibilities, he must be responsible for its realization. The possibilities inherent in man are unlimited; it is our responsibility to decide in favour of their realization in all their plenitude. The individual, reduced to his isolation, senses that humanity is this plenitude. What he is in the process of meaning is measured against what he *anticipates*, not against what already *is* but against what is *becoming*, against humanity.

The charge that such propositions are outmoded humanism leaves me cold. Oddly enough, it is my desire that humanity – this design not yet become reality, this strange semi-manufacture – should achieve immortality. The death of an individual, even if that individual be myself, is not an intolerable concept; and why should we, the failures, the defectives or the only intermittently successful, continue to be a burden through long millennia as the result of inconclusive experiments? What is intolerable, however, is the concept of the death of mankind. I am no more able to applaud the vast increase in population, the explosion in child-bearing, than I am able to see why such child-bearing should be allowed to pursue its course towards misery and the grave instead of being brought under control. And ardently though I believe that two or three thousand million people (the term 'human material' clings gruesomely to masses of this nature) are more than enough, I hope with equal fervour that, given those two or three thousand million, humanity will so take shape as to be immortal.

I

GRAZ

3

Childhood

Childhood: an open window, outdoors shrill voices, the barking of dogs, the cheerful racket of good health and I, confined to my bed, an invalid forbidden to stir for fear of the bony hand that might come clutching at my heart. The sweet fragrance of lilac. I bury my face in its cool clusters, sinking back, far back into the time when I was well – before the auscultations, the rap of the doctor's finger on my chest, the time of not-yet-having-to-go-to-school – the scent of lilac mingling with another, an intoxicating smell. 'Lilac, lilac, poor faded lilac!' I had once said, or so my mother told me, at the age of three or four. It wasn't that but something else, drawing me ever further down, down the stairs where we went to escape the summer heat, underground into the cellar, an eerie spot smelling at first of wine and mouldering walls and then, suddenly, the scent of lilac, overpowering everything else. A woman, her arms and shoulders bare, lifts me up to her lips. Her flesh is lilac, she diffuses lilac. Burying my face in it, I can feel her breasts. Her hair engulfs me in its blondeness. Joy so intense it hurts, the smooth youthful skin, the scent like an abyss. The woman, a friend of my mother's, was called Petra. I was three years old . . .

And then, at the street corner, a little girl in tears. I go up to her, try to comfort and stroke her. Her weeping grows desperate, she screams and pushes me away. A big fat man in a heavy fur coat comes up to me, slaps my face, first the right cheek then the left, with his fleshy hands and, dragging the sobbing child with him, disappears round the street corner. I run home, it's quite near by, fetch a knife from the kitchen, hide it under my coat and, panting, run back up the steps to the street corner in search of the big fat man. Day after day I went hunting for him, up and down every street in the district so that I might plunge my knife into his chest through the little gap in front where his heavy fur coat had fallen apart. I have hated him ever since. I can see him now, the Enemy, striking the defenceless boy, the five-year-old boy who was trying to help a weeping girl, the man with the fleshy hands, the massive jowl, the flabby cheeks, the company chairman, the brass hat, the civil or military dignitary; photographed a hundredfold, he grins at me, the invariable 'smile for the camera please' of the man-eater, the maw of power baring its fangs . . .

My father was an officer, a lecturer at the Liebenau military academy near Graz, 'the old captain with the three bad boys', as he used to be described in our neighbourhood. It was an inordinately long time before he became a major and staff officer. This postponement of his promotion was to him almost as wounding as our resistance, the norm-flouting attitude of his family. Both the former and the latter he attributed to a conspiracy against himself, the simple man who had worked his way up and expected to be recompensed and admired accordingly.

Invariably, when he spoke about his own person, he became so moved that the tears would start into his eyes. His life was a photograph album and, though it contained few snapshots, each one of these was a paradigm: the student whose lantern is the moon, since candles are too dear; the much-respected tutor of a manufacturer's sons, inculcating into them mathematics and a sense of discipline; the young officer swearing his oath of allegiance – to God, the Emperor and the Fatherland; the captain, bouquet in hand, on his knees before his superior's daughter, swearing eternal love; the husband, advancing through life arm in arm with his beautiful spouse; the *pater familias*, heavily moustached, surrounded by his sons, eyes impassive behind his *pince-nez*, severity tempered by kindliness, commanding the highest respect. At this point, however, life began to run counter to the album.

In Samuel Beckett's trilogy of novels, the 'Unnamable' refuses to admit that he is the subject of the photograph they show him. 'But my dear man, come, be reasonable, look, this is you, look at this photograph, and here's your file, no convictions, I assure you, come now, make an effort, at your age, to have no identity, it's a scandal.'

My father's experience was quite the reverse. The photographs refused to admit he was their subject. The album rejected him, snapped shut in front of his eyes. He was left outside. All his efforts to make erring reality conform to the universally accepted photographs proved unsuccessful. It was his misfortune that neither his wife nor his children answered to the ideas of a genteel photographer and obstinately refused to model themselves on situations specially portrayed for their edification.

One of the photographs in this imaginary album was that of the superior and the subordinate, officer and private, command and obedience. Whenever a superior arrived on the scene, the first man who became aware of his presence had to shout to the other subordinates, 'Habt Acht!' (pay attention!), whereupon all those subordinates, whatever their attitude at the time and however incomplete and incongruous it might be, were supposed to freeze. In its evocative ambiguity the Austrian 'pay attention' was not nearly so harsh as the German 'Stillgestanden!' (stand still!). Beware, be on your guard, take care, mind that you pay proper heed to your superiors! All these things were implied in the word of command.

My father delighted in this abrupt freezing of his subordinates which, he thought and privately desired, should be carried out not only by soldiers but also by his spouse, his children, and all other objects, animate or inanimate. The proper ordering of the world required that this should be so.

The batman allocated to my father was called Valentin, a giant of a man who was subject to occasional epileptic fits. He was unwieldy, good-tempered and simple-minded, and we children loved him dearly. When our father was not at home he used to give us rides on his back. He would crawl round the house on all fours, growling, snorting, puffing and blowing, a benevolent monster. But one day the inevitable happened; all of a sudden the door opened and my father came in, having returned home earlier than usual. We scrambled hastily to the ground while Valentin, in dismay, stumbled to his feet. 'Get out!' yelled my father, then, to us, 'And you, go in there!' Obediently, we filed into the drawing-room; outside in the hall his voice could be heard, muffled, yet harsh and cutting. Then he suddenly appeared, ordered us to line up, military fashion, in front of him. 'Valentin's been relieved of his duties,' he said; 'and it's you, with your usual effrontery, who are to blame. He's been doubly disgraced, as a soldier and as a man. You are to ask his forgiveness before I have him punished. A soldier! A man! Crawling on all fours!'

At that moment the realization suddenly came to me: so there are two worlds! One a world of uniforms, of ranks, of conventions, of fetishes, of fixed social attitudes, the other a world of human beings behind this masquerade. A man? A soldier? A component in the machinery of command and obedience? To us Valentin was a human being, a friend, a brother. What did we care about my father's world? We detested it.

The child's experience is totally unlike the fixed concepts of the adult. In his book *Theorie der Prosa*, Viktor Shklovsky quotes what Šperk has to say on the subject:

Children differ from us in that they perceive everything realistically, in a way that adults are unable to do. To us, a chair is part of the concept 'furniture'. But children do not know the category 'furniture', and to them a chair is huge and alive in a way it can never be to us.

Shklovsky comments: 'This is the work performed by the creative writer; he demolishes the category and detaches the chair from the concept "furniture".' To my father, Valentin was a piece of furniture, a man, a soldier, a category in a hierarchically ordered world. We children detached him from that concept. To us he was Valentin, an individual, our friend.

And in the same way Marie, too, was our friend. She had come to my mother as a young girl, to apply for the post of 'domestic servant'. She would, she said, do any kind of work, though as yet her cooking was not up to much, and then – at once timid and defiant she looked my mother straight in the eye – 'then you see, m'm, I'm expecting!' My mother had taken an immediate liking to her. She was delighted with the girl's forthrightness and Marie became our 'maid of all work'. From her we learnt the most astonishing things: that there was a working class; that her father, a carpenter, having swilled away his week's wages, would come home of a Sunday morning and beat his wife and children until, exhausted, he fell onto the bed, whereupon they would turn out all his pockets finding, if they were lucky, one or two kreutzers; that this little ditty was enough to put him into a towering rage:

The little birds sing
Tra-la-lee, tra-la-lee,
Mason and carpenter,
What fools they be.

She further told us that the carpenter's wife regularly gave birth once a year, though fortunately the baby would usually die in the first weeks or months of its life. On these occasions the child's body was laid out on their one and only table. 'It gave us the creeps,' Marie said, 'just a wipe with a damp rag afterwards, and then we'd be dunking bread in our coffee – on the very table where the corpse had been!'

Over the table in our dining-room there hung an extremely ornate paraffin lamp. When it was lit at night it diffused, through its pink shade, a warm, civilized light. But if the wick had been wrongly inserted or had not been trimmed, if it was turned too high or too low, if we forgot to keep a close eye on this insidious lamp or actually left it on its own in the room, it would often happen that it began to flare or smoulder and suddenly the cry would go up: 'It's smoking again!' The chimney would belch forth wreaths of black smoke shot through with rufous streaks, darkening the whole room with an evil-smelling cloud from which soot would shower down onto the table-cloth, the furniture, the carpet; glutinous filth infiltrated everywhere, an acrid smell clung to the curtains. These eruptions of fire and murk, the cry 'It's smoking again!', windows flung open and nerves set on edge, were an intrinsic part of our hearth and home, of our chequered domestic bliss.

Each day clouds would gather above the dining-room table.

We were not allowed to approach the table until father had taken his seat. Before we could actually sit down, we had to go up to him and make our bow. On the command 'Down!' our hands, like recruits, had to remain absolutely still upon the table-cloth. During the meal it was our duty to keep silent. Occasionally, when father had just been reading some new pedagogical treatise, there might be innovations. For instance, we would be invited to make conversation, to fill out the intervals between soup, meat and pudding with sprightly discourse. Through his *pince-nez* my father kept a sharp eye on the way we used our knives, forks and spoons, making sure that we ate our soup without lowering our heads towards our plates, that we wiped our mouths without needlessly soiling the table-napkins, and so forth and so on.

My youngest brother, Otto, was the principal object of this formative process. 'Otto, don't lap up your soup like that! How often do I have to remind you not to slouch? Only yesterday I told you to hold your spoon level when raising it to your lips!' Such reproofs, accompanied by an ominous drumming of the fingers, heralded the arrival of the cloud. When, shortly afterwards, my father suddenly hit out at Otto's temple with the knotted end of his table-napkin, my mother rallied to her youngest son's defence.

'You know I don't like that!'

'The young rascal must be taught manners if he's not to end up in the gutter!'

The clouds gathered.

Otto was a strikingly handsome little boy. He was small for his age and did not really begin to grow until he was seventeen, by which time he was already in naval uniform. He would respond to his father's watchful eye, to the paternal anger constantly crouching and ready to spring, with an indolent composure. It was as though he were not there. One evening he was caught slinking up the stairs that led to the attic. Upon being asked what he proposed to do there, he replied: 'I'm going up to visit my corpse.' He had, he said, visited it often to make sure it had not gone astray. Perhaps this corpse acted as his understudy whenever he became the object of father's disciplinary attentions.

This absurd hatred of his youngest son can hardly have sprung from father's desire to have a daughter and his consequent exasperation when, twelve months after Walter, my mother gave birth to yet another baby of the male sex, though this may well have been regarded as a further act of contrariness on her part. What never failed to enrage him was the impassive mask behind which Otto would take refuge from his angry glare. In order to humiliate him, my father had taken to depositing his scraps on Otto's plate, the bones he had gnawed, the bits of gristle he had been vainly masticating. It was a practice that never failed to repel us; only Otto behaved as if nothing had happened. In addition, father was in the habit of counting every mouthful the child ate and, when Otto was asked by his mother whether he would like another dumpling or some more meat, would exclaim: 'No, he's got enough!'

The clouds gathered. When struck with the table-napkin, Otto had behaved as though the blow had not been intended for him but for some other, non-existent being. But when a knife-handle descended, sharply and painfully, on the little boy's knuckles, my mother jumped up and I jumped up, she seized Otto by the hand and me and my brother Walter, and the four of us left the dining-room. My father sat there, all on his own, dumbfounded at such insubordination and incapable of understanding how reality could differ so greatly from the photograph album.

'What an awful man!' said Marie. 'Shall I fetch the food into the kitchen?' . . .

It was disintegration of the family idyll in the days before world war, revolution and convulsion had become permanent phenomena; except that most women put up less resistance than my mother, most children were not as rebellious as we. And intermittently the paraffin lamp belched forth smoke: the Russo-Japanese War, the German Emperor's fanfaronades, the pounce of the panther* on Agadir, Austria's annexation of Bosnia, the Tripolitan War, the Balkan Wars, the black smoke shot through with rufous streaks . . .

In the album containing pictures of predetermined but never-to-be-realized situations, there was one snapshot called 'The Duel'. Actually there were three photographs. In the first, two women, one a stranger and the other his wife, are kneeling in front of my father, each of them clasping a knee as he stands there imperturbably, his legs slightly bent. In the second picture he is holding a pistol in his right hand and taking aim in copybook fashion, while his *pince-nez* glitter ominously; in the third he is seen magnanimously offering that same hand to the opponent whom his bullet has grazed, forgiving him for having too closely impinged upon an officer's honour.

Of these three photographs, only the first was partially realized while, much to our chagrin, nothing at all came of the second, the third being therefore underexposed, insignificant. Moreover, the first of the three contained a distressing blemish, for though there were indeed two women kneeling in front of my father, neither of them was in fact his wife.

As regards duelling, the position was as follows: though forbidden by law it was, in circumstances more or less rigidly prescribed

*A German gunboat, the *Panther*, sent into Agadir during the 1911 crisis.

by their code of honour, an inescapable obligation for officers of the Imperial and Royal Army. In such cases there could be only one alternative: either to break the law or to forfeit one's honour. This served to remind officers that they were not mere common-or-garden citizens but members of an archaic and higher caste. The fabric of the present was interwoven with archaic institutions and customs of this kind, as is the meat of an old ox with stringy sinews and tough fibres.

The man my father had challenged to a duel was called Kajetan Rieben Edler von Riebenfeld. He had left the army and married the rich owner of a farm which his impetuous activities had quickly reduced to near ruin. It was at this farm, in the environs of Graz, that we used to spend our summer holidays when we were still at school.

The von Riebenfeld family adored histrionics. Only the eldest son, who sported a tiny moustache above a shapeless little baby mouth, had settled down to a conventional existence. In preference to the farm, he had elected to take over a profitable inn, the property of his overbearing wife. The occasional visits of this couple to the farm were heralded by a cloud of dust, for they arrived in a carriage and pair. And on each of these occasions the wheels of that carriage rolled over old Riebenfeld's heart, it being many a year since his stables had harboured anything better than carthorses.

The second son, Rudi, a man of athletic build and classical good looks, was addicted to women and drink. One memorable moonlit night, outside the stables, he tore open his shirt and, confronting his father, threw out his chest with the cry: 'Go on, father, stab me! Right there in my heart! Else I'll strike you dead!' His father, having drawn his Turkish sabre encrusted with imitation gems, began slicing away at the moonshine. Clad only in their nightgowns, Kajetan's wife and Rudi's sister went rushing down into the farm-yard and flung themselves screaming between the two men, who by now were impatiently awaiting their intervention. Kajetan with his Turkish sabre shattered a window pane, Rudi, armed with an axe, smashed a waggon shaft. We children thoroughly enjoyed such happenings.

Rudi's sister, known as Mitzi, had the same classical good looks as her brother. She was rather like Goya's *Maja* (though since Goya was not known to me at the time, I must be attributing this likeness to her retrospectively). After we had been put to bed, we children used to creep down the dreadfully creaky winding staircase from the first floor to the kitchen where Mitzi would be sitting in all her glory before the glowing kitchen range. She would allow us to clamber onto her massive thighs and even, after a brief and half-hearted show of resistance, permit us to play with her ample breasts; we were honour-bound, however, to make no noise, to remain un-heard. But she herself would laugh every now and again, cooing in indolent motherliness and dark desire. It was not our evening games with Mitzi, however, but a complex concatenation of circumstances which induced my father to challenge the Edler von Riebenfeld to a duel.

There was also a third son in the house, a shy seventeen-year-old by the name of Pepi who was in love with my mother, while his brother Rudi's attentions were directed towards our much-courted maid, Marie. At some time or other, while giving my mother a bunch of flowers, Pepi had been permitted to kiss both her hands and possibly also her wrists, on the inside part above the pulse. Somehow this occurrence, as also the relationship Marie was enter-taining with Rudi, came to my father's ears. Perhaps he had, in imagination, confused the two, Marie and my mother, for the mistress's affection for her maid, flouting all conventions, was an abomination to him. Of one thing he was quite certain, however, and that was that the two brothers, Rudi and Pepi, had offended his honour as an officer, his only possible course of action thus being to redeem that honour. But how? It was out of the question to chal-lenge a seventeen-year-old boy to a duel, quite aside from the fact that Pepi and Rudi were farmers and hence, even though nobly born, belonged to a caste incapable of giving satisfaction. After pro-longed reflection my father could see only one solution to the problem: the one-time officer Kajetan Rieben Edler von Rieben-feld must deputize for his sons. Only in this way could the duel be conducted in a manner befitting my father's station.

The proposal delighted the former cavalry officer. To engage in single combat with an officer on the active list might help to re-furbish, indeed lend glamour to, the scant reputation he enjoyed in the neighbourhood. What a topic to boast about at the inn! What an unexpected adventure to brighten up his clodhopper's existence! He therefore shook off his sobbing wife and wailing daughter, remarking that honour was something no woman could understand, that death was preferable to dishonour, and much else of the same ilk. My father was compensated for other situations that had eluded him to the extent that the first picture in the duel series was partially realized: two women, namely Kajetan's wife and the curvaceous Mitzi, knelt down before him, begging his clemency and forgiveness. My mother's absence was, of course, to be deplored; completely unmoved, she had declared the whole business to be a silly piece of play-acting. Some degree of balance was restored, however, by the intensity of the histrionics indulged in by the other two women.

To us children all this was an even greater delight than it was to old Riebenfeld. First there were the officers who came to act as seconds, then there were the pistols, brought out of their cases and subjected to a thorough examination, and then the exhaustive consultations about the location of the duel, our own suggestion of the little field-path leading to the old cherry-tree finally receiving general assent. Again and again the distance was paced out and each time there was a dispute about the count – now one pace too few, now one too many – and, as a background to all these sober preparations, floods of tears, the high-pitched voice of conciliation and the deep drone, now noticeably quavering, of the old cavalry officer, 'Death before dishonour!'

My mother, however, suddenly irrupted upon the scene. 'I've had enough of this,' she said. 'It's perfectly absurd! If you absolutely insist on honour being satisfied, I'm sure that Herr von Riebenfeld will apologize, though what for I can't imagine, and then let's not have any more of this nonsense.'

'Do you know what you are saying?' demanded my father.

'I do know, and there's something else I know. If you refuse to see reason, I and the children will return to Graz this instant, leaving you to do as you please. Otherwise, I invite you all to supper. Marie and Mitzi are already engaged in plucking the chickens.'

Meanwhile my grandfather, the canny old general, had also arrived. Suppressing the smile on his weatherbeaten face he opined that, so far as honour was concerned, an officer should not, of course, follow in the footsteps of Falstaff; on the other hand, the facts of the case were so vague, von Riebenfeld was such a buffoon and his family so determined to apologize on every count, that my father,

he felt sure, would never be able to forgive himself should he be
the cause of these good people's undoing. At that my father declared
himself ready to allow mercy to take precedence over justice, while
we children made no attempt to disguise our dismay.

At the age of six, after suffering from a variety of childish ail-
ments, I contracted pneumonia which subsequently turned into
lobar pneumonia – a mild form of tuberculosis. It was at this time
that my sister was born.

So instead of going to school I had to stay in bed at home where,
with the aid of a primer, I taught myself to read and write all on
my own. When Christmas came, I surprised my mother by writing
her a letter and reading aloud to her from a poetry book. Ever since
that time my greatest pleasure has been the exploration of the world
through books, the attempt to conquer, to hold it fast in writing, to
describe and capture it by means of a system of symbols, the miraculous ability to transform a blank sheet of paper into a communication, description or complaint, into a request or an imprecation.
I read and I wrote. The world took a hold upon me through the
word. Condemned to inactivity among rugs and pillows, I overcame
my impotence by the power of the imagination.

Physically weaker than my brothers and sister, but privileged as an
invalid, I became a tyrant. I invented an explorer and conqueror
by the name of Ernst Fischer who was Columbus, Cortez and Napoleon rolled into one. We built ships and set sail for South America.
Welcomed by the natives as liberators and supported by them, we
drove the British, Dutch and French out of Guiana. The republic
we then founded was modelled on that of ancient Athens, excepting
only the slaves. This involved the construction of a capital city with
a forum, pillared halls and monuments, but built of paper instead
of marble. A constitution was drawn up, a legal code drafted. The
country's history had to be written, its own literature created; a
beginning was made in blue exercise books: 'The Brothers Fischer,
Collected Works.' My brothers soon grew tired of the Republic of
Guiana, the more so since the dictator Ernst Fischer, despite the
country's republican constitution, would permit them to be no more
than his lieutenants. The egoism of weakness, which I had evolved to
a fine art, found itself face to face with a mounting resistance. Grave
dissension shook the republic and it was only by means of cunning
and diplomacy that its gubernatorial legislator, historiographer,

architect and poet was able to foil the firm alliance formed against him by his younger brothers. Skirmishes were frequent. With trays for shields and kitchen knives for swords, the dissident leaders of Guiana did battle with each other until finally the state, once intended to be a model of its kind, collapsed as a result of this internal strife and was consigned to oblivion.

My projected synthesis of adventure and state-founding, politics and literature, science and art had ended in failure. I retreated, read and wrote. I was alone.

One night my mother fled from the conjugal bedroom where the twin beds stood, dark, of ancient provenance, crudely carved, to take refuge with me, who was barely awake. At that time I was perhaps eight or nine years old. Clad only in her nightgown, she knelt panting beside my bed, her body shaken by spasmodic sobbing. She was holding me close in her arms and the odour she gave off was unfamiliar and disagreeable. Instinctively I knew from what it was she had fled.

The process of sexual intercourse was unknown to me. What I had heard about it seemed unbelievable. It was quite inconsistent with my romantic dreams of eroticism that a man should push his stiff member into a woman's vagina and then leap about on top of her like a he-goat. But Marie had intimated as much, adding that the filthy beasts, when their straining and sweating was done, would relieve themselves inside the woman's belly. While my dream of woman certainly involved lying naked with her, inhaling the fragrance of her skin, submerged in her flowing locks, coaxing her lips with kisses, hands roaming gently over her body, I was inclined for the rest to believe in immaculate conception.

The sobbing by which my mother was shaken, the disgust she appeared to be feeling, shocked me into an awareness of sex. So my father had tried to force his way into this woman, had insisted on his conjugal rights. Marie knew what she was talking about; such outrages were not reserved for maid-servants alone. Hideous images thronged my brain. The little turrets crowned with fat knobs, phallic ornamentation of this marriage bed, were instruments of violation. He had used them to impale my mother. Perhaps he had also drawn his sword, an officer even in his night-shirt, demanding subjection. Jack the Ripper – somehow or other I knew the name. From now on I hated my father. So it was he, the gentleman in the fur coat, the man who had slapped my face for trying to comfort a weeping girl, murder in the mask of solid citizenship. 'Shall I go and get a knife?' I asked my mother.

Oedipus complex? Though I worshipped my mother, I never desired her. On the contrary, I felt no physical attraction whatever towards her, and I shrank from manifestations of tenderness. What my father stirred up in me was not jealousy, but rather the hatred felt by the weaker for the stronger, by one without the strength to protect the humiliated woman who had turned to him for protection. It was above all the feeling that he humiliated my mother, she who was far and away his superior, that he sought to subjugate her by physical force, his sword in his right hand, the Civil Code in his left. An invalid's sensibility and my mother's determination to wrest me from the jaws of death may well have helped to arouse in me a spirit of disobedience as opposed to dispirited obedience, a spirit of revolt against the patriarchal world, against the world of officers, bull-necks and riding whips, of gleaming boots and booming voices, against that world which relieves itself inside the belly of humiliated womankind.

That night I said to my mother: 'You must have a bedroom to yourself. And shout for help at once if he tries . . . if he tries . . .' I could find no word for it. 'Shout for help at once. I'll kill him!'

My mother was a beautiful, romantic and passionate woman. I could imagine her as a châtelaine, setting out for an early-morning ride through woods and meadows; surrounded at night by artists, writers and men of the world; at concerts, at the theatre, on the terrace in summer discussing all manner of subjects, delighting in her many lovers. I was convinced that I was not my father's son and implored her to confide in me, to tell me that my father was a poet, an explorer, perhaps even a cardinal. What excited me about this mythical cardinal was the forbidden element and the ceremonial scarlet, the high-sounding pomp of the title.

I found it incomprehensible that my mother should have married this banal, stiff-necked man, twenty years her senior. She did her best to explain it to me and thus, for the first time, to herself. Her mother had died young. Her father, a *grand seigneur* of the old school, had married his self-indulgent, pleasure-seeking niece, and 'Mutz', as we used to call our mother, had been sent to a boarding school for officers' daughters. During the holidays she felt herself a stranger in her home. She admired her father, but his time was taken up with his job, his social duties, his marriage and his library. Her stepmother was concerned with little else besides her mirror, her dressmaker and polite conversation. My mother's only friend was her shy and self-effacing elder brother. She fell in love with a young officer. Her stepmother laughed contemptuously: 'A mere boy, a mere nobody! You think that's a proper match for you?' Her father said: 'You'll have to get that out of your head. He's poor and he's much too young for you. No good can come of such a marriage. What you need is a *husband*, not a playmate.' The lieutenant was summoned to see my grandfather. Politely he was given to understand that it would be most undesirable were he to become involved with his superior's daughter. On 18 August there was a parade to celebrate the Emperor's birthday. My grandfather was watching it from the balcony with his wife and daughters. The young lieutenant was marching at the head of his company. He saluted, drew his revolver and shot himself. The band stopped playing. It was the time of psychological operettas, of the *Merry Widow*, of tragedy in everyday dress. Dust had begun to accumulate on the plush furniture and the artificial flowers. Lunch was eaten off tables where corpses had been laid out.

My mother was distraught, hardly aware of what she was doing. A respectable captain, complete with bald patch, moustache and *pince-nez*, appeared on the scene. Bearing a not-too-expensive bouquet, he fell on his knees before the young lady. '*Gnädiges Fräulein*,' he said, 'allow me to confess my love for you and to lay my heart at your feet.' The object of his address was all too aware of the absurdity both of his posture and his words; but she was defenceless, unsure of herself and the world; she begged to be given time to consider. 'That's the husband for you!' declared her stepmother, 'serious, staid, and correct.' 'An excellent officer,' put in my grandfather. 'And just the right difference in age – like us!' rejoined her stepmother. '*Quite* the best sort of marriage.' Whereupon my grandfather: 'He has worked his way up by earnestness of purpose and his own merits. In marriage, what counts is character, not charm.'

My mother did not dare say no. 'They want to get rid of me,' she thought, 'nobody cares about me.' The engagement was settled. Not until several days afterwards did she summon the courage to speak to her ever-busy father.

'I can't marry him. He repels me.'

'But you've given your consent,' my grandfather replied. 'You can't suddenly refuse now. You must stand by your word. He's a worthy man and he loves you. Besides which, there'd be a scandal.'

The word 'scandal' haunted her like a ghost. 'A scandal!' said her stepmother over her bare shoulder as she sat in front of her looking-glass. 'A scandal!' came the echo from the kitchen, the pantry, the stairs, from the creaking doors, from the whispering walls, from the ticking clocks. My mother contemplated suicide. But how? She had no revolver. Jump out of the window? Drown herself? It was too vulgar and distasteful. Run away, perhaps? But where? And what then? If only some gypsies would come along and take her away with them! If only the house would fall down! If only . . . if only . . . What finally decided her was the advice of her elder brother: 'I don't think he's really that bad. Or would you prefer to be a governess, a spinster, never have any children? It's not your style. By marrying him, at least you'll get away from here, from this enlightened despotism, this tyrannical kindliness that thwarts you at every turn.'

So she married the man she abominated.

'But why?' I asked. 'Why?'

'Don't ask me! I wasn't myself. Why do soldiers stand to attention when ordered to do so? Why do they throw themselves down into the mud and crawl about on all fours? Why do a dunderhead's subjects submit to him instead of forcing him to abdicate? Obedience and authority turn living men into dead things. And by the time the dead wake up, it's too late.'

Therefore one must rebel. Therefore one must acknowledge no authority. Neither that of one's father, nor that of any court of justice, nor that of any institution. Hence, a war against my father, with all it might entail, was inevitable.

Very soon after my mother's flight from the conjugal bedroom, my father became aware that I was obstinately pitted against him, that I was his enemy, the ally of a wife he regarded as eccentric and high-handed.

I cannot deny that I used often to feel sorry for my father. He was incapable of seeing the world other than as depicted by the photographs in his imaginary album. His stereotype of life was more powerful than any argument. What lived, thought and functioned in him was this stereotype. Life owes recognition to the industrious. The state owes its citizens legally defined civic rights. Children owe their parents love and obedience.

'I am a model father. Above all reproach. When, I ask you, have I ever neglected my duties towards you?'

'I don't know anything about your duties, nor do I keep a diary.'

'But I do!'

He took out a big notebook and began to read: 'On 31 March you failed to say good morning to me. On 2 April you gave an insolent reply to a perfectly justifiable question. On 7 April you jumped up from table exclaiming defiantly, "This is too much!" Was this so, or wasn't it?'

'I don't doubt the accuracy of your diary. But that isn't what matters.'

'It's the facts that matter. I know that I am in no way to blame for the pass things have come to.'

In his own way, I thought, he's right. He is the norm. It is we who, as he puts it, have gone off the rails. Why didn't he marry some other woman, one who would have submitted to him, looked up to him, recognized him as the master of the house? Why did he marry my mother who detested him?

'It's not a question of who is to blame.'

'That's the whole question. Any court of law would find you and your mother guilty.'

'And what if we are?'

'Ah, so you admit it! I'll make a note of that. You have confessed that you two are guilty. And I won't let you forget it!'

'But it makes no difference to our relationship with you. We're incompatible, can't exist together. As things are now, my mother's on the verge of a breakdown. Far better to part company.'

'So you propose to drive me from the house, from *my own* house? Away from blood, hearth and home?'

The anthem, I thought. Blood, hearth and home for our emperor, blood, hearth and home for the fatherland. A father's land, a father's world, a father's rights . . .

'In this, your avowed intention, I see additional and aggravating evidence of your guilt. I have the right to an ordered family life, I have a right to your respect and love. Are you able to provide a *single* adequate reason why those rights should be denied me?'

'Is there any such thing as a *right* to respect, a *right* to love? And *in* that case, haven't we too the right to live our own lives?'

'What do you mean, *your* lives? It's my pay, my work you're living on. You children haven't yet attained your majority and as for your mother, a wife owes obedience to her husband. The law, no less than your own welfare, demands it.'

'Must we have the riot act? Can't we speak to each other as man to man instead of as hypothetical son to hypothetical father, as a uniform without rank badges would speak to a uniform with gold stars?' Unable to put into words what I wanted to say, I was trying desperately to find a breach in the wall of categories, an opening that would give me access to a hidden being that might, perhaps, be more than just father, officer, head of family, a being wasting its life away in a dungeon. 'Can't you feel that we're depriving one another of air? That we're on the point of suffocation? Not just my mother, but you too! Can't we come to some reasonable arrangement?'

'There can be no such arrangment between a head of family and the members of his family. It's all laid down, both by the natural order of things and by the law.'

'As it is between officer and subordinate?'

'That, too, is part of the natural order. But to you the word "order" is quite unknown. As I stand here, I am not just your father, I am a representative of the inherent force that keeps the world upon its course. Mutiny, anarchy, the subversion of order – that's *your* principle. What you call an arrangement is chaos pure and simple. The very first concession made by right to wrong, by order to caprice necessarily involves a second and yet a third; it is the first step towards the abyss. This conversation is contrary to nature. But I am the stronger and you are never to forget it.'

'So it's war?'

My father was the norm. But it was a norm that was beginning to go rotten. In the provincial town where I grew up I did not know, was indeed too young to know, the extent to which the breach between fathers and sons foreshadowed a social crisis, nor how representative we were, my father and myself, when thus confronting each other. From the cracks that were appearing in bourgeois society, apprehension oozed. Nietzsche, Strindberg, Wedekind, Sigmund Freud, Karl Kraus, the young poet and diarist Georg Heym – all these presaged the catastrophe. The growth of irrationalism, the mistrust of reason and intellectual argument, the tendency to violence, cannot simply be attributed to the fact that the imperialist bourgeoisie had turned their backs on reason and were staking their all on violence. Although social structures usually have one dominant factor, its influence will not necessarily extend to every sphere. In social structures that lag behind new inventions, requirements, expectations and possibilities, everything is at risk. The sudden ventilation of sexual problems (psychoanalysis, *Les Demoiselles d'Avignon, Frühlingserwachen, Die chinesische Mauer* etc.), or the struggle against the ornate, against plush, against hypocrisy, or the rebellion of sons against fathers, characteristic of the years preceding the First World War, could be regarded only in the most narrow and dogmatic sense as deriving directly from the new monopolistic structure of capital; yet the discrepancy between the new realities on the one hand and the old institutions and norms of living and thinking on the other, the malaise, the premonition of approaching catastrophe, engendered a general condition of instability, of exacerbation, of conflict. From out of the bourgeois world, now that it had sprung a leak, there crept fear, and with it came an outburst of violence.

When, at dusk, my father sat at the piano playing with a sure touch the music of Beethoven, Schubert, Wagner, Verdi and Hugo Wolf, I was moved by his musicality. I found it less agreeable when he made us play at 'guess the tune', which meant identifying a song from the first few bars he played. Again, I would feel sad on his behalf when the song: 'Laugh, Bajazzo, cut the maddest capers . . .' echoed mournfully across the dark room and my father exchanged his uniform for the garb of the deceived clown. And every time my hope would revive that this tormented man, who in turn tormented my mother, might be persuaded by rational argument to come to some sort of understanding. In the romantic role of my mother's deliverer I obstinately pursued the course of enlightenment – as, indeed, I continue to do. Though my expectation that reason must inevitably prevail was repeatedly disappointed, I persevered in arguing with my father, in proposing a separation, without fuss or bother, a gentleman's agreement that we should spend two months out of every twelve together, doing our best during that time to avoid all conflict. But every attempt on my part he regarded as renewed provocation.

One day during my fifteenth year he called me into his study. Seated stiffly in his red armchair, he was breathing on the lenses of his *pince-nez* and polishing them with his handkerchief.

'I have something to say to you. You may take a seat. Your behaviour is becoming increasingly outrageous. People are already beginning to talk about us. There have been some anonymous letters. I find myself compelled to take steps.'

On the desk, among the legal books and the pedagogical treatises, lay a revolver. Was my father trying to impress me?

'In front of your grandfather, you blatantly refused me the respect that is my due. You insisted on discussing that Jew, Heine, with him, although you know quite well that I regard him as a distiller of literary poison. Though I cleared my throat repeatedly, you took no notice and when I tried to speak you cut me short. My patience is exhausted. If you won't listen, then I'll have to make my displeasure felt.'

Going over to the desk, I set the chair at an angle to it and sat down. Among the books lay the revolver.

'Your mother sets you against me, although I am the best and most conscientious of husbands. I don't waste time, I deny myself all pleasure, I work only for you. It's no trifle to keep a wife and four children in a manner befitting one's station.'

'It's not *our* fault that you've got four children.'

'Another of your customary impertinences! In future I'm going to cut down your mother's house-keeping allowance.'

'She can't make ends meet as it is, and if it wasn't for grandfather . . .'

'She accepts money from him in order to lower me in his eyes. Not one of you knows what money is. As a student I used to work by the light of the moon because I couldn't afford to buy candles.'

I had heard the same story so often before that I answered without thinking: 'The moon was brighter then. It's older and weaker now. I, for one, find it impossible to read by the light of the moon.'

'Older and weaker? What nonsense have you been reading?' my father asked without a smile, for he always took everything literally. Once he had exhorted my mother to shop only at Gross's thenceforward. 'Why?' 'Because his goods are the best and the cheapest' – 'Who says so?' – 'It's here in the paper, it's down in black and white!' Anything that was down in black and white was to him as incontrovertible as an official pronouncement. The fact that my mother did not do her shopping at Gross's was yet another proof that she did not know what money was.

My mother had to be extremely economical. She would sew until late into the night, and darn our worn-out stockings. But sometimes she would bring home flowers, or perhaps some unnecessary knick-knack: 'Isn't it pretty?' she would say, 'and it wasn't at all expensive!' In fact, she just didn't know what money was.

'I shall cut down your mother's house-keeping allowance.'

'Might I make an alternative suggestion?'

'It's *my* turn to talk now, and I haven't finished yet. I'm going to take your brother Otto, that lazy good-for-nothing, away from school and set him to learn a trade.'

'He wants to go into the navy. His ambition is to go to a naval academy.'

'Why these eternal pretensions? Father's in the infantry, so what does Master Otto have to do but go into the navy! Why not the cavalry, if it's the cachet he's after? But I'm the one who has to pay. My patience is exhausted. The navy for that whipper-snapper? Putting on the airs of royalty just because his mother's got a handle to her name!'

'Might I make an alternative suggestion?' I repeated. 'You can keep your money. We don't need it. Let's go our separate ways. We'll be able to manage somehow.'

'You're proposing to throw me out, eh?' My father had risen. 'But I'm staying, my fine young fellow. I don't have to treat with you. I order you . . .'

The revolver slid into my hand. I had not meant it to, it just seemed to happen. The object between the law book and the pedagogical treatise had taken possession of me, not I of it. I considered it thoughtfully, then looked at my father. He was trembling. His *pince-nez* had slipped off his nose. His face was even more sallow than usual. 'Put that away!' he exclaimed. 'Put it away at once!' He was afraid.

The unexpectedness of the situation determined my attitude, directed the scene. I was flabbergasted. Is command really so weak that it immediately collapses if not obeyed? The weapon was in my hand, my father was afraid, the roles had been cast and I played the one allotted to me, adapting myself to the situation. The old officer was trembling before a fourteen-year-old boy.

'Put it down at once! At once!' he repeated, sinking back into his red armchair.

For the space of a second I pointed the revolver at him. Then I laid the weapon down on the desk.

'I didn't mean it!' stammered the old man, for that was all he was now, just old, nothing more.

'I didn't mean it, either.'

'Against your own father! An old man! Your own flesh and blood!'

Why didn't he shout at me? Why didn't he have the courage to give me an order? Was this patriarchal world with its law books, its barracks, its prisons, its warrants, its legal authorities and its traditions so weak that an armed NO was sufficient to bring it to its knees?

'I had thought of a cut in the house-keeping allowance only as an extreme measure. Surely you know how kind-hearted I am . . . It's just that I worry about you . . .'

Is recourse to arms, a sudden show of force enough to intimidate these commanders, these rulers, these fathers? Can a naked revolver achieve what no argument has been able to achieve? When reason fails, can the game be won by force?

'Now, you're a sensible boy. Talk to your mother and the rest of the family. And if you need anything, you only have to ask . . .'

From that moment onwards, I was the stronger. The victory did not make me glad. I would sooner have found myself face to face with an unyielding dictator than with this incarnation of fear in uniform, unable to preserve its dignity unless the world were kept on its course. Moreover it was a victory that in no way altered the circumstances.

My mother's house-keeping allowance was not cut down. My brother Otto was allowed to remain at school. When he had reached the fourth form and taken the necessary examination, he left the parental home with a sigh of relief to enter, with my grandfather's help, the naval academy commanded by Nikolaus Horthy. My father treated me as an equal. But he stayed.

When, in the summer of 1914, the band suddenly stopped play-ing – we were sitting in the cafe by the Hilmteich, the day was

shimmering blue and green like an exotic butterfly – and we heard
the announcement that in Sarajevo a Serbian irredentist had shot
Crown Prince Franz Ferdinand, I identified with the assassin and
was delighted that he was called Princip [principle].

In my diary I wrote: 'All honour to the principle of freedom!
Down with tyranny!' I knew nothing about Franz Ferdinand and
his political ideas, or about the problems of dualism and trialism in
the elegantly decaying monarchy, or about the complex relationship between His Majesty's German-speaking, Slav and Magyar
subjects. It was not politics that aroused my passions, nor was
'freedom' a political or philosophical concept to me; rather, it was
something both exceedingly personal and exceedingly abstract.
The Crown Prince as an individual meant nothing to me: he stood
for the world of uniforms and ranks, of command and obedience
– my father's world.

The war that began in 1914 and has been going on ever since
revealed its nature to me through two experiences.

Awkward young soldiers were being pelted with flowers by
women and girls. The streets of Graz were full of excited people
marching towards the Südbahnhof. Their patriotism reeked
of alcohol. Over and over came the roar: 'Death to all Serbs!
Long live the Emperor! Down with traitors!' Outside the station,
in the middle of a knot of howling, screaming, insane people, a man
was dragged to the ground, trampled upon, torn limb from limb.
'A Serbian spy!' someone called out. 'A Serbian spy!' went the cry
from one mouth to another as the remains of a human being were
retrieved from the murderous mob.

'How can you tell if someone's a spy?' I asked one of my school-
fellows. He looked at me suspiciously. 'What do you mean? You
don't, by any chance, mind if people choose to make short work
of spies?'

'But how do they know they're spies?'

'He was speaking Serbian.'

'Is that forbidden?'

'People ought to speak German at a time like this!'

So it was not going to be just a war of uniforms.

'That's the way it begins', said my mother. 'That is war. And it's
also the end.'

Her voice was very sad and fraught with emotion.

That evening there was a big dinner-party at our house. Exclusively officers: a general, two of my uncles and a number of young subalterns. They had brought champagne with them and sat in the dining-room under the paraffin lamp which diffused its civilized light – not, this time, a cloud of black smoke shot through with rufous streaks. Their time had come, a great time that waxed ever greater. They were drinking liberally and were in jovial mood. 'We'll thrash these Serbian horse-thieves to ribbons. In a fortnight the whole affair'll be over, unfortunately. Then it'll be one long celebration, a party to end all parties! But now, how about a toast? To our charming hostess! To victory! Death to all Serbs!' The uniforms stood up and raised their glasses.

My mother, too, had risen.

'You're not officers!' she said, in unexpectedly level tones. 'You're common murderers. Now be off!'

So dumbfounded were the uniforms that, glass in hand, mouths agape, an inane expression on their faces, they froze into what is known in the theatre as a 'tableau'.

My father was the first to realize that something appalling had happened, an insult to the army, under his own roof, a betrayal of God, Emperor and Fatherland. And he himself, compromised by this woman in front of a general – he was finished, ruined.

'How *could* you . . .' he hissed between clenched teeth.

At last the uniforms understood. With a curt bow the general turned towards the door. My father followed him, almost disappearing under a smother of apologies. One after another the officers put their glasses down on the table and silently, with bowed heads, marched out of the room.

When they had all left, my mother said softly: 'What were they saying? What were they saying? It's not true that my brothers are monsters. What terrible poison is this – the desire to trample on those weaker than oneself! The power to murder! The werewolf!'

These were the two occurrences that determined my attitude to the war.

So far as our private life was concerned, the war brought a certain relief. My father was appointed commandant of the Enns military academy. We saw him only in the summer holidays, and during those months we did our best to get along together without conflict.

The release of my mother's 'surety' money and the cash payment that followed came as a godsend to her. When an officer married, the bride's parents had to make over a certain sum as a kind of accident insurance; after so many years of marriage and under certain conditions the Ärarische, or Austrian Exchequer, would place the sum at the disposal of the officer's wife. My grandfather advised my mother to invest the money in war loans, but she was so delighted to have some money of her own at last that she did not follow this patriotic if ill-judged advice. Until that time she had expended all her passion, her desire to love and be loved, on us her children. We were her only compensation for a marriage to a man she loathed, the only justification for her existence. Now that she had a little money of her own, now that her husband was absent for most of the year and we were growing up reasonably healthy and independent, she looked forward to making up for what she had missed.

'Mother of the Gracchi', my grandfather used to call his youngest daughter; he himself bore an undeniable likeness to Scipio. Indeed, it was not just my mother's face that was Roman; there was a classical grandeur about her whole character. The stultifying nature of her marriage, her anxiety for her children and the stuffy provincialism by which she was surrounded had prevented her from developing into a woman of stature.

At the outbreak of war my mother was thirty-seven, doomed, or so it seemed, to share the fate of Madame Bovary. Although she was far more spirited, intelligent and intellectually aware than Flaubert's heroine, the world of stupidity, triviality and narrow-mindedness whose prisoner she remained while seeking to escape it was the same tritely infamous bourgeois world that crushed Emma Bovary. She never found her proper milieu or the experience that liberates; hers was the adventure of the circus horse, galloping round and round in a circle.

By comparison with my father, the bandleader Willy Maier was seductive and even lovable. He played the fiddle while his daughter, with exuberant breasts but careworn features, sat at the piano; two other musicians made up the little orchestra which used to play in the summertime in the Swiss café beside the Hilmteich. My mother was delighted whenever Willy Maier performed for her *con brio*, his eyes as expressive as his violin. I rejoiced in her success and was bored by the daughter who ogled me pensively, as though speculating whether, in spite of my youth, I might have means of my own. I purchased one or two of the photographs which portrayed her in a seductive *décolleté*. Fleetingly she pressed my hand, lamenting that she never had a day off; finally the bandleader's wizened wife, about whose existence we had known nothing, lay in wait for my mother in a dark alley-way, heaped insults on her and threatened to scratch her face. In the course of a long discussion I persuaded my mother, whose youthfulness had been restored by this innocent flirtation, to avoid Willy Maier from then on, along with his wife and daughter.

The years that followed were a curious amalgam: on the one hand, withdrawal into a world of fantasy, of magic-lantern slides upon whose images reality seldom impinged; on the other, naïve rebellion against a world in process of disintegration, the world of the military, of hysterical patriotism, of catastrophe lowering among the war bulletins and casualty lists, all personified in the disabled soldier churning out the *Radetzky March* and the *Blue Danube* on his barrel-organ – a far cry indeed from the 'luvverly funeral' of the Austrian daydream: four black horses, black plumes waving, the pompous cortège of death.

At this time my mother and I were more or less of an age: I was experiencing a first pubescence, she a second. She spent her 'surety' on the opera and concerts, on smart clothes and hats – and today I still feel glad that my mother should have stolen a march on inflation, using the money to catch up on ephemeral pleasures rather than investing it in war loans.

In her box at the opera her applause would earn her the gratified looks of the opera singers whom she would later meet and invite home to supper. My brother Walter and I wore wide-brimmed velour hats and displayed a not very confident *odi profanum vulgus* when we accompanied my mother in the Sunday parade, thereby provoking the corps students, the officers and the patriots in civilian dress. We made a deliberate show of ignoring the war and, childish though the forms taken by our defiance may have been, I do not hesitate to endorse them today.

We would have been perfectly ready to protest against the war in real earnest, but in this town where Karl Kraus was unknown there was not so much as a murmur of dissent, and no echo reached us of the resistance put up by revolutionary intellectuals and workers. In the military circles in which I grew up, politics were regarded as

vulgar and, much though she abhorred the milieu from which it
sprang, this disparaging view had also communicated itself to my
mother. In reading the newspapers we confined our attention to
features and reviews, ignoring the leading articles; we were repelled
by patriotic bombast and knew nothing of the labour movement.
'The workers? That's where they live', we children were told
whenever we went past the sombre viaduct near the station;
beyond that viaduct lay the town's few big factories, lorded over by
retired public servants and erstwhile corps students. Thus there was
something slightly sinister about the workers, a whiff of sulphur
quite unconnected with the working-class children with whom we
played; they were just children like us, but the workers as a body
constituted, beyond the viaduct, a disquieting area of darkness. Thus
in our resistance to the war we stood alone, and the only expression
we could find for it was a Bohemianism not altogether devoid of
absurdity. And when, after Italy's entry into the war, I read d'Annunzio, ostentatiously carrying his books about with me, I thought the
world of myself.

Expelled from grammar school for writing pornographic poems,
I made the most of my freedom. My reading was an unselective
miscellany: literature classical and modern, good and bad; history,
art, philosophy. There was no one who could help form my taste.
As far as my grandfather was concerned, literature ended round
about 1890 (which meant that while Flaubert, Ibsen and Tolstoy
were just tolerated, Zola, Strindberg and Dostoyevsky were definitely taboo) and, as for my mother, her judgement was uncertain
and subjective; she loved Lessing above all other writers, but she
also had some admiration for Theodor Körner, and it was only by
degrees that I managed to wean her from this predilection.

I wrote poetry, novels and plays, in their amateurishness more
caricature than pastiche of Shakespeare, Grabbe, Hebbel, E. T. A.
Hoffmann, Ibsen, Strindberg, Hauptmann, Béranger, Heine and
Dehmel. I vaguely recall the plot of one of the plays, called *The
Spirit King*. Its hero was the junior employee of a very rich self-
made man. When the play opens the millionaire is crawling round
the floor in search of a kreuzer which has rolled away somewhere
into a corner. 'This is how I grow rich,' he says. The little clerk
despises the crawling beast he has to serve, for he himself is really
the monarch of a vanished spirit kingdom who is condemned to

live in this vale of tears. On midsummer night he foregathers with the spirits who, once every year, are permitted to resume their former way of life – writers, painters, composers, actors, impecunious art-dealers, vendors of the spirit world's left-over stock. For the space of twelve hours they have the power to summon the wives of the rich, to chastise monarchs, to strip warlords of their uniforms and compel them to polish the boots of their troops, to force millionaires to crawl round the floor in search of the last kreuzer, their banknotes and securities having previously been consigned to the flames. In the course of this night the spirit king seduces his boss's daughter and the following day is kicked out through the door.

It was a skit, and a far from optimistic skit, on the magic circle in which we were imprisoned.

After two years of this confused existence, another school accepted me as an extra-mural student. I crammed the work of three years into one, though not at the expense of reading and writing, concert-going and visits to the opera; on the eve of my examinations I had a nervous breakdown. Weeks of insomnia, each quarter of the hour recorded by the bells of St Leonhard, while time struck out at me, crept away, stood still and struck, and crept away through the darkness, the enemy, the relentless enemy, until it was subdued by the daytime bustle, and the candle beside my bed went out – the light, deathly blue rising into yellow, flickering away into red, that had illuminated the notebooks of the insomniac.

One of my mother's relations was head of a department in the Ministry of Foreign Affairs. Through him I obtained permission, in the summer of 1917, to accompany my mother to Switzerland whither a rich aunt had invited us.

Restored to health I returned, took my wartime matriculation, joined the army and went to the front.

4

Collapse

The oyster of sleep was beginning to open, its shell prised apart by intruding day but I, still too tired to keep awake, sank back into the gentle roar, gentle no longer, a rolling torrent, rolling, clattering, rattling, the sound of wheels, back into security, the smell of hay, where from? High overhead a tranquil sky, where to, where am I, what was that? Wasn't I riding through the night? Flickering horizons, conflagrations, the approach of dawn, and wasn't I sliding off my horse? '*Mère des souvenirs, maîtresse des maîtresses* . . .' Baudelaire, whom I read at the front. And then retreat, day and night, rolling columns, and now awake, no longer dreaming, instead Sergeant-Artificer Hrdal's familiar face, and horses, uniforms, guns, mulberry trees, autumnal meadows, the road . . .

'We've elected you to the soldiers' council,' Hrdal said.

'You've elected me to . . .?'

'We've sacked the officers and elected soldiers' councillors. Admittedly you're already half an officer, but we like you . . .'

'Sacked? I hope you've included Colonel Kraus!'

'He was the first . . .'

And there, standing between two pretty Italian women in the Renaissance portico of a yellow villa, was Colonel Kraus with his red drinker's face, waving to us, his insubordinate regiment.

'Sacked!' said Hrdal. 'Taking his leave of us. They've signed the armistice. Thinks he doesn't need us any more, the bastard. Those women will have the clothes off his back, you can be sure of that, and he'll be lucky if he's not done in by the peasants. The war's over. We've got to be in some sort of order when we push on.'

'Did I sleep through all this?'

'You needed it. We didn't want to wake you. The men have held a meeting and both Germans and Czechs have given their word of honour to stick together until we reach safety. Then we elected soldiers' councillors so as to have the leadership we need.'

'And what will happen next?' I asked – I, who had been elected to the soldiers' council while asleep and who, though not a party to the upheaval, approved of it with all my heart.

'Nobody knows.'

Thus, in the few hours while I had been asleep, the Imperial and Royal Field Artillery Regiment to which I belonged, half of it Czech-, half German-speaking, had ceased to exist and with it, as likely as not, the Imperial and Royal Army and the Imperial and Royal Monarchy and, so I hoped, the whole archaic load of rubbish. How long such things endure! And then, how quickly it's all over.

Colonel Kraus for one.

Barely a week had gone by since Colonel Kraus, complete with glossy boots and an adjutant glossy as porcelain, had ridden out into the marshy country by the banks of the Piave where the half-battery I had the honour of commanding occupied an advanced position in the middle of a swamp. He was an unexpected guest and I had not seen him once since my arrival at the front. I ordered my men to form up, excluding those who had a high fever although even the physically fit looked in poor shape, with filthy boots and uniforms, the majority unshaven, unsoldierlike and unhappy. This did not at all please Colonel Kraus who bellowed at me: 'Your men look like pigs!'

In somewhat unmilitary fashion I replied that such, unfortunately, was the case and that much as we should all have liked to have clean boots and neat haircuts, we had been ordered to remain here in the mud. Although my tone had been perfectly polite the elegant officer assumed the appearance of a blood sausage exploding in a pan.

'Who do you think you are? If your colonel can wear clean boots, it's surely not beyond you to see that your men don't go about looking like pigs.'

'If you, sir, would let us have your villa behind the lines along with two orderlies, our boots would be as shiny as yours,' I said with the utmost amiability.

'You don't know me yet!' the colonel shouted. 'And you call

yourself an officer's son? We'll . . .' The adjutant was reaching for his holster.

Behind me there was a muffled slap, the sound of a dozen hands striking leather. The colonel wheeled his horse round, his adjutant followed, and they rode away. Behind me the gunners returned their pistols to their holsters and since then I have known what *solidarity* is. Even today, this word brings echoes of the slap of hands on leather pistol holsters.

'Could end badly,' said Hrdal, clasping my hand.

But when the time came it ended badly for the army of His Majesty the Emperor of Austria and King of Hungary, as also for Colonel Kraus who had ridden out to us under the pale blue autumn sky on the day before we were instructed to pull out, the day before the Americans broke through.

'Defeat!' Sergeant-Artificer Hrdal said when our half-battery was ordered to lay down rapid fire on the Italian positions at ten o'clock and withdraw at six o'clock the following morning. The sick tumbled out of their dugouts, the signalmen abandoned the telephone, everyone was happy and excited. 'We're going home!' someone ventured to say. 'Going home?' growled Hrdal. 'If you think any of you'll be better off when you get there, you're wrong. Your masters at home will grind you down the same as your masters out here, and nothing'll be any different. Except for you, of course, Mr Fischer, sir, you'll become a doctor or something, but us? Labourers, peasants, scum. You've always been decent to us, you've given up your extra rations, shared out your cigarettes with us. All pals together at the front. But who are you going to stick up for when you get home, Mr Fischer, sir? For the common people? Against Colonel Kraus . . .?'

By eight in the evening my pack was ready; Baudelaire, Carducci, Oscar Wilde, loot for the newcomers, were left behind on the duckboards. At eight-thirty the battery commander, a canny, self-effacing reservist, came to take leave of us. At ten o'clock the regiment began to withdraw; we were expected to remain in position until six o'clock the following morning. 'Pull out sooner if it gets too beastly,' the battery commander said amiably as he rode away into the darkness. Cold showers of rain, flares, searchlights, heavy artillery to the north. The men squatted beside the howitzers, talked of home in subdued voices, fell silent, every so often puffing nervously at evil-smelling cigarettes.

At ten o'clock that evening all hell broke loose on the far bank of the river, flames ripped the darkness, a thousand guns roared out, shells screamed past, shrapnel burst above our heads, everywhere about us splinters smacked down on the swamp which swallowed them greedily. Then the answer from the Austrian artillery, barking field guns to the left, to the right the roaring howitzers. After an hour there was a pungent reek of cordite, the barrels were heating up, the men sweating. I cannot deny that I was carried away by ambition to excel at this game, that I, who loathed war, kept urging the gunners to load more rapidly, to fire more rapidly. It was not ambition alone but also delight in chaos, the infernal splendour of the battle, the flickering horizons, the pomp of death. At first it enchanted then gradually stupefied me, I grew tired, listless. As more and more Austrian batteries fell silent, so the din on the other side increased. By five o'clock in the morning it was apparent that my howitzers were the only ones still in action on this side of the river.

I gave the order to pull out. The horses were supposed to be waiting for us by the bridge. The twenty members of my half-battery, seven of them in a high fever with malaria, worked doggedly and in silence to drag the guns out of the gurgling, tenacious ooze. At last it was done; two men to each gun-wheel, they grasped the slippery spokes, pressing themselves against the felloes as they sank up to their ankles in mire. After half an hour I thought I could go no further; the slimy mud had me firmly in its clutches. A jerk, and my right leg slipped out of its boot. How long it took me to pull the sodden leather back over my foot, I don't know. Exhausted I plodded on behind the guns, at each step clutching the leg of a boot with aching, lacerated hands lest I should lose one again. Two hours later we reached the bridge where the teams were waiting.

Too weak to swing myself into my horse's saddle, I was assisted by a corporal, who gave me a leg up. I headed for the road in search of the regiment. At every step the exhausted beast sank into the soft, glutinous, gluttonous ground, gave at the knees, to be jerked up again and again with the reins. From the indeterminate background of noise emerged the rattle of wheels, the clatter of gun carriages, the stamping of horses, the human babel of orders, protests, curses. At first I could perceive nothing and then, between the trees, I caught sight of lanterns and hurricane lamps, pale and diffused in the gloom, indistinct silhouettes of riders, guns, heavily laden waggons. From the dark columns faces stood out, ghost-like. Bursting shrapnel sang through the air, rattled against the branches. I rode slowly along the column. The road had been churned up by many thousands of feet, hooves, wheels. Vehicles jostled, squeezed, ground against each other. Men argued, quarrelled, cursed. No one cared what happened to his comrade. From a few miles distant came the roar of the Italian artillery. The bursts groped their way towards the road. All at once the storm broke over us. A hail of shrapnel smacked down on the huge body of the column. My horse shied, my saddle slipped, I hung from the creature's belly, slid to the ground. There was some laughter, no attempt to help. I led the horse by the reins. At ten o'clock next morning I found the regiment in a half-flooded meadow beside the road. The sun, dim and sickly, struggled through the grey dampness. Hungry and exhausted, I reported that the half-battery had ceased fire at five o'clock that morning and then withdrawn. Colonel Kraus, looking old and dilapidated, nodded apathetically as he squatted beside the fire.

At the field kitchen I was given coffee and biscuits. Warming my hands on the hot mug and chivvying the sleep from my burning eyes I listened to the conversation of the others. They talked of a breakthrough by the Americans, of treachery on the part of Hungary and Poland, of an armistice, of a withdrawal as far as the Tagliamento or the Isonzo, of peace negotiations; they blamed the high command, the imperial family, the Prussians; suggested that Austria would come to terms with the Entente. No one knew anything definite. I took no part in the conversation and, when I had eaten and drunk, I mounted my horse and made my way back down the column in search of my half-battery. It was a relief to be returning to people who regarded one as a human being and not as a mere hunk of flesh dressed up in uniform. Having brought them back to the regiment, I was settling down with my head on my saddle when Colonel Kraus's adjutant sent for me. Avoiding my eyes, he ordered me to ride on ahead, reconnoitre the road and bring back a report on conditions.

Once again I was engulfed in the rumbling monotone of the columns of sleepless regiments slowly pushing their way onwards along the wide road. Horses fell, guns stuck fast, wagons became entangled, the press grew ever more impenetrable. Yelling drivers lashed their horses, officers raged, irritated men snarled back.

I observed with curiosity a daredevil N.C.O. in charge of a gun trying to force his way through, although by now four columns were wedged into one solid mass. His horses' muscles bulged as if about to burst as he managed to urge the team into a trot and, by taking the extreme edge of the road, to gain a few yards. Barely had he heaved a sigh of relief than the churned-up embankment collapsed and his gun tipped onto its side; two horses fell, an axle broke and a mass of earth slid into the marsh. A miracle was needed to unravel the tangle.

The miracle happened. Shouted commands, an order coming up the column, passed from mouth to mouth: 'Clear the middle of the road!' It was, I thought, a good and sensible order, but how was it to be carried out? An officer on horseback was threading his way through the confusion: 'What's this appalling shambles? You've five minutes to clear the road. His Excellency is going to see that there's an orderly withdrawal.' 'And what shall we do about this gun?' a sergeant inquired of His Excellency's adjutant. 'Don't ask idiotic questions! Get it out of the way, push it into the marsh – anywhere. That's your affair. I'm not in charge here. You've five minutes to clear the road. Is that understood?'

The commander-type had invariably repelled me, but now I began to understand the value of a leader, the workings of order. After some argument the gun was tipped into the marsh, its wheels protruding from the black morass. At this there was some indignation but the main reaction was one of malicious glee. By dint of furious shoving, squeezing and hauling, the columns were eventually split down the middle and forced sideways towards each verge. Carts skidded over the embankment to splash groaning into the mire and within five minutes the middle of the road was clear. A grey motor-car, lean and elegant, glided through the gap between the masses, throwing out cascades of mud to right and left. In the grey car, conversing with a senior officer, sat His Excellency, the Lieutenant-Field Marshal. Both were wearing fur greatcoats and at intervals they peered out anxiously from the depths of their upturned collars. Everybody saluted; the general, nervous and aloof, nodded condescendingly. The road opened up before him as if by magic; in his wake followed more grey motor-cars, smiling, saluting officers: the General Staff. They vanished as they had come, improbable as wraiths.

'Pleasant journey!' called a gunner, no longer rigid at the salute, after they had passed. 'Give the Emperor the army's regards!' shouted another. 'Did you get a good look at them?' asked a third. 'You won't have another chance.' He was right. Taking advantage of the empty highway I rode on quickly. Soon the columns had again merged to form a thick, congealing porridge. No one was going to see that there was an orderly withdrawal. Our commanders had gone. That was about all they were good for.

At midday a word began to spread among the mass of men: armistice. A few aircraft were circling above us but no bombs were dropped. The artillery had been silent since ten o'clock that morning. The sky was soaking up the clouds, the sun was scorching. I unbuttoned my heavy greatcoat which was plastered with dry mud and put my sweat-soaked cap into my pocket; the reins lay loosely in my hands. My skull was buzzing with drowsiness. Suddenly I heard myself addressed – or was it me? 'You there – the officer cadet!' There was another ferocious bark and I found myself face to face with a major who was glaring at me angrily and gesticulating like a lunatic. 'Can't you salute properly? What's your name?' Wonderingly I gave my name, quite unable to fathom what the clown had in mind. Having written my name in his notebook he returned to the attack: 'Look at your turnout! No cap, greatcoat unbuttoned, girth slipping – a fine example to the men. With people like you, His Majesty couldn't fail to lose the war!' Before I had time to reply, this champion of a properly turned out, respectful defeat had spotted the next target for his imperial and royal wrath.

Austria! I thought, and then I heard someone whistling. A second-lieutenant was sitting on the field kitchen, his cap tilted over his eyes, plucking a chicken and whistling: 'We're the girls, we're the girls, we're the girls from the Chantant, and love we always take lightly.' 'Come here, starveling!' he called to me. 'A man's got to eat, that's what I always say. And if you're like me you do so at your leisure. Only leisure polishes leather – that's my motto. Armistice. A man isn't human when he's hungry; he's got to eat his fill. Fine bird, isn't it? I enjoy plucking it – I've never minded hard work so long as my tum gets the benefit. The cook's going to roast it. I've schnapps as well. Sit down. D'you play tarok? Two of us do but we've still to find a third.' I told him that I had to ride on ahead and reconnoitre. 'Reconnoitre? Are you cracked? What are you going to reconnoitre? The shambles up front and the shambles behind? Tie up your horse to one of the waggons and don't be a bore.' I'd be back, I told him. 'By then there won't be any chicken,' said the second-lieutenant. 'Look at them prowling around. Each to his own taste, that's my motto. When a man's on duty he's not human. If you've no wish to be human, that's up to you. Good-bye.' I saluted and rode off, while the second-lieutenant went on plucking his chicken, whistling: 'Where there's no sun, the rose soon fades away, where there's no love, affairs soon have their day . . .', and plucking his chicken at his leisure.

By four o'clock in the afternoon I was back again with the regiment making my report. The colonel stared at me, the adjutant gave a bored nod. At the field kitchen I found they had reserved a special helping of pork ('Don't you tell the officers!') and black coffee with a great deal of sugar ('Secret reserve, none for that lot!').

But that lot still wielded the power. I was summoned to the adjutant. 'Is that your horse?' 'Yes, he's a stray I found yesterday.' 'Hand it over to the colonel at once. His own has gone lame.' 'And what about me?' 'Go and find another one!' Orders as always. Obedience as always.

The beast they eventually gave me had hitherto done duty as a draught-horse. He had been accustomed to proceed with a horse ahead of him and another on his off-side and he was unable to adapt himself to his new circumstances. It was impossible to make him move straight ahead and whenever I fell into a doze there was always the danger of sliding down the nearside embankment. How I detested that stupid animal! But were we any different? Didn't we still obey, still salute?

Night fell, black; there had been no intervening dusk. But still the horizons glowed red, burning villages, camp fires, flickering reflections over the surface of the dark morass. The trunks of willows shone green, in the black waters the glimmer of torches and lanterns, a smell of burning mingled with the stench of flooded meadows, murk and putrefaction. Shivering with cold, and taxed beyond my strength, I rode on the field kitchen as it rumbled forwards, stopped, remained stationary and then rumbled forward again. My whole system cried out for rest, for oblivion, yet my consciousness kept asserting itself: none of this wild beauty must be forgotten, every detail must be retained, crystallized in the memory, ineradicable. The columns rolling through the noise- and light-torn darkness, hectic monotony, chaos, with death lining the road on either hand, a semblance of order maintained by sheer force of habit, a march into nothingness.

It was past midnight when the battery reached the blazing sheds and barns. Most of us crawled out of the carts to warm ourselves at the flames. The bitter wind blew the flames southwards. North of the blaze it was freezing cold; on the south side the heat scorched one's skin and one's eyes were inflamed by smoke. I listened to the fire singing, soughing, groaning, and though I stood only three paces away, my teeth were chattering. The devil, freezing in hell and unable to shake off the cold, even by setting the world alight.

Shortly before dawn the regiment crossed the Livenza at San Motta. The river, enormously swollen after the rain, was jammed with logs and planks. The roads were better now and the brigade split up, wheeling north and south. The sun crept out from the tree-tops, dim and listless like a bug. Shyly the day began to unfold. In the delicate pink of the clouds a silvery fish, an aeroplane; over towards the luminous rim of the sky a squadron was gaining height. 'Italians!' Hrdal growled. By now they were overhead. 'Why aren't they bombing us?' 'Armistice!' 'Yes, of course. Armistice.' Some subaltern or other began to prattle away about a German victory in France, they were marching on Paris, he said, had used enormous aircraft, miracle weapons, to bomb Paris and London, had made a pact with Russia and the Revolution so as to dictate peace terms to the Entente. His words passed from mouth to mouth. Some were credulous, others scoffed, but most remained indifferent.

By midday we were approaching Portogruaro, a small town which contained a hospital and several headquarters. On either side of us were brown maize-fields, leafless mulberry-trees, barren stretches of plain. 'Take some men,' the adjutant ordered, 'go to the depot on the edge of the town and get hold of all the rations you can.' Accompanied by Hrdal and four hefty lads I rode up to the depot. There were a lot of carts there, empty ones arriving, others leaving full. A corporal had just loaded a couple of barrels. 'Rum!' he said, smacking his lips as he drove off at a gallop. An Italian peasant appeared with a donkey-cart and I ordered him to wait. I felt sorry for him, his sunken cheeks, the fear in his eye sockets, but I needed his cart. 'You understood that, *maledetto Italiano*?' said Hrdal, placing his clenched fist under the peasant's chin. The poor fellow understood.

One man remained behind to keep an eye on him while the rest of us went clattering into the depot.

Behind a desk sat an obese lieutenant, hostile eyes glittering beneath the spectacles he had pushed up onto his forehead; next to him a scrawny N.C.O. with a penholder stuck behind his ear. There was a smell of rum, cheese, molasses, of dust and paper. 'That's the lot!' wheezed the lieutenant, wiping the sweat from his forehead. 'We've stopped issuing!' the N.C.O. added for good measure. I told them that I had orders to draw rations for my regiment and that I had no time to lose. 'What about the returns?' croaked the N.C.O. 'It can't be done!' 'What about the inventories?' groaned the lieutenant. 'We can't just play fast and loose with war department supplies.' 'Returns!' roared Hrdal. 'Inventories! It's grub we want, not paper!' 'Oho!' said the lieutenant. 'Oho!' came his echo in counterpoint. 'A cash payment, perhaps?' suggested the lieutenant. 'A receipt from your regimental headquarters, perhaps?' suggested the N.C.O. 'Show me the way,' growled Hrdal, seizing the N.C.O. by the collar and shaking him like a plum-tree. 'You deal with the lieutenant and I'll see to the rest.' The penholder flew from behind the trembling N.C.O.'s ear as he was dragged away. 'Violence!' screamed the lieutenant. 'Mutiny! Revolution!' When I questioned the advisability of abandoning a well-stocked depot to the Italians, the lieutenant answered: 'That's good order. Don't you know what good order means? Without good order there can be no army, no war, no monarchy. Each item in my supplies is part of that order, but you, you subversive young . . .!'

Hrdal and his men returned with cases, sacks and bales, behind them the N.C.O., his hands raised in despair. 'Place this on record, Julius! Make out a chit.' 'They missed the white flour,' the N.C.O. whispered. He scribbled out the chit and handed it to me for signature. I signed it, a piece of sticking plaster for the injury we had inflicted on good order. An hour later the depot was blown up together with all the remaining supplies, including the white flour.

The sun blazed down on Portogruaro. The streets and arcades were teeming with carts, wagons and guns; the horses had been unsaddled and unharnessed; the men lay drowsing in the shade of houses and vehicles. The sky darkened over: a cloudburst. A few remained in the open, letting the drops patter against their half-naked bodies, but the rest took refuge in the arcades. Ten minutes later the sun had come out again, its light and heat beating down on the town. Once more the sky grew dark; a formation of some thirty aircraft was diving on Portogruaro. Thousands of men stood with their heads thrown back, shading their eyes against the light, blinking up at the aeroplanes. We could see the pilots, the machine guns, the struts and airscrews as the machines manoeuvered a thousand feet above us. Some waved to the Italians: armistice.

Leaning against a pillar I was admiring the display which was at once noisy and graceful. Suddenly there were spurts from the paving stones, dust and mortar came showering down from the walls and, from the cornices, a spattering of little pellets. It was like a hailstorm yet there was not a cloud to be seen, only the metallic squadrons. Why then the man over there, writhing in the street, why the horse collapsing onto its knees, why this panic, this general stampede? It took me a moment to realize that the airmen were firing their machine guns. Then came the dull crump of explosions; stones and timber rose in sheaves into the air. 'Bombs!' someone said. And then we were standing pressed shoulder to shoulder in the arcades watching the dance of the bullets. There was a great deal of merriment each time some latecomer went leaping across the square in search of shelter or when a man, rudely roused from his sleep, crawled beneath a gun carriage rubbing his eyes. The wounded were being bandaged on the steps; loose horses galloped through the town, lathered in sweat. 'Bastards!' shouted Hrdal. 'They've broken the armistice!' He did not know that the cease-fire had expired, no one knew; the agreement with the Austrian high command was known only to the Italians. For ten long minutes we were bombed and machine-gunned and then the drone of engines died away.

Orders to move. The men were irritable, swore because they had been given no rest, chased after the horses, harnessed them, hooked up the traces, hastily tidied themselves as best they could. New orders: cover the withdrawal! Orders countermanded. New orders: back to the Livenza! Another countermand. No one knew what was happening. The regiment, ready to move, awaited the next order. Colonel Kraus was nowhere to be found. Nevertheless the columns, as I could see for myself, needed no one to direct them. One after another the batteries moved off, the entire operation being organized by the N.C.O.s and men on their own initiative. Almost spontaneously, it seemed, what needed to be done was done. At that moment I marvelled at the vast organism, the inner discipline, the mighty structure of the masses. Before my eyes a miracle was happening: the transition from 'command and obedience' to the autonomy of the masses, doing what had to be done as a matter of course. No one sought his own advantage. It was only when the battery's turn came to move off that the gunners laid into the exhausted horses, the traces grew taut, the axles began to creak, the wheels to roll. And once again the road, the tawny landscape, the rhythm of the march. Where to?

An hour later another Italian formation appeared. The machines stooped like hawks out of the soft blue sky. In a display of skill that seemed to be courting our applause, the Capronis hurtled earthwards, banked lazily and, with engines cut, glided down until they were between six hundred and a thousand feet above our heads, when they opened fire and began to scatter their bombs. Under the impact of the hail of metal the road shivered like the skin of a freezing man. Too tired to feel any violent reaction, I stroked my horse's neck and wondered dreamily: why? What's the purpose? What's that horse up forward doing on the ground with dark stuff pouring from it? Why is that young subaltern clutching his chest, sliding out of his saddle, being laid down in the meadow? Is that – death?

'Dismount, Mr Fischer, sir!' roared Hrdal. 'Take cover!' Since I did not immediately obey, I was hauled out of the saddle. The sergeant shook me furiously. 'Are you mad, young man? D'you really want to finish yourself off just when it's so nearly over?' I looked at him stupidly; all at once I had the feeling that the guts had spilled out of my body, that I was empty, drained; heart gone, stomach gone, scared to death. Ashamed of myself, I feigned indifference and then I saw that the faces of the others, too, were looking very strange and unfamiliar.

I crouched down behind the field kitchen and with growing apprehension watched the road being scored and ripped by bullets. It was apprehension born of impotence, of inability to stop the ticking clock of death. All of us were affected in this way. Hrdal picked up a rifle, lay down on the embankment and started firing. He knew that it was pointless to engage the aircraft with a rifle, but anything, however foolish, was better than this nerve-racking inaction. A minute later hundreds of men, myself among them, were lying on the embankment beside the road, firing at the aeroplanes.

Zealously I applied myself; load, aim, squeeze the trigger: I lay on my stomach, lifted my rifle, jumped up, ran a few paces, threw myself down on my stomach again; thus I experienced the soothing power of action. The battle lasted for two hours and then the airmen, who as likely as not had simply wanted to demonstrate their superior strength, left us to ourselves. I crawled onto my wagon, poured some rum down my throat and thirsted for revenge. But revenge upon whom?

Towards early evening the regiment turned off the road into a mulberry grove; apparently the withdrawal was not to be resumed until the following morning. In company with Ensign Steinbauer, the son of a German-Bohemian industrialist, I walked away from the bivouac. Close by was a farmhouse packed with soldiers and, craving sleep, we climbed into the hayloft. But first of all we needed a wash so we went down to the well in the yard. An emaciated woman threw herself sobbing at our feet and clasped us round the knees, screeching incomprehensibly. Several rickety children, monotonously whining, cowered in the doorway. Beneath the arch of the big entrance gate stood an old peasant, legs astraddle, arms outstretched, his swarthy face tense with determination and mortal fear. He was foaming slightly at the mouth. His chest was bare and he was panting. Surrounding the silent man was a milling crowd of soldiers, one of whom swung his rifle at him. 'What's all this?' I shouted, striding towards the group so that the woman who had been clasping my knees fell forward, striking her forehead on the ground. The rifle butt cracked down on the peasant's head. The old man closed his eyes; his body quivered. Nevertheless he managed to remain erect. Grabbing the rifle I roared: 'What harm has the old man done you?' There was muttering and grunting, a grim, perhaps also embarrassed, silence. Then one of the men spoke up: 'The bastard won't hand over his cow!' 'Well, you're not robbers are you?' 'We offered him money but he wouldn't take it. You can't talk to the old swine.' Steinbauer, who was standing close by, whispered: 'Leave well alone!' The mood was hostile to me. The men, breathing rum and wrath, were threatening me. One against all, a novel situation of which I had hitherto had no experience. Unsure of myself, I said evasively with a calmness I was very far from feeling: 'You can't take the old chap's one and only cow away from him. Look at the wretched life they lead.' Yet it was precisely because of this that events took an unexpected turn. The group disintegrated; some now supported me, others were calming down, the many-headed monster became a crowd of single individuals, a crowd which began to disperse one by one into the shadows. 'The good Samaritan!' Steinbauer mocked. 'Even if these ones leave the old man alone, the next lot will have his cow!'

Barely had we settled down in the evil-smelling hay than bugle calls rang out in the yard. Rise and shine! What could it mean? Trumpets, voices: 'Move off! Italians coming up behind us!' The vampire sleep was sucking at our ganglia. Shouted orders, whistle blasts, move off. Brain gone dead but feet still functioning. 'Glad you've turned up!' was Hrdal's greeting when we appeared. 'The bastards are blind drunk. They've been defending the rum barrel with pistols and bayonets. Fool that I was, I brought the thing along with us. We've had to pick a few of them off otherwise we'd never have been able to set fire to the barrel.' Most of them were lying on the ground, the living indistinguishable from the dead. Some were staggering about mumbling, others were draped, green-faced and retching, over the barrels of the howitzers, only a few were tolerably sober. Hrdal and three other N.C.O.s backed the horses and hooked on the traces; four older gunners threw buckets of cold water over the drunken men, trampling about on them, kicking their faces, pouring curses into their ears. I myself was attending to a young lad; mucus was dribbling from his mouth, his eyes were white and staring. All at once he collapsed heavily – dead. We had to heave the drivers into their saddles and lash them securely to the horses; the others were strapped to the guns or thrown like sacks onto the wagons. Hrdal, taking command, yelled at the officers as though they were street urchins. Silently, obediently, they did as they were told. 'Those blokes over there have shot their captain,' said a corporal, grinning. 'We'd already decided at the front to do him in.' Collapse! All at once I understood the term in all its enormity.

'Don't keep getting in the way!' Hrdal was roaring at me. 'You've set this trace up wrong. You're a nincompoop, d'you understand? Now kindly go and saddle your horse and stop mucking up our handiwork, you bleeding intellectual, you!' I had saddled my horse and my foot was already in the stirrup, when Hrdal hauled me back: 'You're to ride on a limber. We need at least one sober man to a vehicle. Mind the sods don't fall under the wheels!' I climbed onto the limber Hrdal had indicated; one man sat on my right, another on my left, the pair of them glassy-eyed and reeking of rum. So we rattled through the night, a tipsy battery in a regiment accursed.

The road was uneven. The sozzled drivers, their saddles askew, rained blows on the horses. Trot, gallop, trot, gallop, helter-skelter; a sudden jolt flung us upwards and a man fell into the road on my left. I thought I could hear the crunch of his bones as the wheels crushed them and I shouted; no one heard me. And then, shot out of my seat again, I fell forwards, grabbed at thin air and slithered down behind the hooves of the galloping horses. I felt something sliding through my hand, my frantic fingers closed round the lead-rope attached to the shaft and I was dragged along, with pounding, roaring, clattering all around me, swept along over the sandy gravel-strewn road; two minutes of searing pain, mustn't lose consciousness, and then the man at the brake was easing the mad rate of progress to a gentle trot and they heard me shouting. Finally the gun came to a halt; covered in abrasions, my uniform in tatters, I crawled back onto the limber. Feeling myself gingerly, I was amazed that I should have fared no worse; a close brush with death. To sleep! To sleep! At the gallop again. Something's going to pieces – what is? The world out of joint. The army, the nations, Europe . . . to hell with it all. To sleep! To sleep! The night is cold, the road endless; collapse, sleep, warmth, a bed . . . The columns thunder across the Tagliamento. Through the brimming gullies the water foams, roars, reverberates. The bridge shudders. Walk, trot, again at the gallop, again at the trot; if it hadn't been so cold sleep would have dragged us under, down under the hooves, the wheels, the alien soil, down . . .

At some time there came the order: 'Dismount!' Lights flickered, houses detached themselves from the gloom. Officers rode along the verges directing the regiments to their billets. At long last . . .

Stretched out in the tickling hay, my body was an alien thing, a corpse; in my hollow skull time hammered away, a death's head. Summoning the last of my strength I lit a cigarette, was enjoying the red glow, the dwindling of consciousness, when I heard a shout. Someone was calling my name, approaching through the night, death, a voice, a voice growing ever louder, the Last Trump: 'Cadet Fischer!' Through the hum of space the cry: 'Cadet Fischer!' Through the mountain of exhaustion, plaintive, insistent: 'Cadet Fischer!' White light scything through my eyelashes, a tormenting hand shaking me, leaden eyelids forced apart. Steinbauer was shining a torch in my face: 'Up! You're wanted at regimental H.Q. They've been looking for you everywhere!'

From out of the cigarette smoke and the fumes of alcohol, the puffy, senile face of the regimental commander, and I, still wrapped in the shreds of sleep, the world a shadow-play, barely credible. With shaking hand the colonel raised the bottle to his lips, swallowed, hiccupped, stuttered: 'You're a young man, you'll . . . renown of the army, the fatherland . . .' Gulp, glug, good luck. 'That's it . . .' Renown, the army's renown, the imperial family, the fatherland. 'Gave me great pleasure . . .' 'Commended by the Emperor himself.' Befuddled, muddled words, gulp, glug, glory. The adjutant followed me out: 'The colonel has taken the catastrophe very much to heart. He's done you the honour of putting you in charge of the telephone exchange. You will be responsible for communications between the artillery brigade and the infantry covering the withdrawal. You'll remain in position until ordered to move. Good luck!' A revenge for the incident at the front a few days previously when he had ridden away in such haste behind the colonel.

Awaiting me were one N.C.O., four signalmen and a wagon bearing the telephone equipment. The N.C.O. reported all present and correct and requested permission to move off. 'Where to, d'you know?' I asked. 'More or less.' 'All right then, let's start.'

We set up the telephone exchange in the last house on the out-skirts of the village. The men knew better than I what had to be done. Should I act the commander? 'Wake me in an hour,' I told the N.C.O. and threw myself down on a palliasse. Midway between wakefulness and sleep I could hear the men talking. My eyes were on fire. Why not allow myself to sink, to sink right down? Why not sleep? Why this pride in keeping awake for so absurd a purpose? Why? Because of the others. The N.C.O. was sitting at the table, headphones clamped over his ears, eyes closed, his breathing shallow and irregular. The slap of hands on leather: solidarity. I lurched across the room and placed my hand on the N.C.O.'s shoulder: 'Go and get some sleep. I'll wake you in an hour or so. The others had better have some rest as well. I'll be able to manage the telephone myself.' The N.C.O. mumbled a protest but nevertheless tottered away and collapsed onto the palliasse. I adjusted the headphones, cradled my chin in my hands and smoked. An hour later the signalmen returned. The line was functioning and I told them to go and sleep.

Was my attitude one of solidarity and nothing else? I remember how proud I felt to be awake when everyone else was asleep, the vanity of solitude. The room was thick with the breath of sleeping men, the pungency of sweat. The night pressed damply against the windows, sombre eye-sockets. From time to time the earphones sprang to life with an order or a report. Others too, then, were awake out there, ghosts carrying on through sheer force of habit. I smoked incessantly, lighting each cigarette from the dying glow of the last. Suddenly I started, the stub had burned away, ash lay on my slumbering mouth. Ashamed of myself I planted a bayonet under my chin to prick me whenever I was overcome by sleep. Seventy cigarettes and a weapon to ward off sleep. Time measured by the flaring of each match, by the glow-worm's pulse, bright when I inhaled, dim when I expelled the smoke from my lungs. The cold was creeping up my body from my legs; only behind my forehead was there heat, glowing ash. I was no longer alive, as yet not dead, poised in a limbo, a lump of ice, its scintillation a reflex of my expiring consciousness. At four o'clock in the morning the brigade pulled out. At five o'clock came the roar of the Italian artillery.

A shell struck the house next door but the sleepers did not stir. I woke the signalmen who gaped at me in a dazed way on being ordered to bring the line in. The same old obedience, the same old force of habit. I stayed behind, alone. Explosions shook the house, plaster broke away from the ceiling, pieces of wall came pattering down. From the landing a sinister whispering, rustling, creaking. Revolver at the ready, door flung open, men and women scurrying away, hesitantly returning, propelling each other forwards; suddenly a shot rang out, plaster spurted from the wall above my head. I raised my revolver and fired at random, once – no movement. A second time – wavering. A third time – flight. Shouting, they ran off. I leant against the door-frame, waiting for the next attack. This lying in wait and listening, this aggression was exhilarating – aggressive vitality, murderous glee. A violent detonation threw me to the ground amid a shower of dust and masonry; the opposite wall had collapsed. The signalmen reappeared, flung their equipment into the wagon, harnessed the restive horses. A dozen vehicles were approaching at a wild gallop, the drivers in their panic flight laying into the horses like madmen. Ever intent on the preservation of good order, I grasped the horses by the reins and shouted: 'Who's in charge here?' 'We can't stop! The Italians are right behind us! We're the last to get away!' 'I'm taking command!' I shouted, faithful to the regulations. It was, I thought, a ludicrous pose, but in fact the men were ready to recognize the authority of anyone who had not lost his head. After three hours of tolerably well-ordered flight we came up with the brigade rearguard. I informed a captain of what had happened, handed my party over to him, rode on, and at midday found the battery. By now too weak even to dismount, I mumbled something, broke off in mid-sentence and collapsed into a pair of waiting arms, stiff and unconscious. They loaded me onto a wagon, bedded me down in hay, pushed a rolled-up greatcoat under my head and poured rum and soup down my throat. Of all this I knew nothing.

When I woke up I was a soldiers' councillor.

What changes had there been? Many caps no longer bore the imperial cockade, but as before the officers rode along the verges, as before the drivers lashed their horses, as before the columns rattled onwards in orderly progress. Gas masks, steel helmets, ammunition boxes lay in the ditches, so much useless junk now that the war was over. Yet each individual knew that on his own he would be lost, only as a mass could we get through, our final destination, home.

First meeting of the soldiers' council. And lo, who should come riding up astride a donkey, clad only in a shirt and long drawers, ankle tapes aflutter, plumage plucked by pretty women, trounced and pillaged by peasants, but Colonel Kraus, sorry remnant of a dictatorial commanding officer. Although they laughed, the men felt sorry for him, bundled him into a greatcoat, placed a cap on his head; and thus arrayed he appeared before us, the assembled soldiers' council, to hold forth in a croaking voice with genuine emotion, unctuous solemnity, faithful to his oath of allegiance to His Imperial Majesty ... bound to his regiment by ties of loyalty and duty ... with his regiment through thick and thin. Tears were coursing down the cheeks of the plucked, pillaged Colonel Kraus, back once more in the bosom of his regiment.

And for those who had hitherto rejected the knowledge, there could no longer be any doubt: this was defeat.

Coming towards us was a party of Italian soldiers, released

prisoners of war homeward bound. We talked to them as to old friends, gave them bread, preserves, cigarettes. 'The war's over!' and '*Maledetta guerra*!' and handshakes, laughter, fraternal sentiment.

And who comes here, waddling along on his stumpy legs, his baby-face sallow and gleaming with sweat, sad eyes wide with alarm, eyes improbably big in so small a countenance? He sits down, out of breath, on a milestone and wipes his forehead with a brightly coloured rag. 'You'll not get far on those short legs of yours!' says Hrdal grinning. Shyly the diminutive figure raised his baby-face: 'Napoli, how far?' Everyone crowded round him laughing, snorting, whinnying. The midget stood up, his eyes round and sad. 'Napoli!' he said in a firm, high voice. I offered him my hand, he gave me a helpless look and then went waddling off into the setting sun, brave, lonely, ridiculous.

Napoli! How far to Napoli?

And as for us?

How far? Where to?

5

Homecoming

'Beware, in this labyrinth whose name is home! In its passageways the minotaur's carcass lies rotting. Take care, my friend, that you do not suffocate in its stench.'

Thus Hans Lebert, in a recent novel, warns the soldier returning from the Second World War. Having served with the British Army in the war against Hitler, he is now on his way home to Austria, to Styria, and his half-sister, a former 'werewolf'* in the service of the Gestapo.

In those days, after the First World War, there was as yet no minotaur's carcass. What lay rotting somewhere in the passageways was a diminutive monster. And it was only when the air lay motionless above the town, a miasma without wind or oxygen, that suffocation was near. At other times there were still old gentlemen in the park feeding the squirrels and doodling with their walking-sticks in the sand or the snow.

As I passed by I overheard two of them talking. One was pointing with his stick at a diagram he had scratched on the ground: 'And these, you see, Excellency, were our positions here and the Prussians were over there, and if only Benedek had wheeled his left flank inwards at the right moment, the Prussians would have lost the war!'

'A pity,' replied the other.

'How d'ye mean, a pity?'

'That they didn't lose the war.'

'Think so?'

'Everything'd be different.'

'True.'

*A paramilitary organization under S.S. leadership.

That was in 1919. They were discussing the Battle of Königgrätz. Eighteen sixty-six. Then the Prussian breech-loaders had prevailed over the antiquated Austrian guns. The battle for supremacy in a Germany that was massing for action had been decided. Austria withdrew into the kingdoms and countries represented in the *Reichsrat*. Into Kakania – imperial and royal cloud-cuckooland.

What did he want to do when he grew up, I asked a four-year-old.

'Retire on a pension.'

He chose his way of life without a moment's hesitation.

On Sundays between twelve and one a procession of students would parade in orderly rank and file along the Ring, decked out in their distinctive insignia – Goths, Allemani, Vandals, Cheruscans, Lango-bardians and so forth – the members of the duelling clubs. Their heads were predestined for coloured caps, their faces for sacrifications, those carefully nurtured scars incurred in glorious duel. Every now and again one of them would suddenly march up to a bystander and transfix him with a look. 'You were staring at me, sir! Are you in a position to give me satisfaction?' Whether this accusation of staring concealed a primitive fear of the evil eye or whether it betrayed uneasiness on the part of Teutonic 'comers-in', anxious lest they be viewed askance by the peoples who had arrived before them, I cannot say; whatever the case, it was advisable either to give the challenger a box on the ear or else demonstrate one's lack of academic status and hence one's inability to give satisfaction.

It was during one such student's duel that young Alexander Sacher-Masoch was wounded. In a state of semi-consciousness he heard someone say: 'Where's that ear? Where the devil can it have got to, that damned ear that's been sliced off?' Finally the ear which Sacher-Masoch had severed from his opponent's head was discovered underneath a chest. So dusty had it become that it had to be cleaned with alcohol before it could be restored to its owner. Despite this severe dusting, the ear grew on again beneath the coloured cap sported by the injured party. Even at the time this combination of dust and severed flesh seemed to me a portent.

The Austrian monarchy was no more; the cockchafer lying on its back, its carapace intact, its quick devoured by ants, had forfeited even a semblance of being alive, only the carapace of bureaucracy still simulating the existence of what was no longer real. In fact the

Austrian monarchy had died with Franz Joseph, the legendary Emperor of Schönbrunn who, perhaps, having long since ceased to be, was no more than a phantom, a waxwork image of one who had passed away. His successor Karl seemed like a tailor's dummy, placed on the throne because there had to be somebody to administer the Crown Lands and to answer for the defeat – the war that had been lost and of which, in 1914, the then Foreign Minister, Graf Berchthold, had said that it had already grown insipid. With the end of the insipid war came the end of the insipid monarch.

The new state, first called German Austria and then Austria, found itself completely at a loss. Unlike the 'Succession States' it was not the product of revolution, but was a remainder, a leftover. On 21 October 1918 the Social Democrats submitted a proclamation 'To the German people in Austria', which was unanimously adopted by Parliament. In the course of the debate, Victor Adler, the Social Democrat leader, then mortally ill, read out a declaration that called, either for free federation with the Succession States or, since German Austria was not viable, for union with the German Reich. 'We demand that the German Austrian State be allowed complete freedom of choice in respect of these two possible alliances.'

On 11 November Victor Adler died. The same day the Emperor's manifesto was made public:

I acknowledge in advance the decision to be adopted by German Austria, as to the future form to be taken by the state.

The people, through these its representatives, have taken over the Government. I renounce all claim to participation in affairs of state . . .

On 12 November 1918 the Republic of German Austria was proclaimed.

No one believed in the new state's viability. Everyone regarded it as an interim measure.

Internally, too, the unwelcome republic was torn asunder: on the one hand the metropolis, Vienna; on the other, the Alpine areas which had always been mistrustful of the capital city. It was with undisguised hostility that the people in these provinces spoke of Vienna as the 'city with water on the brain'. Only in the Habsburg state did Vienna – the '*salon* of the peoples', as it was described by the Czech Socialist Smeral – represent Austria. This city of three hundred thousand Czechs and two hundred thousand Jews was the adoptive home of an élite, of whom the majority stemmed from Bohemia, Moravia and other Crown Lands and only a small minority from the Alpine provinces. To the Emperor's average subjects, Vienna meant the court opera house, the Spanish Riding School and the delights of the *Heurige*. For a couple of decades, however, Vienna was in fact one of the most interesting cities in the world: the 'Vienna schools' of medicine, of music, of political economy; positivism, Austro-Marxism, psychoanalysis, Sigmund Freud, Gustav Mahler, Arnold Schönberg, Karl Kraus. As a rule, things tended to come to Austria later than elsewhere; not so the premonition of impending catastrophe, the heightening of sensibility, the loss of reality. Something was coming to an end – not only the monarchy, not only the century, but a whole world, 'fawned upon by decay', as Georg Trakl has it in one of his poems. It was as though Vienna was preparing for its citizens' dream of life and death, the 'luvverly funeral', the pomp of the last journey, the theatricals of transience. Those who were most sensible to all this, because so ambiguously poised between civilization and anti-Semitism, between privilege and ignominious rejection, were the intellectual Jews; along with the old patrician families, a stratum of cultivated bureaucrats and the élite of the Social Democratic Workers' Party, they were Vienna at its most interested and interesting.

And that Vienna, its numbers swollen by pension-hungry officers and officials from all over the former Empire, now stood confronted with the embittered rural areas and was regarded with horror by the Alpine provinces as 'red' and 'Jew-ridden', the 'city with water on the brain'. Unfortunately the Social Democrats failed at this time both to restrain the arrogance of the Viennese workers towards the 'crop-heads', the peasants, and to neutralize, if not win over, the young countrymen who were returning home as rebellious ex-servicemen. The stark antithesis between Vienna and the Alpine provinces, together with the prevailing conviction of Austria's non-viability, was the fundamental ill by which the unwanted state, a lost war's legacy to the Austrian peoples, was beset.

In the over-large metropolis was stored the dwindling stock of what had once been a greater Austria. The fact that intellectual Vienna, though starved of new blood, continued to function and even for a time to exert fresh magnetic force was due, not to those conservatives intent on preserving the past, but rather to the achievements of Social Democracy. 'Red Vienna', with its Socialist financial policy, its up-to-date housing, its school reform and public education system, was able to contend successfully against the encroachment of provincialism. The city boasted men such as the municipal treasurer Hugo Breitner, the councillor for social welfare Julius Tandler, the school reformer Otto Glöckel, the head of the Social Democratic arts centre Josef David Bach (who secured the collaboration of Anton Webern, organized workers' symphony concerts at which classical and modern music was performed, exerted a considerable influence on the repertoire of the Volkstheater and, in 1924, gave the Vienna municipal arts award to Hanns Eisler), the head of the Social Democratic educational centre Josef Luitpold Stern, the chief editor of the *Arbeiter-Zeitung* Friedrich Austerlitz, the intellectual leader of the Social Democrats Otto Bauer: all these played a vital part in keeping at bay the stagnation that was threatening to engulf the country.

Little of all this percolated through to Graz.

The long-standing jealousy felt towards Vienna by this backwater of Pan-German persuasion was exacerbated by the fact that Austria had dwindled to an Alpine province. Huddled round the Schlossberg under the protection of the square clock-tower with its enormous dials and the round tower with its big bell, 'Liesl', the town lay sleeping, and as it slept it growled. But its sleep was disturbed by a flurry of ghostly figures, ridiculous freaks, talents run to seed, existences come to grief, and we who grew up in it suspected that its air of respectability was no more than a façade.

At school we had been taught that the stalwart Bajuvars, tired of constant migration, had plunged their swords into the ground at this spot and, seizing their spades, had uttered the grating cry: '*G'rät's so g'räts!*' ('If it succeeds, it succeeds!') Thus it was at random that they settled and, since nothing succeeds like success, their '*G'rät's*' became Grätz and finally, in more enlightened times, Graz; let us therefore extol reliability, a wholesome outlook, successful achievement, as virtues inherited from our Bajuvarian forebears, and take cognizance of the reprehensible as the dregs left behind by a now extinct primeval population. Moreover, it should not be forgotten that the Landhaus in the Herrengasse is one of the most beautiful Renaissance buildings I know, with its gently curving façade and its arcaded courtyard, as though a cloud from Tuscany had showered down its magic on this particular spot. And, come to that, Nestroy died in this city.

'Napoleon, an arch-enemy of course, but nevertheless . . .', the local-government official, an expert in the history of the area, cautiously sought to convey the information that the man he spoke of might be numbered among the great – having, moreover, been son-in-law to the Emperor. 'In praise of our city, Napoleon said: *La ville des grâces au bord de l'amour!* Have you got it? Graz on the banks of the Mur, turned into a Gallic pun meaning the town of the graces on the banks of love.'

The Bajuvarian aspect was an outer shell only: the semblance of uprightness just a décor of decorum, the town by the light of day. We suspected it to be otherwise, from the sudden silences of grown-ups, from their sidelong glances of complicity, a chink in the night, juveniles not admitted.

With beating hearts we waited for it to reach us, as it crawled through the streets, the hundred-breasted dragon, the bloody-clawed *Tatzelwurm*, the disallowed, the disavowed, leaving a slimy trail behind it for blow-flies to feed on then go humming past the houses, into the windows, the dark buzzing, the prattle, the tittle-tattle, the dragon's seed. Raped, did you say? The Chief Justice's wife? But then they're all no more than . . . no more . . . We found a rhyme to it: whore, the forbidden, the alluring word, brazen like the great bells and, somewhere, the red lantern, the eternal red lantern outside the *maisons de joie*, the bawdy-houses, whore-houses, debauchery, Sodom and Gomorrah, *la ville des grâces au bord de l'amour, au bord*, bawd, bawdy-house, brothel, the Chief Justice's wife, the general's wife, the professor's wife, but then they're all no more than . . . Children run away from home during the night. The gentlemen arrange a stag-party. Their wives grow weary of the marriage bed. Tittle-tattle becomes a dream, a fearful dream, a pleasurable dream, the Mur overflows its banks, *l'amour sans cesse*, *excès de l'amour*, the deluge, ladies and gentlemen, licentiousness, rebellion, anarchy!

*

The kingdom of Yugoslavia had refused to allow us, the defeated army, to cross her territory. Since we knew nothing of what had been happening behind the front lines we had never heard of a kingdom of Yugoslavia. The soldiers' council met and decided to declare war on this unknown kingdom. We swaggered off and brought our howitzers and field guns into position, warning the Yugoslav spokesmen that, unless allowed to pass, we would bombard the neighbouring villages. After long and arduous negotiations and thanks largely to the Czechs, an agreement was reached. We handed over our artillery to the new kingdom but retained our personal weapons – wisely, as it was to prove in the event.

So we went on marching until we reached Cilli. There we forced our way onto a homeward-bound train. Someone in one of the coaches tried to keep us off with machine-gun fire. It was not the pistols we were holding that saved us, but the Czech language spoken by some of my companions. We managed to find seats on the footboard.

Just outside Graz soldiers wearing red armbands confiscated my blanket, the only thing I still possessed.

To be ringing at the door of our old flat seemed utterly unreal. But so irresistible was my mother's joy that at first my only feeling was one of security. A few days later my brother Otto also arrived home. He, the youngest officer in the Imperial and Royal Navy, had done better than I, having brought with him a large bundle of food, tobacco and linen. This helped us through the early days. Then poverty stared us in the face – the humiliating, grinding poverty of those who have gone down in the world.

My father, too, had returned, arriving home from Enns in a threadbare civilian suit. Though officially a citizen of Bohemia, he was entitled to choose between Czechoslovakia and Austria. He opted for the latter. A year went by before his application was approved and a thin trickle of money, depleted by inflation, at last began to come into the house. We sold the few trinkets my mother possessed as well as books, clothes and furniture, all at a fraction of their real value. We owed money to the grocer, went out looking for work, smuggled tobacco from Yugoslavia into Austria, touted cigarettes in cafés and went hungry.

The poverty of the *déclassé* is worse than any other kind. It reeks of disgrace, improvidence, social ostracism. There hangs about it an aura of desolation, cynicism and anarchy. Day after day and hour after hour my father would stand by the window drumming with his fingers on the panes, or else he would stay in bed, getting up only for meals. Occasionally he would sit down at the piano and play the eternal 'Laugh Bajazzo . . .' or perhaps the Funeral March from *Götterdämmerung*. Meanwhile we cleaned the rooms, aired the beds and tried to keep one of the stoves going on fuel that did not burn but only smoked. We cracked jokes in an endeavour to hide our shame over our loss of status.

A real revolution has sufficient impetus to carry the *déclassé* along with it, to transform and remould him. But what had become of this real revolution? In what way did the Republic's representatives differ from their predecessors? The provincial dignitaries of the Styrian Diet, Christian Socials, Pan-Germans and Social Democrats, were such as I had hoped to see overthrown. Though the monarchy had been abolished, there was nothing about the Republic that was new, radical, or in any way inspiring. On top of that, we were told by our rulers that the Republic at whose baptism they had officiated was in fact stillborn and that nothing could save us from chronic hunger and misery but union with Germany, or again – though this was rumoured rather than publicly avowed – the restoration of the monarchy. In the face of these alternatives, my answer was: 'You can go to hell. Without me.'

The first time I walked down the Herrengasse wearing the only clothes I possessed, namely my uniform, I was attacked by several youths. Two of them held my arms while a third ripped from my collar the officer cadet's insignia I wore. I had set no store whatever by those insignia and would have been glad of their removal, but I was very much put out by the manner in which it had been done. I was pleased, therefore, when a burly officer, who was the next object of the youths' attention, put them to flight with kicks and blows. I, who had felt an extreme satisfaction when, during the retreat, the soldiers had dismissed their officers and elected soldiers' councils – I, who had myself been a member of such a council, now found myself suddenly siding with an officer. It was an uncomfortable feeling for, while still dreaming of revolution, I was confronted by its travesty – up there in the castle, the philistinism of our new provincial elders, the principle of order personified; down here in the street, those repulsive youths who were certainly not industrial workers but simply *Lumpenproletariat*. It was a travesty that repelled me.

What could I do?

Absolutely nothing.

At Graz University I enrolled for courses in philosophy, history and German language and literature for which, as an ex-serviceman, I did not have to pay. I tried to avoid the Pan-German students, made the acquaintance of a number of Jews and other 'outsiders' such as painters, sculptors and writers, was sometimes invited out to supper, wrote poems and went hungry. What I really wanted to do was blow up the town, the Republic, the whole of the Continent.

A patron of literature and the arts, Gräfin H., gave a reception to which she invited artists and students. Poetry was read aloud, speeches were made, no offence was given. Despite mutual mistrust, the Pan-German students with their coloured caps and the cosmopolitan artists with their anarchist tendencies did not fall out. The atmosphere of high-minded tolerance was respected by all.

I refused to read any of my poetry. But when we had all drunk a great deal and had reached that stage midway between fraternization and irascibility, I recited my latest poem. Some of it had already been written, some I improvised on the spot. It ran more or less as follows:

> *Round the tipsy pig dance we,*
> *the sacred, snouted one.*
> *Wildly we dance, we pant, we groan,*
> *and tomorrow will no morrow be.*
> *The moon decays, night crashes down*
> *and tomorrow comes the sea.*
> *Dances the flesh, dances the Nile,*
> *dances the sacred crocodile,*
> *dances the giant griffin*
> *upon his tail so stiff in*
> *circles with the sphinx,*
> *waggles his rump and winks.*
> *And where we dance will grow no bread,*
> *just desert sand and salt there'll be.*
> *We dance the seed and harvest dead*
> *at the tipsy pig's decree.*
> *We are the lust that turns to dust*
> *and tomorrow comes the sea.*
> *The blood that spatters the stars is lost*
> *to all eternity.*

The waters rise, night crashes down
and with it hurtles the dead moon
into our midst, our dance, our round.
And tomorrow will no morrow be,
but heedless gawps the pig.
Tipsy is he,
German and blond.

The room was empty. The students, not wishing to offend their hostess by lynching me in front of her eyes, had left the room in a solid phalanx – Goths, Allemani, Cheruscans and all. The artists had slipped away into adjoining rooms. 'Delicious!' said Gräfin H., 'but it really shouldn't have been German and blond!'

In Austria there were no horizons. The Russian Revolution was a storm in the distance; I knew little about it, read no newspapers, dreamt of an upheaval that would be a kind of apocalyptic *Vie de bohème.* So provincial was the atmosphere in which we lived that it sometimes drove me to indulge in childish pranks. A young painter, Pipo P., and I went to a carnival ball dressed in black from head to foot, black high-necked shirts, black scarves, black masks. We stood motionless, our backs to the wall, neither of us uttering a word but every now and again pointing at nothing in particular. It had the effect of disturbing, irritating and generally upsetting the other guests. In the end we were thrown out.

We could not possibly have known that black shirts would one day be the badge of Fascism, but what was fermenting in the confusion of our ignorance was ultimately to become the ingredients of counter-revolution. To the revulsion we felt towards the bourgeois world lingering on, malign and shoddy, beyond the war, was added our fear of a proletariat whose standard of living was now higher than our own. At the front I had been on friendly terms with the gunners in my half-battery, never realizing that these men in uniform were locksmiths, turners or electricians in disguise. Now, however, in the twilight of this early post-war period, my childhood welled up again – the sombre viaduct behind which the workers lived, the table Marie had told us about on which corpses were laid out, and the children's coffins came tramping into town as living men and women – the, to me, unknown and menacing proletariat.

At the university a 'student company' was formed to defend the town hall against the workers; among its members were my brothers and myself. Why? In order to defend the bourgeois world we abhorred, the property we did not possess, our own misery against theirs? Nothing of the kind; it was the instinct of the well-bred combined with the demoralization of the 'newly poor', a craving for excess, for the mass, for violence which drove us to occupy the town hall along with the hated Pan-Germans. We stood shoulder to shoulder with the upholders of law and order yet were entranced by the anarchical nature of the enterprise, the occupation of an official building, the provisional seizure of power, the kaleidoscope of disorder in the name of the principle of order. Not a shot was fired; the negotiations continued until midnight when we escorted a doddering major back to his house.

'Where have you been all this time?' my mother asked. 'The town's in such a state of turmoil. I've been worried about you.'

No sooner had we begun boasting about our heroic deeds than she broke in harshly: 'Aren't you ashamed of yourselves? Do you mean to say you were prepared to fire on people just because they were workmen protesting against injustice? And you actually boast about this disgraceful behaviour? I don't want to have anything more to do with you. Go away!'

It was the most salutary dressing-down I have ever received.

My father did not long survive the war.

One morning we found him on the floor; he had fallen out of bed and was covered in blood.

He died of cancer of the throat.

His last words were: 'Be on your guard against Jews and Socialists!'

6

Decision

My mother had gone on strike against life.

The husband she detested was dead. Her brief period of flowering was over. Poverty had ground her down. Because our struggle to provide even the rudiments of existence had proved unsuccessful, because an unbearable, all-pervasive poverty-stricken atmosphere drove us away from home for nights on end in search of the redeeming adventure, the saving grace, her suspicion that she was completely played out and that her constitution was being undermined by some mysterious disease had grown to be an *idée fixe*.

She spent her time in bed, only getting up to help my fifteen-year-old sister with her depressing household chores. My brother Otto got a part-time job in a briquette factory run by a scoundrel who mixed clinker with sand for sale as fuel. I soon followed him there, since the wages of one part-time worker could not provide enough for a family of five.

At the time the 'Freiland' society of artists organized the first exhibition of modern art in Graz. It was April 1920. No police were brought in to prevent the intrusion of this very mild form of Expressionism which did, nevertheless, outrage the majority who went to see it. To me this exhibition was the manifesto of a revolution of which hitherto I had known virtually nothing. I wrote:

We are astonished that in this latter-day Gotham the New should speak out so clearly and courageously ... Art, not as an aesthetic and formal re-experiencing of nature, but as the crystallization of independent dynamic forces, a passionate dialogue between the artist and the world ...

The piece ended thus:

Something new has begun, the dawn of a new age, perhaps; and it is to the New that we pledge our allegiance, for if there is one thing we detest, it is ossification – if there is one thing we cherish, it is dynamism!

With this piece of criticism, I bearded the editor of the *Tagespost*, the Graz newspaper read by the respectable bourgeoisie.

'Do you seriously imagine that we'd print such stuff? It's a disgraceful exhibition! Know what it is? Cultural bolshevism! Never heard of such a thing, I suppose? It's a degenerate form of art, and yet you apparently think that we at the *Tagespost* would actually encourage such outrageous stuff! No thank you!'

I recalled a friend's approbation of some other paper. What had it been? The *Arbeiterwille*, yes, that was the name. And if the editor of the *Tagespost* described the exhibition as cultural bolshevism, what paper if not the *Arbeiterwille* would be prepared to encourage a form of art that outraged bourgeois sensibilities?

After waiting a long time in the offices of the *Arbeiterwille*, I was admitted to the editor-in-chief's office. A small bespectacled man was sitting at a big desk; he was chinless and his eyes were large and dark: he was called Moritz Robinson. At first sight it seemed to me that I would only have to clap my hands thrice for the little fellow to vanish into thin air and reappear as a black cat, arching its back in the waste-paper basket.

He was polite but uncommunicative, said he had already heard of me though in what connection he could not recall; he would look at my manuscript and get in touch with me very soon. The next day my criticism appeared in the *Arbeiterwille*. I went to thank Robinson, whom I found extremely busy. However, he suggested that I should write criticisms of all future art exhibitions.

But you couldn't live on that.

The work at the briquette factory beside the Southern Railway's ash tips, an inexhaustible source of raw material, glimmering, smouldering, exhaling foul vapours, was assuredly no picnic. My brother Otto, robuster than I, had been more or less accepted into the bosom of the workers' community; but they were far from pleased to see yet another student arrive, a scrawny intellectual with narrow, nerveless hands. No one spoke to me, their looks were hostile, their every gesture intimating what I already very well knew – that I was an intruder.

Otto, who possessed some technical knowledge, was by now working inside the factory. I, however, had to push a heavy barrow, carefully balancing it across the unsteady planks that led to the tip. Having got there, I had to load it up with the glimmering, smouldering, evilly reeking waste-matter from the locomotives and, hideously straining my underdeveloped muscles, push the barrow back to the sheds outside the factory and tip out the load in a single heave. It was a movement I simply could not master, being unable to co-ordinate the rhythm of my body with that demanded by the operation, and I would gasp, sweat and tremble, feeling myself seared by the others' scorn; an innocent at the stake. Most of all I was troubled by the looks I received from a raw-boned young working girl. She had to do the same work as myself; but how strong, how skilful she was in loading her barrow, how sure-footed as she pushed it across the wobbly planks, and how admirable the motion with which she tipped out her load! At that moment the gawky, unlovely girl was almost graceful; the rhythm of her body was so completely attuned to that of the operation, the heavy labour was so easily done that it seemed entirely effortless: the barrow was manipulated like a musical instrument, thus evoking something tantamount to aesthetic satisfaction. I watched her and saw that she worked three times as fast as I. And every time she tipped out the barrow she would smile. To me it seemed the mocking smile of one who is strong and censures the weak.

I was wrong. On my third day at work she came up to me. 'Give me your barrow. I'll show you how it's done.'

She took the barrow from me.

'Finish your cigarette and rest for a bit. It's heavy work for you.'

And as she, the raw-boned girl, gracefully tipped out my barrow, she remarked casually: 'That's booked down to you!'

She was doing it, not for her own profit, but for mine.

There it was again for the second time – solidarity. The first time had been at the front when, behind me, I had heard the slap of hands on leather and seen the colonel in front of me tremble. And now this gawky girl, helpful, friendly, demonstrating her solidarity with one weaker than herself.

I cannot deny that I was close to tears – and that I continued to accept her help. Every now and then, having loaded her own barrow, she would also load mine, push it across to the shed and tip it out whilst I, smoking my cigarette, would relax, watching her.

She asked nothing in exchange. Neither to be taken out nor to be kissed, no *quid pro quo*. Nothing except that a human being should be able to be a fellow human being. Solidarity.

The workers accepted me. I was no longer a stranger. We drank beer together, and there was no false pride about accepting the occasional drink. My new mates explained to me what a trade union was. Having become a worker I joined the union.

The briquette factory lay on the far side of the viaduct, the one beyond which the workers lived. In the evening after work my brother and I used to walk through the middle-class part of the town, grimy with coal in our blue overalls; people were beginning to cut us, student workers being rare at that time. To call someone a 'prole' was offensive in the extreme. We had become 'proles', at first with some embarrassment, but soon with self-conscious defiance. We – the proletariat.

One evening after work I went to the *Arbeiterwille* with a piece of art criticism in which I declared war on good old bourgeois 'realism'. 'We must fight ourselves clear of the stagnation imposed by nature! Are you blind to the technique, the dynamism, the rhythm of the new?' The old methods were quite incapable of depicting the grace and solidarity of the young, raw-boned working girl.

Robinson looked at me in surprise. 'Where have you come from?'

'From the factory?'

'I thought you were a student.'

'I've got to earn some money.'

'Do you *like* working at the factory?'

'What else can I do?'

'Might you, by any chance, prefer to work for this paper?'

'*I'll* say!'

'Can you do shorthand and typing?'

'Yes,' I lied. 'But I know nothing about politics. I haven't read anything by Marx. My only political experience has been in a soldiers' council.'

'Well, we can give it a try. Three months on probation and then we'll have to see. Not that I can promise anything yet. I do need a young reporter, but the decision rests with the party committee. Come back and see me in a week's time.'

A week later I had become a reporter.

'A remarkable coincidence,' Robinson told me. 'At first everyone was against it. "An officer's son – Fischer?" old Pongratz, the provincial chairman, suddenly asked. "*Colonel* Fischer? Very decent people they are. Our children used to play together in the Industriepark and Frau Fischer would sit on the bench next my wife, no side at all, though she knew very well who we were. And in the days of the old monarchy, too. I'm in favour of Comrade Robinson's proposal." '

That was how I became a reporter on the *Arbeiterwille*.

Unfortunately local news items can't be written in verse, and to describe a tram accident is infinitely more exacting than writing a love poem. The Wila publishing house in Vienna, a concern run by ex-officers, had accepted a volume of my poetry. The poems were mediocre and the whole was called *A Bird called Desire*, a title which elicited the ribald comments of my colleague Otto Egger.

After several strenuous weeks of apprenticeship reporting local news such as tram accidents, brawls, murder and theft, and acquiring in the process a style that differed materially from that of the Expressionist novel, I was introduced into the courtroom by Otto Egger. He was a courtroom reporter of enormous originality. One day he told me about himself.

'I think I can truly boast,' said this man with the fine Celtic face, 'that I have never done an honest job of work in my life. When someone comes out with all that crap about the dignity of work it makes me wild. You idiot, I tell him, it's the parasites who invented it, this dignity of work you're on about, it's the profiteers, the capitalists – so that you'll toil and moil for them and, what is more, poor oaf, shout "Up with work!" instead of downing tools. A strike is the only truly human kind of relationship that a worker can have with his work. And as for all that blather about horny hands, sweat and honest toil, to hell with such balderdash and poppycock!

'In my youth I was an ecclesiastical wood-carver and I says to myself, Otto my lad, this isn't your cup of tea. You're too much of a layabout ever to make an ecclesiastical wood-carver. However fine a piece of wood you've got, your carving'll turn it into an ugly devil's mug. And so I went on the road, and you can take my word for it, there hasn't been a day, in any country anywhere, when there's been the remotest connection between work and Otto Egger. Not even in England, and that was quite a feat in a country where medievalism is tarted up to look like democracy and morality sets traps for vagrants and, hey presto, you're caught! Then they whip you into the workhouse and it's straight out into the woods with you to chop down trees, but when it comes to avoiding work no effort's too great for me. So what do I do but pick up the biggest axe of all and convey by gestures – since they speak nothing but English and I nothing but German – how heavy the thing is. Hanging my tongue out and dragging my feet, I go across to the smallest tree and strike its little trunk; the axe is so big and the tree so small that I begin to sob for very pity. And then I take the smallest axe to the biggest tree, go tap, tap, tap like a woodpecker, shake my head and tap, tap, tap again. I tell you, it made the Englishmen laugh, in spite of their being so solemn by nature, and so, while I was in England, I became the clown of the corvée. You've no idea what efforts I had to make to keep them laughing while they did their beastly duty. The overseer and the buffoon – we two were the only ones who didn't do any work; and that's the world for you – if you can't be the master you have to be the clown.

'Now I'm a journalist, a courtroom reporter, but can that really be called an honest job of work?'

His courtroom reports made thousands laugh. To many they were the sole incentive for buying the paper. Often an edition of the *Arbeiterwille* would be sold out because word had got around that it contained some new journalistic outrage by the ecclesiastical woodcarver, that enchantingly vulgar man whose wild sense of humour and aggressive imagination took language by the hair to drag it through bog, bush and briar, a clown risen up in rebellion against the bourgeois world, against injustice and hypocrisy.

He introduced me to the courtroom. Now, in a law court, every case is 'living theatre'. I soon learnt not to be just a courtroom reporter, but to take sides, to become involved, to be an active participant. And in some of the big trials, I participated passionately, usually on the defendant's side, more rarely on that of the public prosecutor. I was always on the *qui vive*, listening carefully, acquiring a feeling for detail, for the apparently insignificant feature – crucial, perhaps, to the fate of the accused; listening, too, for the false inflection and the genuine undertone. It was a school second to none, and no theoretical knowledge could have so convincingly persuaded me of the existence of the class struggle as did my daily experience of class justice. It was not simply that in political cases the right administration of justice precluded a verdict favourable to the left, but rather that a proletarian was at a disadvantage whatever the circumstances. Most of the judges and lawyers, I knew, were upright men concerned to reach just decisions; nevertheless, they were instinctively inclined to allow extenuating circumstances where the accused was an educated man, whereas their attitude towards a proletarian tended to be cautious rather than considerate. Hence it was with all the more ardour that I espoused the cause of proletarian defendants, and if I had helped to demolish the prosecution's case and to secure a verdict of not guilty, or even the acceptance of extenuating circumstances, the report I wrote would be a proclamation of victory.

In Graz there were three outstanding lawyers: the Pan-German Dr Walter Kless, the Social Democrat Dr Arnold Eisler, and the Zionist Dr Otto Spiegel. I soon made friends with this aggressive and intelligent advocate; like a panther, he was always crouched ready to spring and, if the prosecuting counsel or one of his witnesses showed the slightest sign of wavering, would pounce ruthlessly, fangs and claws bared, upon his prey. Our friendship began by his occasionally asking my advice or drawing my attention to some weakness in the prosecution's case; with increasing frequency we found ourselves allies in the endeavour to rescue an accused from the 'man-trap of justice', as Otto Egger used to call it. If he was defending rogues, I would be his adversary; it used to amuse him when I was able to demolish his arguments with others which had been overlooked, both by himself and the public prosecutor. He invited me to his house, and the social circle of Jewish intellectuals and attractive women to which he introduced me was intensely refreshing after the usual tedium of a provincial town. It was at this time that a Pan-German student remarked: 'You're worse than a Jew because you aren't one, as we've taken the trouble to ascertain. You're a Jew by choice!'

It was a twilight existence I was now forced to lead. On the one hand there was home, a sick mother and, despite my admittedly modest reporter's wage, insurmountable indigence; the old silk upholstery was in tatters and, upon the seats of chairs that were disgorging their springs and webbing, sat the motley crowd of men and women who were our friends – painters, writers, students, aristocrats, Socialists – enlivening my mother's bedside with boisterous discussions on art, politics, philosophy, Socialism and sex. Then there were my days spent in court, in the reporters' room, many nights spent in cafés and bars or at champagne parties, suppressing my craving for meat and bread-and-butter after a lunch of watery soup, rice, peas and sauerkraut; not suppressing my craving for women, enjoyment, love, burning the candle at both ends, self-destruction; extracting from my already over-taxed constitution poems, stories, plays – more, ever more, and yet still more, and always an awareness of antithesis, fever pitch and arctic chill, resentment at the abuse of a compulsive vitality, at the fragmentation of the self, more, ever more and yet still more, and suddenly the desire to blow you all up, you, the survivors, the surfeited, the remnants of a vanishing, perhaps already vanished world. Was it really me?

I knew that Graz was ruining me and that here decay preceded maturity, so that I was sometimes unable to distinguish a flame in the mist from the glimmer of putrefaction. I had many friends who were kind, intelligent, talented, but there was none who could help me educate myself, overcome my inconsistency, my grasshopper mentality, my destructiveness. The world I needed was larger than this one, tucked away and parochial as it was, and yet I could not leave it for my mother needed me. My brother Walter was a medical student, Otto was alternating between his studies at the Technische Hochschule and survey work on a new railway, and the housekeeping devolved on my sister who was learning shorthand and typing. I have often reproached myself for the fact that she did not go to grammar school, though it is hard to see how this could have been managed. It was not easy, during those years of inflation, to turn an honest penny and, brash though our behaviour may have been, we were innocents so far as money-making was concerned.

I could see no way out. It was no longer any good my trying to turn a blind eye to the situation. I compelled myself to control my craving for pleasure, to work harder than ever before. But this was not the answer. One's private life, whatever its range, is a dead end in the absence of any social goal, of historical content.

In the disillusionment that followed 1918 a few of us young

intellectuals in Graz toyed with the idea of starting a secret society of 'Catilinarians'. We knew what we *didn't* want – the already extant. What we did want was something indeterminate but different. When, later, I turned towards the labour movement, I encountered one of the angry young men who had been a party to our project. What price Catiline now? He was on his way from the left to the right, to the Bund Oberland, the Silesian Freikorps, to the S.S., I on my way to the left. But what precisely was that left?

In the Styrian Diet, Social Democrats sat cheek by jowl with Christian Socials. The leader of both Christian Socials and Diet was the enigmatic Rintelen. Under the aegis of his deputy, the adventurer Jakob Ahrer, ex-officers, fanatical philistines and demoralized ex-servicemen were being recruited to form what was known as the Heimatschutz. Although this militant organization's ostensible purpose was to protect the country against neighbouring states, its real object was the struggle against the labour movement, against 'Bolshevism'. The Heimatschutz, in concert with the commandant of the provincial gendarmerie and other high officials in the Styrian Government, was in close collusion with the forces of the Hungarian counter-revolution. In the Tyrol, in Salzburg and in Carinthia the same thing was going on. In July 1920 the leaders of the Austrian Heimwehr groups foregathered in Munich to meet Escherich, organizer of the Bavarian counter-revolution. On 5 March 1921, at a meeting of the leading industrialists' federation at which representatives of the major banks were also present, Ahrer demanded a yearly subsidy of five million kronen towards the expansion of the Heimwehr. Objections were raised by certain representatives of the *grande bourgeoisie* but nevertheless Ahrer got what he wanted.

Having spent too long over my 'Catilinarian' daydream before finding my way to the labour movement, I had not been fully alive to the existence of the Soviet Republics of Hungary and Bavaria, their eventual collapse and the White Terror. But I was beginning to find the spectre of the Heimwehr disturbing. Was it indeed a spectre? From Vienna it may have looked like one. In Graz, however, and in Styria it was all too palpably real.

Was the labour movement too weak, I asked myself, to banish that spectre? I, who was aware of my own incompleteness, longed for a complete, a total revolution.

I recalled vague discussions at the front about the Russian Revolution. Then it had been something remote, the dawn of a new day or the threat of a holocaust. Suddenly I saw it as an actuality. I collected together everything I could find in Graz about the Russian Revolution – pamphlets, newspaper cuttings, manifestos. Fragmentary and inadequate though it may have been – it was what I had been looking for. If the country was to be protected against Bolshevism by the Heimatschutz, then Bolshevism was needed to preserve the country against its protectors!

When, in 1922, I travelled to Leipzig on borrowed money, I was fleeing, not only from Anny – of whom more presently – but from my own divided self, from the reality of Austria. I had been invited to go by my friend Friedrich Lorenz. One of his aunts, who was involved with the Schule der Weisheit in Darmstadt, had procured him a post as a publisher's reader, and he had promised me a job. The job proved to be a figment of his imagination, and my time in Leipzig was lean and unsuccessful, highlighted only by one event, the performance of Bertolt Brecht's *Drums in the Night*. It was as though I was seeing myself in a mirror which 'distorted me to the point of recognizability'.

When I returned to Graz – where my brother Walter had been keeping my reporter's seat warm for me – I was able to arrange a performance of *Drums in the Night*. As artistic director of the Workers' Theatre Group I succeeded in securing the cooperation of the producer, Helmut Ebbs, for a performance that was infinitely more original and 'alienated' than the one I had seen in Leipzig. The day before the performance I wrote in the *Arbeiterwille*:

The bourgeois are saved. Everything's set up as they want it: sentimentality and business, domesticity and turpitude, highmindedness and opportunism, with peace as a substitute for war; the gramophone plays *Deutschland, Deutschland über alles* as of yore, and the song of 'the dutiful man beside his hearth who's worth his weight in gold' rings out loud and clear. But the candle flickers, the moon rises red and menacing, drums sound in the night, bourgeois society's gramophone grinds on, but outside the drums grow loud – a spectral figure enters, stark and wan as a visitor from the nether world, and stops the gramophone. This is Andreas Kragler, the dead soldier whom everyone had forgotten. The old song is ended and now *the other thing* begins . . .

The man who returns from mass murder, from chaos, from hell, suddenly feels that it has all been in vain, that he no longer fits into the bustling world, that there's no room for him, and that all the barrages and gas attacks he has been through have not even earned him the paltry, the humble right to a prodigal son's welcome. And Kragler stands up, with a painful effort brings himself to say: 'Feeling as I do that I've no right to be here, I beg you, from the very depths of my heart, to go with me, at my side.'

The tragedy was written when the drumming in the night drowned the voice of the individual, and its author, who had seen the concept of revolution submerged in blood and horror as once before the concept of fatherland turned in horror and despair against all proclamations, manifestos and concepts in whose name the earth is ravaged again and again by madness and murder. Drums, machine guns and artillery fire – and tommorow it will all be over. 'Drunkenness and puerility. Now's the time for bed – the big, white, wide bed . . .'

Later, when he had become a Marxist, Brecht violently criticized *Drums in the Night* for not being sufficiently definite. For myself, I felt that the escape to the 'big, white, wide bed' did not provide the answer. True, the old gramophone had been stopped — but already it was beginning to blare and rasp once more – in the houses of the Balikes, in the squares where the Heimwehr exercised. And what of the other thing? The drums in the night had fallen silent. But Kragler did not find repose in bed and went badly astray when, in the belief that 'every man does best to remain in his own skin', he himself became hidebound in the endeavour to shut himself off from all concepts, proclamations, manifestos. There was no getting to rights with this, one's own skin, from which it was essential to extract oneself. Hence, out of what was past, we – Kragler and I and many others – hearkened, sceptical and believing into the future.

And was it the future that was happening in far-off Moscow? Was it the answer, not only politically in terms of Socialism but *the whole thing* – the *other things*, renewal from the depths of our hearts?

7

The Speaker

The girl at my table attracted me very much. She was a miner's daughter and the wife of a young trade unionist. We were waiting for the speaker to arrive from Vienna. It was the evening of 1 May 1921. At all the tables round about us people were drinking beer out of heavy ribbed convex glasses known as *Krügel*, provided by the Graz breweries. The attractive young woman, her husband and I were drinking a light, dry, red wine.

A half-hearted attempt had been made to decorate, with fir branches and red cloth, the timbers of this large, dark room where the workers, clad in their Sunday best, had fore-gathered to celebrate May Day. Although some of them were radically inclined, the general mood was affable and relaxed. The group of Young Socialists in their blue shirts, a little bit of spring sky, wind and light in the big, sombre hall, formed a mosaic of impatience among the patient majority. But as time went on and the speaker from Vienna had still not arrived, the impatience began to become general. Finally we learned that the train from Vienna had been unaccountably delayed and that the speaker would not be turning up after all. Furthermore all the leading comrades in Graz were otherwise engaged. What was to be done?

Two men approached our table.

'We need a speaker. How about you, Comrade P.?'

'I'm no speaker,' replied the young union secretary, 'but Comrade Fischer here . . .'

Just then I was busy trying, by dint of all sorts of metaphors, to make a surreptitious yet comprehensible declaration of love to Comrade P.'s wife. 'I can't speak!' I said.

As a boy I was a stammerer. A word would loom up, become a reef that made a landing impossible, shipwreck inevitable. Because of my exiguous vocabulary I could neither sail round nor otherwise avoid that reef.

The commonest consonant, the one I most detested, was *N*. But B, P and T were also unmanageable. The most kindly were M and L, music and light, mouth and love, mild, magic, motherly, limpid, lovely, lilting.

On the other hand, I found exalted speech helpful; the sublime, declaimed in ringing tones, came more easily to me than everyday language. But to adopt such a tone at school would have been ridiculous. If, when I was called upon by the teacher to answer, the words refused to come, unable to get past the barrier of my lips, I would grin sardonically. Through shunning a reputation for weakness, I gained a reputation for insolence.

When I was twelve years old my mother said: 'Read this aloud to me!' It was a very large book with very small print, all Shakespeare's plays comprised in a single volume, in the translation by Tieck and Schlegel. Thus began my struggle for speech.

For the second time I had to learn to talk, not by the unconscious process in the course of which a child assimilates language and the world about him, but by painful and conscious effort. I clung to the beautiful vowels, rich in intimations and dreams: to say rose without stammering, to say flame, breath and wind; to salvage the foundering gondola of euphony, to make whole again her timbers, her fabric, was my constant endeavour.

This went on for a year, closeted alone with my mother while a whole world opened up before me.

The last play I read was *The Tempest*; without a stutter, for the first time participating in language, cured by the magic of the word and, like Ariel, set free from cramped confinement, I read without stammering about Prospero and how he sets the spirits free into the 'thin air', breaks his staff and abjures magic, and I, recuperating from my condition of speechlessness, was so entranced by the epilogue that in my delight I lost sight of the meaning.

> Now my charms are all o'erthrown
> And what strength I have's mine own;
> Which is faint . . .

... Now I want
Spirits to enforce, art to enchant;
And my ending is despair ...

'I can't speak,' I told the woman sitting at my table.

'But you *can*,' she said, 'as you've just been doing, and very well too!'

'I can't speak in public, won't ever be able to, and don't really want to.'

'Suppose I ask you to do it for my sake? For love of me?'

The two men had already left our table, but she called them back: 'Comrade Fischer's going to speak.'

She filled my glass to the brim and I hastily downed the contents before being seized upon by the two men who, ignoring my protests, half dragged, half propelled me between the tables towards the platform. And now a thick-set man was rising ponderously, stolidly, to his feet at the speaker's table, already he was saying apologetically that the speaker from Vienna had been delayed and then, confidently, that Comrade Ernst Fischer of the *Arbeiterwille* had kindly agreed to speak instead. And almost before I knew it, I was standing there, not very convincingly, behind the speaker's table, aware of the murmur of disappointment, the heartening applause of my two companions visible a long way away at the back of the room, the woman's pretty face as she tenderly raised her glass in encouragement, and then nothing, except the interplay of light and shadow, blurred contours, patches of colour, pale dots in the beery, smoke-laden atmosphere, scraps of blue sky, the shirts of the Young Socialists, and then all of this vanished too, and there was only a cornfield swaying in the wind, water rolling away into the distance, a wave, the woman's pretty face rising, falling, swallowed up by the foam. And so, in a voice that sounded strangely in my ears, I began to speak into the troubling silence, to speak for love of you, of my love, my declaration of love to the first of May with its red flags fluttering in the light, of solidarity, the slap of hands on leather, disrupting discipline and stronger than war; of those who cry 'Heimatschutz' meaning no more than property, whereas we, the working class, the International, when we hear the word 'country', when we hear the word 'fatherland', finding valleys too narrow, rivers too wide, we burst asunder what constricts us, reach out into the distance, humankind my people, the earth my fatherland! As I spoke I could feel myself merging with the people sitting before me, the woman's pretty face was no longer far away but enlarged as in a film close-up, her face, detaching itself from the whole, filled the entire room, became the face of all, and suddenly the unexpected happened: applause, rumbling from cloud to cloud at the approach of a thunderstorm, the electric fluid in which audience and speaker are united, out of the many the one begins to take shape – the mass.

To my astonishment they were clapping. I was taken aback, amazed, delighted and, whereas I had begun confidently enough, I was now positively forging ahead, or rather being carried away by my speech, for this was no longer solely the product of my own obscure conception but was also emanating from all those 'others' in whom I was discovering my self, a self of which I had not previously been conscious.

Speaking at a venture for love of you, and relying almost wholly upon intuition, I had made a beginning and the 'electric atmosphere', fortified by reciprocal action, had then set in.

Language as a curb, a brake, had been all too desperately familiar to me as a stammerer. I had overcome that condition with my mother's help and that of Shakespeare's language. But what had just taken place, with the help of an electric fluid not wholly devoid of mass eroticism, was the experience of language as the congruent partner of thought, the unconscious at the hub of the conscious. Once again came the applause, interrupting and urging me on to yet bolder metaphors, to a freer use of language, yet at the same time destroying the innocence of the speech: the speaker became an orator.

As, with applause surging about me, I went back to my table where the pretty woman was enjoying my, her *own* success, it was no longer for her that I had spoken; I had been moved by 'love of her' – a love which had escaped from the fortuitous confines of individuality to spill over into the pure being of the International.

I had discovered that I was a speaker, all unbeknown possessed of the power to seduce people by means of the spoken word. It was the most fateful discovery of my life.

By fateful I mean two things: on the one hand, the temptation to obtain the maximum, albeit entirely ephemeral, success with a minimum expenditure of time, application and hard work; on the other, the inevitable routine of rhetoric that distorts life and literature into its own likeness. A speaker makes a direct impact. His speech is not a work that has to come *ready-made* into the world. The speech creates itself with the cooperation of the audience, in that the echo the latter returns to the speaker provides fresh material for his speech, the impulse for new associations. The speaker's work is done as he goes along, breaking down resistance, obtaining surrender, delighting in seduction.

At this time, and quite unaware of its close affinity with the circumstances I have just described, I was working on a play about Don Juan. In this comedy Don Juan indulges in verbal seduction only, finding no pleasure in fulfilment – perhaps, in fact, impotent. The woman thus seduced is passed on to Leporello, an unimaginative phallus, who consummates the willing flesh in silence and darkness. It is the egoism of the weak man, narcissistic enjoyment uninhibited by any thought of the consequences.

Thus it would sometimes happen that the erotic would also be infected by the rhetorical. Worse than this, however, I was myself seduced by the power of the spoken word into a more facile form of artistic expression. My first experience of extempore speaking was unrepeatable in its intensity. Later I not infrequently prepared my speeches with conscientious care, collecting material, considering my arguments, anticipating rejoinders, for it was the cause that was at stake and my object was to convince. But even during this preparatory stage the audience was taken into account so that I tended to neglect concision and purity of language in favour of an inflammatory style that pandered both to my own voice and the probable mood of my audience – a process tending to obfuscate the thought.

I have, alas, indulged in all forms of rhetorical masturbation. I have spoken at innumerable meetings, have been acclaimed like an operatic tenor – electoral speeches, parliamentary speeches, speeches at conferences – yet of all the verbal dust I have stirred up, of all that swarm of words, what remains? The momentary stimulation evaporated into thin air and who knows how much intellect squandered, how much strength gone to waste, though not for the most part in political speeches, for my persuasive powers were equally effective in ordinary conversation.

For a man like myself who needs to be overstimulated and overtaxed if he is not to lag too far behind his potentialities, the rhetorical mode invites self-deception: the as yet indefinite feeling, the still immature idea are fallaciously presented as definite and mature. The abridged procedure of rhetoric suppresses the process of fermentation.

A prelude to my first attempt to introduce political agitation and rhetoric into drama, thus bridging the gap between stage and audience, was the performance in September 1924 of my play *Attila's Sword* at the Burgtheater in Vienna. It was a bad play and I had written better if unproduceable ones before it. A medieval fable provided the vehicle for the romantic's horror when confronted by the power of objects to which man, not possessing but possessed by them, is subservient. The result was a series of sketches hastily put together, amongst which there were a few lyrical scenes and a very great deal of imitative, jejune amateurishness. With Stefan Zweig and Josef David Bach for sponsors, I was vain enough to entrust this abortion to the Burgtheater. I used to enjoy the rehearsals, although with every day and with every scene it became increasingly manifest that there was nothing here of the hazy vision I had pursued, and that, furthermore, an allegorical play of this kind was completely out of tune with our own era.

A year later, on 12 November 1925, the Workers' Theatre Group put on a performance of my passion play *The Eternal Rebel* in the Graz opera house. It was economical, concentrated and effective but here, too, poetry had all too often to play second fiddle to rhetoric.

Nevertheless, during the performance of the passion play the footlights dividing stage and audience ceased to exist. The fourth scene finds the rebel on trial. The bench is presided over by the devil with, for his fellow justices, a cowl and a uniform. Downstage, next to the footlights, the grey chorus. 'Who's in favour of acquittal?' asks the devil. The grey chorus raise their hands, a dense forest of hands. 'No one!' says the devil. 'Who's in favour of a death sentence?' The three incumbents of the bench hold up their hands. 'Unanimously sentenced to death!'

Uproar in the big proscenium box. An old working woman leapt to her feet. 'It's a lie! A hundred votes to three!' And others next to her leant over the balustrade gesticulating violently. 'Rogues! Swindlers! It's a fraud! Take another vote!' For some it was their first visit to a theatre. The play was to them reality, though actually so very far from naturalistic, with its verse, its choruses and its fiery rhetoric.

But it was not in fact the rhetoric whose effect was so elemental as to eliminate the footlights and turn the audience into a chorus that intervened in the action; rather it was the gestures, the mime, the increasingly evident discrepancy between saying and doing and, manifest in that discrepancy, the social reality – the many who are nobody, the few whose votes count; it was the starkness of the situation, spurning any kind of naturalistic trappings, that entirely abolished aesthetic objectivity and provoked the intervention of the audience . . .

During one of the rehearsals in the Burgtheater I was approached by an elderly actor who had only a few lines to speak. A young actress had just asked me to write, not medieval but modern plays in future, and one with a scene in which she could wear a bathing dress which would show her figure to so much better advantage than voluminous petticoats, when the old man bore down upon us with measured tread. He raised his right hand to his brow, shielding his eyes as though dazzled, advanced a few steps more, again raised his hand to his brow and asked in a voice such as only the tradition of the Burgtheater could have produced: 'The author???' When, with some embarrassment, I said I was indeed the author, the old man's face assumed a dazed expression as though he were confronted by a supernatural being.

'How fortunate I am to make your acquaintance! For my artistic conscience is being tormented by a question which I shall, with your permission, put before you. I have a line to say at the end of which there isn't a full stop but a dash; in other words the sentence breaks off, is incomplete, which means that my voice must go up and stay up, soaring high into the air. But the director, Herr Herterich, insists that my voice go down.'

In the word 'down' the rounded vowel sound went rolling down into the bottom of the primeval pit, and in the old man's eyes there was a look of distress, as though it were being demanded of him that he bury a sentence alive.

'You are the author. It's for you to decide. Is it your wish that my voice should go down, or may it go up?'

His 'up' was like a joyous exclamation, a blackbird's song, a triumphal fanfare.

'Your voice should go up!'

'The author's verdict! Thank you. Now I know where I stand

and I'll cite your authority, even if it means opposing the director of the Burgtheater himself!'

And I? Hadn't I, too, allowed my voice to go up? Up and up? 'Soaring high into the air', my sentence uncompleted? For too long I remained a speaker.

8

Letter to Anny

The air is shimmering moist and silver, the mountainside so close that I stretch out my hand and stroke the fur of its forests, the skin of its meadows; the quiet light after storms; memory. In this air and in this light I am writing you the letter I have never written, the one that has been repeatedly begun, broken off, never completed, my declaration of love.

At first you were no more than a piece of gossip. Here in this town there's a girl with red hair and a red car, with golden eyes, white gloves, a sensual mouth: the lubricious whispering of a provincial town . . .

'Love!' we called out in unison, with aggressive irony. Then, mockingly, you gave me your hand, a murmured 'Perhaps'.

We had been invited to a New Year's Eve party given, I think, by art historians, in some studio or other. A local-government official, specializing in folklore or something of the kind, made a speech in a tone redolent of bonhomie and self-satisfaction. He bewailed dissension, party strife and self-interest but, the Lord be praised, and it was well to recall this at the start of a new year, there was one unifying, conciliatory element, a common bond linking each and every one of us – at which point the word was snatched out of his mouth as you and I yelled it in unison. It struck a jarring note, evidence of heterodox hard-heartedness – typical of course, what else can one expect of a Jewess and a Red – and the damage could only be partially made good, as the speaker was now at pains to do, by a sonorous repetition of the word, fraught with emotion, all stops pulled out, '*Love*, yes my dear, my beloved friends!'

'I'd like to see you again . . .'

In your legendary red car you drove off into the winter night . . .

At last! I thought. At long last! The first word in common, ironical perhaps and motivated by ribald high spirits, and yet it took us so much by surprise that you gave me your hand: love. What did I know of it? In love from childhood onwards, each woman never more than a cloud, a wraith, a product of my imagination. I wrote you a letter, the first, tore it up, not one word that was to the point, not a sentence that contained an echo of the two of us.

My memory refuses to tell me when I saw you next, nor can it recall any detail between our first meeting, our first embrace, our first quarrel; instead, it fills in the gaps with earlier, fragmentary figures, those who prepared the way for you.

There was the singer, called Maria like your dark-haired sister, with whom at the age of seventeen or eighteen I fell hopelessly in love, writing her poems and eventually making her acquaintance in the champagne tent at an opera fête, when I found myself too shy to talk to her. But her parting words were: 'I should be delighted if you would come and see me . . .' She was forty and beautiful, and she lived in a house on the outskirts of the town. In reply to a fresh batch of poems she sent a little note: 'I'll expect you here at eight o'clock tomorrow evening.' I stood outside the gate, two of the windows were lit, occasionally I saw her silhouette and still I stood there, invisible among the bushes, a finger on the bell. At ten minutes past eight she opened a window. It was a cool autumn night, I saw her face, beautiful and pensive, and I didn't press that bell, she closed the window, at ten o'clock the light went out. I never saw her again except on stage and, when she came to take her curtain call, there were no longer any gratified looks for me. Nor did I write her any more poems, only a letter from the front, a declaration of love, an ineffectual attempt to explain my feelings to her, my love that shunned reality, the love of a foolish boy who was bold enough when nothing serious was at stake and took fright when too powerful an emotion threatened to overwhelm his meagre breast. Though I expected none, an answer came: 'You sweet, silly boy! I don't understand your letter. I was fond of you. What a pity!'

And then there was another whose name, like yours, was Anny. It was in Switzerland, beside the Wallensee in the summer of 1917. I had just taken my wartime matriculation as an extra-mural student, after a year of overwork during which I had had to assimilate a three years' curriculum. I was suffering from insomnia, an aunt as rich as she was corpulent invited my mother and myself to spend a holiday beside the Wallensee and an uncle in one of the ministries obtained a permit authorizing me to stay in Switzerland for a month. I very soon recovered my strength, did a great deal of swimming and boating and became the pet of an octagenarian lady who told me all about her past love-life, reiterating at frequent intervals: 'Don't waste your time with me! Run along and find a young woman and put into practice what I, an old one, have told you.'

Towards the end of my holiday I was lying in the sun, congratulating myself on having acquired so pleasing a tan, when my attention was caught by the clumsy efforts of an over-elegant young man and his beautiful, willowy companion to climb into a boat from the wooden jetty without getting wet. I ran across to help them, pushed the boat off into the lake and swam after it for some distance – at which juncture the sequence of events becomes blurred.

In this woman time was annulled. What happened subsequently was her and only her. All that was ephemeral was embodied in her, became manifest in her person, extrinsic movement contained, brought to a standstill in a profound state of motion, an arrested wave, a continuous moment. It was not love but rather a feeling of astonishment that such pleasure could really be, submerged by the blue, the moist air, the island in the middle of the lake, a flock of birds startled by bells rising in a silver galaxy, and white fear in her face, fear of the flapping and fluttering, she sought the protection of the scrawny youth, her white face, till tomorrow then; and she on her own, without the dressy young man, a little way removed from the country house, in the warm night; 'my name's Anny', he was only a cousin but what did it matter who he was, submerged in lips and hair and shimmering opulence; desire which she knew how to appease and how to intensify, and nothing but pleasure, no soul in the intoxication of the senses, unromanticized enjoyment more powerful than dream, intimation or imagination. When I had pulled her blouse off her shoulders, down over her breasts as far as her waist, and my hands caressing her could get no further with her undressing she, with a little laugh of impatience and a 'Better this way, perhaps', captured my fingers in her own, with her other hand removing her blouse, then asked with gentle raillery: 'Do you often go to bed with women?' 'This is the first time,' I said. Instantly she paused, looked into my eyes and then, as though my words had been a charm, she became deliciously transformed; laughingly, she surrendered herself with the utmost passion and tenderness as though intent that I should forgo nothing in the way of pleasure, surprise and erotic discovery. I took it all for granted: this exuberance in the art of love, in improvisation, in joyous play, this sweet delirium, this extremity of rapture was, I believed, no more than the essence of womanhood and consequently I thought that this woman, so exceptional, so self-revealing in the sudden spasm of love, was offering no more than others of her sex were able to offer. For all my excitation, there was a small part of me that remained cool and detached so that, while all my senses were fully engaged, I continued to observe every detail. So *that's* how it is, so *that's* what it is, and I wished that there should be no end to this glorious intercourse.

What I felt then I was to rediscover much later in Picasso's erotic drawings, the concentration of the body upon the sex, the throng of breasts, shoulders, thighs, softly parted lips, the ecstatically clouded eye in the clear surface of the mirror – but devoid of horror, the horror of the faceless, hundred-breasted monster that grinds men's bones, embodiment of the collective woman.

Once you asked me whether I was sensual. In mid-career. 'Don't be so passionate. Keep still. Let me enjoy my pleasure.'

Sensual? There was too much torment in my love for you. I didn't dare be as sensual as I had been in the liberating embrace of the first Anny, who taught me to know her body and my own in the inexhaustible possibilities of enjoyment. For you I wrote: 'Flesh, the white flame . . .' but in reality it was the flame that consumes everything material, that strives improbably upwards.

Into such a turmoil did you stir my senses that they transcended themselves, their state became one of hyperabundance, or hyper-sensuality. In my desire there was too much imagination, over-reaching reality. Like the tumult in those Baroque paintings in which everything in this world is only an allusion to the world beyond, arms raised, faces upturned, ecstatic gestures, all alluding to what is happening up there above the clouds. It was a kind of Catholicism of the feelings that made me virtually incapable, when with you, of the pagan enjoyment your nature demanded. You, whose enjoyment was pagan . . .

As we, the first Anny and I, lay in a happy state of torpor, her cousin opened the door, flooding the room with the dazzling light of the summer morning. 'Go away!' she said, waving an indolent hand at him and I, for want of anything better to say, murmured something about 'situations'. He nodded sympathetically: 'The situation as regards myself is that I'd like some breakfast. Would you care to join me? Us?' Whereat she: 'I'm sorry, but if you could be patient just a little longer . . .' He went out into the garden. 'Stay with me, today, tonight, the next day and . . .' 'I shall have to nip back to the hotel, or my mother will worry.' 'Don't go away, come back, and come and come!' I rang up my mother. Then we had breakfast.

The cousin was vivacious, witty, boastful. He seemed to be wooing me and my admiration, spoke of the Clarté with which he had some connection, of Romain Rolland and René Schickele who were his friends, of his decorations, one presented by the Pope because, he confided chattily, having first written a pseudonymous pamphlet attacking the Vatican, he had then refuted it under his own name; change, he averred, eloping with your self from identity, was the spice of life. I had no idea then, nor do I know now, what his purpose was or what his relationship to Anny. I believe that she really was his cousin and, on occasion, his lover; maybe, too, some sort of secret service work was involved, but at the time in Switzerland his stories amused me, though with Anny's white face in front of me, her fragrance, her breasts under the dressing-gown, all I could think was: Why don't you take me back to your bed? Why this interruption with coffee and roses and all this light going to waste? We have so little time . . . but this I forbore to mention. Two more days, two more nights, then we would have to go back to Vienna. A pity, I thought, but can bliss surpass itself? In those two days and two nights there was not a single moment of descent from the heights, of disenchantment. We were in the isles of the blessed and the closer our parting drew – though she knew nothing of it – the more bewitching, the more prodigal and self-abandoned Anny became. 'Is that what you like?' or 'Would you prefer something else?' or, 'Come further into me, still further, really deep, so you plunge right into my heart!' And when I had plunged really deep inside her, had penetrated, flowed over into her heart, the night was nearing its end and, as I plunged deep inside her, I said: 'My train leaves in four hours' time.' Her face grew whiter than I had ever seen it and she looked at me aghast: 'But you *can't* . . .' and fell silent. Then she said: 'You can't go. Stay, stay with me! What do I have to do to keep you with me? Don't you understand that nothing's the same any more, not me, or anything else?'

Four hours later I was sitting in the train. Over there, in the trail of smoke from the engine was the country house. And here, standing on the embankment, was Anny. She waved, then threw herself down in the grass. Her body was heaving, but not now in the throes of pleasure. I was hardly conscious of the parting; all I felt was: how sweet, how sweet you were to me!

In memory what had been no more than delight, no more than sensuality, turned into love. The next woman I slept with left behind only the stale taste of not being Anny. So Anny was more than just Woman, and women were not the miracle in which for a few nights I had been engulfed. Too late I fell in love with Anny. And I didn't write to her. And she didn't write. It was – as had been intended – paradise lost.

And you?

Your father was an urbane, middle-class Jehovah, governing wife and daughters with a heavy hand; your mother nervous, with diffident charm putting up a timid resistance against the patriarch on behalf of you two, your dark-haired sister who ran away from home with an actor and went on the stage, and yourself, who did at least marry an irreproachable timber merchant. He had chosen this career in order to win your hand, to keep you in comfort with a house and motor-car of your own and the freedom that only money can give. A clever, brittle, enigmatic man whose ambition it was to become a journalist (an ambition he was to fulfil many years later, in Paris when, after losing you, he entered that profession); but in order to possess you he gave up any idea of abandoning a business which, unsatisfying though it was, at least guaranteed prosperity. He was helplessly addicted to you, Anny, as was anyone who had been drawn into your magnetic field. Though able to enjoy your own magic without restraint, you invariably became the prisoner of those addicted to you. You fought against it, not wanting just to be an object of desire, of sensuality. 'Revolting!' you once said of a lover on the eve of his dismissal. 'He rang me up and actually panted into the telephone, "As you got into your car I saw your naked thighs – come to me at once, you must come at once!" Foul, don't you think?' 'And you . . .?' 'Disgusting, don't you think?' 'Did you go?' 'Yes. Can you make it out? But never again . . .'

The word 'sex appeal' was not in use at that time, and what emanated from you was more than that. It was elemental sensuality and vitality, the 'lusts of the flesh' as attributed by medieval Christianity to the 'gods in exile': Venus in the mountain, Diana lusting after blood, witches, sylphids, the *Belle Dame sans Merci*. You were, with every fibre of your being, so *cupida rerum novarum*, so insatiable was your hunger for the as yet unknown, that you had to love and be loved as the eagle has to fly, as Columbus had to follow the quest for new paths across the ocean: ever seeking a fresh sea-route, the young wind on your cheek and, from the crest of the wave, still scanning the distant horizon, the empty space where there was no landfall, only luminousness. The very ease of your conquests made things harder for you since, between you and the one who was calling you into the future, between you and the one awaiting you, there was always the thicket of your beauty and magnetic power. In conquest after conquest you fell a prey to your own self.

In the Bible, the term used for sexual intercourse is 'knowledge'. 'And he knew her . . .', when he slept with her. The penetration of the body, the in-dwelling, the coalescence *is* knowledge, even though only physical, elemental, primordial; from phallus to eros, from the sexual act to love, intercourse is knowledge progressing towards the identification of knower with known. You were waiting for such 'knowledge', hoping that it would come from me, and hoped in vain; I never 'knew' you. That knowledge would have meant your freedom and mine in relation to our selves, the surmounting of our insufficiency, our equivocally unfulfilled existence.

My use of a romantic vocabulary is not fortuitous. There is about it something ominously reminiscent of Perseus and Andromeda, of Ariadne and Dionysus, of those ambiguous liberations which obfuscate the transition to male supremacy. Nevertheless, your inexhaustible vitality enabled you, at once imperilled and redeemed, to become what you are by your own efforts, without any help from me. In my love for you there was and still is all the radiance of romanticism as well as all its poison.

It was Lou who finally taught me how to escape from the ancient land of romanticism. In lines dedicated to another woman, though written with you in mind, I took my leave of this exquisite nonsense, this melodious egoism, of Narcissus in the role of Romeo.

> *Would I were drained of blood, all empty, hollow,*
> *Light-blind my night, in blackness saturated!*
> *Oh, could I be at last annihilated*
> *So death might ease the pain of parting's sorrow!*
> *Parting from you were death, did it not borrow*
> *Life's trappings; restlessness, grief unabated*
> *In sleep, and longed-for peace in vain awaited,*
> *Envying the dead their night without tomorrow.*
>
> *Parting, ah slow, inexorable bleeding,*
> *Stream without shore, unfathomable deep,*
> *Into the aching void of my heart's needing*
> *You pour fresh anguish, from dark clouds descend,*
> *Breathe new life into death and, when I weep,*
> *Bring back things past, in torment without end.*

It is not a leave-taking from you; on the contrary, it being easier to love Helen than a living woman, the object of my leave-taking is the phantom which I so often mistook for you.

Was it a phantom? And even if it was, is a phantom not as real as the reality of the fluctuating, vanishing, recurring moment? Does it not possess identity and permanence?

> *Thou Moon beyond the clouds! Thou living Form*
> *Among the Dead! Thou Star above the Storm!*
> *Thou Wonder, and thou Beauty, and thou Terror!*

Moon beyond the clouds, deep inside you; not yet, keep still, and next door, voices, noise, but we the star above the storm; our host slipped me the key, and you, drunk with so much night and proximity, so prodigally ripe, so ready, you and I together in the next room, divan, candlelight, a cloud, you, integument of cloud, cloud flesh and, as gently, deliciously you open up, moon beyond the clouds, next door forgotten, already veiled over by the other planet, and what an idiotic expression, to sleep together, when every sense is awake, wakefulness magnified a hundredfold, and you absorbing me into yourself, deep into the shimmering, flexible, firmly enfolding cloud steeped in moonlight, not yet, lie still, and I absorbed by you, into the envelope of your skin, your flesh and blood, your body, all one mouth with which my own is mingled, deeper still than once the other Anny, the early harbinger of this delight, deeper into the heart, the network of veins, into all that moist fountain-head, and again lie still, again not yet, and never any end, never again to be an I, always and only you, and next door, those of the vanished planet, listening walls, gloating eyes, let them all come, the whole town can watch us, see us high up in the bell-tower, naked and interlocked, beneath the rocking bells, swaying with the rhythm of the bells, rising, falling, unbroken, unspent, never to be forgotten, imperishable wave of delight, moon beyond the clouds and nothing but mouth, was woman ever so deep an abyss, so overflowing with fragrance, with terror and tenderness? The eyes of most women, when orgasm overwhelms them, cloud over, become remote as at the point of death. Not so yours, flaming beacons of joy, 'living form among the dead'. Did I say 'nothing but mouth', forgetting the eye, the looking? Your golden eyes, huge, wide open, opening wider and ever wider, unflinching in their gaze, looking into my face so as to miss nothing of the reflection of your magic there, so that my pleasure should find itself in yours and yours in mine, so that we, an hermaphrodite in the exchange of our sexes, should mutually enjoy each other, sucking mouth and seeing eye, and the delight of your breasts communing with my hand so that neither of us knew whose substance was whose, for me the pleasure felt by your breasts, for you the pleasure felt by my hand, and each the other's mouth and eye and looking. You were the more conscious, Anny, the more pagan, and I, drowning in you, emotional Catholicism, *unio mystica*, I was the weaker.

'Forget tonight,' you said afterwards. 'No, don't forget it. But not another word about it. It was a celebration – an unrepeatable one.'

I was determined that the celebration should be repeated. And then again not. And then again, yes. And what I wanted ... Who – I? Wanting what? I had become your addict, and the fiery shirt of Nessus, indestructible, now in process of weaving, was precisely what we had ironically shouted on New Year's Eve: love, fantastic, ineradicable, imperishable love. And you? At first you wanted what you said: a celebration, no more. And yet you did want more, for me not only to become addicted to you, but to conquer you, sweep you off your feet, hold you fast. What you wanted – what I wanted . . . yet at the backs of our minds, behind the back of our wishes, we knew it wouldn't work out and went on hoping that perhaps . . . One thing, however, was certain: we had made such deep inroads into each other – lie still, not yet, and never any end – that though between us there might be dissension, discord, anger, parting and reconciliation, reconciliation and parting, there could never be an end.

You reproached me for my weakness; I wasn't strong enough to make you my wife. But what you failed to understand was my poverty, the chilly chasm dividing you and me. Mine was no proud, rebellious, proletarian poverty; it was the grinding, humiliating indigence of the *déclassé*. The kind where your house is laid waste, the bookshelves grow emptier and emptier, the entrails come spilling out of the tattered furniture, and you have to make a detour round the grocer's shop because you owe him so much money, and you shiver in bare rooms and you can't light the senile geyser in the bathroom and have to wash in the cold water you detest, and you see your mother's misery as she lies ill and worn in bed, and you go to borrow money from friends, you discuss art and politics with them, you read them your poetry, you're witty and amusing, and when it comes to begging the words stick in your throat, and your mother's waiting for you, what if you come empty-handed? and you turn back abruptly as you're leaving and mutter 'Oh, by the way, I forgot . . . do you think you could possibly . . .?'

As a reporter I was not paid enough to maintain a family; moreover we accumulated so many debts that nothing was left by the end of the first week of the month; on top of that I was frivolously inclined and preferred to spend my evenings elsewhere than in the desolate flat but, since an invitation was not always forthcoming, I was forced to buy my drinks from the waiter on tick. It was an absurd situation and I did my best to close my eyes to it; it was not rare for me to have nothing in my stomach but rice or sauerkraut yet be invited out in the evening, by your friends or mine, to drink champagne and innumerable cocktails, and I was too proud to tell them that alcohol and cigars don't satisfy hunger. And when I used to sit in your room beside your desk, drinking glasses of this and that and nibbling almonds, unable to bring myself – no thanks, I've already eaten, not hungry – to ask for a sandwich, only wanting to kiss you, talk to you, drink with you, build castles in the air, it wasn't just because of my foolish delight in your presence, in the fragrance of your skin, the shining of your eyes, it was also a feeling of being safe, a mollusc on the sea-bed, a dreamlike unworldliness. Leaving you late at night, I would have to cross the whole town from the suburb where you lived to my flat on the eastern perimeter, an hour and a half's walk, and the further I got from you and the closer I came to the sober world of reality greyly emerging out of the night, the more I lost hope of ever being able to comprise you permanently within my existence. And what an existence! It wasn't, of course, that you needed wealth, but to drag you down into poverty, to jeopardize the fragrance of your skin, the sweetness of your smile, seemed a vile thing to do. And what an existence! How was I going to live without you?

'Don't stay in Graz!' you said. 'Come with me to Paris!'

My mother loved you and you were fond of her. Nevertheless: 'Don't tie yourself to her apron-strings. You must cut yourself free. You'll go to pieces here, along with all your gifts and potentialities!'

I couldn't leave my mother in the lurch. It wasn't an infantile 'mother fixation'. I was immeasurably indebted to this exceptional woman. That she had now gone on strike against life, had simply let herself slide, was wretched for her and a burden to me. Precisely because I tended to be irresponsible, it was imperative that I should not shrug off this responsibility. My brothers were students and could make no contribution towards the household, my sister was un-provided for and, because my mother was oppressed by all this, because she trusted me implicitly, it was my bounden duty not to betray that trust, not to inflict upon her this final disappointment.

So my love for you was not an overriding love?

You were quite right when you advised me to break away from that spectral province, and I know how much my development was hamstrung through my failure to escape – no matter whether to Paris or Berlin – at the earliest opportunity, through my failure to lay any foundations somewhere else for our future together. But I believe that were I once again to find myself in the same horrible dilemma, my decision would be no different from what it was then. I would, of course, have one advantage I lacked at the time through being too young, too unstable and unsure of myself: I should be sufficiently uninhibited to discuss 'practicalities' with you, without fear of detracting from the glorious plenitude of the 'other aspect'.

It was the discrepancy between this excessively romantic love on the one hand and material insufficiency on the other that was responsible for introducing into our relationship a distorted, contorted form of 'class struggle'. My ineptitude which spoilt so much, my supercilious diffidence and helpless defiance were only partly conditioned by inexperience; more often it was the rebellion of the guttersnipe against the beautiful, spoiled lady who has so graciously invited him to her table, granting him a favour at one moment only to withdraw it the next. Many years later, after your dark-haired sister and I had unexpectedly fallen in love, she once said: 'You mustn't forget that Anny was very nearly as young as you were and, though sexually experienced, she had no idea how to behave towards someone like yourself who was not, after all, exactly a simple case. You were like two stones striking sparks off each other . . .' Like two stones! Stone clashing on stone to make fire, a fire that never went out, stones that never broke. It wasn't just inexperience, money too played its part and even if money doesn't smell, as the Roman who had grown rich building cloacas cynically remarked, it can sometimes be the manure upon which scented orchids feed. You would probably have been capable of suddenly deciding to throw everything to the winds. But what then . . .? 'And even if it means going on the streets for you in Paris, I'm capable of it!' I was very touched, and you meant it, for just as long as it took to say. But, foolish though I was, I did not – fortunately – take it very seriously even then.

I had no room of my own, that was the trouble, and no money to rent one, no refuge for our love. Alone together in your husband's house, we used to talk endlessly, fireworks of the intellect, a state of insatiable excitation. Or else it was in company with others, the many who knew about our love and were willing to abet it – never more than hasty, clandestine explosions of accumulated desire, in the next room, haphazard, fleeting – something I longed should be without end, inexhaustible until the moment of the most extreme, the most exquisite and most tender exhaustion, to be with you for once with no limits set, a night and a day and a night, and you, too, however much you might sometimes deny it, wanted more than just a celebration, that trembling drop of happiness and, even as you fought me off, would suddenly draw me to you. A passion that spread its wings so wide yet was so meagrely nourished bore in itself the seeds of conflict, a conflict it could not without damage endure.

Once, when we were again snatching our pleasure in the usual haphazard way – this time for some inexplicable reason underneath a Christmas tree – I was clumsy. You spat at me like a cat, pushed me away, kicked out at me. 'Never again!' you said, 'I don't want it. Now go away, leave me!'

Months of separation. You and I, each asking everyone about the other, whether I had another girl, whether you were saying unkind things about me. And finally, arranged by friends, the small party at carnival time in the house of a beautiful young sculptress, each pretending to know nothing about the other, of each other's presence, and strict injunctions to wear masks and fancy dress, and mask spoke to mask and knew. You knew that I knew, and each pretended not to know the other, a game of make-believe at once so foolish and so wise that the two who loved one another fell in love all over again and, having been left alone together, were too shy to fall into each other's arms, so that voice mingled with voice, not flesh with flesh.

Thus union, parting, reunion . . .

And then there was your child. When I saw you again, after some New Year's Eve – which, I don't remember – you were pregnant. Your husband was the baby's father. You told me about the birth. 'Bliss, you know. Painful? Of course, but not too bad, yes, of course, conceiving . . . nothing as compared with the bliss of giving birth, though!' It was your child that kept you, a boat yearning for the open sea, moored to the bollard of security. What could I have done? Today, allowing myself to lapse back into the self I once was, into you, as you once were, while at the same time remaining my present appraising self, I feel able to take a more lenient view of my weakness.

But at the time, in 1921, I was shipwrecked upon you, weaker than Odysseus who, having surmounted the breakers, scaled the cliffs to conquer the nymph. You had your child and I no money – such are the simple formulae to which the problem can, in effect, be reduced.

How about my writing? Was there nothing? Neither present possibility nor future prospect? A newly established Viennese publishing house – run by ex-officers, as I was later to discover – had brought out *A Bird called Desire*, the book of poems mentioned above. The same publishers provisionally accepted *The King of Sodom*, a novel conceived in strong colours, on condition that one chapter be excised – a chapter in which an ageing temple prostitute, Aholibamah, takes her pleasure with a black he-goat. Wilfully, I said no and turned a deaf ear to all persuasion so that the novel was never published. And then, even before meeting you, I had begun work on a short-story cycle, *The Black City*. 'In these cities of black basalt; where magic fire fled the dark . . .' (*Verhaeren*), and thus, too, the city in my story, a grotesque amalgam of Sodom and provincialism, myth and technology, yearning and revulsion, the black city, built on a disproportionate scale from a grandiose plan after the old one had been blown up, only a few ruins being incorporated into the modern Nineveh or Babylon.

The third story was called *Electra*. You had given me *Les Fleurs du Mal* in which I had found the line: '*Pour rafraîchir ton cœur, nage vers ton Electre.*' And you with your amber eyes, electron, Electra, Orestes' sister, brother-sister love, and the black city, fire everywhere, a flood of light, electricity, the electronic era, the spark leaping from nerve to nerve, current of electrons. You insisted on hearing the unfinished short story and where I erred was in giving way for, in as much as you were depicted in *Les Fleurs du Mal*, so too your likeness would have been more true to life in the completed story than in the fragment I read aloud to you. Yet it was all there, your chaotic desk, your voice over the telephone, disembodiment of your so much desired body, and your erotic supremacy, and then – the final episode in the fragment – the carnival, the fancy-dress party. I described the hectic, restless, intoxicated atmosphere, of this party, inflation, devaluation not only of money, better spend it, money or self; tomorrow it may be too late, tomorrow comes the sea. Be profligate, take the plunge, swim your way through the deluge, an island, Electra, *nage vers ton Electre*! You were the presiding goddess. Sumerian, Hittite, Assyrian, Ashtaroth, archaic Aphrodite, blissful descent into hell. Upon your bare shoulder a bird of brilliant plumage, a fantastic parrot, pecking savagely at anyone who tried to touch you and screaming: 'Not you! Not you!' No one was allowed to lay hands on you, desire incarnate, voluptuousness, frigidity, under your skin a shadow, anguish of loneliness, no one capable of doing you justice, of recognizing the human being in the goddess. Not you! Not you! All around you turbulence, sweating flesh, panting ecstasy and you, unapproachable, watchful, waiting, Electra waiting for her brother. With an indolent gesture you took the parrot from your shoulder, raised it aloft, tossed it into the air above the masks, above the hands outstretched to catch it.

'Whoever brings it back to me,' you said, 'can hope . . .'

Bemused, shrieking in terror, the brightly coloured bird flapped heavily, uncertainly through the close, dusty air, the crowd of dazed, bedazzled drunks in hot pursuit. They snatched the harassed, by now scarcely fluttering, bird out of each other's hands, tearing out its feathers until each possessed his own relic of gaudy plumage and the luckless creature, now plucked and hideous in its nudity, fell lifeless to the floor. Whereat . . .

Your lips were vividly painted. Your lashes and eyebrows black, with a dusting of gold. Your face was alien and stiff, framed in flaming red hair. Motionless you sat enthroned, the goddess of lust and death. And then the dead, denuded bird, laid out upon a silken cloth, borne aloft by two men and two women – a funeral march, Chopin, perfumed, parody or macabre kitsch while, shocked into sobriety, the guests formed a gruesome funeral procession and paced through the hall in a pageant of masks and solemn music, until the two men and two women, arriving before you, raised aloft the booty, the sacrifice, the dead bird.

The last page fell from my hand.

'And that's supposed to be me? Get out!'

You were on your feet, your face such as I had never seen it, frighteningly like that of the Electra in my unfinished story.

'So *that*'s how you see me? Get out!'

Whatever I might do would be wrong. Should I leave without saying a word or first pick up the pages that lay scattered about on the floor? Should I try to make you change your mind, when your face was so cold, your mouth set in so hard a line?

'You don't love me,' you said as I began to gather up the ill-fated manuscript, the *Electra* that would never now be finished.

'What you love is my skin, my hair, my lips. Perhaps the way I smell. Perhaps the wine you drink here, wine and *schnapps* enough to get squiffy on. It's your own desire for me that you love – not myself. I've had enough, Now take this and go!'

You handed me a dainty revolver inlaid with silver and ivory.

'All right,' I said.

'I don't want a farewell letter. I shall know what's happened from the papers.'

'All right,' I said, toying with the revolver.

I had put the pages together, the ashes of our love.

Gripping them firmly, I put the revolver into my pocket and, without sparing you another glance, was at pains to leave with my head held high, with as much pride and dignity as I could muster, when I tripped over the steps of the dais on which your desk stood, fell flat on my face, felt your scorn cutting the nape of my neck like a knife, got up not very gracefully and trotted away, a nothing, a nullity, the empty husk of the man I had been only a few minutes before.

My one thought was to get away from Graz. Even animals, when they are going to die, leave their usual habitat. I travelled, why I cannot imagine, to Bruck-on-the-Mur intending to die there, booked a room in an hotel, exactly where or which one I have forgotten, ate amply and well, sent for a litre of red wine. 'All on your own, then?' asked the chambermaid, clearly puzzled by this customer. 'If you need anything, you only have to ring.' Thanks. I had a sense almost of security, released from the effort to exist. Weary of striving. Let yourself slide into nothingness. Medusa's smile, allure of death, 'fawned upon by decay'.

Isn't the revolver altogether too filigree, too dainty a lady's toy? Can the heart be brought to a halt, the skull shattered by these small bullets, this flimsy piece of metal? And supposing it doesn't work? How risible, how pathetic this buffoon, incapable even of killing himself!

Anny. Love. What is it, actually? You love my skin, my hair, my mouth. Perhaps the way I smell. So when exactly does it begin to be *love*, this fragrance, this desire, this intoxication? Weren't you in love with her *before*, in love with a dream-image, daydream, imago, all there beforehand, leading up to her, Helen, and the first one to come along *was* Helen, her double, anyone who happened to be there at just the right moment? It may have been *partly* that, perhaps, but I'm not in love *because* I'm in love, this letter's addressed to *you* and it's *you* who has opened it, not just anybody, you're not nameless, you're not faceless. What excites me in you isn't just your sex – exciting to the point of madness, of distraction, though that is – but rather a combination of . . . qualities, intentions, possibilities? You as an incomplete being, finding completion in me, rhythms, radiations, vibrations, complementary, predestined for each other?

Because I am powerless to hold fast the woman I love so immeasurably, I recite pathetic monologues, fit consolation for milksops. Hold fast – but *whom*? How about her allegation that when I say love, I don't mean her at all but my own dream, my own creature, a self-invented puppet? *Whom* then would I hold fast, the lovely wraith, Helen's reflection in the magic mirror, the rainbow over the troubled waters, plummeting sexual desire? Is it *you* I love, your self, the latent I, uncomprehended otherness, or is it the *possession* of the cloud, of the shadow, of the mask, imaginary owner of an imaginary essence? I tear myself apart, am torn by self-doubt, by dissension, by uncertainty, am torn in twain, and know without a doubt, with a certainty more absolute than ever before, that I love you. But what I mean by love I am unable to say.

I drink and consider. What's the best way of doing it? Temple, mouth, heart? Of all things, not the shame of being found wounded, ambulance, hospital, police inquiry, in this idiotic provincial town. Give me a proof of your love! My death will provide the proof that I can't live without you. Will you be sorry?

Repulsive sentimentality! So I still want, not so much that you should be sorry, but that you should be sorry *for me* because I was too weak to settle matters with you one way or the other. Enough of that!

Since I am incapable of hating you, cannot, will not hate you, I order my memory to retrieve out of the shades of the deep all the happiness, the blessed isles bathed in light, so breathtakingly near, so unattainable that he who has failed thankfully takes his leave . . .

I see your face, not cold and stony as it was last night; bright, tender, happy, half veiled by moist eyelashes, and open my mouth to you, the dainty, the little silver revolver . . .

A sudden booming, a salvo, a roar of gunfire, from the inn below, opposite my window, men's voices singing:

> *O I'm a Styrian boy,*
> *Of sterling stock am I,*
> *'Gainst them that do me wrong*
> *My arm is strong . . .*

A male-voice choir. A glee club. Round table, men of sterling stock. This, then, is what's going to survive ... Like a thunder-clap from the high Dachstein, to the Rhine, to the Rhine, to the German Rhine, from the Dachstein where th' grey Teagle dwells (the grey Teagle, to us children a fiend, a fabulous monster, a nightmare), th' grey Teagle dwells, the pride that swells the manly breast, the glass flows o'er, dear fatherland mayst rest secure, waves crash, swords clash, this lovely land my Styrian land, 'gainst them that do me wrong my arm is strong, the thunder-clap, the manly breast, the glass flows o'er, mayst rest secure, good fellowship, good fellow-ship, here's to good fellowship! Jack boots tramping over graves, to the Rhine, to the Rhine, to the German Rhine, sterling stock male-voice choir, and here's – ready now – three cheers – steady now – here's to good fellowship, vanquished but uncowed, and death to all Serbs, a dead Russian's a good Russian, good fellow, good fellow-ship, wonderful indestructible good fellowship ... And here we have an intellectual, neither ready nor steady, toying with a filigree revolver preparatory to shooting himself dead for love. Laugh? I thought I'd die!

> *Tell me lass, where dost tha sleep o' nights,*
> *Sleep o' nights?*
> *Where dost tha lay thi sweet head?*

Take that revolver out of your mouth! Puerile, deadly plaything. Kill yourself laughing.

> *First tha must find thi way up three stairs,*
> *Up three stairs,*
> *For the street's no right place for a bed.*

If them, why not me? A hand reaching out from the grave, against male-voice choirs, against thunder-clap and the roar of good fellowship, against the sham-dead war, beerhouse today, slaughter-house tomorrow – and I? A filigree revolver against field guns, nevertheless, must go on living, against this macabre, massive, unsubdued sterling stock.

Carefully packed in a cardboard box, the revolver was returned to you through a friend.

I suggested to my brother Otto that we should make our way to

Italy as tramps. My other brother Walter deputized for me on the paper. I needed fresh air, violent physical exercise, to put new life into me, to restore my vigour. At the beginning of March crossing the Alps, fresh snow up to our knees, soft and feathery, fatal to leave the path, push on, survival depends on it, what more beneficial for muscles grown slack? Self-chastisement, a ghost arming itself with a body, painful laborious rebirth, feet blistered and raw, Cortina d'Ampezzo, sheltering in barns, stables, presbyteries, the house-keeper, nice young men yer reverence, wine from the cellar, old bottles, dust, yes yer reverence, three more trips to the cellar, new bottles, old wine, deep slumber, balmy sea air, the plain, behind us steep and white, mountains under snow, salty tang. Mestre – every-where, along the road, on the walls, in huge, untidy black and red lettering, *Evviva il Fascismo, Abbasso, Evviva Lenin, Abbasso, Per d'Annunzio e Mussolini, Evviva, Abbasso*, a trip through a civil war, Venice, invited by a friend to stay, a quiet *pension* near the Colleoni, dreams of you, Giorgione, Titian, the Assunta, an introduction from my paper to the Socialist Party, arranged with a gondolier, *abbasso Mussolini*, to attend an anti-Fascist gathering in Chioggia, waited in vain for the contact, understandable reluctance to trust inquisitive foreigners, Pablo Veronese, *palazzi*, class struggle, and then on, through the Romagna, firing in the villages, Italy, blood and wounds. The tip-dispensing traveller never really gets to know a country, but we tramps experienced the kindliness, the helpfulness, the generosity of this nation, more lovable, perhaps, than any other in Europe; unlike the Czechs and the English, democracy no mere convention but the very blood of life.

A crumbling mosaic of memory, small, brightly coloured frag-ments which I assemble for you out of the time when, fleeing from you, I was secretly making towards you, away from yet back to you. Through Bologna, already beyond it: '*Daitser Svain! Daitser Svain!*' behind us, shouting, panting, gesticulating, a rallying cry and, having finally caught us up, '*Daitser Svain!*' with an inflection almost of tenderness as, indeed, was the intention, these being the only words of German origin he knows with which to hail us – German pigs! '*Siamo fratelli, tutti fratelli!*' and he invites us to have a drink with him and his friends. In the heart of the Appenines a road-mender, a tiny, bare stone cottage, wife, two kids, only one bed for the lot of them in which we, he insists, must sleep, taking umbrage when we protest, a portrait of Lenin, *Evviva Lenin*! *Bandiera Rossa*, we talked all night long. And outside Florence the little *trattoria*, rain dripping from our broad-brimmed velour hats, wet through, hot soup, the last of our money. Something to drink? No thanks. Food and no wine? I have a good one, why not try it? No thanks. He opens a bottle: have a sip. Drink some! Don't you think it's good? And after the soup? We've had enough, thank you. Young men must eat. He brings out another dish. What matter? In any case we can't pay, so why not another dish? Yes, of course, a second bottle, and cheese and fruit, of course, and some of this delicious cake. *Il conto, prego*! Despondent, brazen. He wrote out the bill, folded it, and handed us the disaster on a plate: 'Send me a postcard from Rome. You were my guests. Thank you.' On through the rain. Bello Sguardo, Baroness Franchetti's *palazzo*. The doorman looks us up and down superciliously, tramps, shivering in our wet clothes, unshaven, muddy. We hand him a letter of introduction from a friend of the young Baron's, a composer. Exit doorman, centre, shaking his head. Enter a pretty chambermaid, as in a Mozart opera. Observes us, not altogether without sympathy. 'Do you think we could have a wash?' 'With pleasure!' Exit centre. Enter doorman. 'The Baroness regrets . . .' With lowering obstinacy we insist on speaking to her, just to pay her our respects, nothing more. Enter the Baroness, daughter of Lenbach the painter, amiable, aloof, exit just as the maid re-enters, her sweet soprano echoing down the hall: 'The bath's ready!' A bath? What bath? 'Well, then, gentlemen, since it would seem that a bath is ready – may I invite you to remain as my guests?' Our own apartment, waited upon by a liveried servant, stony contempt. Three days had gone by when, for the first time, we were invited upstairs, big party, to display the tramps, a *contessa*, artist, took a liking to us, I flirted outrageously with her, was discovered kissing her in a dark corner and was admitted without more ado into the aristocracy .

Ten days in Florence and then, on foot, through Tuscany, through the spring, through Umbria, often hungry, often befuddled with too much wine, picked up by American women somewhere in the purlieus of Siena, left in the car outside the château, cadging cigarettes off the chauffeur and then, at dinner with the ladies, waited on by this same chauffeur, white gloves and stony contempt, stupefied by the rich banquet and little inclined for a sexual *quid pro quo*, we escaped through a side door, gesture of complicity on the part of the chauffeur, roars of laughter.

Ten days in Rome. An uncle who had once been in love with my mother and hence never married, a librarian in the Vatican, gentle and diffident, a brilliant scholar, invited us to stay. Audience with the Pope; former mountaineer, listens to an account of our wanderings, then turns to give a final blessing, a valediction, *ere perennis* and, blessing us, seeks the parting word, 'Sleep well, now!' and again, 'Sleep well!', an unsentimental, unforgotten, benevolent word. And at night in the Colosseum, wine, moonlight, arguing with a crowd of students, *per d'Annunzio e Mussolini, no, no, no, soltanto per d'Annunzio, no, no, no, per Mussolini*, our rejoinder *abbasso* finding little support, d'Annunzio the god, the pilot who flew over Vienna, the hero of Fiume, a braggart in full fig, arguments, voices, metal on metal, and vehement opposition, but without brutality, without physical violence. And then, for the first time since my obsession for you, in love again, idiotically, absurdly, with Phidias's Amazon, marble seduction; when the attendant wasn't looking I fondled her hips, her breasts, my hand gliding hot over the cool surface, feeling the form of her in its unyielding hardness. This, too, was you, translated to the plane of perpetuity, 'in lineaments divine'; Ovid, Rousseau, Pygmalion, the Romantic dream of the sleeping statue brought to life by lips of flesh and blood: the Venus of Isle, by night persecuting the bridegroom who had placed a ring on her finger, crushing him, squashing him, monstrous lust, murderous vampirism, gods and heroes resurrected from the rubble of antiquity and from Christianity's crypts.

Southwards, via Appia, the Pontine marshes, Terracina, Naples, *Dormitorio Pubblico*, a roof for the night shared with a tubercular negro, we squat on the floor so as not to be eaten alive by the infernal armies of monstrous and bloated bedbugs; in the harbour, filth and light and congestion, carobs to dispel the pangs of hunger, 'pig food' say the sailors, laughing, and then the fourteen-year-old boy with the rolling gait of an old salt, ran away from Styria, two years spent aboard ships of all kinds, if we liked we could sail with him for Egypt, he'd fix it with his shipmates, stow away in the hold and, once at sea but not before, straight into the galley, quietly doing the washing-up as though that was what we'd been signed on for, astute and experienced, this boy. Running a temperature, sunstroke, scarcely able to stand on my feet, must go home, my brother touchingly concerned. I, stumbling, burning, sweating, back by workmen's train, they were building a new line, and then by normal passenger train: Tickets! Haven't got any. Then pay. We can't. Then get out. We won't. We're backed up by our fellow passengers, at the next station carabinieri, please arrest us, have us repatriated to Austria, Santa Madonna! too much fuss and bother, official report, official confirmation, waste of time, stay on the train, for goodness' sake, pleasant journey and we're away! A few days in Rome, still running a temperature, then a student, formerly one of my brother's fellow cadets at the Imperial and Royal Naval Academy, presented me with a ticket to Graz and, as we crossed the Piave where once we confronted each other we, the Italian workers and I, all rose to our feet with: '*Maledetta guerra, siamo tutti fratelli, abbasso gli signori, generali, fascisti!*' Farewell to the people over whom, only a few months later, Mussolini was to ride roughshod.

When was it I next saw you? I cannot recall, only memory, a floodtide of memory, bears you towards my lips, the waves rise and fall, flinging you into my arms, carrying you away again, between each wave a vacuum, and so, without order or sequence, situations tumble over each other, bliss and torment and never so much as a week, three days, or even a day, a night on our own, without the world outside tapping at door or window, without the rift of parting that cut across all our times together. And yet when you did come, when you were actually there, time stood still and no one else counted, however importunate he, however beguiling she might be – evanescent, unforgettable interstices.

Beside a lake in the Salzkammergut, the enchantingly beautiful Heliodora, fair-haired Gothic madonna, classical in her strength and grace, the Amazon of Phidias, adorable perfection. You thought her delicious and so we all three of us went rowing on the lake and, when we were far out, abandoned our oars, the madonna exorcised by your lips, the Amazon coming to life under my hands and then, suddenly and without warning as so often among the lakes, the storm broke and all the luminous brilliance of blue and green and naked flesh was swallowed up in sombre purple, in livid, leaden cloud. Heliodora was trembling, her arms clasped round our knees, head ducked down below the gunwales, a bundle of terror. We rowed, you and I, knowing our muscles had got to hold out, now flung aloft, now dragged down, and the weeping girl, water splashing in her face, wet tongues lapping up her tears, and you, laying into the oars, arms, legs and breasts taut, the wind set upon you, forced open your lips, only to be bitten, crushed by your teeth, and between your thighs the wind raging with desire, unable to violate you, its fellow element, one element against another, and thus side by side at the oars, we the hermaphrodite, and it was not the wind that entered you, to which you surrendered, by you engulfed, by me transpierced, a whirlwind of intercourse.

That night you left your door on the latch, light filtering through the narrow aperture. I didn't come in. Under the same roof your husband, your child lay sleeping, after all the delights of the storm there must be nothing surreptitious, clandestine, furtive between us. The crack of light round the door, *entre-ouvrant la porte*, the angel of death in '*La mort des amants*', and my desire for you was too great for me to be satisfied with such scrappy, catch-as-catch-can love-making; rather possess you whole in verse than 'Tell me lass, where dost tha' sleep o' nights, Where dost tha' lay thi sweet head', and the next day, 'But my door was open!' you said, in surprise and not without mockery, and you may then have presaged the last three lines of the poem which last night I translated, sleepless with thoughts of you.

> *Un soir fait de rose et de bleu mystique,*
> *Nous échangerons un éclair unique,*
> *Comme un long sanglot, tout chargé d'adieux:*
>
> *Et plus tard un Ange, entr'ouvrant les portes,*
> *Viendra ranimer, fidèle et joyeux,*
> *Les miroirs ternis et les flammes mortes.**

Then you went away to Paris.

A year later, in April 1930, I arrived in Paris to visit you. I had come from Majorca, penniless, tanned, strong and healthy. Stefan Zweig had persuaded S. Fischer, the publisher, to give me an

---

*In dieser Bläue, diesen Rosenschatten,
verschmelzen wir im samtenen Ermatten
und atmen Abschied in das Abendwehn.

Ein Engel naht und lässt mit treuen Händen
und heitrem Blick ein Leuchten auferstehn
aus trüben Spiegeln und aus toten Bränden . . .

advance (or else had provided the money out of his own pocket), and suggested I find somewhere beside the Mediterranean where I could work at my novel. A few weeks without responsibilities, holiday without pay, Genoa, Las Palmas, Puerto de Sollèr. In Las Palmas, in a half-overgrown park, lying on my stomach writing, I lost the ivory cigarette case with my dead sister's photograph. It was almost as if I had lost her for the second time, as if my careless-ness and self-centredness had been responsible for her death. After spending a whole day in a vain search for the missing case, I moved on to Puerto de Sollèr where it was cheaper and there were no foreigners except for a Baltic count, fair-haired and pallid, who came sauntering up to me and drawled: 'What do you say to a gentle-man's agreement that we ignore each other completely, eh?' Joy-fully I assented, no conversation, just sea, light and work. In my dreams, the dead girl and you.

My novel was called *An Impossible Way to Live*. S. Fischer sub-sequently turned the book down as being too left-wing. Hermann Kester, Kiepenheuer's reader, said: 'Too negative! Everybody knows it's an impossible way to live. Go away and write about how life ought to be lived. Then come and see me again.' Wieland Herzfelde of the Malik Verlag criticized the novel for not being sufficiently left-wing and for its petit-bourgeois pessimism. No working class at all. Was the town wholly devoid of workers? A sudden inspiration: 'Call your book *City Without Workers*. One or two amendments and it'll be done! Its present shortcoming then becomes an asset – *City Without Workers*, we've got it! You can't live without a proletariat, or a class struggle!' But Hitler came between the novel and its publication. The manuscript was lost during my years abroad.

Was it a coincidence that I lost so many manuscripts? So frequent and persistent a coincidence would seem to indicate something in-built. There is no such thing as perpetually recurring coincidence. What I had done I felt impelled to undo, nor did I ever have any propensity for completion, for consummation, always preferring futurity, the project, the indeterminate possibility. It was an un-acknowledged desire for self-destruction, for the negation of identity, which made me lose one thing after another. You alone, when I lost you, lost you time and time again, were never beyond recovery, an eternal return.

So I came to you in Paris and when you kissed me with such a wealth of tenderness, with such fathomless joy, I realized as never before: 'This is the only way to live!' You were there just for me, divorced from your first husband and still refusing the man who wished to be – and later was to become – your second; naked on the divan, more beautiful than ever, a plenitude of beauty, a naked *Maja* but without those breasts that seem almost to be straining apart as though reluctant to surrender, without, too, the harsh expression about the eyes and mouth; rather, it was unqualified promise, a blissful preparedness: take what you want, take everything and more! It had never been like this before, so overwhelming, so natural. Too much! My body would not respond. You laughed. 'So tanned and strong, with muscles like steel – all except this one, that won't cooperate, refuses to stand up. But much though I want him, I'll contain myself, patiently seduce him because now, for the first time, I want the whole of you, I don't want just to be a cloud, but to be your wife. Do you understand? Your wife, wholly and entirely yours. There's been too much imagination between us.'

Never sure of my body when love was at stake, I wanted you to be my wife and yet knew that you would not be, and imagination came between us yet again, flying down from paradise on powerful wings but with feet too crippled to grip the ground and incapable, its wings once folded, of bearing us up against the weight of gravity. I had never known so much paradise as in that week with you, when you showed me Paris, the Louvre, Notre Dame, Montmartre, the fresh green of the plane trees, the watery blue of the sky, the breath of the sea, the whole permeated by a sense of unreality, delight fraught with foreboding, happiness with valediction, for always paradise is what is lost.

What was enchanting about you, what inspired love, was and still is the characteristic you share with Lou – the capacity for enthusiasm, sudden, immoderate, irrepressible enthusiasm, whether for a person, a town, a book, for a happening or vision, for spirit, courage, solidarity, for the kibbutzim, the Resistance, or revolutionary fortitude. How marvellous your way of bursting into flame, of breaking out of your own self, and the absoluteness of your spontaneous abandon, in love as in hate, in acceptance as in indignation: 'Don't you *see*? Can't you *hear*? You must *feel* it, completely and absolutely!' Again, comparable only with Lou, the white heat of the moment, fire without smoke. Resisting no impulse, saying yes, the immediate, the unpremeditated, the unexpected, snatching up the receiver, headlong to the airport, the leap into the blue – caprice? A paltry word for such insatiable, untamable, uncontrollable vitality; and yet fidelity, again common to both of you; not in terms of sex, needless to say, no body-servant you, in fee to a man, never what is known as wife, spouse or anything else signifying possession, but fidelity in terms of love, the certainty of love in whatever situation, a love not frittered away in sensibility, but active, helpful, practical. In my love for you, Anny, your hair also played a part, your skin, your mouth, insensate hypocrisy to decry the physical, the skin is more than a husk, the mouth more than desire, yet these attributes, these external attractions, conducted me deep into your essence and, that time in Paris, I *understood* my love and was *afraid*.

It now seems to me – though I don't know, do you? – that you might then have been prepared to become my wife, to have me hold you fast, never let you go again. But there is one thing I know today which I only suspected at the time: I did not believe I would be able to do justice to, meet the requirements of, a beautiful, spoiled woman accustomed to plenty, a woman who needed Paris, the *ambiance* that only an expansive if not substantial way of life can provide. That she was equal to a catastrophe and steadfast in the face of danger, she was to prove later on in the Resistance, but I do not believe she could have endured the common run of things with me, the more so since a wealthy, cultivated, congenial man was then absolutely determined to marry her. My inability to offer you what it was not in your nature to do without was an obstacle more difficult to overcome than momentary physical impotence.

Perhaps this was why, all unaware of the connection, I began talking about my dead sister. We had strolled across Versailles and out into the sunlit woods where we lay closely entwined. 'See that *voyeur* over there?' you said laughing, as I stroked your thighs, and then I began telling you about the girl who had died, about the photograph I'd lost in Majorca, about the small flat we'd shared, about our agreement not to commit incest, not to expose our relationship to the hazards of sex, about her death, the awful, despairing shriek that shattered the hospital walls, about the way her eyes gradually turned white, a blank nothingness from which she struggled to re-emerge, and how, you having become my sister, she had found resurrection in you, at which you pushed me away, trembling, your features frozen, 'Let's go! I'm alive. I'm me, no one else!' – and the man, the one behind the trees, the *voyeur*, who followed us, resembled a corpse more than a living being. The witness, the ghost at noon.

That, if I am not mistaken, was the moment of decision: you didn't become my wife. Infinitely you remain my sweetheart.

What you withheld from me, what I withheld from myself, was given me in full measure by Lou twenty years later.

A dead sister, two living women, you and Lou.

In every love there is a hidden element of incest.

A crack of light round the door. I push it open, step into the past, the imperishable present. Profusion of light: memory.

II

VIENNA

9

Assistant Editor on the *Arbeiter-Zeitung*

In the spring of 1927 I became an assistant editor on the Vienna *Arbeiter-Zeitung*.

Ernst Toller had come to see me in Graz. We discussed the possibility of the Workers' Theatre Group staging his play *Hinkemann*. From one day to the next we became fast friends. His face, nobly handsome if somewhat too soft, the passion and melancholy of his temperament, his craving, now that he was out of prison, to make up for what he had missed of love, enjoyment and success, seemed to me both touching and attractive. He had been one of the initiators of the Munich Soviet Republic and was able when talking about it to convey his own excitement to his listeners, but what I found utterly captivating on such occasions was the combination of revolutionary ardour and youthful – I had almost said boyish – high spirits.

The theme of *Hinkemann*, the man who is a failure with women, and the urgent question: is Socialism capable of·relieving the individual's existential distress, does it really represent a world truly satisfied, truly redeemed? – such were the deepest problems with which this tormented, lovable, love-starved poet was concerned. His over-ebullient talent, his quivering sensibility, his depressive insatiability I recognized as akin to my own, and his vanity – alien to me – as compensation for a tragic incapacity. He was a man so vulnerable, so impatiently intolerant of himself, that he needed constant reaffirmation from others.

'What are you doing here in Graz?' he said. 'Come with me to Berlin.'

Not long afterwards he spoke to Otto Bauer about me. Why Berlin? Why not join the editorial staff of the *Arbeiter-Zeitung*?

Toller advised me to follow him to Berlin, indeed urged me to do so. Vastly superior though Austrian Social Democracy was to the German variety, I must not, he averred, remain in too restricted a setting. He was right. All the same I went to Vienna. Mainly out of concern for my mother. And besides . . .

'On this editorial staff you'll be working cheek by jowl with the greatest Socialist now alive!' Such was Oscar Pollak's greeting when I joined the *Arbeiter-Zeitung*. 'It's both an honour and a great responsibility to work on the same paper as Otto Bauer.'

I admired Otto Bauer, he was the most persuasive, the most convincing speaker I have ever known. When approaching the climax of a speech he would lower instead of raising his deep, expressive voice and speak quietly into the ensuing hush. More than a mere rhetorical trick, this was evidence of his desire to convince people rather than sweep them off their feet.

His style was simple, cogent, entirely free of baroque effusions. His every sentence must be comprehensible, his every thought intelligible to even an uneducated man. Once the editor-in-chief of the *Arbeiter-Zeitung* called him a 'genius of the commonplace'. Otto Bauer replied with a laugh: 'It doesn't necessarily follow that a thing's commonplace because it's easily understood.'

Otto Bauer was said to be arrogant, as indeed he was. This was due in the first place to his contempt for the provincial politicians, the sly *bien-pensants* with whom he had to wrestle, and in the second place to the disturbing problems with which he, a Jewish intellectual, was confronted in the labour movement. It was in defiance of Austrian anti-Semitism that, though a positivist, he adhered to the Jewish religious community. 'How could you possibly understand?' he said. 'You've never heard anyone muttering "dirty Yid" behind your back.' Nor was it always confined to muttering. There was nothing of this kind to be feared from the Socialist workers. Some Social Democratic officials, however, particularly in Lower Austria, invariably referred to the 'Jews in the Wienzeile''* And the philistine Austrian petit-bourgeois class was rabidly anti-Semitic. 'The Yids!' – not so much Jewish businessmen as Jewish doctors, lawyers, scholars, writers, journalists: Sigmund

*Social Democratic Party Headquarters and offices of the *Arbeiter-Zeitung*.

Freud, Karl Kraus, Arnold Schönberg, Arthur Schnitzler, Josef Roth, Franz Werfel – these were 'the Yids'. Social Democracy's intellectual élite, Otto Bauer, Friedrich Austerlitz, Siegmund Kunfi, Hugo Breitner, Julius Tandler – these were 'the Yids'. In Austria, anti-Semitism and anti-intellectualism were rolled into one abhorrent ball.

Otto Bauer's respect for workers was such that it amounted almost to awe. Once, in his editorial office, I listened to a conversation between him and a Social Democratic factory spokesman, whose blustering stupidity grated on my nerves. To my astonishment Otto Bauer several times deferred to this man's opinion when in fact – or so I thought – it invited contradiction. 'But he's utterly bone-headed,' I said when the man had gone. 'You're arrogant,' replied Otto Bauer. 'He's a worker.' It sounded as though he were reproaching, not only me, but himself, for being an intellectual.

By contrast, his arrogance sometimes found such concentrated, such vitriolic expression in leading articles or parliamentary debate that his opponents, deprived of the power of speech, were reduced to shaking their fists at him.

In October 1932 the Heimwehr Fascist Major Fey made his first speech in Parliament as Secretary of State for Public Security. From the front bench of the Opposition, Otto Bauer called across to Chancellor Dollfuss:

'That's what Mr Dollfuss is thinking this week. Not so long ago he was voicing a different opinion. One week you're wearing your democratic bonnet, the next your Heimwehr hat!'

Dollfuss sprang to his feet: 'And you're constant in your opinions, a Bolshevist who endorses the dictatorship of the proletariat, but never genuine democracy.'

Bauer strode across towards Dollfuss and brought the palm of his hand crashing down on to the ministerial bench: 'I am prepared to respect anyone who is a sincere Bolshevist. For common time-servers, sir, I feel nothing but contempt!'

During the ensuing tumult Dollfuss hurried out of the chamber and while the Heimwehr deputy Heinzl, a huge troglodyte of a man, was hurling thunderbolts at Otto Bauer, the little Chancellor went raging up and down the corridor outside exclaiming: 'It's the end! Never again shall I remain in the chamber when that man's speaking!'

The most dangerous of Otto Bauer's political adversaries was the only one whom he invariably respected – the prelate Dr Ignaz Seipel, a man of cold intellect and unwavering fanaticism, and a consistent counter-revolutionary. They were antagonists who were intellectually a match for each other, and whose horizons were not confined to the immediate events of the day; in these two men were writ large those problems by which their small country was beset. It is no recent discovery that Seipel and Bauer were 'too big for Austria'; in their own day it was already being said of them that they had outgrown their provincial context and that the desire of the one to restore the monarchy and of the other to integrate his small country into a large German Reich was born not so much of his political convictions as of his own personal need. The counter-play between these two exceptional men endowed the course of events with an aura of tragedy. In the confined space, the flickering candlelight threw two vast shadows upon the uneven walls, shadows that impinged upon each other, became fused together, now shrank, now grew, now climbed, now fell, an engrossing shadow-play. When Seipel died in August 1932, Otto Bauer wrote an obituary of his great rival which aroused considerable displeasure in Social Democratic circles. And I too wondered whether it was necessary, at a time of intensive struggle against Fascism, to 'lower the flags' in honour of a man who had been partly responsible for inducing that state of affairs. The reproach may have been justified so far as Bauer the politician was concerned; but as a man, the obituary he wrote redounds to his credit.

But it was not only Otto Bauer who provided a noteworthy experience for a young assistant editor on the *Arbeiter-Zeitung*. There was also Friedrich Austerlitz. He was a thick-set man with a fascinatingly hideous face, as though an anti-Semitic cartoonist, commissioned to draw a Jewish caricature and carried away by some quintessential quality, had ignored his commission and had endowed the drawing with a kind of grandeur. He was feared by many because of his lack of self-control, his sudden rages. Though it can be disagreeable to have a thunderstorm for an editor-in-chief, it may lend zest and flavour to a newspaper. This is just what Austerlitz succeeded in doing.

After I had joined the editorial staff, my colleagues and the compositors waited all agog for the first storm to break over the newcomer's head. For three weeks nothing happened. I wrote, and learnt how a newspaper is made up. The proofs were submitted while still damp to the editor-in-chief who signed and returned them. 'I shouldn't do that, if I were you!' said the maker-up Salzborn, when one evening I made up a page otherwise than in the usual manner. 'The old man'll create!' I insisted on having my way and a few seconds later was summoned to the editor-in-chief's office. It was the moment everyone had been waiting for. All abandoned their work – reporters, makers-up, proof-readers, revisers, compositors and copy boys – to assemble outside the editor-in-chief's door.

From behind his desk Austerlitz glowered at me. 'Are you responsible for this layout?'

'Yes.'

'You must have gone off your head! So you imagine you're going to start innovating, eh? Any idea, young man, where you are? These are the offices of the *Arbeiter-Zeitung* where there happens to be an editor-in-chief, if you follow me, but innovations there are none! Then along comes someone from Graz – from Graz, of all places! – and instead of showing a proper respect, instead of cons-cientiously calling to mind that this is the *Arbeiter-Zeitung*, that this is how it looks, has always looked and will go on looking as long as I sit here, if you follow me, and I *am* still sitting here . . . but you . . . do you really suppose I'm going to vacate this chair for a young whippersnapper from Styria?'

At this point I, too, began to shout.

He stared at me incredulously, struck dumb with amazement. Then he tried to shout me down. I raised my voice still more. We were both bellowing. It was a regular shouting match. We continued to bellow at each other until we were completely hoarse.

'Get out!' he panted.

'And is the page to stay as it is?'

He did not deign to answer. I left the room and walked straight into the arms of the eavesdroppers outside the door.

'The page stays as it is.'

Salzborn shook his head incredulously. Hardly had I reached the compositors' room before I was called back. Would my vocal chords hold out? Behind his desk Austerlitz was slumped down in exhaustion.

'How could you have done such a thing?' he said hoarsely. 'Shouting at me like that – an old man like me . . . it's outrageous, shouting at an old man . . . But let me tell you that if you shout like that again . . . well, then you'll have things all your own way in the editorial department.'

Never again did he shout at me. I loved the old man. He was a miraculous monster.

When the paper had been made up I would often sit with him until late into the night. He would recite Shakespeare and Karl Kraus, and we argued about Schopenhauer whom he preferred to all other philosophers, until suddenly he fetched a detective story out of his pocket: 'Have you read this?' 'As it happens, I have.' 'On what page did you realize who the murderer was? No cheating, mind!' His flair in criminal and judicial matters was exceptional and he used it to serve his no less exceptional passion for justice. Judges and lawyers admired and feared the numerous articles he wrote in defence of men in the dock, establishing their innocence by means of brilliant arguments and syllogisms, or at least revealing the thread-bare nature of the prosecution's case. It was his secret hope that he, the autodidact, the Jew, the expert, would, on the occasion of his sixtieth birthday, be awarded an honorary doctorate by the Faculty of Law. At the University of Vienna even Sigmund Freud got no further than professor extraordinary.

Austerlitz had been a commercial traveller until Victor Adler had taken him on. He was not a Marxist but a radical democrat who loathed injustice, regardless of its complexion or provenance. Guided rather by impulse than reflection he was capable of writing, in a sudden access of passion, something that he might later regret. I recall one article in particular, 'The Hour of the German Nation', which he wrote at the outbreak of war in 1914. Some people, how-ever, have been more inclined to reproach him for his leading article of 15 July 1927 – an article of which he had no cause to be ashamed, either at the time or later.

This headstrong man disliked being addressed as 'comrade' by all the rag-tag and bobtail of the Social Democratic Party. On such occasions he was wont to say: 'I'm not your comrade by a long chalk. To you, I'm Herr Austerlitz, and I'd rather decide for myself who is to be my comrade and who is not.'

With growing bitterness, indeed with despair, Austerlitz watched

German Social Democracy give way before Hitler without a struggle. He, who was neither a Marxist nor a revolutionary Socialist, regarded methodical resistance, not only to Hitler but to reaction in general, as the only safeguard. When on 19 June 1931 Seipel unexpectedly proposed a coalition with the Social Democrats, the move was opposed not only by Bauer but also by Renner. In his book *Austria 1934*, Pertinax (Otto Leichter) wrote:

Then Austerlitz spoke; it was the last speech he made at a party conference. 'Make no mistake,' said Austerlitz with prophetic foresight, 'about what's going to happen in Germany as a result of the policy pursued by the German Social Democrats. The last division in the German Reichstag will cost Social Democracy thirty seats.' (On 16 June the Social Democratic Party had once again voted for Brüning, despite his second emergency decree which had considerably eroded the rights of the unemployed and demolished the social services.) And Austerlitz concluded his speech with the words: 'Let us take cognizance of our responsibility before the entire International!' ★

After making this speech – only a few days before he died – Austerlitz came into my office. He looked decrepit and this always excitable man was now in a state of unprecedented excitement; there was something different, alarming, shocking about it, as though he had just suffered some dreadful blow. 'It's the last conference I shall take part in. And I'm telling you, Hitler's coming. No one will stop him. German Social Democracy will go under ignominiously, I'm telling you! And here too – Hitler will come here! And no one's going to stop him. First the Heimwehr, then Hitler! And our party as well, still steadfast today or apparently so, it too will give ground, more and more ground until it's too late. In today's "no" I can hear tomorrow's half-hearted "yes" – and that'll be the end of us. I refuse to have any part in it.'

His eyes seemed to be starting out of his head. Afraid that he was about to collapse, I tried to take him by the arm. He shook me off and went out of the room.

His death left a gap in the editorial department that no one else could fill. In actual fact Oscar Pollak had long been in charge of day-to-day administration and it had become rare indeed for the thunderstorm to go growling along from door to door. Sometimes,

★ p. 132f.

however, a halting sentence, a vapid phrase might be enough to start the old man's anger rumbling down the corridor. 'To you the German language is nothing but a freak-show, a rubbish-heap of trivia. So far as you're concerned, everything always "takes place", whatever happens in the world, whatever matures, comes into being, decays, dies and becomes, finds its echo in language. For you, the word "takes place" suffices; a gathering takes place, war and revolution, fairs and catastrophes, they all take place. At this rate, it'll end up by sexual intercourse and death taking place, language the burial-place of what has taken place!' Thus he would make his presence felt from time to time, leaving the administrative, technical and editorial aspects to others; and, when he died, business went on as usual but, though few people noticed it, the newspaper was different. The life had gone out of it, it lacked an aura.

Deeply affected though I was by this death, I had been affected even more deeply by one that preceded it, the death in November 1929 of the Hungarian revolutionary Siegmund Kunfi. In the summer of 1920 I was still an illiterate so far as Socialism went and Kunfi's personality had a decisive effect upon me. I cannot deny that for me the most effective arguments in favour of an idea were the people who represented it. Indeed I owe much less to books than I do to those who have set me an example. The greatest idea is questionable if its advocates fail to live up to it. Kunfi's rigorous attitude towards his own mistakes brought the concept of revolution, of Socialism, to life for me. Those who insist upon being in the right are the death of ideas.

In the editorial department of the *Arbeiter-Zeitung* Kunfi and I worked in adjoining offices. Finding me congenial, he would often come in for a talk. On one of these occasions I brought up the subject of the 1920 Social Democratic Party school at which he had given a highly self-critical account of his part in the abortive Hungarian Revolution. He paused for a moment before replying: 'Yes, but that was only part of the truth. Now I'll tell you the rest of the story.' And then he, this insomniac, this conscience-stricken, tormented man confessed that he had not devoted all his strength to the service of the cause, but had betrayed the revolution with a woman. And apropos of this he expressed some concern about 'Eros and the International', a recent pamphlet of mine that had evoked displeasure within the party. The pamphlet recorded the interior monologue of a young Socialist an hour before a meeting at which he is to speak on the theme of the International. It was the constantly recurring experience of my first speech, made long before in Graz, which I had set down in almost graphic detail.

'Such states of mind are suspect, not to say dangerous,' remarked Kunfi. 'Eros is an unpredictable god; whenever there's an important decision to be made you must drive him out, admit nothing, serve nothing but the cause . . .'

Then he suddenly paused, looked at me reflectively and asked: 'What exactly are you doing in this place?'

'My work, I write and . . .'

'And . . .? Any plans? Any future? Destination . . .?'

And with sudden and disquieting vehemence he added: 'Don't stay with this paper! Don't stumble into politics! You're no politician.'

'I haven't any political ambitions.'

'Eros and the International! Odd place for a butterfly, I'd have thought. What business can it have here, on the central organ of a labour party? Better follow Eros, don't lose sight of the International but go your own way – as a freelance writer, not as prisoner of a political party.'

And, friendly though his tone was, it also betrayed a kind of desperation.

He hoped to overcome his chronic insomnia by undergoing psychoanalytical treatment. But instead of recovering he grew rapidly worse. From the antithesis Eros: Revolution the latter was gradually eliminated. This caused the defection of some of his friends, but I stood by him.

Siegmund Kunfi died of an overdose of sleeping tablets.

Though I gave some thought to his advice to leave the newspaper, I did not follow it.

That I was not cut out to be a politician was incontestable. But as a political journalist who believed not only in the International but also in Eros, and who defended the latter against the attacks and calumnies of the bourgeois world, there was much that I could do.

While remaining on the fringe of politics?

All at once we found ourselves in the thick of it.

15 July 1927

'Victory! Victory! Victory!' the Vienna *Arbeiter-Zeitung* proclaimed exultantly on 25 April 1927.

'To bring about our downfall, they banded together,' Austerlitz wrote, 'they set out to destroy us; these elections, or so they thought, would be the Social Democrats' *coup de grâce . . .*'

It was true: Ignaz Seipel who, in October 1922, had curbed the inflation, had placed the country's finances in the hands of the League of Nations' Commissioner General, had deprived Parliament of all say in crucial financial questions, Seipel who had promised to clear away the 'débris of revolution' and to proceed thence to spiritual 'slum clearance', this same Seipel had, in the spring of 1927, united the anti-Marxist parties into a bourgeois bloc which would, he hoped, enable him to repulse the Social Democrats.

'Not an inch of ground have they wrested from us! Not only have we brilliantly contended every single Social Democratic position, but have also occupied new ones, thus enormously improving on our victory of four years ago . . .

'What a party we have! Social Democracy in Austria, Social Democracy in Vienna!'

On the previous day the Austrian voters had returned a new Parliament. The Social Democrats had gained 1·5 million votes as against 1·3 million in 1923; the parties and organizations of the anti-Marxist bloc (Christian Socials, Pan-Germans, Monarchists, and various National Socialist groups) had increased their tally by only 150,000. The agrarian Landbund, of Pan-German persuasion, which had not succumbed to the lure of Seipel's 'united ticket', polled 230,000 so that, as before, the bourgeois parties as a whole still constituted a substantial majority. The Social Democrats' share of the poll amounted to 42·3 per cent.

But there were infinitely greater forces at the disposal of Social Democracy than an electorate of 1·5 million. In Vienna alone more than 350,000 people belonged to Social Democratic organizations, the Social Democratic trade unions comprised 750,000 industrial and other workers. The Social Democratic Party could count on the support of the factories, the railways, and the postal and telegraph services, not to speak of thousands of soldiers in the city's barracks; all Vienna's municipal institutions were at the party's disposal and thousands of workers were receiving military training in the Republican Schutzbund. The élite of the intelligentsia were Social Democratic sympathizers. Moreover the masses trusted their party and were prepared to obey its directives. Never before or since, I believe, has a Social Democratic Party been so powerful, so intelligent or so attractive as was the Austrian party in the mid-1920s.

Proudly and self-confidently the Austrian working class professed its loyalty to this party with its exemplary Socialist cultural and social policy in the Vienna municipality, a party which, in Linz in 1926, had set itself a programme bolder, more far-sighted, more heartening than that of any Social Democratic Party before it. This programme marked the party's definitive step along the democratic road to Socialism, a step which did not, however, preclude the possibility of revolutionary action; should the counter-revolution resort to force against a Social Democratic government, it would be answered with force: the dictatorship of the proletariat.

Even though the electoral victory of 24 April had not resulted in a majority, the Social Democratic workers looked forward to radical political change, many being convinced that an actual seizure of power by the working class would immediately ensue. They put their own interpretation on the leading article in the *Arbeiter-Zeitung*:

Not one election result anywhere with which to bolster up the legend of a shift to the right; everywhere an increase in Social Democratic votes and, in certain places, new successes which presage a future majority; everywhere a well-nigh irresistible advance, prelude to a Social Democratic majority. The 'united ticket' which set out to swing Austria to the right, a retrograde step, now finds itself discredited and compelled to withdraw . . .

Compelled to withdraw? Did Seipel resign? Did he observe the democratic rules of the game?

The workers remember . . .

On 30 January 1927 the so-called 'Frontkämpfer' [front-line fighters], allies of the Hungarian counter-revolution, planned to stage a demonstration in Schattendorf, a village on the Hungarian frontier. That morning the village crier announced that there were going to be two demonstrations; the Republican Schutzbund had decided to oppose the systematically organized 'shift to the right' – a favourite catchphrase of Seipel's.

Beneath the shadow of democracy, murder lay in wait. The 'débris of revolution' was being cleared away, and those guarding that 'débris' were sometimes shot down. The murderers, Frontkämpfer and National Socialists, found judicial protection. February 1923: Birnecker, a works councillor, killed, two workers seriously wounded. May 1923: Still, a railwayman, killed. September 1923: Kowarik, a seventeen-year-old worker, murdered by National Socialists. May 1925: in Mödling, Frontkämpfer opened fire on workers, and with knives and spades so viciously assaulted a municipal councillor called Müller that he subsequently died in hospital. Carefully selected and well-briefed conspirators smiled their complicity. Still's murderers were convicted of grievous bodily harm and the illegal possession of weapons and were sentenced to fines that were later remitted. Of the five men who set about Kowarik, two were discharged, the others fined for illegal possession of weapons. The two ringleaders responsible for the attack at Mödling and the death of the municipal councillor Müller received sentences of no more than twelve and eight months' imprisonment respectively. The murder of workers was a 'gentleman's' offence.

The workers were up in arms. In Schattendorf 200 Social Democrats marched against the Frontkämpfer. The latter retreated; the Schutzbund men surrounded the station and persuaded the Frontkämpfer arriving from Vienna to go home again on the understanding that both demonstrations would be called off. Outside an inn, the headquarters of the Frontkämpfer, some of the now dispersing Schutzbund men shouted: 'Come out if you dare!' The next moment shots were fired from the windows. A child and a half-blind ex-serviceman were killed. The following day there were workers' demonstrations throughout the country. Even the conservative

Neue Freie Presse wrote: 'In this case the Frontkämpfer have been guilty of a quite exceptionally despicable deed' (afternoon edition, 31 January 1927). On 3 February Seipel informed Parliament that the Governor of Burgenland had sworn on his honour that there was no pro-Hungarian movement in his province. It followed that the fatal shots had not been pro-Hungarian but merely anti-Marxist.

When would the murderers be brought to book?

Clear away the refuse of revolution! Make room for the constitutional state!

And, in the name of that constitutional state:

On 2 March 1927 carefully picked troops occupied the Arsenal. In the days after the fall of the monarchy, a certain quantity of arms had been deposited in the building and there was said to have been an agreement between the Christian Socials and the Social Democrats concerning this stock of weapons. Now, on the eve of the elections, Seipel thought fit to frighten the citizenry and provoke the Social Democrats; he therefore seized the armoury. Huge crowds of workers gathered outside the Arsenal. The lights went out. The men charged with clearing away the refuse of revolution found themselves groping about in the pitch dark. In the near-by barracks there were Socialist soldiers fully determined to come to the aid of the workers. Would the party leaders mobilize the Schutzbund, proclaim a strike, use force to prevent the 'shift to the right'? They did none of these things. To them the ballot-paper was answer enough. Their way was the way of democratic decision. The workers were placated. The Christian Social War Minister, they were told, had seized no more than a few rusty old weapons. Accounts would be settled with these ridiculous gentry on 24 April . . .

Now that the election had been won, everything was going to be different.

The *Arbeiter-Zeitung* declared:

'The real loser in this election, however . . . is Dr Seipel himself. Having sallied forth to wring the necks of the Social Democrats, he must now slink off home, derisory hero of an almost unprecedented defeat.'

And the next day Otto Bauer wrote:

'The old Christian-Social/Pan-German system has collapsed, and Seipel's Government must go . . .'

But Seipel stayed. He knew what *power* was. Were he at this moment to cede to a democratic decision, the result of the election would be a *real* defeat. If, ignoring that democratic decision, he were to remain and enter into league with the Landbund so as to be able to invoke the right of majority, if he, 'the derisory hero of an almost unprecedented defeat', were to declare, in answer to his prematurely triumphant foe: 'Slink off home yourselves! I'm staying where I am!' – then he would be the victor.

Seipel knew what power was. When, on 2 February, the Schattendorf victims, the child and the disabled ex-serviceman, were carried to their graves, the sirens wailed in every factory throughout the land. Trains and trams came to a halt. Factory bosses and government ministers found that their telephones had suddenly gone dead. In restaurants and cafés waiters stopped serving, remained rooted to the spot. 'Waiter!' 'General strike, sir!' 'But surely you're not one of *those*!' 'We belong to a trade union, sir. We'll be serving again in a quarter of an hour.' For fifteen minutes Austria was as if turned to stone, a memorial to the two who had died in Schattendorf. That, as Seipel knew, was power. A few deputies more or less in Parliament presented no real problem, but this! One word from the trade-union leaders and the country had been brought to a standstill: the power of solidarity. It was imperative to break it.

Seipel the ascetic, devoid of all vanity, self-indulgence or cupidity, desired nothing but power – power that was pure and unadulterated, that flaunted no insignia. He felt himself to be the representative of a harsh God, of a divine master who had ordered his emissary to crush the serpent, to overthrow the anti-Christ. It was the enemies of the *Lord* who were exulting in their victory and he, the representative, whom they taunted, was the only man they feared in this unstable Republic, telling him to slink off home. But he would not budge, would turn the empty victory of God's enemies into its opposite. Austria, democracy, the people's well-being – none of these mattered. Bigger things were at stake, the principle of divine order, the power of the *Lord*, the proof that democratic victors were powerless. On 2 February they had challenged *him*, on 2 March *he* had answered with the act of provocation in the Arsenal; Parliament was not the arena where the struggle for power was going to be fought out.

His decision to stay, so baleful for Austria, was logical in terms of power politics.

A few days after he had written about the collapse of the system and demanded Seipel's resignation, Otto Bauer gave a carefully guarded address before a mass meeting.

Just one or perhaps two more [such elections] will put paid to bourgeois government. That is what this election really means to us. We have rendered the Vienna Town Hall impregnable, and in Parliament we have again appreciably extended our salient. They are still entrenched in their fortress there, a fortress that isn't going to fall either tomorrow or the next day, but that it *will* fall, we know. Not in some future generation – it is we, all of us, who want to experience its collapse!

The exultation of victory had made way for cautious rejoicing. Many of us were disappointed, feeling far from assured that an increase in votes with each new election would put the workers into power and abolish bourgeois government.

During the course of the next few weeks it became all too evident to the Social Democratic electorate that nothing had changed. Thousands were asking themselves in dismay: 'Was it really a victory?' In Parliament the Social Democratic fraction had been reinforced by the addition of one or two deputies – but in the police stations workers were still being beaten up, in the barracks soldiers victimized for their Social Democratic views, in the factories revolutionary workers were still being sacked. It was exactly as though the elections had never been, parliamentary democracy, theoretically unassailable, was in practice teaching its adherents a cruel lesson.

In the contradictory weeks that followed the elections and the installation of the bourgeois bloc under Seipel's new Government, there was one incident that troubled me more than many of the 'wider' political issues. 'The Government', my friends in the editorial department had said, 'has to keep within certain bounds. Admittedly, it has Fascist groups of one kind and another at its disposal through which it can instigate acts of provocation, but the Vienna police will never open fire on the people. We're so strongly represented in the police force and have so many comrades in the Federal Army that the Government couldn't risk any really drastic course of action.' And then one day a workman came to see me at the office. He had been badly beaten up in a police station, where one policeman had held his head clamped between his thighs while another, armed with a rubber truncheon, had rained blow after blow onto his bare buttocks, rupturing the skin. The procedure had been heralded by the cry: 'Put him through the mincer!' I wrote an account of the incident in the *Arbeiter-Zeitung* which elicited dozens of letters relating similar experiences in other police stations – and also a complaint from the secretary of the Social Democratic police union in person. This man objected to my report which, he claimed, had offended the members of his union; the police force was not a benevolent society and anyhow we ought at least to have consulted him before publication, since only harm could come of such meddling on the part of starry-eyed intellectuals. While the man was there, Austerlitz stood by me, but afterwards he pointed out that, whatever the merits of impulsiveness, the fact remained that the other side of the case also deserved a hearing; not, of course, that one should allow oneself to be brow-beaten by bureaucrats, and he himself had always had a very soft spot for Don Quixote, considering the knight of the sorrowful countenance to be infinitely more admirable than Achilles, Siegfried *e tutti quanti*, but on the other hand, a party newspaper could not afford to disregard the interests of party organizations, though this did not mean that it must tolerate too much interference from the various officials of those organizations.

It was at this time that I began to concern myself with the general problem of power. It would seem, then, that there were police officials who belonged to a trade union, Social Democratic voters in uniform, executive organs of an anti-Socialist régime. The Social Democratic trade union represented their material needs and demands vis-à-vis the Government; on the other hand, with their weapons and rubber truncheons, they were part of the power apparatus, each of them being himself a particle of power. To them was entrusted the preservation of order not only against criminals, but also against disturbers of the peace, agitators, 'undesirable elements'. Their consciousness was split: to vote for Social Democracy is a private matter, but duty is duty. The ballot paper and the 'mincer' belonged to two distinct spheres. Now, hashish and power have this in common, that their use implies their abuse. How, then, would this power apparatus, even if it comprised many upright and sober-minded men, how would it react if sent in against trouble-makers by the reactionary régime? Would it do its 'duty' as the law decrees? And if it obeyed the decree as was to be expected – would not the brutal, aggressive, megalomaniac elements instantly gain the upper hand? Only an organized, determined 'counter-power' would be able to throw the power apparatus out of gear, if not actually subvert and disrupt it. At the time these were no more than vague speculations, which never acquired the density of formulated thought . . .

It was 5 July, the day on which the trial of the three men who had admitted to firing the fatal shots at Schattendorf was due to commence. Parliament had not met for ten weeks. The Heimwehr declared its solidarity with the accused. The leader of the Tyrolese Heimwehr, Richard Steidle, speaking in Wels, said: 'It's up to those of us who are prepared to defend the freedom of their fatherland, not with words alone but, if need arise, with their fists' (*Neue Freie Presse*, 5 and 6 July 1927). In Favoriten, the largest working-class district in Vienna, Frontkämpfer disrupted the funeral of a Social Democratic shop steward. At a Social Democratic athletics meeting in Klosterneuburg near Vienna there were violent clashes with Fascists. The *Reichspost*, the central Christian Social organ, spoke of the murderers as angels in time of need. Though the public prosecutor demanded that these 'angels' be punished, it was with the rider that the moral responsibility for what had happened in Schattendorf rested with the Schutzbund, thus all but assuring an acquittal. The courtroom was filled to overflowing. On 14 July, in the late evening, the jury returned after deliberating for three hours. The accused were acquitted.

On 15 July the *Neue Freie Presse* wrote:

The onlookers remained mute. Not a sound, not a movement, not even a stifled exclamation to be heard. The silence was oppressive. Was no one sufficiently horrorstruck by the violent death in Schattendorf of two human beings, an unfortunate child and a disabled ex-serviceman, by the fact that those who fired the fatal shots were to get off scot-free, without even a light sentence? No one . . . I hoped for some show of disorder . . . at the very least, some protest by a minority, some expression of dismay . . .

The *Reichspost* bore the headline 'A clear-cut verdict'.
And the *Arbeiter-Zeitung*?
Assembled in the editor-in-chief's office, late in the evening of 14 July, there were, besides Austerlitz himself, Otto Bauer, Julius Braunthal, Oscar Pollak, Otto Leichter, Hans Zeisel (a student) and

myself. Thus Bauer and Austerlitz were the only members of the executive who were present in the party headquarters.

The porter telephoned to say that two shop stewards from the power station wanted to talk to the party executive. Pollak, who took the call, looked inquiringly at Otto Bauer as he passed on the message. Bauer hesitated. Braunthal said: 'Better come with me! There's no point in your talking to these people.' Taking the receiver he said: 'Send up the lift. Ask the comrades to wait down there for a moment and then let them come up.' Bauer was still hesitating but Braunthal propelled him out of the room. As Bauer was on his way down in the lift, there was a sound of heavy footsteps – the shop stewards climbing up the winding stairs.

'We want to speak to Comrade Bauer!'

'Sorry, he's not here.'

'To Comrade Deutsch, then.'

'Sorry . . .'

'Comrade Seitz.'

'Sorry . . . We might be able to contact one of them by telephone.'
None was available.

'Well, how about you, Comrade Austerlitz? You're a member of the party executive. What's the party decided to do?'

'Protest against the outrageous verdict, protest in the strongest possible terms.'

He turned to the copy boy. 'Fetch the leading article from the composing room.'

'We demand a general strike!' said the shop stewards. 'A general strike and a mass meeting in the Ringstrasse.'

'One can't demonstrate against a verdict returned by jury.'

'Why not?'

'Because . . .' Austerlitz felt that the shop stewards were right, that their sense of justice was outraged, but his own primal feelings were overlaid by legal formalism if not by something deeper – a passion for justice in the abstract. 'Trial by jury is a great democratic achievement. Even if the jury is mistaken, you can't come out into the streets to protest against it.'

'To hell with that. The strike is on. We'll come out into the streets. Protest against the jury, you say? Against the whole system, against the murder of workers, against class justice and reaction! We'll send Seipel packing!'

'And what then?'

'Workers' power!'

The copy boy returned with the brush-proof. Austerlitz read his leader aloud to the shop stewards: ' . . . This acquittal is a dastardly trick such as the annals of justice have seldom if ever seen before . . .

'In the view of these jurymen, to fire on human beings would seem to be a mere bagatelle; and, moreover, if those who do the shooting are Frontkämpfer, no more than a permissible form of hunting. But men who so contemptuously spurn underfoot the oath they have taken, who so impudently disregard justice and legality, cannot call themselves a jury. They are dishonourable law-breakers whose shameless verdict must earn them the hatred and contumely of all right-thinking men. Most assuredly they will stand condemned . . .'

'There! You've said it yourself, Comrade Austerlitz!'

'There's more to come. Listen!' And Austerlitz went on:

'But whenever during the course of the proceedings in the court-room an opportunity offered to confuse the jury, to influence them, to induce in them the conviction that to fire at Schutzbund members is really a public-spirited act – that opportunity was taken . . .' As he read, Austerlitz waxed even more vehement. 'The bourgeois world is constantly warning us against civil war, but is not this blatant, this provocative acquittal of men who have killed workers *because* they have killed workers, is not that in itself civil war? Let them be warned! For injustice sown on the scale that it was yesterday can only be productive of disaster.'

The shop stewards had listened attentively.

'Is that the right kind of language?' asked Austerlitz.

'Yes, it's the right kind of language all right. But we need more than that. We need the right kind of directives.'

'I've no authority. It can only be done by the party executive.'

'Where *is* the party executive? You're the editor-in-chief, com-rade Austerlitz, you're a member of the E.C. Put it on the front page – general strike. Everyone to the Ringstrasse.'

Austerlitz looked at us inquiringly.

I now butted in, with great volubility and even greater political inexperience, to propose the wrong thing. Of course a general strike, a demonstration in the Ringstrasse, I said, but *spontaneous*, not as a result of a party directive, but of the workers' own revolutionary feeling; revolutionary spontaneity, infinitely more effective than an organized demonstration!

What was the party there for, replied one of the shop stewards, if it remained silent at moments of crisis? It ought to be *leading*. Of course, I opined, but action first, leadership afterwards, the masses taking action off their own bat, the street reverberating to the tramp of the masses, that's what would shake the foundations of the régime! My eloquence pleased the shop stewards but, more experienced than I, they shook their heads; the party must not remain silent. 'How about my leading article?' said Austerlitz. That was good, they said, spoken straight from the workers' hearts, but a party that was always demanding discipline of the masses must help to make such discipline possible by itself taking the lead, providing an objective for the strike and the demonstration.

It was a ding-dong battle. Otto Leichter opposed my view and rightly so, but he also argued that the editorial department could not take the initiative without confirmation from the party executive and in this he was wrong, for what didn't happen ought to have happened, even without confirmation from the party executive – the strike call for which the workers were waiting. Disgruntled, the shop stewards took their leave – no more time to lose, back to our comrades in the power station, and tomorrow the balloon will go up in all the factories, see you again in the Ringstrasse.

The next day, 15 July, a blue sky above Vienna. At eight o'clock in the morning I was in the Ringstrasse.

The trams were at a standstill. The electricity workers, with the shop stewards in the lead, were on the march, audible a long way off. As yet only isolated voices: 'Death to the workers' murderers! Down with the Government! Seipel to the gallows!', but already the shouting was beginning to resolve itself into the voice of the masses; as yet it was an orderly procession, but already a ferment was disrupting the orderliness. On the terrace of the university some theology students stood pointing their fingers at the workers and laughing. A surge up the steps, and the students fled. The entrance doors banged to. A smashing of panes. A police officer disarmed. 'Smoke out the Fascist rats!' Stewards argued with those intent on breaking into the university, persuaded them to rejoin the march.

Strike in the factories. The municipal workers are marching along the Ringstrasse. The working-class districts have risen, are moving in from all directions towards the centre of the city.

Even today I find it incomprehensible that the leading men of the Social Democratic Party could really have supposed that the workers would not rise up in protest against the acquittal, against class justice, against the Government and Seipel.

Yet, to quote from the account given by Robert Danneberg in his pamphlet, *The Truth about the Police Action on 15 July*:

On the evening of 14 July the Socialists informed Schober (the Chief of Police) that no demonstrations were planned.

Seitz, too, when contacted by telephone very early next day, expressed his conviction that Deutsch would have little difficulty in placating the workers. (Julius Deutsch, head of the Schutzbund, had been sent to the power station early that morning to pacify them. Nevertheless they decided to stage a one-hour strike, between eight and nine a.m.) At eight o'clock Deutsch telephoned the police to tell them that the workers were marching towards the centre of the capital. He expressed the hope that, after a short demonstration, stewards would succeed in leading them back again.

The police were alerted. The first squads were directed to the Ringstrasse. They formed a thin cordon on either side of the Parliament building, thus damming back the advancing masses and giving rise to what common sense should have bade them avoid – aggression. The obstacle was an incitement to attack; at that particular moment uniforms and swords constituted a challenge rather than a deterrent. The nervousness of the armed policemen did the rest. And no less nervous than his men, the Chief of Police, Johann Schober, frantic with incertitude behind his well-tended goatee. 'I'm only doing my duty! I'm only doing my duty!'

There was one man who was not nervous. A car glided through the capital; behind the curtain a sharp silhouette, an Augustan profile – Ignaz Seipel. In such a situation the best policy is to be absent, to wait and see, so argued this mathematician of power: leave the initiative to the enemy, who's not as hard, not as relentless as yourself, leave the responsibility to the secretly despised bureaucrat with his well-tended goatee, his vanity, his ludicrous kowtowing, his anxiety to keep in with everybody; let him see if he can manage this leaderless mob.

Inside the Parliament building the Social Democratic deputies were beginning to arrive; behind it the mounted police waited in readiness; on either side uniformed men with drawn swords were pushing back the crowd; but still the masses pressed on, growing ever more dense, refusing to be held up. Those behind didn't know that the police were barring the wide street, forcing the demonstrators back against the gates of the Volksgarten, hounding them onto the grass in the Schmerlinspark, and they pressed forwards, seeking to break down whatever it was that was holding them up, to clear the congestion. Those ahead of them in the front ranks, face to face with the power of state, were still individuals – Schmidt or Meier from Ottakring or Favoriten, employed at the power station or Siemens and Halske; they were indignant, certainly, but not unsympathetic, although the blind masses were building up behind them, an irresistible floodtide. They were trying to persuade the police to go home, what does Seipel pay you, how much d'you take home? A sword doesn't help a man to fill his belly! Can't you leave us in peace? You're workers just like us! To which the police, uncertain of their position, retorted, now be sensible and disperse, we have our orders, what's it all in aid of, anyway? And the answer came back, to hell with your orders; restore order, you say? Who *for*, eh? It's *us* that'll restore order today, our *own* kind of order and that doesn't mean class justice or murdering workers, see? The cordon was slowly retreating, the police beginning to give way, the masses to break through, when a young police officer cried: 'Forward! Clear the street!' And swords flashed through the air, the lightning of the power of state, answered by the thunder of a thousand voices rolling over the Ringstrasse: 'Shame!' A workman who a minute before had been talking to a policeman now snatched the sword out of his hand, brandished it in the air, broke it across his knee and flung the pieces in the faces of the unwilling assailants. Instantly the thin cordon was swept away and, in the triumphant roar of the crowd, the voice of the individual mingled with everyone else's while the individual himself ceased to be, was no longer Schmidt from Ottakring or Meier from Favoriten; he had been absorbed into the masses.

This was the moment when the inspector in charge of the mounted police ordered his men to attack. Suddenly a horse shied, reared, whinnied, the rider dug his spurs into its flanks, tugged at the reins in a vain attempt to curb the now terrified beast and was carried away as by a tornado, into the heart of the whistling, howling, bellowing storm. Never shall I forget that horseman of the fifteenth of July. With the incidents still fresh in my mind, I wrote a description of how he, the 'Mistelbacher', followed by the rest of the troop, charged into the crowd. Mistelbach, the name of a village in Lower Austria, was then used as a term to denote the quintessence of doltish rusticity. Thus the young countryman recruited into the police force, especially into the mounted police, was dubbed a 'Mistelbacher' by the Viennese workers, and the word expressed not only the city dweller's sense of superiority, but also his realization that the forces of reaction, in order to combat 'red Vienna', were recruiting their cohorts from amongst the 'sons of the soil'. The hatred felt by the workers for the farming community may have been excessive but it was a fact, and one that manifested itself in hatred for the man who, deriving from an outmoded social structure and mistrustful of the city, assumed the uniform of the power of state.

'The horse is out of control,' I wrote at the time, 'and fury, too, is out of control as the horseman, snatching his sword out of its scabbard, goes galloping into the middle of the maelstrom.'

Rather a bloodbath than admit that you feel insecure in the saddle, that your grip on the reins is not tight enough, straight into the maelstrom. He rides into the crowd, into flesh and blood, his blade cleaving the city. At full gallop he plunges into a crowd of people being herded towards him by other horsemen, driving them back whence they came, then, with his fellows, pushes his way into the Stadiongasse where barricades are being erected out of granite setts, carts and pieces of scaffolding, finds himself being showered with stones and planks, gallops off into the Rathauspark, green silence, cool fountains, overcome by uneasiness he hacks at the young branches, slashes the dense foliage, utters a bellow and, still bellowing, at the gallop across the Rathausplatz, his face congested, his eyes bloodshot and unseeing, he slices at thin air, at emptiness. Summer frocks hurry past, yellow and mauve, and silken legs, out of the shadowy town-hall arcade, across the empty square; and suddenly, behind them, the rabid horseman. With little shrieks, the girls run for their lives, here an alley, there an alley, at last a doorway but the door's locked and so, cowering down, clinging to each other, eyes wide with fear, they wait for death, the sword cutting into the tender flesh, but then the horse rears up, throws his rider, gallops away, riderless, unbridled, across the empty square, in a lather of frightfulness.

Together with the poet Fritz Brügel, secretary of the Chamber of Labour, whom I had accidentally encountered, I watched the mounted police go into the attack, the crowd dispersing as though a fire were being scattered, particles of fire sent flying in all directions, only to reunite, a flock of fire-birds, into a flame that grew as it consumed itself, striving for permanence in ephemerality. 'Fly then, o flame, o red flag!' exclaimed the poet, translating for me a Russian revolutionary song, and suddenly we became aware of the absence of flags, of the flaring red flags that usually headed the workers' demonstrations in Vienna, for this demonstration was different, continually being dispersed by the police and as continually recomposing in the Schmerlingplatz, the little park between the Parliament building and the Palace of Justice. The Palace of Justice where the Land Registry Office, the Chancery Court and well-ordered files were housed, a building which hitherto had escaped notice amid the general air of expectancy as though all were awaiting some inflammatory gesture. Where was the Schutzbund? No directive had been issued to its group leaders, its members had joined the demonstration as individuals, there was no organized counter-power, but the police, too, seemed at a loss, now attacking now retreating, and Otto Bauer, it was said, had intervened, and Schober was giving orders only to countermand them again, and Seipel was nowhere to be found, and fresh masses kept flowing in from the working-class districts, and suddenly another police attack, but the crowd, the growing crowd, was crouched and ready to spring even as it gave way, and was now on the look-out for something on which to vent its rage – not individual uniforms but the power of state itself.

A squad of frightened policemen was using the Palace of Justice to cover its rear and endeavouring to stem the slow advance of the masses – a slow advance and not as yet a storm. Then the first shot rang out. The crowd held its breath, listening; another shot and yet another – the first shots whose perpetrators will never now be known. The crowd uttered a roar. There was a smell of burning, of smoke. Not far from the Schmerlingplatz, in the Lichtenfelsgasse, a police station had been set on fire after being evacuated by its inmates, who had taken refuge in a flat in the same building. And whereas the shots had galvanized us, the hot smell that now came wafting across was a release, a liberation, fly then, o flame, o red flag, we'll wait no longer, the time has come! And whereas the building over there in the background had hitherto been no more than cover for the policemen's rear, an anonymous structure, it now evoked the cry: 'The Palace of Justice!' Like a spark, it flew from group to group, 'The Palace of Justice!' At last an objective for the demonstration – the Palace of Justice! The masses their own midwife, abetted by powerful symbols. There, before our eyes, the pretentious building turned into a symbol: Palace of Justice, class justice, murderous justice, a bulwark for the murderers of working men. And the masses were ravening for another symbol – a flame, fly then, o flame! . . .

When the Bastille was stormed it housed no more than a handful of political prisoners, among them the Marquis de Sade; but it symbolized power, injustice and repression. And so, too, the Palace of Justice in Vienna, a repository crammed with files though not the seat of the guilty, had nevertheless become a symbol towards which every face was turned. We all wished it to happen yet all were waiting for the perpetrator, for the firebrand, for the deed. Again the stridor of bullets, the crowd wild with rage. Action was on its way. Emerging from the crowd, lifted on their shoulders, steadied by their hands, breaking a window, forcing an entry – not skilled workers, these, not young revolutionaries, but sinister figures. Particularly noticeable, a cadaverous man, his cap pulled well down over his eyes, beneath it a long, crooked nose; not someone whose path I'd care to cross, but at this moment he seemed to me as to thousands of others to be the deed – the deed engendered by us all, being committed at our behest. The crowd not only tolerated what he and his henchmen were doing but endorsed it, identifying with them. Tension and silence.

To begin with the intruders contented themselves with throwing files out of the windows, bundles and bales whose string gave way in a flurry of paper. Suddenly a picture of vast dimensions framed in gilt. At the window a man was holding it up for all to see – a portrait of the erstwhile Emperor, Franz Josef. A cry arose: 'The Emperor, the Emperor in the Palace of Justice! Now we know who's governing Austria! Monarchist judges! Executioners of the republic!' The imperial portrait fell with a crash onto the heap of files outside the window but refused to catch fire for mould and dust do not readily ignite, but over there a petrol pump, forced open, petrol spurting out of it, containers passed from hand to hand, and up go the flames, soaring up from the picture and the files to lick the façade of the building, the fire demanding to be fed, to rise yet higher, to spread its attack, it is the will of the masses, the will to be a flame, until at last it comes billowing, flaring out of the windows, the fire, the flag we had lacked up till then, fanned by the breath of the masses, the bravely flying, flaring flame. The Palace of Justice is burning down.

The flag, then, was flying – but where were the leaders? There was no turning back now and the symbol no longer sufficed. If the spontaneous deed was to result in anything more than ashes, it must be organized into an uprising, a revolution. At the time I knew nothing about the objective criteria for a revolutionary situation and all I felt was: yesterday evening the party made itself scarce but now, if its courage fails it now, if it does not accept responsibility, refuses to risk an encounter and all that such an encounter involves, then, or so it seemed to me, spontaneity would end in disaster. For already people were shouting, 'To the *Reichspost*!', the Christian Social newspaper which had applauded the jury's verdict, the acquittal of the workers' murderers. It was only a short way from the Palace of Justice to the Strozzigasse, and Brügel and I followed the crowd and watched while they broke down the door of the building, watched while they set the place on fire. I recall the schizophrenic state of mind in which we, as young intellectuals, found ourselves – we still remained rational enough to deplore this as senseless, pernicious arson, but so much did we partake of the crowd that unreason got the upper hand and we exulted in the burning.

Back from the Strozzigasse to the Palace of Justice, the volcano at the heart of the city. The police had withdrawn and there was a curious hush broken only by the roaring of the flames. The crowd stood silent, staring at the fire. The police station in the Lichtenfelsgasse was no longer alight; the fire brigade had dealt with the blaze, aided by Schutzbund men. But when they tried to get through with their fire engine to the Palace of Justice, they found their way barred. The crowd would not tolerate the subjugation of their own image, the flame. Then the most popular among the Social Democratic leaders climbed up onto the front of the fire engine: Karl Seitz, Burgomaster of Vienna, General Theodor Körner, Hugo Breitner and Julius Tandler. We admired their courage, some even applauded, but the majority, expecting their leaders to do something more than just put out fires, refused to let the vehicles through, shouting: 'We want arms for the Schutzbund!' Again and again the Social Democratic leaders adjured the crowd to make way and eventually they saw their efforts rewarded. The Schmerlingplatz was cleared and the fire brigade was able to set to work. A Schutzbund detachment, its total equipment one thin leather bandolier per man, had made its way to the Parliament building.

At this moment there was a sound of rifle fire, its crackle louder than that of the flames. Squads of police officer cadets were advancing in extended order. Volleys ripped into the unarmed crowd.

In an interview which Anton Wagner, chief of the fire brigade, gave to the *Neue Freie Presse* on 18 July, he said:

When, with the help of members of the municipal authority, we had succeeded in advancing far enough and were about to deal with the fire, we heard volleys of rifle fire all around us. As a result of these shots and the ensuing panic the square in front of the Palace of Justice remained clear for a few seconds, just long enough for us to advance still further and gain control of the hydrants . . .

It was midday and things seemed to be quietening down. Fritz Brügel and I were on our way home. In the Stadiongasse, a little way ahead of us, we heard the crackle of the first volley. Fugitives came running towards us. A wounded man collapsed. And there, all alone in the middle of the road, lay the body, and bearing down on it with measured tread the line of policemen. With their carbines pointing forwards and downwards, right hand on the butt, left on the breech, the armed men moved forward in hatred and fear. A few of the workmen, Schutzbund men armed with small wooden slats, turned back to pick up their companion's body. Several of the policemen raised their carbines and took aim. We went across to them: 'Who's in command?' We said, 'You can't shoot at people who've done no harm!' One man fired, the others hesitated and an officer yelled at us: 'Clear off! No one has any business here unless specially authorized. You're interfering with police action! Shoot you down if you don't make yourselves scarce!' Jostled by carbine muzzles, threatened by carbine butts, we made off round the corner, saved only by the clothes we wore, clothes which testified to our non-proletarian origin. More shots, here, there, all over the place.

What had happened?

In the interval between the first shooting and the attack by the cadet squads, something had occurred which we could not have known about: the leading Social Democrats had had a meeting with Seipel. They had suggested he resign to make way for a coalition government, for unless he was prepared to do this the situation could not be brought under control. Seipel's manner was cold and inflexible. He was convinced that, fearing civil war, they would never proceed to extremes. And even if they were to take the plunge the fact remained that the Schutzbund had not been alerted for such an eventuality, none of its formations being armed and ready. So, 'I shall stay, gentlemen!' As soon as he had dismissed the Social Democrats he ordered Schober to suppress the turbulence without mercy and at whatever cost. Schober armed six hundred men with rifles and carbines. The cadet squads were told horror stories about policemen being trampled to death, torn limb from limb and finished off in various gruesome ways. And thus, having been gorged with blood, the principle of order was invoked for a blood feud. Like a bird of prey inflamed by the scent of blood, the power of state swooped down on the people.

A few disconnected pictures arise out of the heat-haze of memory: the worker on the heap of rubble tearing open his shirt and shouting: 'Shoot me if you dare!', and they did dare; he had been standing erect and, as he fell dying, rifle butts smashed in his skull. In the town-hall courtyard a dressing station, doctors, stretchers, ambulance men and then, right into the middle of it all, a hail of bullets through the grating in the gate.

And the fifteen-year-old boy escaping up the scaffolding, climbing from plank to plank, just you wait, my lad, we'll get you, target practice, a welter of foul language, guffaws, riddle the little bastard with bullets, the boy somersaulting from one plank to the next until the small bundle of flesh and blood exploded on the pavement below.

Dying and wounded were being carried into the Parliament building. We followed them in. It was cool like the bottom of the sea. Marble and composure. Corpses and deputies. Into the silence of this vault I shouted: 'Arms! The Schutzbund must have arms! The people are being shot down like dogs!' A tall figure advanced towards me: 'Your place is out in the streets, young man; ours is here.' It was a well-turned sentence, unforgettable the sonorous voice, the regal gesture of Burgomaster Seitz (he who, two hours earlier aboard the fire engine out in the street, had shown himself fearless yet was now playing Cicero to my Catiline). I was too much enraged to appreciate these classical attitudes: 'What are you waiting for?' And more wounded and dying were carried into the building, and pushing in behind them some Schutzbund men, meagrely equipped with straps and sticks: 'Is this what we're supposed to fight with? Give us arms!' And more volleys, outside, out there, in another world, and again: 'Give us arms!' and cool air, marble, composure, then a sudden irruption of soldiers into the pillared hall, envoys from the barracks where there were still plenty of old hands from the days of Julius Deutsch and the Volkswehr: if you need us, we'll come. And Körner takes us on one side: 'Be reasonable!' he says, 'I can understand just how you feel and I sympathize with you, but we don't want civil war. You can't play at revolution; it was Lenin who said that, not a Social Democrat.'

I wondered whether to speak to Otto Bauer, began walking towards him. So worn were his features, so distraught did he seem that I didn't dare address him still less demand what I felt, despite Körner's sage admonition, to be indispensable: armed resistance, the hazard of revolution. Bemused, disappointed, discouraged, I went out again into the hot city, out of the cool refuge of irresolute policies, into the bloody streets, the smoke, the chatter of rifle-fire, and the blue summer blaze, into the chaos without hope where, I had been told, I belonged.

The slaughter had begun at two o'clock. At three I was still convinced that the Seipel régime had collapsed. At five o'clock the man-hunt was over and I suspected that Seipel had won, although I continued to hope that the party, the working class, would succeed in snatching his victory from him.

During the night the Social Democrats printed a news sheet; it was the only newspaper available on the morning of 16 July. The police were blamed for the disaster but, the article added, the crowd had been infiltrated by several hundred irresponsible individuals whose actions had been incompatible with the dignity of the working class.

The news sheet contained four directives:

1. A twenty-four-hour general strike.

2. A strike of unspecified duration by the railway, telegraph, telephone and postal workers.

3. Constant readiness on the part of the Schutzbund.

4. A total ban on public demonstrations.

Though the general strike was universally observed, the situation itself was paradoxical. Despite the slaughter, the eighty-nine killed, the thousand or more wounded, despite the three hours' mass murder, organized labour had in fact seized power. To me, driven to the point of distraction by the loathing I felt for the killers and by anxiety about the attitude of the party executive, it was a marvellous thought that members of the Government could not telephone each other without the express permission of and censorship by the Social Democratic Party workers,* that for the space of twenty-four hours the workers' directives carried more weight than the word of the highest authority in the land. None of us slept. The editorial department of the *Arbeiter-Zeitung* was a camp with sentries, truckle beds, dispatch riders, and, in the midst of all the comings and goings, the din and discussion, our typewriters clicked away as we set to work on our stories and the first commentaries.

Austerlitz defended his leading article against the reproaches of numerous party officials. Domes, the elderly General Secretary of the Metal Workers' Union, rebuffed everyone who attempted to criticize the attack on the Palace of Justice; haranguing these critics, he cried: 'Woe betide a working class that is willing to put up with too much injustice!' When I asked my colleagues on the paper why Social Democracy had not simply seized power on the strength of a general strike and with the support of the Schutzbund and the soldiers, they replied that we had no right to destroy parliamentary democracy, that even the radical Linz Programme adopted a year previously had only envisaged the dictatorship of the proletariat in the event of an attempted counter-revolutionary coup, and that little Austria was not able, in a far from revolutionary situation, to reproduce what had been achieved by a vast country like Russia in 1917 at the cost of untold sacrifice such as could not be asked of other peoples, and of efforts that might never see any reward.

Meanwhile a stream of Social Democratic politicians and journalists was arriving in Vienna from the provinces. They were as furious

*Or *Vertrauensmänner*, annually elected voluntary workers, an integral feature of the party organization.

about the *Arbeiter-Zeitung*'s leading article as they were outraged by
the rebellion of the capital, by the 'megalomania' of the Viennese
proletariat, and demanded the unconditional suspension not only of
the general strike but also of the railwaymen's strike, and an immediate reversion, at whatever cost, to the rules of the democratic
game. In Innsbruck, they said, Federal troops had occupied the
station together with Heimwehr squads; this was correct, but what
they omitted to tell us was that the railwaymen had fought back to
such good effect that the troops had subsequently been forced to
withdraw. Again, we were informed that in Styria 20,000 members
of the Heimwehr, equipped with rifles and machine guns, were
marching on Graz. It was untrue. This ostensibly invincible Heimwehr army, led by the blustering advocate Pfrimer, consisted in fact
of no more than a band of drunken rowdies, and not only had
workers in Bruck and Leoben erected barricades but, under the
leadership of the radical Social Democrats Wallisch and Pichler, had
to all intents and purposes seized power.

In the corridors of the newspaper office we paced up and down
arguing fiercely, stood about in groups with Schutzbund members,
deputies, dispatch riders, and journalists from Vienna and from the
Federal provinces, furiously refuting the hysterical emissary from
Styria and editing reports, while all the time scraps of information
kept coming in – about talks between Christian Social and Pan-
German politicians, about threats from Hungary or Italy, about the
icy contempt with which Seipel, at his back the deliberately inflated
bogey of the Heimwehr, had declared his determination to make
absolutely no concessions: the strike must be unconditionally called
off, there could be no question either of an amnesty or of a declaration that both sides regarded what had happened as a 'cataclysm'
whose effects must be dealt with jointly. And the Social Democrats
from the provinces were also demanding that the strike be unconditionally called off.

'And how about Otto Bauer?' I asked. 'Domes? Austerlitz?'

'What can they do?' came the answer. 'What do you expect
them to do? Civil war? Dictatorship of the proletariat? Wouldn't
stand a chance! Economically and politically doomed to failure. A
coalition government, perhaps? Renner and the moderate Christian
Social wing? Not up your street? Not up Seipel's street, either, and
he's still the man who makes the decisions.'

'Because we're frightened of our own strength.'

'Because we are the weaker.'

'And supposing we seized power all the same, set the example for everyone else?'

'What kind of example? A few days of minority rule and it'd be all over, the end of Austro-Marxism.'

At a party workers' meeting on 17 July, Otto Bauer said:

'I have to justify a course of action which culminated in our decision that it would be unwise to attempt what would necessarily be an uncoordinated and irregular distribution of weapons to the wildly excited proletarian masses. At a time when passions were running so high the distribution of weapons on a large scale would have meant open civil war. And it is our primary duty to refrain, so long as we are able, from any action that might lead to civil war.'

On 17 July the Burgomaster of Vienna issued a proclamation from which we learnt that a municipal guard had been set up, whose 'collaboration with the Federal Police', so the proclamation ran, 'has been assured'. A government statement read:

The political disputes that will inevitably result from the events of the past few days must be conducted in their proper setting, namely Parliament. The exact date for the convocation of the National Assembly is subject to negotiations at present being conducted between the Government and the political parties. The Government insists that the National Assembly be able to meet without let or hindrance; this will involve the cessation of the transport workers' strike in all its aspects before the convocation of the National Assembly.

The transport workers' strike was called off 'in all its aspects' on 18 July, having achieved nothing at all. Only the Innsbruck railwaymen refused to comply with the directive; though in the heart of the Heimwehr country, they did not call off their strike, nor did they resume work until the military had cleared the station.

The day before the funeral of Seipel's victims Otto Bauer said:

'I'd like you to write an article in honour of the dead.'

I was amazed. Why me? Otto Bauer knew very well what I was feeling and thinking. He had called for restraint. He could hardly expect it of me. I wrote the article. No one tried to tone down a single word, to dilute a single sentence.

On 20 July the *Arbeiter-Zeitung* carried the headline: 'The Legacy of the Dead'.

After a brief unvarnished account of the man-hunt, the article went on:

Most terrible of all is the senselessness of their death ... it was no revolutionary struggle but a *battue*, an unplanned, vicious, blind carnage in which a hundred human beings lost their lives – died senselessly and to no purpose ... Is this really true?

Whether the deaths of these hundred human beings remains senseless or whether it acquires meaning and revolutionary content rests with us, all of us ... Seipel and those like him have no care for the dead; what they bewail is the damage done to the tourist trade, the destruction of the land registers, the loss of confidence abroad. The horror of those searing days meant no more to them than a tiresome suspension of business and means no more than a convenient pretext for political transactions ... Already they are calculating the cost of the disaster, not in terms of blood and despair, but in terms of schillings and groschen ...

Conciliation? There is no such thing ... We have experienced the hatred of the bourgeoisie, the unrestrained rabid hatred that discharged itself in the volleys fired by the police. That hatred we reciprocate ... Beside the graves of the dead we shall pledge ourselves, not to conciliation, but to an impassioned struggle against a bourgeois-capitalist world in which workers are shot down like game, we shall pledge ourselves to a profound and implacable hostility towards the abominable system whose arguments are dum-dum bullets.

But our hatred will use different methods from those employed by the bourgeoisie; we shall not answer bullets with bullets but with mightier, more radical means. They shoot down individual workers, we shall destroy, not individuals, but the entire system. In the Bartensteingasse a group of men dipped their hands in the blood of the dying to write on the walls the terrible word 'Revenge!' We find this understandable but we reject the idea of a blood-feud with as much vigour as we repudiate conciliation ...

Not conciliation, not a blood-feud, but complete self-surrender to the labour movement – organized passion and unwearying struggle, that is what the dead demand of us. Their blood will be atoned when Socialism triumphs.

It was not just anti-Marxist newspapers that expressed outrage at this obituary. Many Social Democratic politicians also reprobated it.

When today I look back to the young Socialist I then was, I find my sorrow, anger and rebellion in no way abated. At the same time I cannot rid myself of the uncomfortable feeling that what I wrote in a state of emotional stress has not stood the test of time; it has a hollow ring about it. However right I may have been to look to the future, beyond the senseless loss of life, beyond the serried ranks of coffins, and to translate the desire for bloody retribution into commitment to the revolutionary class struggle, I am nevertheless startled by the discrepancy between word and deed. For all the sincerity of my feelings, I played my part in the deception, in the discrepancy between word and deed that was inherent in Austro-Marxism, though by no means peculiar to it. Since then we have all too often witnessed the use of flags to veil a reality which contradicts them – a lack of sincerity which could not be imputed to the article I wrote at the time.

All the same, I was determined to oppose the general trend of the party, even if anarchically, as a lone wolf, having no answer to the question 'What now?'

For the first time I found myself involved with such problems as crowds and power, loyalty and responsibility, idea and reality.

And then, on 26 July, came the great confrontation in Parliament between Ignaz Seipel and Otto Bauer, on the one hand power, on the other conscience, on the one hand politics, on the other humanity, on the one hand victory at any price, on the other hesitant scrupulousness.

Cold, hard, incisive, the Chancellor in clerical robes: 'We have to remember,' he began, 'that among the wounded – not, praise be, among the dead – there is the Republic of Austria; this is the casualty with which we are concerned today. Probably no country or government has ever been so innocently precipitated into bloody confusion as we have been . . .

'And now I stand before you in the name of this sorely wounded Republic and call upon you to conduct the present discussion solely with a view to finding ways and means of preventing any additional – and perhaps far more dangerous – blow being dealt the Republic by her children!

'Do not ask anything of Parliament and the Government that smacks of clemency towards the victims and those responsible for the disastrous interlude . . . We are very far from wanting to act harshly, but . . .' – and here Seipel's voice rose, every word a stone flung into the chamber with unerring aim – 'but we shall be firm. To be firm does not mean being harsh any more than clemency necessarily implies weakness. But either of these things presupposes choosing the right day and the right hour.'

The man who replied to him, Otto Bauer, was no representative of infallible Providence, and he was concerned not with injured authority, but with less abstract wounds. His speech began with the admission that it had been a mistake not to call for an organized demonstration. 'There were grave considerations militating against holding such a demonstration and we could not make up our minds to do so, believing as we then did that it would be wiser to pacify our comrades in the factories. In this we failed. The demonstration was a spontaneous manifestation. Today I admit quite openly that we were wrong; it was a disastrous misreading of the situation. But the very fact that the demonstration was spontaneous made it exceptionally difficult for us to assemble those members of the Schutzbund who were leaving their factories – to assemble them either quickly enough or in sufficient numbers ... The Schutzbund would have had no difficulty in coping with the thousand or so people who were impeding the fire brigade's activities in the Lichtenfelsgasse and at the Palace of Justice and, had they been given the opportunity, the worst would never have happened ...

'We have not come here, you see, to repudiate either our guilt or our mistakes. To those who have lived through this horror any such claim would seem unbearably hypocritical; and only a man who has already accused himself and admitted his guilt has the right to level accusations at others.

' ... For years the workers of Austria have endured with super-human patience economic distress and the demoralizing effect of unemployment. No amount of economic distress, no amount of unemployment has ever incited them to violence. One thing and one thing alone exacerbated them beyond bearing ... And if an outraged sense of justice leads to a wilder outburst of indignation than does the worst economic distress, would you not be inclined to regard that indignation as a token of something which no one is better able to appreciate than yourself – moral integrity ...?'

Besides an independent inquiry into what had happened, Otto Bauer demanded an amnesty for those who had been arrested on 15 and 16 July.

'I did not expect the Federal Chancellor to propose an amnesty today . . . that would have been too much to hope. What I did expect was that the Federal Chancellor would feel some sort of obligation to relieve at least to some extent this untold human suffering, if only as a palliative – not out of compassion. For I am aware that in a statesman compassion is no virtue. Not out of humanity, for authority, not humanity, is the order of the day. Not out of any kind of religious conviction, for duty bids him stand firm. No – purely and simply out of considerations of state, in order that not too much bitterness be left to accumulate at the grass roots of society . . .

'This is an hour that would, I should have thought, have called for an idiom of a different kind – not the idiom of pharisaic accusation nor that of "authority" and of "remaining firm", but the idiom of pacification, a gesture calculated to propitiate the exacerbated masses . . . The Federal Chancellor is too petty to choose such a path and to that all I can say is "Woe betide a country so unfortunate as to be thus pettily governed at such an hour!" . . .'

The antagonists were talking at cross-purposes.

Seipel's desire at this particular moment was not to be a great *man* but to divest himself of all human attributes, to be the representative solely of power, of authority. To Otto Bauer, the central problem was the politician's personal responsibility for the lives, the welfare of his fellow human beings whose fate depends on the decision he makes at crucial moments. Ignaz Seipel felt himself to be free of all such personal responsibility; he had been entrusted with a higher mandate. The idea which Bauer served was a humane one, it bore a human face; the principle which Seipel represented conceived of human beings as no more than figures in the interplay of eternal powers and, come what may, Lucifer must be overthrown, Sodom must go up in flames, the anti-Christ must be made to topple. To regard this merciless man merely as an instrument of capital would be superficial; he cooperated with the leading banks and the leading corporations because they were part of the Establishment, the props of an order, an authority which the prelate of power contended as God-given. To Bauer, reason was the supreme court of appeal; it was to reason that the rationalist, the apostle of enlightenment appealed, to reason that he looked to overcome violence, to educate humanity. Seipel knew more than the rational humanist about the subterranean, impulsive, irrational nature of a crowd; it was imperative, he believed, to subdue by force masses that rose in revolt against the established order, to organize counter-masses (the Heimwehr he regarded as providing such a possibility and, subsequently, National Socialism), to shoot at the right moment rather than talk. Seipel, an experienced moral theologian, had smiled when Bauer spoke of 'appealing to what was moral in man' as being the more difficult method, nothing like so easy and convenient as shooting people down. And the fact that Seipel remained adamant, refusing to make the slightest concession, was not the result of any pettiness but rather, and much more, a well-considered method whereby the principle of power is so clearly demonstrated that an opponent's defeat, his impotence at the crucial moment, is made plain for all to see.

Hence he was concerned, not with the 'wounded Republic', not with the 'unfortunate country', but with a victorious battle in the international crusade against the anti-Christ. Thus, as Otto Bauer had said, two different outlooks were indeed confronting each other, not so much Marxism and anti-Marxism, as the humanist view and the view that subordinated everything to the triumph of a principle.

The fact that Otto Bauer admitted the grave errors made by the party and by himself was impressive. But were those mistakes *fortuitous*? Had they not been preceded by earlier and more radical mistakes? Can humanism and revolution be reconciled? Are not moral scruples an obstacle to all action, and will not the Seipels of this world invariably emerge victorious from any contest with a Hamlet? Must not a revolutionary be equipped with Seipel's harshness *as well as* the humanitarianism which Otto Bauer represented? A humanitarianism that does not shrink from violence, a humanitarianism that dares to squeeze the trigger? Does such a thing exist? Can such a thing exist?

My Sister

Between the slats of the green shutters, the fingers of the summer day came probing in after us, painting the shadowy room with stripes of gold. We – a group of politicians and newspapermen – had fore-gathered in this summerhouse somewhere outside Vienna to discuss a topic which I have since forgotten. Suddenly the door opened. Fair hair cascading about her shoulders, inundated with light and sky, a young woman came in. Everyone's eyes were turned towards her, no one spoke, and then all rose to their feet in homage to my sister's beauty . . .

The hideous black imp once carried to the bedside of the ailing six-year-old so that he might see his new-born sister, had grown into a girl of ravishing charm, and that girl into a young woman of exceptional loveliness. It had not been easy for her to extricate her-self from the atmosphere of indigence, provincialism and Bohemian-ism, from the oppressiveness of her circumstances and the threat of demoralization. She had left school at the age of fourteen to look after our wretched household and, although she took part in our discussions and extravaganzas, she longed for freedom and friends, for a richer, more dignified existence. At that time in Graz we brothers did not have enough money to enable her to continue her studies and our mother was ill and needed help. Today I am haunted by the question whether it might not after all have been possible to let her finish her schooling, whether our decision not to do so wasn't influenced by that form of egoism which is peculiar to the male sex. However, I brought her to join me in Vienna as soon as I could find work for her and my mother had been able to wind up the Graz household.

Josef David Bach gave my sister a job in the Social Democratic arts centre where she was part secretary, part shorthand-typist. She was anxious to make up for what she had missed, to learn foreign languages, to acquire a knowledge of literature; she read and wrote and strove to achieve material and intellectual independence. Again and again I was astonished at the way this beautiful young woman, who was so much courted and admired, evolved with such conscious lucidity into a personality of outgoing friendliness and bewitching vivacity. Like me, she was susceptible to the charm of the moment but, though younger than myself, she was more determined, less volatile. And, for all her apparent exuberance, she was intrinsically reserved.

Together we rented a house, a former stables in a quiet patch of garden; it contained a big vaulted room, not unpleasing architecturally and, on the other side of the small entrance hall, a little bedroom. There were all sorts of good reasons why I should have the larger and my sister the smaller room – the fact that I worked in the evenings, that my desk was large, that I entertained a great deal. In addition I could plead the fact that the arrangement was made at my sister's own behest – and yet I know today (and must have known at the time) that it was not my sister who decided the matter but my own egoism, the damnable egoism of the male. Both rooms were agreeably cool but both were damp, my sister's bedroom more so than the vaulted room inhabited by myself. True, during the gruesome, deathly cold of the winter of 1928–9, she mostly slept with me, but sometimes she was supplanted by one of my girlfriends. Why, in that winter of a new ice age, when towns were half buried in snow, when the alley-ways grew narrower as the snowy embankments rose higher, gigantic white slopes, and when every morning we had to shovel our way out of our snowbound fastness along the path that all too soon would be buried again, why, during that winter, didn't she spend every night with me? Why didn't I exclude all other women for the benefit of my sister?

We had agreed not to indulge in any kind of sexual relationship and to that agreement we adhered. The love between brother and sister, this familiarity in otherness, this halfway house between objectivity and tenderness, erotic approbation and unruffled candour, this total freedom from any obligation to ape a style or feelings not one's own, was something we were not prepared to put at risk in the

chancy game of sex. Our decision was in no way influenced by that
most powerful taboo of a patriarchal society, the taboo on incest;
while understanding its significance in the hated paternal world, I
felt in no way bound by it. Ours was a purely individual decision
which we had arrived at as a result of individual insight, and for that
very reason we never contravened it. There was no fear, when we
slept together during those frozen nights – all the colder because our
stove so often went out – that our senses would suddenly catch fire.
Perhaps, if she hadn't had to sleep in her own room from time to
time, my sister would never have caught cold, the cold which had
at first seemed so innocuous.

'I shouldn't care to be your lover,' she once said. 'It must, I suppose, be rather nice for her to be worshipped as a goddess in the first
act, but quite horrible when in the second or third it dawns on her
that she's just a puppet of your own contriving. Those high-flown
feelings of yours more often than not are mere self-delusion, a piece
of elaborate play-acting. Perhaps you have to do it because you're
basically unfeeling. I'm less unfeeling, and therefore more down-to-
earth. Sometimes I envy you your ability to be carried away, the fact
that you can throw restraint to the winds and plunge headlong into
an adventure as though it were an ocean – a boundless ocean. That's
something I can't do because for me there hasn't been an ocean yet,
much though I long for one. But then, it has to be the real thing, not
a figment of my imagination. You're either up in the air or down
in the depths, blazing hot or freezing cold, overflowing with high
spirits or cold stone sober. Because it's yourself you're out to enjoy
in any woman you're with, you can't observe yourself and her and
the ebb and flow of your feelings. Unlike you, I do observe such
things. And if it's love it must be able to stand up to that observation.
You're apt to take every quickening of your pulse for love, and then
you're disappointed and unjust towards your cloud turned goddess . . .'

Some fool once told my sister that, though very lovely, she was
unfeminine. She laughed when she repeated his remark to me, but
all the same she was hurt. 'What exactly does "unfeminine" mean?
Pretty, oh yes, but somehow not right, imperfect, not quite up to
what a man has a right to expect? In other words, a gorgeous
monstrosity! Needless to say, I want to be found pleasing, even by an
idiot – evidence enough, I should have thought, of my femininity,

as they call it! But when, into the bargain, you've gone to bed with the oaf, surely you're entitled to slap his silly face?'

'Cleopatra used to chop their heads off. One night in her service – then off with your head!'

'Very sensible too. But I'm not cruel and a lot of things seem just funny to me that other people take seriously. Instead of chopping off heads I keep records.'

She gave me one of those records to read.

While we were driving somewhere or other I was suddenly struck by an uncomfortable thought: 'Surely to goodness he won't feel obliged to start a flirtation?' It was a tiresome thought and I decided to make it quite plain to him that he was under no such obligation.

Tired by the journey and the change of air and a little unsure of myself as a result of my reflections, I didn't know quite what attitude to adopt and felt I wasn't behaving naturally.

The next morning when I woke up I felt marvellously rested. I'd slept like a log; no dreams.

We had meant to climb up to an upland pasture but stopped halfway there and lay down in the grass. I stretched myself out in the sun and wished I was a cat so that I could stretch even better. But suddenly, out of the sunshine and my lethargy, a question crystallized. Can't he really see what a good body I've got? But that wasn't what I wanted; too idiotic! For a second a curious, nagging pain radiated through me; my lips were pressed against my arm and all of a sudden I realized that I'd been biting myself. Then I buried my face in the grass which was moist and cool . . .

He was talking to some man from Vienna about things which at that particular moment were of no interest to me. Then he spoke to me, looked at me. A charmer? Surely to God I should be able to control my body by now!

That evening we went to have supper at Maishofen. My limbs felt heavy and I allowed myself the rare pleasure of surrendering to an immense lethargy and passivity; delicious after all these weeks of hard work, nervous tension, inexorable ambition, self-centredness.

While we were at the inn he asked me: 'Do you think they'd be immoral enough to let us have a room here?'

I blushed and hoped he wouldn't notice.

Outside once more, I felt an arm thrust under my own. A strange arm so close to my body. It was delightful to talk about indifferent things while conscious of this strange arm and of this morning's little nagging pain. When was he going to kiss me? I wasn't going to make a move, for just then I wanted everything to happen of its own accord. But I was worried in case I should find it funny. I really am worried by this feeling, a mixture of merriment and pity. Why are men apt to be so terribly funny – and then sulk if they're told so or if you laugh? I observed him out of the corner of my eye: no, he wasn't going to make a fool of himself – so that was one weight off my mind. Then, under some trees that smelt of night, I felt his body pressed hard against my own, felt his lips on my throat and on my shoulders.

I was glad that everything was going so smoothly and that I could give myself up completely to my feeling of passivity, and for some unknown reason I felt like laughing, in a sudden and unexpected access of merriment. All trace of nervousness had disappeared and I was in full control of my voice and movements . . .

I got into bed and unhurriedly lit a cigarette. He had said: 'I'll come and say good night to you.' How I love those funny old euphemisms! As the door opened I thought: 'I must remember to put out my cigarette in good time, otherwise I'll burn a hole in something.' Then suddenly I couldn't understand what this man was doing in my room, noticing at the same time that I had raised myself slightly and given a little laugh. I'll catch cold, I thought, with the window open onto the lake.

With great deliberation I put out my cigarette, wanting to stay lucid for as long as possible, a point upon which I am, perhaps, over-insistent. Slowly my body sank into a torpor; beginning with my legs, it crept slowly up my back, arms and chest, my head still remaining conscious for a moment longer, a consciousness as after a sleepless night, every sound, every movement more acutely perceived, and which one knows will only last a moment before being overwhelmed by a wild, dark unconsciousness.

We emerged from our embrace. For several seconds I felt horribly sober and wondered what this stranger was doing in my bed. But my body was grateful, and once again my body took over and I was filled with gratitude and gaiety.

'How nice that you don't feel bound to come out with the usual inanities, spoiling what's lovely and light-hearted with stupid sentimentality. Today I feel grateful to you and that's all.'

He was kissing my back, my breasts, and I surrendered to his kisses and the cool breeze blowing over the lake. One final lapse into torpor, then we laughed, smoked a cigarette and said good night. I was alone again and nothing had happened, except that my body was heavy with an agreeable tiredness.

When I woke up I felt gay as a lark. Driving up into the mountains I surrendered to the gentle, rhythmic swaying of the car. We climbed up towards the glaciers. In the good, sharp air everything seemed bright and simple. Life was unburdened by yesterdays and tomorrows. The here and now was an end in itself. We lay in a hollow, the ground moulding itself to the shape of our bodies, and love seemed utterly natural, a part of the sunshine and the trees. All I thought was that today one ought to be very young and very brown.

We had supper together. He had another appointment. Saying he'd be back very soon, he asked me to wait for him.

I waited, read a couple of newspapers and was just stretching out my hand for a book when suddenly I wondered: 'Are you jealous?' A curious thing, that question. Very often it's the way you begin asking yourself whether you're in love. Carefully I examined myself before answering my question with a no. I love people who come from other countries. In the same way it might be possible to love a man who has come from another woman, because he would bring with him some of her fragrance. But maybe to feel like that you have to be able to love women too.

He'd come back and find me, he had said. I hadn't liked to answer, 'You'll be tired; better sleep,' for fear he'd misunderstand – the sort of misunderstanding I detest. And even if he really thought I'd meant no more than I'd said . . . men are so vain! I believe that in certain circumstances a man would be quite capable of starting a love affair with a woman he didn't find at all attractive, simply because he was afraid she'd otherwise think him impotent. And his fear would not be wholly unjustified, for there are few women who aren't completely convinced that they are desirable at all times to all men. Hence, should an encounter end in failure, the woman will put the blame on her wretched partner's physiological condition – not, perhaps, without a tinge of malice in compensation for her disappointment. For aren't men always running after women? Do they ever willingly forgo an opportunity? Kindness would seem to demand that one should overlook such failures. But this hardly ever seems to be done, and I find it rather puzzling.

He did come back and he was tired, as was only to be expected. And with him he brought, not the fragrance of another woman, but only his tiredness. Perhaps that *is* a cause for jealousy, the only adequate cause. I was pleased with my discovery.

Another breakfast, a short train journey, a caress or two. It may be a long time before we meet again.

I was touched by the reserved melancholy of the concluding sentence.

'You know a lot about our weaknesses.'

'Male vanity and sexual bad manners, those aren't the worst. One can get over things like that with the help of a little humour.'

'Tinged with regret . . . ?'

'That as well. Natural human relationships can be so pleasant if they're not bedevilled by self-esteem and hypocrisy. What's really bad is that no one will recognize us as equals. One of the things I like best about you is the fact that you do. You don't look on me as – unfeminine because I go out to work, because I'm ambitious, want to achieve something.'

'Why are you offended when some ass makes you out to be unfeminine?'

'I'd like to tell the idiot . . . Can I read you what I've written?'

And this is what she read:

' "Because of the established social order, it is only with the help of the male that woman has hitherto been able to achieve a tolerable existence, or to obtain any influence, not to mention power. Therefore she does her best to make him dependent on her. This she has only been able to do by means of sexuality, the sole method not forbidden to her. She has therefore had to perfect herself in this sphere and concentrate all her efforts on pleasing the male. Almost all allegedly feminine qualities spring either directly or indirectly from woman's dependence on the male, from her desire to please and thus to rule him, or at least to achieve a more endurable form of existence.

"Hence all qualities acquired by woman in her struggle for existence, in her struggle for the male, have been dubbed feminine, and unfeminine any quality acquired by modern woman in her struggle for her daily bread and for material independence . . ." '

She looked up at me. 'Perhaps in these days a woman ought to be ugly. One is constantly being reft away from the struggle for independence through being desired and through wanting to be desired. Sometimes I even catch myself wondering whether I shouldn't marry a rich man and so get all the money and freedom I want. I shan't do that, because there's nothing so demoralizing as mixing money with sex . . .'

I can hear my dead sister's voice, see her pensive, mocking face. Memory is the realm of the dead. In *Ulysses*, the young poet Stephen Daedalus feels on his lips the 'moist ashes' of his mother. The winter of 1928–9 with its white gulleys, snow all around us, rising higher every day and every night. The borderline between the living and the dead was obliterated, the realm of the dead overflowed its bounds, the state of non-being that left its mark on you, infiltrated the here and now which itself had grown fragile and unstable.

We opened the window. The little black kitten I had given you crept into your bed, seeking a warmth that had long since evaporated, and inside your bed she answered the call of nature. Seizing her by the scruff of the neck, I rubbed her nose in the damp patch. 'Leave her alone,' you said, 'she's cold.' The kitten stared at me, her eyes wide with hostility and disgust. Then out she went through the open window. 'Was that really necessary?' my sister asked, and for a brief second there was something in her voice reminiscent of the kitten's eyes. We hurried out to retrieve the little creature. Nowhere to be found, she had been swallowed up by the winter.

Day after day we asked all round the neighbourhood. Nobody had seen the kitten.

An incident of no importance. Why did it upset us so much?

'She'll come back in the spring,' I said.

'She's dead!' said my sister.

It was very cold.

In March I went to Salzburg to report a very unusual trial.

My sister had caught a cold. Her throat was inflamed and she was running a slight temperature.

I asked a doctor I knew to take her into his hospital.

'Why?' my sister asked.

'You'd be warm there and they'd look after you.'

Leaving her on her own, I went to Salzburg.

In the dock of the magistrate's court stood an unemployed waiter, Josef Stampf, self-styled 'stop-gap of the law'. His medical report stated: ' . . . Again the circumstance that for fifteen months he has been drifting round out of work is characteristic of his criminal fecklessness.' Especially in a country like Austria where unemployment was rife.

Noble châteaux situated in the Salzburg area had been repeatedly burgled. Whoever had been responsible had known enough to distinguish between valuable *objets d'art* and less valuable ones; in other words he was a connoisseur. There was a persistent rumour abroad that the owners of these stately homes were being robbed by their sons. It was a distasteful rumour which impelled the gendarmerie to investigate the matter. They interrogated the young Prince Thurn-Taxis and his friends. The old Prince Thurn-Taxis turned up in Salzburg. 'What he was doing here,' I wrote, 'no one seems to know, but very soon the dust was allowed to settle, obliterating all trace of this inquiry, though a handful was kept back specially to fling in the public's face.' In short, the police announced that the perpetrator was not to be found. There were awkward questions in Parliament; the Vienna Federal Police put their finger in the pie. The plum they pulled out was the waiter Josef Stampf. In 1926 he had broken into a château belonging to the Rothschilds; as a notorious burglar of stately homes, so opined the Vienna police, he must incur the grave suspicion of having committed the burglaries in the Salzburg château. The rest was a matter for the Salzburg police.

My journalistic ambition and my passionate desire to come to the rescue of the crumpled little waiter and his tubercular wife banished everything else from my mind. I persuaded Stefan Zweig to occupy a front-row seat in the courtroom throughout the trial, and his presence created anxiety on the bench, an anxiety that was enhanced by my pugnacious articles. I hoped to exert sufficient influence on the magistrates to obtain an acquittal or at least a lenient sentence. In this I was not altogether successful. Nevertheless, the accused was acquitted of the main charges. For a number of other offences he was sentenced to two and a half years' hard labour.

. . . And then there was Madeleine, the gentle cloud brimming with eroticism, ready to overflow at the slightest touch, who begged me to stay just one night longer.

When I got back to my hotel the morning after the trial, I found the telegram. 'Condition alarming. Return at once.' It was from my brother Walter, now a doctor . . .

We went past the porter's lodge into the bleak hospital landscape, ringed round by dirty-white buildings. Spring was in the air, for the first time, and there was something else, as yet indeterminate but somehow frightening: a distant sound of wailing. And Walter began to tell me what had happened: my sister's condition had suddenly deteriorated; first tonsillitis, then gradual septicaemia which blood transfusions had not been able to alleviate. Hence we could only . . . And this wailing filled the air, stopped for a second or two, then began again, like a motor or an animal, hideously long drawn-out, monotonous, all-pervasive. I looked at my brother walking beside me, his face knife-sharp cutting the air; he didn't return my look. We were approaching the wailing which issued from somewhere at the back of the building and rose to such a pitch that it was the shriek less of some living creature than of the very fabric we were about to enter, a mouth of stone screaming to the sky, this brilliant blue spring sky. Although I knew 'that's my sister screaming; that's my sister dying', it seemed to me impossible that a human voice could attain such a volume of sound. Silently we walked into this wailing, went up the steps, through the white gulleys, along the corridor to the white door which my brother opened, up to the bed where my sister lay grappling with death. The struggle had already lasted twenty-four hours and, though it was a hopeless one, her young organism would not give in.

Her hands clawed at the blanket, her fingers convulsively clutching and helplessly releasing it as though trying to gather together what was escaping her and at the same time sweep it into the void. So too her unnaturally distended eyes; they rolled to and fro in their sockets, white as the walls, the pillows, the bed, then the flickering pupils turned back from nothingness, desperately trying to fasten on some object, to perceive it, to use it as a shield with which to ward off death. Suddenly I was that object; she stared at me, making an enormous effort to recognize me, to find herself again in me, to return to existence through the windows of nothingness. She was no longer screaming. Slowly she raised her trunk, lifted her hand towards me. The silence was ghastly, the gaze of these eyes from the realm of shadows. Then she said softly: 'Go away!' She stared at me, repeating the words, hoarsely, with vehemence: 'Go away!', her hand still pointing at me. I turned away, she sank down and again the room was filled with her wailing. Rejected, condemned by the dying woman, I left.

'She didn't know who you were,' my brother said afterwards. But I knew she had recognized me. Repudiated, damned, the one who had absented himself instead of staying to help her, helping to save her; who had battled against injustice instead of against her death; whom ambition and Madeleine's embrace had caused to forget her.

In all my life I have never felt so guilty as I did then, and the years have in no way attenuated my sense of guilt. The fact that I could have done nothing to stop the fatal course of the septicaemia is no justification. When I left for Salzburg she had been, or so it seems to me now, a little upset, but she was convinced that I would return as soon as the trial was over. I, however, taken up not only by the trial but by a love affair, I had arrived too late.

The memory of my sister's death at the age of only twenty-four is the *surviving party's sense of guilt*, as though he, the survivor, were alive at the expense of the dead woman he loved. As though it were her 'moist ashes' he was consuming. As though a greater, more active, more willing love might have been capable of preventing her dying. As though his own egoism had fed on the other's vitality and helped to bring about her death. As though he had secretly conspired to murder her.

Why not me? Why her?

The question was not a rhetorical one. Even as a child I had been on nodding terms with death. My sister was strong, healthier than I. The premature death of this beautiful, serious-minded girl who had worked so doggedly at her own education was a loss far greater than mine could have been. Was not the final 'Go away!' with which she had pushed me back into the land of the living an intimation of this?

So absurd is death that it's almost impossible to take it seriously. My relationship with it is as casual as my relationship with reality. Only once did it seem to me monstrous, insensate, the self-exposure of a world engaged in an imbecile game between nothingness and nothingness – and that was when my sister died.

To talk about her death would have been idle chatter.

So we sat, when it was all over, on this first, brilliant day of spring, in my mother's bedroom and talked of unimportant things. Our voices rattled like skeletons' bones.

Then I went home, to the dismal house that was home no longer.

On the window sill, outside my sister's bedroom, sat the little black cat, blinking its eyes at the spring and purring.

12

Crisis

After the shock of 15 July 1927, Austria was in its death-throes. It was a slow death, a prolonged death-struggle. Ashes, cold ashes, smokeless chimneys rearing skywards, like the huge, threatening fingers of one condemned to die. Grey mortification, the grey sunken faces of the unemployed. Carrion crows battened on the country; to them its fibrous flesh was tasty enough. Time wove its web, a black spider, dark time, a net in which the people become enmeshed. There was a stench of wretchedness, of blood and putrefaction.

Against this back-cloth a macabre farce was taking place, its protagonists the leaders of the Heimwehr, provincial lawyers, master butchers, embittered failures, a middle class in which dry rot had set in. But Ignaz Seipel, the producer, the man behind the scenes, was not a *farceur*, far from it; no blood-stained harlequin he, with his Augustan profile, his cold hatred. Out of nettle fibres he wove a net, a shirt of Nessus, a shroud. The dying country fought against it, dying takes time, leaden-footed time, time for a crisis to crawl across the land, eating it bare. Ashes, cold ashes.

In October 1927, at Seipel's request, the banks and industrial federations agreed to give the Heimwehr financial support, described by the Tyrolean Heimwehr leader Steidle as 'handsome'. In October 1928 Seipel permitted Major Waldemar Pabst, Rosa Luxemburg's German assassin who specialized in murder and putsch promotion, to spend a few days at the headquarters of the Vienna police, for the purpose of preparing and directing a Heimwehr parade in Wiener-Neustadt, an industrial centre some thirty miles south of Vienna. In December 1928 Seipel made a speech in Graz: 'The desire for true democracy is one of the mainsprings of the Heimwehr movement. That is why I have confidence in it and why I give it my support.'

Contrary to all expectation, Seipel resigned in April 1929, leaving others to shoulder the responsibility. 'One can engage in political activity,' he declared two months later, 'by refraining from it and by allowing a political concept to ripen apparently of its own accord – in fact, through the work of others.'

The others did the work, abetted by money, stupidity and arms.

While Seipel gave lectures about 'true democracy' and urged German industrialists to accord their respect if not their money to useful and worthy persons such as Hitler, the Styrian Heimwehr chief Pfrimer made an initial attempt at a putsch.

The putsch failed to materialize.

Panic began to spread.

American funds were withdrawn from the larger Austrian banks.

In the autumn of 1929, when Schober assumed power, the Bodenkreditanstalt, one of the country's largest banks, collapsed. Its chairman Rudolf Sieghart was among the Heimwehr's most ardent supporters. Before 'true democracy' could open its doors to him, he was compelled to put up his shutters.

Seipel did not lift a finger. Schober must be put through his paces; the political concept must be allowed to ripen, apparently of its own accord.

Where, then, was the deliverer?

Where the richest man in the country, Baron Louis Rothschild, the head of the mighty Kreditanstalt?

Gone hunting, and God alone knew where.

The police, the gendarmerie were ordered to institute a search for Baron Louis Rothschild. No cut-throat was ever hunted with greater assiduity. The hunters caught their quarry in the act of hunting and escorted him back to Vienna. There he was received by Schober, pen in hand, who begged him as a gentleman to sign on the dotted line without delay and accept liability for the Bodenkreditanstalt. Gentleman though he was, Baron Louis Rothschild demurred, saying he would like to look into the affairs of the bank that was being thus foisted upon him. No time for that, said Schober, the matter was urgent. Being a gentleman, Rothschild signed.

That was the first item settled. A dashing signature had sufficed.

The second was rather more difficult. Schober had promised the

Heimwehr a new constitution, 'true democracy', the corporate state. The major banks were continuing as before to subsidize the Heimwehr to the tune of 25,000 schillings a month, the sum being handed over to the Federal Chancellor as trustee. Not a great deal, but still enough to grease a patriotic palm. At the same time, however, the chairman of the National Bank informed that same Chancellor that between 15 September and 15 October his bank had lost gold and currency to the value of eighteen million schillings, and that the representatives of those same banks which were continuing as before to subsidize the Heimwehr must therefore, in the interests of the economy, request that same Federal Chancellor to withdraw the proposal for the constitution which the Heimwehr had demanded. And in early October, at the Social Democratic Party Conference, Otto Bauer, while urging the workers to maintain discipline, said: 'If those who are a law unto themselves destroy the constitution, then the principle of law ceases to exist, and where there is no principle of law there is a state of revolution.' And night after night, the Social Democrat Robert Danneberg, apparently indefatigable and utterly imperturbable, negotiated with an exhausted, hard-pressed and increasingly perturbed Schober until, on 7 December, a constitution was finally agreed upon. 'We have won a defensive battle!' as Otto Bauer rightly remarked, adding less rightly that it was the 'Battle of the Marne for Austrian Fascism'.

It had been nothing more than an interlude.

On 14 September 1930 the German electorate went to the polls. Where previously there had been twelve National Socialists in the German Reichstag, there were now 107. 'It is undemocratic,' remarked Seipel, 'to refuse to cooperate with a party that has won an electoral victory.'

Ten days later Schober fell.

Believing it would be premature to assume the Chancellorship, Seipel contented himself with the post of Foreign Minister. Starhemberg, leader of the Heimwehr, became Minister of the Interior while Hueber, Starhemberg's friend and Goering's brother-in-law, took over as Minister of Justice. Carl Vaugoin, the man who had served as Minister of War under all preceding governments, now took over the Federal Chancellor's office.

Pfrimer and the other Heimwehr leaders wanted a putsch, not parliamentary rule.

Parliament was dissolved on 26 September 1930; the new deputies were to be elected on 9 November. Pfrimer and his men continued to clamour for a putsch. Starhemberg told them: 'We're almost there, and we'll keep the reins in our hands whatever the election results.' Earlier, in a public speech violently attacking the 'red municipality' of Vienna and its financial adviser Hugo Breitner, he had said: 'Only when this Asiatic's head rolls in the dust will victory be ours!' The following day he qualified this remark; 'No harm was meant,' he said. Indeed, in this land of 'threadbare *Gemütlichkeit*' no harm was ever meant. The greatest dramatist Austria has ever possessed, the Shakespeare of the suburbs, Johann Nestroy, was responsible for bequeathing this dictum to the world. He wrote farces, the most disturbing, grisly, malevolent farces ever written. No harm was ever meant. Holofernes beheaded by Judith was, in Nestroy's facre, no more than a puppet, while the real Holofernes, sly and smiling, peered out from behind a curtain, nor was Judith a real Judith any more than the head was a real head, and nothing was quite real, no harm was meant, except that the corpses lying in the street or hanging on the gallows turned out to be real corpses, and the murderers were real murderers who had not meant any harm but merely done it. And anodyne as were the tragedies written in Austria, the ostensible farces were gruesome and sanguinary in the extreme.

On the night of 12 September, or rather on the thirteenth at four o'clock in the morning, I had just got into bed when the telephone rang:

'Heimwehr putsch in Styria!'

I was tired, not quite sober, and half-asleep and I dropped the receiver. Back to bed. The telephone rang again, and yet a third time. 'A putsch in Styria!' 'Idiots!' I shouted, 'if you can't think up anything better than that, leave me in peace!'

Only after the third telephone call, when Otto Leichter had spoken to me from the offices of the *Arbeiter-Zeitung*, was I prepared to credit what had at first seemed incredible, a stupid joke.

'Koloman Wallisch rang up from Bruck at two a.m. to tell us that the Heimwehr were assembling. They're armed. And it's not just in Bruck but other places in Styria. We've informed the Minister of the Interior [at that time the conservative democrat Winkler, leader of the Landbund], and he telephoned Rintelen who described it all as "tipsy twaddle", as much ado about nothing. Since then rather more detailed information has been coming into the Chancellery. The Styrian Heimwehr's doing a putsch. You'd better catch the next train to Bruck.'

What the devil had happened?

The election results on 9 November 1930 had been a victory for Social Democracy and an unexpected defeat for the Christian Socials.

They were the last parliamentary elections to be held in Austria.

The Social Democratic Party was now predominant, with 41 per cent of the votes and seventy-two seats. The Christian Socials had fallen to second place with 35·7 per cent and sixty-six seats, while the 'Schober bloc', consisting of the Landbund and the Pan-Germans, had attained 11·6 per cent and nineteen seats; the Heimwehr which, to the horror of the Christian Socials, fought the election on its own platform, was left agape with a paltry 6 per cent and eight seats. As for the National Socialists, they did even worse, with 3 per cent and no seats at all.

It had been Starhemberg's and Pfrimer's intention to have a putsch on 9 November, not an election. They had been restrained by Vaugoin who assured them that they could count on obtaining an overwhelming electoral victory. On election night Starhemberg again pressed the now distracted Vaugoin to 'take steps'. Vaugoin did not dare to do so.

Did this mean that democracy was more strongly entrenched in Austria than many of us had hoped?

The Heimwehr split up into warring groups and seemed on the verge of complete disintegration.

In December 1930 there were nearly 300,000 on the dole, not to speak of all those unemployed who no longer had any claim to assistance.

And in May 1931 the Creditanstalt collapsed out of inability to digest the Bodenkreditanstalt, for which Baron Louis Rothschild had accepted liability with such elegant nonchalance.

Meanwhile unemployment was eating its way ever farther into the traditional industrial areas. The civilized integument grew daily thinner and more rotten. A 'social epidemic' is the name given by Marx and Engels to a periodically recurring condition of economic crisis.

Society suddenly discovers that it has reverted to a temporary condition of barbarism; famine or a general war of attrition has apparently deprived it of all its food supplies; industry and trade have apparently been destroyed, and why? Because it has too much civilization, too much food, too much industry, too much trade.

During the economic crisis which struck the entire capitalist world in 1929, this surplus of civilization was used up, reduced to a minimum.

I visited the young unemployed in Steyr and Donawitz, in Bruck and Kapfenberg. I stood with them on mountain slopes, the forest behind us, and looked down on the great industrial works, those slowly expiring monsters. Not yet dead, they would soon be corpses, rotting away in the general process of social putrefaction. The young men's sense of being rejected by these factories, where even their fathers now only worked on sufferance, festered inside them till it became a hatred of all that had anything to do with regular work, a contempt for those who continued to sell their labour power and, underneath the rage, the scorn, the disparaging gesture, always a desperate longing to be productive, to be needed.

The young unemployed whom I met were activists, those whose spirit had not yet been broken. Like all the rest they had formed themselves into gangs with their own leaders, customs and conventions reminiscent of an earlier, barbarian age. They drifted around together, met up with different gangs with whom they shared their bread and their girls, and planned common enterprises. What distinguished them from the other gangs was their political outlook. They called themselves Jungsozialisten (Young Socialists), whose abbreviated form, 'Jusso', they pronounced hard and sharp, the sibilant like the stroke of a lash. It was their political outlook that preserved them from corruption.

Necessity's pinch is sharp. Sharp enough to nip the human spirit in the bud? These young people were the offspring of the war, they had grown up during the war. They had been reared on watery cocoa and oatmeal porridge, turnips and crusts. Their early years were spent in unheated rooms from which they were sent out with bread cards, milk cards, sugar cards, to queue for hours in the streets. Unsupervised, uncontrolled, they idled away this, the 'finest hour'. For them the 1918 revolution did not signify a turning-point, merely the prolongation of a state of disorder, the endless hanging about outside food shops, the primitive barter of any and every kind of commodity, the foraging expeditions and smuggling usual at that time. And when they became old enough to work, jobs were hard to come by and grew ever more so, particularly in the domain of the Alpine-Montan-Gesellschaft and of Styrian heavy industry, but elsewhere too the young worker could only sell his labour power at the expense of his political outlook.

Socialists need not apply. If you've got a job, ditch your undesirable opinions unless you want to be jettisoned yourself. If you're waiting for a job, then bear in mind that there are thousands of others waiting too, thousands who, having no change of shirt, may be prepared to change their opinions, may be prepared to shelve their characters rather than remain on the shelf themselves. The Alpine-Montan-Gesellschaft was known in the Republic as the 'Alpine Kingdom'. It was to have been nationalized in 1918 but never was in fact nationalized, being bought instead by the Italian speculator Castiglioni and later sold to a German concern. Encouraged in every way by the Governor of Styria, Anton Rintelen, the satraps of West German capital who ruled the 'Alpine Kingdom' recruited mercenaries for the Heimwehr. Many of the workers joined the Heimwehr, wore hats adorned with cocks' feathers and, in return for a payment of five schillings, took part in parades and rallies. These recruits to the forces of domestic and foreign reaction, acquired at so cheap a price, were nicknamed 'five-schilling mannikins' by Socialist workers, though in fact the five schillings meant less to these men than their jobs and their livelihood . . .

It was to this 'Alpine Kingdom' that I was now travelling. On the Semmering, at the border between the Lower Austrian Federal Provinces and Styria, there was a long wait.

I got out of the train and followed a man in a Heimwehr hat, hoping to find out what was happening on the far side of the Semmering.

We stood side by side in the urinal, a place well suited to informal conversation, and where there are no searching glances to provoke mistrust.

'What's up in your part of the world?'

'How do you mean, what's up? What's up in Vienna?'

'In Vienna? Nothing.'

'The reds in Vienna are having a putsch. Call that nothing?'

'How come, the reds in Vienna? It's you who are having a putsch.'

'Us? Know why I've been called out? Because there's a red putsch going on in Vienna. So we're going to have our own putsch. You from Vienna?'

Suddenly he darted a suspicious glance at me, buttoned up his fly and settled his hat more firmly on his head; a look of hostility began to invade the vacant features beneath the peak.

'So that's it! From Vienna!'

Abruptly he turned his back on me. We were enemies. I was from Vienna.

Our train had come in; we journeyed into the putsch, stopped at almost every station, talked to people of all sorts, memorizing details, collecting rumours and drawing ever closer to the scene of events, the industrial region of Styria. There were placards on the walls. A proclamation: 'To the people of Austria!' signed by the 'Staatsführer' Walter Pfrimer. 'In their hour of extreme need, the patriotic and loyal people of Austria have nominated me the supreme guardian of their rights.' The Heimwehr, it went on, had seized power. All soldiers and public officials were released from their oath.

The hour of the corporate state had come. The second placard contained a form of constitution. Thenceforward all ministers and provincial governors were to be appointed by the Staatsführer Walter Pfrimer whom it was their bounden duty to obey. His decrees would carry the force of law.

The further I travelled into this putsch, the more risible, the more incredible it all seemed. I was over-tired and at the same time terribly wide-awake. Each one of my senses performed its function unerringly, recording every detail, but these details remained disconnected. Reality grew increasingly unreal. My memory reconstructs the condition I was in at the time. Faces emerge from the mist, situations and episodes in brilliant definition, to disappear a moment later, change inexplicably or assume the appearance of a double exposure, of fragments incongruously jumbled together in a dream.

I see this reporter as a figure distinct from myself, talking to Heimwehr men, asking them what they really want; to the shy, hesitant, secretly apprehensive 'five-schilling mannikins' under the command of an engineer, who only want to keep their jobs; talking to massive coxcombs, stiff as ramrods, flaunting their paunches, bloated reactionaries of the *Stammtisch*, blood- and liver-sausage decked out in made-to-measure Heimwehr uniforms, with only a hazy idea of what they want – power, to be master in their own house, to get their own way, to stop the prole's mouth for him – and they, the respectable citizens, how well they get on with the bureaucrats, same kind of people, same lingo, same clubs, a bow here, a handshake there, a word in the ear of the Provincial Governor, the Commissioner of Police, the Chief Justice, beg to inform you, Heimwehr's about to seize power, what's that you say? Political power? No harm meant, clean up the country, restore order, high time, don'tchah think? Drink to it, what d'you say to a brandy? *Prosit!* What d'you say to a spot of lunch? Many thanks, *prosit*, a putsch, a *prosit*, a handshake, a wink, and then a word on the telephone, confirmation from above, we'll cede to force, see how it goes, no harm done, men of honour to the very marrow.

It was a fluffed putsch, a bungler's putsch, for though the town halls and provincial government offices were occupied with meticulous zeal, exchanges and telegraph offices were not; anyone could telephone anyone else, no lines were cut, and this was all the more astonishing in that, besides the bourgeois who had gone off their heads, besides the heavily armed imbeciles, Pfrimer's action was also abetted by professionals, seasoned officers, technologists of civil war, spare, muscular men with arrogant expressions, pale, penetrating eyes, jack-booted, legs astraddle, hands in pockets, cold tones, a blast on the whistle reducing men to the status of dogs. Pfrimer, being hard of hearing, had to be shouted at, the professionals bellowed at the Staatsführer – what? Can't you hear? Shots had been fired in Kapfenberg, the workers were up in arms. There'd been some casualties, deuce take it, something must have gone wrong, they yelled into his ear, he goggled at them: hadn't everything been arranged in advance, gentleman's agreement with the Provincial Governor? Could Rintelen be double-crossing us? Or Starhemberg, the rival, stabbing us in the back? A top-hole plan, placards announcing the seizure of power, Graz captured by Reuter, the Chief of Staff, a popular insurrection carrying the putsch beyond the Semmering, an irresistible popular movement, the march on Vienna, the Federal capital taken by storm or starved into surrender, a top-hole plan, undoubtedly, and again they were shouting at him, the swine

have left us in the lurch, and Pfrimer, grown nervous, hourly shifted
his headquarters, thanking God the while that he had remembered
his passport, never a putsch without a passport in your pocket. At
three a.m. he signed a proclamation calling off the revolution, the
Staatsführer resigned, was driven to the frontier, his passport was in
order, the fugitive found asylum in Yugoslavia.

The reporter interviewed young members of the Schutzbund who
were standing to throughout the industrial area. In Pernegg the
quarrymen had, on their own initiative, driven off the Heimwehr. In
Hönigsberg near Mürzzuschlag the Schutzbund had succeeded in
capturing four machine guns and eighty rifles during a Heimwehr
assault. In Kapfenberg two working men had bled to death after
being shot down by the Heimwehr, but the latter had fled before the
wrath of the working people. The faces of the Schutzbund men to
whom I spoke were sullen. 'When are they going to let us fight?
What are we waiting for? It's always the others who attack but for
us it's "discipline, comrades!" Given the chance we'd knock hell out
of that lot! What are they waiting for in Vienna? While the others
have their putsch, we have to kick our heels. For how much longer?'
On hand to give the answer was a man they trusted, Koloman
Wallisch if my memory serves me right. 'Our comrades in Vienna
presented the Government with an ultimatum, either the army was to
be sent in immediately against the Heimwehr, or the Schutzbund
would go into action. The Federal Chancellor agreed to send in the
army.' 'To hell with the army. Officers, the gendarmerie, the Heimwehr, all thick as thieves. As for keeping on the right side of the law,
we've waited long enough.' 'Don't get excited, comrades. Be
patient just a couple of hours longer. If by then nothing's happened
it'll be our turn to attack.'

Then the news began to come in. The Federal Army was on its
way from Graz to Bruck whence the Heimwehr was beginning to
withdraw.

Buresch, a middle-of-the-road mediocrity, was Federal Chancellor. On the evening of 13 September, when the putsch began, he
was about to leave for Geneva to seek sympathy and aid for his
country in its disastrous financial plight. He spoke to Rintelen over
the telephone; order must be restored within twenty-four hours.
The Styrian Governor dug his heels in, demanded an amnesty for all
who had taken part in the putsch – men of honour to the very

marrow, no harm meant – failing which he couldn't ask them to call off their venture. Vaugoin, the War Minister, adopted the same attitude. Buresch gave way. Now Schober and Winkler brought pressure to bear on Rintelen. What good, they asked, could come of a putsch at that juncture? International financial aid was what they needed.

In his book *Between Hitler and Mussolini* * Starhemberg wrote:

A collision with the army had to be avoided at all costs, and I hit upon an idea which probably could only have been carried out in Austria. I managed (in the early afternoon of 13 September) to get through by telephone to the Minister of War, Vaugoin . . .

'My dear fellow, as Minister of War I can't negotiate with a rebel leader.'

'. . . I am no more a rebel leader than you are . . . I am only asking that you advance with your military columns slowly enough for me to get my men back to their villages and valleys without being hampered by you.'

'I can't make any promises, but see that you get away . . .'

In consequence, Starhemberg tells us, 'the military columns, advancing on lorries, suddenly had all sorts of engine faults and other repairs to attend to and, consequently, the Heimwehr had time to retreat.'

At a snail's pace, the power of state crawled along the Mur valley from Graz to Bruck and, when the troops entered Bruck, not one member of the Heimwehr was to be seen.

I was in Leoben when the Heimwehr men were handing in their weapons, in an hotel run by a local factory. The farce was over, the principal players had long since made off and behind the scenes the supers were angrily divesting themselves of their props. Commiserating officers kept a tally of the items as they were handed in. Machine guns and rifles, hand grenades and ammunition were all thrown onto one heap, to the evident displeasure of a group of gentry who, though wearing civilian clothes, were quite unmistakably Heimwehr officers. 'You little shit!' hissed one of these at a weedy youth with a frightened, childish face wizened like that of an emaciated nonagenarian. 'How dare you treat your weapon like that?' Though not a loud hiss, it had a keen edge to it, a knife blade held at the lad's gullet. The little fellow had just rid himself of his heavy

*New York and London, 1942.

rifle with a relieved 'Ouf!', had taken off his Heimwehr hat with the cock's feather and pushed it inside his tunic, wiping the sweat from his forehead. He stared in horror at the wrathful gentleman, seeming to recognize in him the boss, the employer; trembling, he retrieved his hat from inside his tunic, stood twisting it round and round in his hands, dry lips crumbling an apology, gave a little bob and crept away with me behind him, remained standing in a doorway, his hat still in his hand till, hesitantly, he put it on, a gesture which earned him a rude thump on the shoulder from a comrade, don't let yourself be seen in that, mate, the reds'll beat you to pulp, and again taking off the hat he examined it, threw it down, gave it a kick, picked it up, sod them, sod the whole bloody lot! And with that, he trotted away into the darkness.

An ancient, childish face, embittered and forlorn, so ended the putsch of 13 September 1931.

And I – what did I believe in at that time?

Not in democracy any more, nor in the possibility of changing the world by democratic means. How could it seriously be supposed that by gaining votes, 45 per cent, 49 per cent, we would gradually become strong enough to bring about a major upheaval? 'The older generation's optimistic belief in progress,' I wrote in 1931 in a short book entitled *Crisis of Youth*, 'is no longer comprehensible to the younger generation. The young no longer believe that there is some intrinsic law in accordance with which the world is progressing towards the good and the beautiful; rather they are firmly convinced that this process must be furthered by *violence* . . .'

The age of democracy had run its term; the century of violence had begun. Violence was repulsive to me, for I have been thin-skinned ever since childhood, absurdly vulnerable. What hardly touches others, threatens to lacerate me. Hence, if I considered violence to be indispensable, if I looked to violence to decide the issue, it was a decision that ran counter to myself, counter to my nature, counter to the constitution of a sensitive intellectual. But was it possible in this world, this disrupted, intractable, distracted world, to take *my own side*? Whose side? That of a touchy, opinionated, superfluous intellectual? In a sudden flash I realized: you have to decide *against* your own self! As you are now you're of no use to anybody, least of all to the proletariat. Basically, you're an aesthete who'd like to make a work of art out of life. Art? Who needs art?

Music, poetry, literature, what point have they in a world whose only rhyme or reason is revolution? To hell with all art that doesn't help to pave the way for revolution! Decide against yourself, useless intellectual that you are! Utility – what a dirty word! To utilize, to use, to be used, filthy utilitarianism of the bourgeois world. Is there such a thing as the utilitarianism of revolution?

There was at this time a young typographer working in the Social Democratic Party building, quiet, friendly, unassuming. He was learning Latin in his spare time. When his fellow workers got to know about it they jeered at him, regarded him as suspect, a dubious intruder. Latin? What for? To climb the social ladder, eh? Take your degree, be called *Herr Doktor*? No, that wasn't why he was doing it. Then what *are* you doing it for? Why Latin? What use can it be to you? He enjoyed it. Something you can't use? That's just why. From then on he was ostracized, his yearning for what was unutilizable, unusable, superfluous, for a language that no one spoke, for the shadow or the mirage of a non-existent world, was inadmissible individualism. The fact that I sided with him was no help, rather the reverse. If he didn't want to play tarok, then at least he ought to do something that was of some use, like working for his local party branch or in the trade-union office. What possible use is Latin? To take his side meant taking my own side and that I was not entitled to do in a world which no longer had any business with Latin and could only be brought to its senses by violence. Well and good, but if what exists is to be totally negated, then what do we want the world of tomorrow to look like? The concept was hazy, tended to be negative – no violence, no boot in the face of humanity, no hegemony whether of capital or of an apparatus or of a mechanism, but alternatively not logical rationalization, normalization, with everything planned, utilizable, useful; an opportunity rather for my quiet, unassuming friend the typographer who was learning Latin because he enjoyed it, just for the joy of it, indeed altogether more joy, kindliness, cheerfulness, away with the wild beast of earnestness, no more of the clenched fist but, in its stead, the outstretched hand . . .

The coming revolution – I hoped that it would come very soon yet doubted this in view of the instability of the young manual and non-manual workers, of the unemployed and the intellectuals, liable as they were, in this world in crisis, to drift this way or that way or into nothingness. But it might, I thought, be possible to rally to our

side those who had fallen under the influence of National Socialism –
possible, that is, if we succeeded in uniting Social Democrats and
Communists. The editor of the Social Democratic *Arbeiter-Zeitung*
wrote:

Our immediate task is to mobilize our hearts and brains to combat the
split in the proletariat, the disastrous internecine strife dividing the working class; if the Socialist movement has two wings, this means in effect
that it is deprived of wings, that in Europe today it cannot fly, but only
crawl . . .

So, I told myself, you sitting here at your desk inquiring into the
darkness and opacity within you have set yourself and others the
task of concentrating your energies upon the unification of the
working class. True, the Austrian C.P. isn't anything much, no more
than a small band, but you can't choose either your country or your
partners, and where you happen to be, there you have to begin. For
behind that small band, the Austrian C.P., stood something which,
in that decaying world, was uniquely stable, great and credible,
uniquely so to me at any rate, beset as I was with doubt and struggling against total negation. To me this – the socialist Soviet Union –
brought strength, hope and confidence.

In the violent alternation of heat and cold, delirium and sobriety,
enthusiasm and doubt that characterized the rhythm of my existence
during this year, my involvement with the Soviet Union was proof
against all attack. The victory of the Revolution had refuted the
prognostications of educated Westerners, as did its outcome, an
outcome that differed from what Marx had thought and Lenin
planned, a virtual impossibility become reality, however inadequate,
but a reality which – only partially known, blown up into a myth
interspersed with dream, legend and illusion – represented to us the
powerful antagonist of the established order we were determined to
overthrow. And thus, no matter what the situation or the argument,
I would invariably take up the cudgels on behalf of the Soviet Union.

In January 1930 I reviewed Leo Trotsky's memoirs for the
Arbeiter-Zeitung. I quote: 'After the tremendous exertion comes the
withdrawal. How far will it go? Not, at any rate, right back to the
starting point. No one, however, can foresee the full extent of this
withdrawal . . .'

I went on to say that Trotsky's great heart had beaten too strongly to be able to compound with the new circumstances. It beat as it had beaten in October, and hence its rhythm endangered stabilization. The epigones' personal struggle against him was merely an incomplete expression of an historical process; if the Revolution was to go on, October had to be liquidated. But October – October was Trotsky; as an obstacle to the withdrawal he was overthrown; 1917 was sent into exile by 1927 . . .

The withdrawal, I went on, was over. The Revolution continued. What was happening then in Russia was the greatest revolutionary experiment in world history. But it was happening without Trotsky. Would he find his way back to Russia? 'We must not succumb to subjectivism. Lenin is dead, Trotsky has been driven out. But their work, the work of revolution, lives on, growing, vastly expanding. And whether this takes place in Trotsky's name or in Stalin's name is of little moment to the working class.'

The final passage of this article upset a great many Social Democrats – and not only in Austria. Friedrich Adler, the Secretary of the Second International, travelled from Zürich to Vienna to investigate. He was told that the article was the work of an opinionated journalist who had gone too far; it did not express the view of the editorial department, nor yet that of the party executive. Such things, he retorted, should not be allowed to appear in the central organ of the Social Democratic Party. Otto Bauer spoke up for me and afterwards very gently took me to task: 'On this paper you are privileged in being able to write anything that comes into your head – wrong-headed more often than not – and you're allowed the right to be provocative. Don't abuse it. It's a good thing sometimes to stir up controversy but, all the same, what is happening in the Soviet Union is of such vital importance to all of us that we can't afford either to condemn it outright or to give it our unqualified assent. I agree with you about the second revolution that is taking place there. Stalin has put an abrupt end to the N.E.P. with its concessions to the peasantry and its proposals for gradual economic development. The collectivization of the agrarian economy represents a revolutionary upheaval. But what will it lead to? A question-mark seems to be called for here.'

Two weeks later, in a leading article, Otto Bauer produced a closely reasoned critical analysis under the caption 'A Second Revolution in Russia'. The opening sentences read:

For the past few months in the Soviet Union an upheaval has been taking place which portends nothing less than a second revolution, nothing less than the most tremendous agrarian revolution the world has ever known. Stalin's dictatorship, having completely broken with the 'N.E.P.' – the 'New Economic Policy' initiated by Lenin in 1921 under pressure from the rebellious peasantry – has now made a completely new departure . .

And here is the concluding passage of that article:

European Socialism has every reason to observe with the most intense interest this exceedingly bold experiment which is about to revolutionize the lives of a hundred million people. But we have no less reason to feel serious concern at the course taken by this, the second phase of the great Russian Revolution.

Otto Bauer's critical tone was more appropriate to the historical circumstances than my emphatic one. A retrospective survey of historical events now gives reason to suppose that compulsory collectivization was a mistake fraught with grave consequences, a significant factor in the deformation of Socialism which today we describe summarily as 'Stalinism'. A retrospective survey of my own development reveals the 'Stalinist' embryo in the Socialist I then was, a Socialist struggling to suppress his critical thinking, one who was determined in all circumstances to recognize the Soviet Union as the Socialist reality, rudimentary though that Socialism might be and still laboriously forming itself out of the raw material. None the less, having made my retrospective survey, and being now in a position scrupulously to evaluate the experience and knowledge gained in the course of past – at that time future – decades, I can endorse my unqualified affirmation of the Soviet Union as it then was. Although in the early thirties there were disquieting portents of the 'Stalinism' to come, the Soviet Union was the only state whose construction was based on Socialism, the only guardian of the concept of Socialism with all its manifold unexploited possibilities. There was no alternative. If there was much that I didn't care for, I was the sufferer, I and my snivelling individualism – not the reality, for all its imperfections.

And so I wrote in *Crisis of Youth*:

None of us regard Soviet Russia as a paradise, none of us suppose that Socialism has already been realized there. The Russian working class suffers from want, superhuman efforts are demanded of it, life in the Soviet Union is hard, cruel, ruthless. That we should not close our eyes to any of these things goes without saying; but we have also to recognize the fact that, over and above all this, the Russian Revolution is the most momentous event the history of Socialism has ever known, that the building up of the Russian economy is one of the greatest of all Socialist experiments and that what they are striving for out there in Russia is the fate of us all, the future of us all. We are bound to do everything in our power to make this experiment succeed; for if it does not succeed it will be a terrible defeat for international Socialism, for the international working class, whether Communist or Social Democrat organized. Should it eventually succeed, it will be a powerful victory for international Socialism, for the international working class, whether Social Democrat or Communist organized . . .

With the pathos of a voluntarist manifesto the slim volume concluded:

Socialism is bound to come: too late for the present generation if it waits for it to fall into its lap – as its unique bequest to all future generations if it is determined to fight for and attain this goal. The time is ripe for the overthrow of capitalism. All the indications are in favour of Socialism. The old world has failed. Its death throes have begun. How long they will last depends on you!
In the future there will be *one* name for the failure of the young: Capitalism! *One* name for their victory: Socialism!

The first edition of the book sold out within a few weeks. I had raised the banner of hope for thousands of young Socialists. Although I did not immediately become aware of it I, hitherto so anarchic and irresponsible, had assumed a responsibility that was too great for me.

I am a politically committed man, not a politician. Ill-equipped though I was to become one, I was compelled to do so by force of circumstances.

13

Opposition

I must alter my way of life, I told myself. Everything's going to pieces. I'm losing my grip, I must pull myself together. Too many women, life dissipated, time squandered, adolescence trailing right on into the years of manhood – and what the devil have I accomplished? Poetry, plays, journalism, a recently completed novel called *An Impossible Way to Live*. Quite so – an impossible way to live. My sister dead and no prospect of marrying Anny. Fleet of foot, with a ready gift for exploiting the moment, for improvisation, I'm trying to escape my own self. Like the age in which I live, I am irresponsible. Hence responsibility must be my aim.

I had met Ruth at an informal party. Eight years younger than myself, she enchanted me with her beauty, vivacity and intelligence. She was courageous, determined, imperturbable in the face of danger, while change, stimulation, acclaim were to her the breath of life. Unreliable in ordinary, everyday situations, she could be absolutely depended upon in a tight corner. She was in no way to blame for our eventual separation.

When I met her she was engaged to a member of the German nobility. Her father was managing director of a colliery in Teplitz-Schönau, an extremely active, sincere and conscientious man; her mother who, physically speaking, stood head and shoulders above her husband, was a German aristocrat, arrogant and irritable, with an ailing and often umbrageous disposition.

As a child, Ruth had dreamt of being kidnapped and living with her kidnappers; at the age of sixteen she had run away to join Max Hölz, the rebel and Communist; finally she settled for architecture. In Vienna she attended the Hochschule für Welthandel from which

she was expelled for having opposed a bunch of rowdy anti-Semites
and for having laid the chief blame for these excesses at the door of
the academic authorities. She remained in Vienna for a time, con-
cealing from her parents the fact that she was no longer a student.
When she finally went home to complete the preparations for her
marriage I found I was missing her. Weary of hectic Bohemianism
and a loneliness tawdry with distractions, I decided to take the plunge,
to try the experiment of monogamy. I wrote her an impetuous
letter, dashed off in the heat of the moment. Ruth got it just when
her engagement was about to be officially celebrated. Having read
the letter twice she went downstairs where her fiancé, his parents
and her own were waiting for her and told them that it had all been
a mistake, that she had no intention of getting married, at least not
to the man to whom she had hitherto been engaged, and that she
would rather go on with her studies in Vienna.

When, later on, there was an immediate prospect of her marriage
to me, her parents were appalled. They asked Theodor Körner, the
'red General', with whom one of their relatives was on intimate
terms, what kind of a person I was. The report was favourable; I
was a very promising young writer, he told them, and came of good
officers' stock. They gave the marriage their blessing.

We took a three-roomed flat in a little villa in Ober-Sankt Veit.
A miniature fountain played in the small garden. It was surprising
how that fountain grew, becoming a legend from which rumours
showered down on me when the party apparatus began to traduce
in every possible way those who were attempting to form a left-
wing opposition. Not content with marrying a rich German coun-
tess, not content with owning a luxurious villa, virtually a small
palace, on the fringe of the Wienerwald, Ernst Fischer had actually
indulged his extravagance to the extent of having a fountain
installed in his garden, and this in a world where unemployment was
rife! That the roubles were rolling in went without saying, an ever
more lavish supply feeding a secret bank account, to rise up in a
golden fountain as high as the treetops of the Wienerwald and visible
from the most distant quarters of the town, a perpetual cause for
scandal . . .

My little book *Crisis of Youth* had increasingly involved me, who
was no politician, in political activity. My ability to inspire an
audience, the influence this gave me, the applause I received,

promised to change the tenor of my life in a disquieting way. I knew
that I was not a politician and that I lacked, not only the tactical
skill and organizing experience, but also the will to power which is
indispensable to anyone in politics. I cannot deny that I have allowed
the power of the word to seduce me; this, however, has been the
only form of power to whose allure I have all too long remained
susceptible.

What was happening in Austria was a reflection of developments
in Germany, an answer, a rebuttal. A trip to Berlin left me depressed.
An answer, a rebuttal – mustn't be like that here, we'll have to learn
how to do things differently!

Ruth and I had gone to Berlin at Ernst Toller's invitation.

'If you get a chance of talking to German Communists ...'
Otto Bauer had said as I took my leave of him.

'I shall be meeting Wieland Herzfelde and hope to have the chance
of talking to others besides him.'

In the drawing-room of a Social Democratic hostess, a clever
woman with whom I had once had a love affair clumsily broken off
by me, I met and talked to clever men belonging to the circle of
Otto Braun, the Prussian Prime Minister.

'So you went to the Sportpalast yesterday to hear Goebbels.
What did you think of him?'

'Goebbels is uncommonly intelligent, a first-class speaker. He
knows what's going on inside the masses, not just on the surface,
but deep down in the social bloodstream!'

'Oh yes, the *system*, what the Nazis call the *system*! A vague term,
covers everything – big shops, rich Jews, well-fed bourgeois and
starving unemployed, pitch into the lot, attack 'em all, and at the
same time make promises all round. You can't lose ...'

'The Sportpalast was full to overflowing. I talked to a lot of
people, unemployed, embittered lower-middle class, angry intellectuals. The system is precisely what they *do* hate. A vague term,
admittedly, but highly explosive; it expresses anti-capitalist feelings,
an inarticulate longing for Socialism.'

'Socialism?' The man I was talking to smiled, a smile that slid
from face to face, till the tastefully furnished drawing-room was one
big smile.

'He's from Vienna,' someone said.

'Oh, of course,' said a third. 'I beg your pardon ...'

'It's so old hat!' remarked a fourth, 'Those categories – class struggle, the proletariat, Socialism! We were all young once . . .'

'Naturally, to anyone who doesn't know Berlin the crowds in the Sportpalast must seem very impressive. Don't imagine we underrate the N.S.D.A.P., but . . .'

'Hitler will never come to power!'

'The Army'll see to that!'

'Hindenburg . . .'

'Schleicher . . .'

'And even if he were to come to power . . . ?'

'Impossible!'

'Let us suppose he does. He'll soon be played out. All that industry's subsidizing is a threat, not adventurism *in perpetuo*. Industry needs calm. The people need calm. Socialism? Flags don't fill men's bellies. Drums don't provide 'em with jobs. You see . . .'

'Hitler in power?'

'Won't ever happen!'

'Let him come! In a year's time he'd be played out, if not before. Then it'll be our turn!'

This latter exchange took place, not in the drawing-room of the clever, smiling Social Democratic hostess, but in the flat of the Communist publisher Wieland Herzfelde. The room was full of people sitting about on chairs, tables, boxes. One little man was perched up on a cupboard. This was John Heartfield, the brilliant inventor of photomontage.

'Once Hitler's in power,' I ventured to reply, 'he'll be there to stay.'

'Now, listen! Do you know what the German proletariat's like?'

'I know what Italian Fascism's like. Mussolini . . .'

'Germany isn't Italy. The battle-hardened German C.P. . . . .'

'He's never come across 'em. He's from Vienna.'

'Of course. The Austro-Marxist variant.'

'Hitler's a puppet of monopoly capitalism and, though he doesn't know it and his backers don't see it, he's the blind tool of history. He's paving the way . . .'

'Who for?'

'For us, of course. The class instinct of many proletarians has not yet reached the stage of revolutionary class-consciousness. For them, Social Democracy's finished, but they're not yet rallying to us. They vote for Hitler. His function consists in detaching them from Social Democracy. Then, when he disappoints their hopes, they'll come over to us. It's self-evident.'

'Is it as self-evident as all that?' I asked.

'The facts speak for themselves, for the inevitability of the pro-letarian revolution.'

'That being so, wouldn't it be more to the point to block Hitler's path, to anticipate his seizure of power by forming an alliance of all the labour organizations?'

'I rather think he's right,' someone agreed, a Communist who had not spoken before.

'The social mainstay of the bourgeoisie, as everyone knows – now surely you can't have forgotten, comrade? – as everyone knows, is Social Democracy.'

'Still?'

'Oh, come now!'

'Hasn't National Socialism taken over that function? And the bourgeoisie . . .'

'No longer exists – is that what you mean?'

'Is divided, isn't it? Only some of them support Hitler . . .'

'And the remainder? You propose we cooperate with that mys-terious remainder? Class harmony?'

'I didn't say that. All I mean is we shouldn't even contemplate the idea of Hitler's coming to power. Our comrade from Austria is right.'

There was a regular set-to between Communists. Soon everyone was talking at once. Wieland Herzfelde tried to keep some semblance of order. 'Let him finish what he's saying!' Interjections, complete bedlam. 'Give him a chance to speak!' I remained silent, listening. So there was some hope here after all, a clash of opinions, a search for a new concept, an orientation towards a united front.

Suddenly a voice cut through the din. It came from the top of the cupboard, where John Heartfield was sitting.

'Comrades! I demand that this discussion cease instantly! There's a Social-Fascist in our midst!'

I looked about me. Silence. Who could it be?

'It's completely inadmissible to discuss internal party matters in the presence of a Social-Fascist.'

I turned my head this way and that. Silence. Everyone was looking at me.

So I was the Social-Fascist.

I rose to my feet in embarrassment and took my leave.

'May I accompany you?' said a man with a Russian accent, whom I had not heard speak before.

We went into a café. My companion was from the Soviet Embassy.

'I just wanted to shake your hand and tell you that I think you're quite right. Hitler's coming. Everyone's to blame. The price will be high, terribly high. And, as always, it's we who'll have to pay it, we, the Soviet Union.'

★

Once back in Austria, I understood better even than before that what was imperative was the unity of the working class and, within that unity – to preserve not destroy it – the formation of a revolutionary nucleus as a dynamic progressive force.

'Do you believe it's possible to form such a nucleus actually inside Social Democracy? The nucleus of a revolutionary mass movement that could break out of the sarcophagus of the apparatus without destroying the organizational structure?'

'I'm no politician,' replied Elias Canetti.

'But you know more than anyone else about the building up and disintegration of a mass. Social Democracy is a mass in process of disintegration, but still it's a good deal more than just a corpse with an organization for shroud. Within it is still preserved the original fighting community of hundreds of thousands.'

'Preserved or mummified?'

'Still preserved, with its common fund of struggles, symbols and memories. I once spoke at a meeting where one of my fellow speakers was the Burgomaster of Vienna. As you know, I'm not too bad a speaker myself – but when Seitz came into the hall everybody sprang to their feet, clapping and shouting for minutes on end. Identification of the mass with a person, a name, red Vienna, the Socialist metropolis. It's still a mass, alright. But it's starting to disintegrate. And the paradox is that those with whom the mass identifies are the very men who are accelerating that disintegration – by their speeches, their retreats, their irresolution. So what are we to do?' . . .

When we moved to Ober-Sankt Veit, Ruth and I had a great many acquaintances but few friends. My mother, with whom we had shared a flat before our marriage, was cold and reserved towards Ruth. The more politically committed I grew, the more estranged we became from my colleagues on the *Arbeiter-Zeitung*. Our flat – with its legendary fountain – came to be a gathering-point for the left-wing opposition then in process of formation. New friends were Elias Canetti and his wife – little trace of whose pretentious name, Venetia, remained in the modest Veza.

Veza had adopted the surname Magd [Maid]. This choice of name was in keeping with her nature. For all her pride, she was extremely modest. Her goodness was the distillation of a dark, smouldering passion. A beautiful white face; snow-capped volcano. One black glove, however hot the weather, for she had lost an arm. Instead of an artificial limb, she wore a sleeve filled with stuffing which hung limp at her side. No one ever asked about it, no one ever spoke about it, yet this defect was a part of her personality. She had schooled herself to move in such a way, so regally, as to discount the lost arm, had schooled herself to disregard what was missing and what was doomed to remain unfulfilled. She loved Elias, worshipped him, suffered at his hands, reproached herself for thus suffering and, while longing to be the only woman in his life, refused to let this feeling get the better of her. She never talked about herself although once, during an English conversation lesson she was giving me, she asked casually: 'Are you ever jealous?' 'No.' 'Even though you love Ruth?' 'I don't regard her as my property!' 'That's marvellous, really marvellous!' To be a maid is no humiliation if you have dubbed yourself such and take yourself at your own word; pride chooses the garb of modesty, service as a badge of honour, voluntary resignation. Her capacity for love was inexhaustible, never possessive, always ready to help anyone at any time.

At first I took Elias Canetti to be an attractive *diable boiteux*, a character such as Goethe describes as 'daemonic', with an 'evil eye' for all that was evil, finding pleasure in the horrifying, the distorted, the deformed, the mad, in uprooting and in giving pain. But behind the evil which Canetti so doggedly pursued there yawned an abyss deeper than hell: death. Behind the mask of evil lurks death. Behind power there is death. The *principium individuationis*

Above Ernst, Walter, Otto
Below Grandfather, General Viktor Planner

Ernst at the age of 10

Ernst at the age of 17

Ernst's sister

Ernst's mother

Ernst at the age of 21

Ernst and Ruth in Salzburg, 1931

Speaking at the Rathaus, 1945

Party card, 1945

Lou in 1948

Lou in the 1960s

Ernst in 1950

In the three sisters' garden, 1970

is the death principle. The extreme individualist that was Canetti hated the individual as one in fee to death, bringing death into the world by virtue of his birth. Hence the individual must be exposed, be stripped to reveal what he is at pains to conceal – behind his inflated vanity, behind his rabid, lecherous sexuality that rends its victims, behind his grinning, artless, man-eater's mug – the individual as the producer and executive organ of death. Evil and power as the incarnation of death. Return to the masses, the absorption of the individual by the mass as a reprieve from death, as the principle of immortality.

In the course of several conversations we had at this time, Canetti propounded the theory which he puts into the mouth of Dr Georges in his novel, *Auto da fé*:

> Mankind had existed as a mass for long before it was conceived of and watered down into an idea . . . There will come a time when it will not be scattered again, possibly in a single country at first, eating its way out from there, until no one can doubt any more, for there will be no I, you, he, but only it, the mass.

Canetti's important studies of crowds and power have led him to abandon this gloomy myth, but in those days he was obsessed by it. To him Communism was the social prerequisite for the attainment of this goal, this future, the mass that has ceased to be scattered. That the mass would 'eat its way out' from Russia he thought improbable; what he had in mind was Asia. I told him that I would have nothing to do with such a form of Communism. So far as I was concerned the individual, the personality, was the *raison d'être* of every revolutionary movement.

'So what can we do?' I said, bringing the conversation back to the problems of the left-wing opposition. 'Social Democracy is disintegrating. Its inherent mass is disintegrating within the still intact carapace of the organization. For the first time a counter-mass is arising, one with great magnetic power – the Nazi Party. In Germany it's absorbing the new poor at all levels, from the ruined middle classes to the unemployed. In Austria that process is just beginning, though not on the same scale. So what we must try to do is to form the nucleus of another mass within Social Democracy, but without disrupting the party. This presents us with a major problem: we cannot become a mass movement without coming into conflict with the party leadership. But in such a conflict there comes a critical point at which attachment to traditional leaders turns into hatred – greater than the hatred felt towards the real enemy. Besides, the Communists are making things difficult for us. Theirs is a small party and has no opportunity of rallying the masses and leading them into battle.'

'But aren't you a Communist?' he asked.

'It's still in the air.'

'Can't you discuss things openly with the C.P.? Or haven't you any contacts?'

I can no longer remember when or through whom I made contact with the Austrian C.P.

I spoke at a meeting from the same platform as Communists against the policy of my party executive and in favour of the Soviet Union and a united front.

Two days later Oscar Pollak, editor-in-chief of the *Arbeiter-Zeitung*, came into my room bearing the *Rote Fahne*, the organ of the Communist Party.

'Have you read this?'

There, for all to see, was an account of the meeting. I hadn't read it.

'You must issue a correction at once. That's what comes of your carelessness. They've twisted what you said to suit themselves – as always. There's only one thing for it and that's a correction in accordance with the Press Law.'

'First read, then correct.'

I read the account.

'There's nothing to be corrected. It's what I said.'

'You *can't* have said it!'

'But I *did*!'

'Even so, you can't have said it. It's impossible that a member of this paper's editorial staff could have said such a thing. Can't you see that? You've got to have it corrected, at any rate the worst part.'

'I wouldn't dream of it. It's what I said.'

'You stick to that?'

'Yes.'

It meant a breach with Oscar Pollak. I cannot deny that I regretted it. However imperturbable I may have seemed, I was pained by my colleagues' growing distrust. One of the bitterest things about the formation of a faction is this estrangement from many whom one esteems, when the personal sphere becomes infected by the political. Endeavouring to protect myself, I assumed a mask of superciliousness, of indifference, of irony. To what purpose? Open confrontation with an enemy tones up the nerves and invigorates the hearts – but how was I to regard as enemies those who, though no less concerned for the labour movement, were of an opinion different from my own and hence reprobated my attitude? That is what makes factional struggle so demoralizing – the hostility it engenders; not a healthy hostility such as is felt towards one who has always been an enemy, but a disease, a growth within one's own system. It is not easy to take on this sort of thing out of political duty, and all the harder for a man who by nature prefers harmony to hatred or fanaticism.

What was I to do?

Resign from my post on the *Arbeiter-Zeitung* and thus forgo a possible field of action? When I consulted my comrades in the left-wing opposition about it, they rejected such a course on the grounds that personal sensibilities must be subordinated to the cause. Whether I liked it or not, I must keep my job. It was imperative not to give up any position inside the party apparatus.

A young Communist intellectual, the physicist Alex Weissberg, who was later arrested in Moscow and found guilty of 'spying', was responsible for my first meeting with leading functionaries of the Austrian C.P. He put a house on the Kahlenberg at our disposal. I informed the Social Democratic secretary of the Nineteenth District, my friend Karl Mark, about this arrangement which had been made at very short notice, and asked him to come too. In some dismay he refused, warning me against the unforeseeable consequences that might result from associating too closely with Communists.

So, late one evening, I sat at a big table in the lonely house where Weissberg had taken me, the only Social Democrat among a group of some six or seven leading members of the Austrian C.P.

'You lead off,' said one of them, 'then we'll join in the discussion.'

I spoke briefly, suggesting that it was of vital importance, firstly to rally those elements within Social Democracy who disagreed with the policy of least resistance and were convinced of the necessity for armed insurrection against the Fascist régime; secondly, to combat the tendency in the party towards demoralization, disintegration and despair, and thirdly to bring increasing pressure to bear on the party and Schutzbund leadership with a view to inducing them to call a general strike and to conduct the struggle with all the means at their disposal. Unless, I went on, we acted within the context of Social Democracy, our effectiveness would be fundamentally impaired. I asked them to show understanding for this particular problem. The cooperation we for our part sincerely desired was being jeopardized in certain quarters by Communists who regarded the recruitment of party members and the creation of discord in our midst as more important than the consolidation of the united front. In a situation such as the present one there should be no question of party politics, the only thing that counted being the common cause, the revolutionization of the working class to counteract Fascism.

While I spoke I was struck by the fact that, of all those present, only one was looking at me in a friendly manner; all the rest, stony-faced, looked straight through me. Every now and then, as though bowing before an imperceptible wind, they all simultaneously bent their heads towards the table where they silently scribbled notes, then raised them again and looked straight through me. The silence round about , the deserted villa, the carefully fastened shutters on the windows and, seated opposite me six or seven men, severe and unfamiliar, only one looking at me in a friendly manner – how odd, I thought, the light above the table, the shadows on the walls, a shadow-play on the fringe of reality.

'Finished?' asked the first when I paused, although I still had much left to say.

'For the time being.'

I hoped in the course of the discussion to have an opportunity of going more thoroughly into certain points.

The first man glanced at his notes and, looking straight through me, began to reply, the other five, or maybe six, listening to him attentively, silently scribbling notes, all nodding their heads simultaneously.

It was, of course, to be welcomed, he said, that the left-wing opposition should desire to build up and deepen its relations with the Communist Party. This meeting would help the left-wing opposition to make a big step forward. For however worthy of recognition and, in his personal opinion, however honourably meant our intentions might be, our failings and weaknesses must not be overlooked. The question must be posed politically. Our manner of posing it had not yet shed its Social Democratic skin. It was after all perfectly clear – not just by definition, but on the almost unlimited evidence of the facts – that the Social Democratic Party would not fight but that it would, on the contrary, betray the struggle of the working class, since such betrayal was its essence and its function as the social mainstay of the bourgeoisie. In no circumstances would Otto Bauer or Julius Deutsch or any one else ever issue a call to arms. Hence it was basically mistaken to think in terms of possible armed insurrection. Our mission was rather to unmask the Social Democratic leaders, to stigmatize their radical slogans as a manoeuvre calculated to mislead and, above all, to attack Otto Bauer who was ten times more dangerous than Renner and his associates, those self-avowed reformists and traitors whom all self-respecting workers must hold in contempt. Our attempt to bring pressure to bear on our leaders, though right in itself, would be of no avail unless we rid ourselves of the illusion that we could deflect them from their treacherous course. If the class was to fight, it needed a Communist Party. Of course the Communist Party was prepared to ally itself with the left-wing opposition but since they, the Communists, were our superiors, theoretically through their clarity of principle and practically through the experiences of the Bolsheviks and the Communist International, it would be of the greatest advantage to ourselves were we to recognize the C.P. as the leading force – of our own free will, since the C.P. did not intend to impose any conditions on us but to regard us as allies and equals. It was their proletarian duty, however, to wean us from the fallacy that it would be possible to achieve the unity of the working class within the context of Social Democracy; our aim should be, on the contrary, to detach the workers from their leaders, and to that end the adhesion of left-wing opposition individuals or groups to the C.P. was essential since it would not weaken but, indeed, strengthen its fighting unity. Whether such adhesion took place publicly or, in certain cases, under cover of secrecy was merely a question of tactics. The C.P. fully appreciated the need for tactical considerations and would do everything in its power to help the left-wing opposition. But in the absence of a strong C.P. there would always be the danger that our party leadership would manage to outwit us or even exploit us as an instrument to prevent radicalized workers from leaving the party and to paralyse their ability to act. Thus if the question was politically posed it became apparent that it was essential to unmask the party leadership and to bring the workers round to the Communist standpoint.

Barely had the first of the men seated opposite me completed his speech, and before I had time to reply that in my view his was a false concept, than the second snatched, as it were, the words out of his mouth. This trite metaphor acquired in the process a new plasticity, for the last word spoken by the previous speaker was still upon his lips when the second snatched it, made it his own, and so it went on, on and on, from the second to the third, from the third to the fourth, on and on, and each of them spoke for half an hour. The second speaker said that he fully endorsed what the first had said, that the question must be posed politically, consequently he too would pose it politically, and not only would he endorse but emphatically reiterate that the unmasking of the party leadership was the most important task, and in so doing he would lay particular stress on the fact that Otto Bauer, and he above all, must be unmasked, for the more left-wing the opportunist slogans with which he sought to mislead the workers, the more dangerous he became, and it was precisely against embarking on the slippery slope of left-wing opportunism, left-wing in quotation marks went without saying, that the left-wing opposition must be warned so as to help it to march forward to Communism by way of the class struggle, and this fraternal help, and already the words were being snatched out of his mouth by the third so as to fully endorse, emphatically reiterate, and lay particular stress on, and similarly the fourth, and each of them a full half hour, and what's the point anyway, I thought, wanting to get up and leave in anger, but all the same I stayed, no longer listening, seeing only the shadow, the huge shadow, behind the man who was lecturing me . . .

and would fully endorse . . .

Lenin's shadow, the eloquent gesture of the hand outstretched, the torso leaning right over the edge of the platform as though he were about to launch himself into the world, take off into the unknown . . .

emphatically reiterate . . .

and his name in gigantic letters, blocks of stone, lumps of clay, written laboriously, the hand more accustomed to axe or gun than to holding a pen, the clumsy hand of the illiterate, the learner, spread out across the continent . . .

and lay particular stress on . . .

and, spread out across the continent, the body of the giantess, the great mother, painfully giving birth, her womb teeming with colossi, children of the Five-Year Plan, cranes, drilling rigs, lathes, tractors, electrification plus Soviet power, a world in process of becoming, hear the call, O ye peoples!

What matter if the great river's paltry tributary reflects the becoming world but dimly or if, in this instrumentation, the trumpet call of the Revolution loses so much of its appeal? Things are difficult for this small party, I thought. The constant pressure exerted by the big Social Democratic Party has embittered and distorted it. Not only does it hate Otto Bauer, but it mistrusts us as well, fears the left-wing opposition as its rival. It won't be any help to us, probably the reverse, in fact. None the less . . .

It's not as though Austria alone were at stake . . .

31 July 1932: German Reichstag elections. Nearly fourteen million Germans vote for Hitler. The N.S.D.A.P. has become the most powerful party. Whereas before there were 107 National Socialists in the Reichstag, now there are 230. On the other side the Communist share of the poll has swollen till it totals nearly five and a half million.

17 October 1932: Major Fey, the chief of the Vienna Heimwehr, is appointed Secretary of State for Public Security. Heimwehr rally in the Heldenplatz. Engelbert Dollfuss, Federal Chancellor since 20 May, the gnome in the military tunic, takes part in the rally. Social Democrats, Communists and National Socialists forbidden to hold processions, parades and open-air meetings.

6 November 1932: more Reichstag elections. The N.S.D.A.P. loses two million votes. Six million electors vote Communist. A turning-point? With his creditors hard on his heels, Hitler finds his followers taking to theirs. His rise to power can be stayed. It isn't. This is the great opportunity. It is thrown away.

4 January 1933: Hitler travels to Cologne at the invitation of Papen who is seeking to diminish Schleicher in the eyes of Hindenburg. The two erstwhile opponents form a new alliance at the home of Schröder the banker. Once again heavy industry begins to pour cash into the

N.S.D.A.P.'s coffers. Hitler, now rolling in money, concentrates the whole weight of his propaganda and party machine on the small province of Detmold-Lippe, gaining 48 per cent of the votes.

8 January 1933: the *Arbeiter-Zeitung* reveals that arms are being smuggled into Hungary *via* the armaments factory in Hirtenberg, whose managing director and principal shareholder, Fritz Mandl, is a friend of Starhemberg's and Mussolini's.

28 January 1933: Schleicher thrown out by Hindenburg. Hitler, Reich Chancellor designate, has to give an undertaking that, even after the coming elections, he will not make any changes in the cabinet and will defer unconditionally to Hindenburg and the German Nationals. Fruitless talks between Schleicher and Leipart, the chairman of the Association of Free Trade Unions. Army putsch and general strike dwindle away, a rumour, no more.

30 January 1933: the Hitler-Papen Government makes its public début.

11 February 1933: France and Britain protest to Dollfuss. The smuggling of weapons is a blatant breach of the St Germain Peace Treaty. Austria must either destroy the arms or send them back.

27 February 1933: the Reichstag fire. Hitler, Goering and Goebbels are instantly on the spot. Lit by the sinister glow of the flames, a man with a wide open mouth, above it a little moustache dancing to and fro like a blowfly as he yells: 'It's a sign from God. Nobody can prevent us now from crushing Communism with a fist of iron.' And turning to an English journalist, 'You are witnessing a great new era in German history. This fire marks its beginning.' And then Goebbels: 'A torch!' Whereupon Hitler: 'This is the point where our enemies bleed to death.'

28 February 1933: press and radio announce: 'A signal for Communist revolution. It was the Communists who set fire to the Reichstag. The Dutch Communist Van der Lubbe has made a full confession. The Reichstag fire was the work of the Communist-Social Democratic united front.'

1 March 1933: a two-hour general strike by Austrian railway workers against the management's breach of the collective agreement.

4 March 1933: meeting of the Austrian Parliament. Motion proposed by the Social Democratic deputy König censuring the general management of the Federal Railways. He demands that no

disciplinary action be taken against the strikers. When the session is resumed after a division, the government parties claim that the division has been improperly conducted. Dr Renner, presiding, when asked to rectify the matter, decides that this is unnecessary. Uproar. Renner resigns as President of the Nationalrat, his resignation being followed by those of the Christian Social Vice-President Ramek and the Pan-German Vice-President Straffner.

5 March 1933: Reichstag elections in Germany. 44 per cent of the electors vote for Hitler, 8 per cent for the German Nationals. A coalition gives the two parties an absolute majority.

6 March 1933: demonstration by the Vienna National Socialists in the main hall of the disused Nordwestbahnhof. Twelve thousand take part and thousands more for whom there is no room march into the city. Panic in government circles.

8 March 1933: the Austrian Government prohibits all public processions, parades and assemblies, issues an emergency amendment to the Press Law forbidding 'abuse of the freedom of the press'. The emergency decree invokes the wartime Enabling Act passed on 24 July 1917 and never rescinded by the Republic.

9 March 1933: the Pan-German Vice-President Straffner calls for a session of the Nationalrat for 15 March. This is declared unconstitutional by the Government, which further states that if necessary Parliament will be forcibly prevented from meeting.

10 March 1933: Otto Bauer addresses Viennese Social Democratic shop stewards and voluntary workers:

We know that, should the decisive battle take place, it will be at the cost of sacrifices which we could only demand of Austria's mothers if everything in our power had already been done to reach a peaceful settlement on a democratic basis ... Should our opponent choose otherwise, should he spurn our desire for peace ... then he must know that we are ready for anything – *really* anything ... In these hard times if there is one thing that makes our sombre lives worth living it is the fact that in this country we still stand shoulder to shoulder in support of what we believe in, the fact that we pursue our ideas and our ideals, the fact that we are able to fight for a better and a greater future. The bourgeoisie knows all this and it is to them an earnest of our determination. Were we to be deprived of that as well, then life would no longer be worth living.

A thousand hands were raised in an oath of freedom and then clenched to make a fist.

And the following day the *Arbeiter-Zeitung* bore the headline 'Freedom Oath'.

Parliament was scheduled to meet on 15 March, in direct contravention of the Government's wishes. The Schutzbund prepared for military intervention; an uprising was planned for the eventuality of Parliament's being forcibly prevented from convening, and of police action against the deputies. On the morning of 15 March Schutzbund messengers were sitting on their motorcycles ready to ride out to all districts with the signal from Schutzbund headquarters. Weapons were handed out. The Schutzbund men waited for the word that would enable them to implement the oath of freedom they had sworn.

It was a long wait, during which they grew increasingly restive, angry, and wracked by doubt. No directive? No. More waiting. Parliament was scheduled to meet at three o'clock. The hands moved over the clock face. The shorter time grew the more heavily it weighed. Nothing at all? No. More waiting. We were all staring at clocks, at watches. So too were the Social Democratic deputies assembled in the parliamentary Members' Room. Three o'clock was the time when Parliament was scheduled to meet. At two o'clock everything was still in a state of flux.

The euphoria that had followed the freedom oath of 10 March had given way to dejection. While the commanders of the Schutzbund had been preparing for military action, the party executive had spent 13 and 14 March deliberating the wisdom of having called for this session of Parliament, thus providing the Government with a date as well as a pretext for armed intervention. The majority of trade-union leaders, as a rule cautiously inclined and averse to action of a radical nature, were this time in favour of a fight, whatever its consequences. In this they were supported by old Ellenbogen, that most circumspect of politicians, who surprised everyone with his impassioned plea for militant action. More surprising still, however, and ultimately to be decisive, was Otto Bauer's adherence to Renner's view which called for a consideration of the incalculable consequences of civil war. On the other hand, General Körner's objections to action by the Schutzbund were only to be expected; he had always rejected the idea of a large armed formation, arguing that, from the purely military point of view, the Schutzbund could never be a match for the state executive, but that in a revolutionary situation the masses would arm themselves, at which juncture small, militarily trained groups could pass on to the workers what they themselves had learnt. No decision was reached, either on 13 or 14 March.

And thus it came about that, on 15 March, the deputies foregathered, their eyes fixed upon the clock. Once again the trade-union leaders urged the party not to avoid the risk of a decision. For to shirk the battle now, as the Germans had done, would be to throw all labour's social achievements to the winds and to forfeit the workers' confidence in their party. And while in some districts weapons were already being handed out and the Schutzbund men were awaiting the call to action, Körner issued yet another warning against the use of force. The hands moved on. The police had been alerted. What was to be done?

Suddenly a woman deputy, Gabriele Prost, exclaimed: 'How about going into the chamber now, this very moment? Then we can open the session, and conclude it before three o'clock!' Her suggestion was approved. The Pan-German Vice-President Straffner, who had convened the session, had done so only for the purpose of formally closing the session of 4 March, thus making it more difficult for the Government to plead that Parliament had brought about its own suspension. He was delighted by the ruse thought up by the Social Democrats. The Pan-German and Social Democratic deputies hurried into the chamber; messengers were dispatched to bring in those who had not yet arrived. At half past two the session was opened. Most of the Social Democrats and Pan-Germans were there. Late arrivals were kept out by the police who had meanwhile been posted outside the doors of the chamber. Straffner elucidated the legal position. Everyone's eyes were fixed on the clock. The session lasted ten minutes. As they left the chamber, the deputies laughed at the sight of the dumbfounded expression on the faces of the police. But the Schutzbund men who had been waiting for the word to act did not laugh. They flung down their arms. Many of them tore up their membership cards. In a number of places the Schutzbund dwindled overnight to a third of its former strength.

The 15 March was a milestone in the defeat of the working class. Had an armed insurrection taken place it would almost certainly have brought about the overthrow of the Dollfuss Government. What would then have ensued was neither predictable at the time

nor can it be retrospectively construed. Certainly not the dictatorship of the proletariat, which was what we of the left-wing
opposition were demanding. At best, an alliance between Social
Democracy and the democratic elements among the Christian
Socials. Maybe something worse. The concept of the Popular Front
did not emerge till much later; whether anything of the kind would
have been feasible in the Austria of 1933 it is impossible to say. I
rather doubt it. None the less, we ought to have joined battle, as
Otto Bauer himself was later to admit. A victory for the working
class, even if only transitory, even in a country as small as Austria,
would have encouraged and strengthened anti-Fascist forces throughout the whole of Europe.

The period between 15 March 1933 and 12 February 1934 saw
the progressive deterioration of the proletariat's fighting potential
and, at the same time, a growing resistance to that deterioration.
When they spoke at meetings the majority of the Social Democratic
leaders portrayed the horrors of civil war – weeping wives and
mothers, the misery of orphans, smoking rubble and the end of
Austria. Intended as an appeal to the conscience of the rulers, it
proved in effect to be an admonition to the workers to go home, not
to resort to extremes, not to take up arms. Meanwhile we of the
left-wing opposition – like the Schutzbund members and trade
unionists who disassociated themselves from us – were doing our
utmost to inhibit this process of disintegration and deterioration
and to bring strength and confidence to those whose feelings were
vacillating between anger and doubt, radicalism and resignation.

And what strength there still was! On the evening of 30 April an
illegal rally of Young Socialists and the Jungfront on the Drei-
markstein in the Wienerwald. The sea of blue shirts and, above the
meadow, the sudden billowing of red flags, hitherto furled, mere
nondescript bundles, the voices, the songs, the spring, and over
there Otto Bauer speaking, we're too far away to hear what he says,
the words are carried away, and here young lads are lifting me
shoulder-high, holding me up, 'Speech! Speech!' And what I say
is carried away, and other speakers emerge from other groups to be
submerged again in the blue sea, and again an individual is raised
aloft to represent the masses and no matter if *what* he says is carried
away – it is the mere fact, since open-air meeting are prohibited, of
these words being openly spoken, carried away into the free, the

open sky above this meadow, that is so vitally significant. And at the end, 'Arise ye starvelings from your slumbers!' Then the order to disperse, not to march back in rank and file, only to be countermanded by words circulating from mouth to mouth: No dispersal. Stick together! Enter the city in close formation. And now the dam breaks, a pale flood streaming down the hillside, channelled into a sunken path, onward, no stopping, swinging towards the city and then, like wild-fire, the first cry of 'Shame!', shrill catcalls, the menacing 'Shame!', police, we'll force our way through, rubber truncheons, force our way through, swords and stones, force our way through, scattered we reunite, join hands, all together now! And beaten, kicked, harried though we are, we feel as though we have won a victory.

And then May Day, a giant circumscribed by barbed wire, no longer striding freely along the Ringstrasse but already part chained, although he holds his face upturned, ignoring those who keep guard over him. There's a barbed-wire entanglement round the inner city, machine guns at all the road junctions, tanks posted wherever a charge is feared, infantry in steel helmets, guns mounted on trucks. And thus, surrounded by soldiers and police, confronted by all the paraphernalia of civil war, the hundred thousand who had been forbidden to march in close formation, not a parade but a leisurely stroll, dispersed, yet still a mass, still ready to become one body, one will.

We of the left-wing opposition, instead of abandoning this mass to the disintegration by which it was so gravely threatened, sought to conserve it and to restore its inner stability, and in so doing came into conflict with the C.P. We were, moreover, already burdened with the far from easy task of forming an effective whole out of the conglomeration of various groups and temperaments that went to make up the left-wing opposition.

A great deal of time was wasted in debating fictitious problems and irrelevant formulations before a declaration of principles was finally agreed. The declaration sought primarily to combat the historical fatalism to which historical materialism had, through oversimplification, been reduced, namely the view that historical development proceeds with a remorseless necessity that is beyond all human control, and that social laws are, as it were, natural laws not susceptible to subjective decisions.

'So you're arguing against Marx,' Otto Bauer said to me a few days after the illegal meeting at which the declaration of principles had been agreed.

'No, against Kautsky.'

The nearer we came to agreeing a programme and to achieving a stable organization, the more disgruntled the C.P. became. They inveigled some of our number into their ranks, induced them to submit to Communist Party discipline and to undertake fractional work inside the left-wing opposition. Within the context of Social Democracy they organized a rival oppositional group consisting largely of Communists. They began to denounce myself and other left-wing Socialists as 'agents of the party executive'.

The break finally came after the emergency party conference which took place on 14 October. By this time we were reasonably well organized and many of the delegates either belonged to the left-wing opposition or were in sympathy with its views. I myself was unable to take part in the deliberations; the original intention had been for me to have an opportunity of putting forward my opinions as a non-voting delegate of the *Arbeiter-Zeitung*. Feelings were running so high, however, that in the end I was to be admitted to the conference only as an observer. I refused to put in an appearance unless I were permitted to speak and, together with Ludwig Wagner and other non-delegates, I set up a left-wing opposition headquarters in a pub immediately adjoining the Arbeiterheim [where the conference was taking place]. There we drafted a resolution to be put before the conference: firstly, the game of grandmother's steps must cease; secondly, the present defensive policy must make way for an offensive policy with all the consequences that this might involve. Impressive speeches were made by Otto Fischer, Franz Schuster, Richard Strasser and other oppositional delegates who, in crossing swords with the Lower Austrian group led by Helmer and Schneidmadl, elicited an increasingly sympathetic response.

During a break in the proceedings Otto Bauer and other party leaders talked to a number of the left-wing opposition speakers. 'Now supposing,' they said, 'you obtain a majority vote – which you probably don't expect anyway – what then? You have neither the authority nor the experience nor the organizational facilities that would enable you to lead labour into battle. You'll split the party, and drive the right into the position of traitors, and that at a time when nothing could be more welcome to the enemy than our disintegration. Or supposing you remain a minority – what then? That, too, has its own logic, tends towards schism and internecine strife, and can only debilitate you and the common cause we share. How can you go over to the offensive if you cut yourselves off from your own source of strength, the working class – still an entity despite deep internal conflicts?'

We could not prolong the discussions indefinitely but had to reach a quick decision. We therefore determined to withdraw our resolution and to agree, with certain reservations, to a joint one.

The C.P., isolated from the mass of the working class and made up of unemployed and intellectuals, had little understanding for problems of unity. Instead of pursuing their discussion with us after the conference, instead of listening to our arguments – whether these were right or wrong – the Communists accused us of treachery. At a time when we were exposed to increasingly virulent attacks, to the suspicions and the slander of the Social Democratic party apparatus by which we were castigated as 'agents of the C.P.', as 'vermin' and 'schismatics', the Communist Party published a leaflet which ran:

A special task has been assigned by the party executive to the so-called 'left wing' – Ernst Fischer, Strasser *et al.* They are playing at opposition in order to deceive the workers. In practice they are just as much opposed to any form of struggle as are Otto Bauer and Schneidmadl. In actual fact this so-called opposition has only one task: to prevent the formation of the revolutionary united front. They are nothing but an obstacle to the development of genuinely left-wing workers into a single revolutionary class-front party, into the Communist Party of Austria, into the Communist International.

The leaflet went on to appeal, not for armed resistance, but for a 'storm of protest', for a 'general strike', for the 'expulsion of all professional traitors', and contained the exhortation:

Against the Heimwehr and Hitler-Fascism! Against the Dollfuss–Fey hangman's régime! Against the traitors in your own ranks, ranging from Renner through Otto Bauer to the left-wing agents of the party executive! Create the revolutionary united front! Rise up in a general strike!... Unite under the red flag of the Communist International!

To appeal for all this was easy enough. But to proclaim a revolutionary united front in opposition to Social Democracy, the trade unions, the Schutzbund command, and the left-wing opposition was certainly no way to bring about a general strike or armed insurrection. This ready use of revolutionary cliché showed a blithe disregard for the existing state of affairs.

Arraigned by both left and right as mischief-makers, spies and traitors, it was not always easy for us to stay our course. I confess that I found it hurtful and that I sometimes asked myself whether this really had to be. It was the first, though it was not to be the last, time I was compelled to assume that most uncomfortable and thankless of roles which consists in steering between the devil and the deep blue sea, between two established powers, two experienced political machines, two dogmatic creeds, solely by the light of my own conscience – which might be deceptive – and on the strength of my own responsibility – which might lead me astray. In everybody's life there seem to be situations that repeat themselves – not by chance but because, by a subconscious decision, an unknown, incomplete self has predetermined its own existence.

The attitude of the Austrian C.P. after October 1933 was disappointing; but during that same month of October, a man stood in the dock of the Supreme Court in Leipzig, a man whose stature was such that he towered high above the pettinesses of individual parties and above the inadequacies of their members and methods, a man who embodied all that is comprised in the idea of Communism: Georgi Dimitrov.

In court the accused declared:

'The Communist International desires the matter of the Reichstag fire to be fully elucidated. Millions are awaiting the answer.'

The President of the Court: 'Who is presiding here? I insist that you hold your tongue!'

Dimitrov: 'Millions are waiting for an unequivocal answer!'

Who indeed was president of that court? Who the prosecutor? Who the judge? The world replied: Dimitrov. Everyone succumbed to his spell. Not only the peoples in their hundreds of millions, but those actually present in the courtroom: newspaper correspondents, judges, court officials, S.A. guards. The latter had to be relieved daily, for they admired this Communist, they thought him a tremendous man.

On 4 November Dimitrov and Goering stood face to face.

In riding boots, legs astraddle, hands on hips, his over-abundant flesh held in check by his tightly fitting uniform, such was the picture presented by the Prussian Prime Minister and President of the Reichstag when he appeared as a witness in court.

Bellowing like a bull, he claimed to have saved Germany and Europe from Communism. The Reichstag fire had, he asserted, been meant as a signal for arson, looting, murder, mass poisoning. And as for foreign accounts of acts of terrorism by the S.A., 'Yes, acts of terrorism were in fact perpetrated, but by Communists disguised as Storm Troopers. And,' he went on, 'I have left my police in no doubt: if there is any shooting, it is my hand that shoots. If somebody is shot dead, it is my hand that has shot him. But one thing I demand – that not a single shot be fired into the air.'

With slow deliberation Dimitrov rose, his pale features taut, his right hand resting on the rail, calm, matter-of-fact, confident: 'On 28 February Ministerpräsident Goering gave an interview on the subject of the Reichstag fire in which it was stated that, at the time of his arrest, the Dutch Communist Van der Lubbe was carrying not only his passport, but a party card. Now how did Herr Ministerpräsident Goering know at that time that Van der Lubbe was carrying a party card?'

Goering: 'I must admit that I haven't bothered much about this trial hitherto . . . I don't go running around personally turning out people's pockets. In case you don't already know, let me tell you that the police search all criminals and inform me of what they find . . . I'm not a detective but a responsible minister, so I'm not really concerned with catching out one miserable little crook, but with unmasking the party, the ideology responsible for it. No stone will be left unturned by the criminal investigation department, I can assure you! . . . To my mind the crime was committed for political reasons, and I am further convinced that the criminals are to be found within your party. That party is a party of criminals and must be destroyed!'

Dimitrov: 'Is the Herr Ministerpräsident aware that this party which must be destroyed rules over one sixth of the whole world, in other words the Soviet Union? Is he aware that the Soviet Union maintains diplomatic, political and economic relations with

Germany and that those economic relations are of benefit to hundreds of thousands of German workers?'

President of the Court: 'I forbid you to indulge in Communist propaganda here.'

Dimitrov: 'Herr Goering is indulging in National Socialist propaganda.'

Goering: 'In my opinion you're a scoundrel, fit only for the gallows.'

The President of the Court (to Dimitrov): 'I've warned you before not to indulge in Communist propaganda in this court. It should not, therefore, come as a surprise to you if the witness flares up as he has done. I absolutely prohibit propaganda of this kind. Your questions must be purely factual.'

Dimitrov: 'I am completely satisfied with the Herr Minister-präsident's answer.'

The President of the Court: 'Your satisfaction or lack of it is of no concern to me. You must now stand down.'

Dimitrov: 'I want to put one more factual question.'

The President of the Court: 'You must stand down.'

Goering: 'Out with the blackguard!'

The President of the Court: 'Remove him!'

Goering made as if to hurl himself at Dimitrov. He was anticipated by the police who dragged the prisoner away. Turning for the last time to look at the exploding mass of flesh that was Goering, Dimitrov asked: 'Are you by any chance afraid of my questions, Herr Minister-präsident?'

It was this that carried more weight than anything else. Not to go under without a struggle as in Germany! To follow Dimitrov's example! In these circumstances of defeat his figure stood for future victory.

14

February 1934

'No politics today!' said Otto Bauer.

He had come into my office one day early in February 1934.

A few weeks previously at a conference in the Third – his own electoral – District, he had been outvoted by the left-wing opposition. This had hurt him and, with the arrogance that forms like a crust over a wound, he had taken me to task:

'Your people aren't properly informed. They argue at a very low level. One of them shouted at me: "You've got plenty to eat! Try going hungry for once and then you'll sing a different tune!" What kind of an argument is that?'

'That such a thing should have been shouted at *you* is certainly regrettable. But hunger and unemployment *are* arguments, even if not intellectual ones.'

'They're not *political* arguments. Besides, even *your* people should know that I'm not indifferent in the face of hunger and unemployment.'

Before I had been able to answer him, he had gone back to his room and so distant had his manner been that I had not dared follow him so as to say how greatly I desired to be on good terms with him, and how much the *unity* that was essential to our struggle depended on him, for all his inner contradictions. Since then we had not talked to one another. Otto Bauer had been withdrawn and cold and I had respected his reserve.

But now, friendly and magnanimous, he had come to seek me out.

'You spend nearly all your evenings out speaking, going from one meeting to another. What else do you do? Do you read at all?'

'Oddly enough I do!'

'What do you read?'

'Plato.'

He looked at me in surprise.

'*The Republic*,' I said. 'Not just out of interest in philosophy. Philosophically speaking I regard Plato as a disaster. But at meetings where politics are forbidden I talk about Plato's model state. I argue against the authoritarian régime he favours and talk about Athenian democracy – and if the police officer appears to be restive and starts reaching for his hat, I quickly revert to Plato's forms and to his concept of the power of music.'

For in accordance with a time-honoured Austrian tradition, when the police officer donned his cap it meant that the meeting was over.

'Plato as camouflage for agitation?'

'Not only camouflage. Sometimes the means assume more importance than the ends and all at once I become engrossed in philosophical problems.'

'You're no politician . . .' Bauer looked me straight in the face, then looked away again. 'But what else can we do?'

'Music as the guardian of the established order. The *Radetzky March* and the *Blue Danube*. "For the introduction of a new kind of music must be shunned as imperilling the whole state . . ." '

' "Since styles of music are never disturbed without affecting the most important political institutions." ' With a smile, Bauer concluded the quotation . . .

The music which ushered in the year 1934 was the crump of bombs and mortars, the explosion of Nazi terror; and, inaudible behind these sound effects, the game of intrigue – Dollfuss and Hitler, Starhemberg and Mussolini, Fey versus Dollfuss and Starhemberg, contacts between Renner and the Provincial Governor of Lower Austria and farmers' spokesman, Reither. Then, on 10 January, a leading article in the *Arbeiter-Zeitung*: 'Were the National Council to be convened today, the Social Democratic deputies would not hesitate, within the limits of constitutional procedure, to authorize a democratic government to turn its sharpest weapons against the Nazis.'

The next day, 11 January, the hangman went into action. A tramp, Peter Strauss, suffered the death penalty. The mentally deficient son of a domestic servant, he had set fire to a barn out of revenge against the farmer who had chased him, a beggar, away from his door. A short time before, the Federal President had pardoned the first man to be sentenced to the gallows, a rich farmer's son who, having got a girl with child, had then murdered her because she stood in the way of his marriage. No guinea-pig he for the apprentice hangman.

'For a political constitution,' Plato says, if not in precisely these terms, 'once it has made a right beginning, spreads outward in ever-widening circles . . . And it is against the law to speak slanderously of rulers or even to assert that the unjust man thrives while the just man succumbs to misery . . . at which point Plato's wisdom is drowned amid the general laughter and the police officer dismisses the philosopher for a knave.'

And on 18 January the Italian Secretary of State, Suvich, arrived in Vienna. According to information divulged by diplomatic circles, he and Vice-Chancellor Fey had agreed the liquidation of Social Democracy. Dollfuss, however, launched an attack upon the Nazis, appealing to the 'honourable labour leaders' and the 'more reasonable circles in the nationalist camp'.

On 22 January the *Österreichische Abendzeitung* published a statement by Vice-Chancellor Fey:

The appeal to the workers was not aimed at the red leaders or at the red organizations, but directly at the workers themselves. In the corporate state there can be no room either for the Social Democratic Party or for Marxist trade unions . . .

'Do you remember the passage in *The Republic* about the useless activities of self-styled statesmen – if one, being unable to measure, is told often enough that he is six feet tall, won't he believe it of himself?'

'Little Dollfuss! And do the police really swallow that particular bit of Plato?'

'I invariably go on to say that, according to Plato, the true legislator must observe religious practices and revere the gods, demigods and heroes. That satisfies the police . . .'

On 25 January an official announcement declared that, on the previous day, three machine guns, sixty rifles, two hundred hand-grenades and a quantity of small arms ammunition had been found in municipal buildings in Schwechat. To *whom* they belonged was not made clear. But Fey had a number of Social Democrats arrested.

Starhemberg threatened the Nazis and gave orders for an 'active anti-terror campaign'.

With all this going on, it was strange to be discussing Plato. What Bauer wanted, I think, was a respite from politics, an unpolluted atmosphere in which to talk to me and to convey that, while not regarding me as a politician, he felt me to be a kindred spirit. 'Perhaps,' he said, when our discussion about Plato was over, 'we shall manage to survive the worst. Mussolini and Fey are putting on the pressure, Starhemberg is trying to outmanoeuvre his rival. Dollfuss is vacillating. Powerful voices abroad, voices to which he pays attention, are warning him not to resort to extreme measures. Kunschak and Reither are not the only advocates of moderation – other Christian Socials also fear that an Austria without Social Democracy would fall an easy prey to Hitler. The longer this goes on, the more effective will the contradictions in the Government's camp become.'

'And the greater will be the disintegration among the workers.'

'All the same, we mustn't lose our nerve. Don't force your people into making an over-hasty decision.'

Circumstances did nothing to substantiate these illusions.

On 28 January the Social Democratic executive, some of whose members were radical Socialists, declared:

If the reform of the constitution were to be carried out along constitutional lines, at the same time safeguarding the right of manual and non-manual workers to set up trade unions, then those manual and non-manual workers would be prepared to cooperate in constitutional reform. The party executive emphasizes the willingness of the workers to defend their country in every possible way.

On the same day Starhemberg warned the Lower Austrian Bauernbund [Farmers' League] that the purpose of the Heimwehr was to create Fascism, not to preserve a democratic state.

And on that same day Dollfuss emphatically ruled out any possibility of an agreement with what he described as the 'Marxist misleaders'.

2 February: the Tyrolean Heimwehr demands the dissolution of Social Democracy, the voluntary liquidation of the Christian Social Party, the setting up of a standing provincial committee to assist the Provincial Governor, a body consisting of six members – two

Heimwehr, two Sturmschar [Schuschnigg's special force] and two farmers' representatives.

3 February: Schutzbund chiefs Major Eifler and Captain Löw arrested on the orders of Vice-Chancellor Fey.

Social Democratic rallying campaign. 'A poor response,' reports the Upper Austrian Schutzbund chief Richard Bernaschek. 'Many workers simply stay away . . . When I tell my comrades in the mining district that we shall fight, come what may, they don't believe me any more. They're even tired of discussing it. They just grin sardonically . . .'

5 February: the *Reichspost* reports: 'Since midnight last night the Tyrol has had an authoritarian government . . . its explicit intention being to obviate a putsch. This threat has sent the Nazis creeping back into their holes . . . The rider is in the saddle. Now let him show us what he can do.'

And Bernaschek, in a letter to Vienna: 'The rate of disintegration is speeding up. Within a few months we have lost whole districts.'

6 February: Kunschak and other democratically-minded Christian Socials protest against the Heimwehr coup in the Tyrol.

7 February: the Heimwehr demands that steps be taken in Styria and Burgenland similar to those in the Tyrol. Fey orders the mobilization of large sections of the 'Voluntary Schutzkorps'. Not only did the weapons found in Schwechat belong to the Schutzbund, he claims, but stocks of weapons and explosives had also been found in Vienna: he announces the arrest of Major Eifler, Captain Löw and other Schutzbund commanders.

8 February: the *Arbeiter-Zeitung* premises and other rooms in the Rechte Wienzeile party headquarters searched by the police.

9 February: the search continues until seven p.m. 'Nothing found,' the police report. 'Reds prepare for civil war!' proclaims the *Reichspost.* In the Vienna Municipal Council, however, the Christian Social workers' leader Kunschak addresses an appeal to Dollfuss in which he states that the enemy is National Socialism. To combat it and to work constructively for the people's spiritual and material well-being is, he says, the need of the hour. Many discordant elements will have to be reconciled in order to make common cause against the impending danger. 'God grant that the divisions by which the hearts and minds of our people and leaders are torn be rapidly healed before the country and its people stand weeping at the graveside.'

An hour after the Vienna Municipal Council had concluded its session Fey signed an order instructing the police to arrest every Schutzbund commander they could lay hands on.

On 10 February, in an interview with the editor of the *Reichspost*, Dollfuss said: 'We neither can nor will have anything to do with the stubborn followers of the Marxist–Bolshevist ideology . . . From time to time one politician or another may express himself otherwise but . . . this has nothing to do with my own way of thinking.' Notwithstanding the nature of the Chancellor's reply to Kunschak's appeal, Otto Bauer seemed to feel relief. 'I believe,' he said, 'that we can really take an evening off for once. I'd like to go and see Greta Garbo. Would you like to come to the cinema tomorrow?'

'Perhaps, but I rather think my wife and I have arranged to do something with Elias Canetti.'

On that day, 11 February, Richard Bernaschek sent two couriers from Linz to Vienna with a letter for Otto Bauer. The following is a passage from that letter:

. . . If tomorrow, Monday, an arms search is started in any of the towns in Upper Austria or if any key men, either of the party or of the Schutzbund, are arrested, these acts will be met with armed resistance followed by offensive action. This resolve no less than its execution is irrevocable. When you in Vienna receive our telephone message, 'An arms search has begun, arrests are being made', we shall expect you to give the workers of Vienna and elsewhere the signal to attack. We shall not turn back. I have not informed the party leaders of this resolution. If the Viennese workers leave us in the lurch, may they be covered with ignominy. Should the above-mentioned contingencies not arise, I shall come to Vienna tomorrow, Monday, in the afternoon together with Comrade Koref, who doesn't know about the resolution, and I shall account for all this to the national party executive . . .*

On the same day, 11 February, Karl Münichreiter came to see us in the Veitlissengasse. This emaciated, mercurial, vehement comrade, the father of three children, was unemployed, and the purpose of his visit was to find out when the action was going to start.

On this same day, 11 February, the combined forces of the Vienna

Österreich Brandherd Europa, Genossenschaft Universum Bücherei, Zürich, 1934, p. 278 f.

and Lower Austrian Heimwehr carried out manoeuvres in the Wienerwald, concluding with a memorial service in honour of those who lost their lives in the First World War. Fey made a speech in which he said: 'Our discussions of yesterday and the day before have convinced us that Chancellor Dollfuss is on our side. I can go even further and tell you in so many words that tomorrow we shall set to work, and that this work will be well done.'

It was past midnight when the couriers from Linz handed the letter to Otto Bauer. He warned against separate action on the grounds that the Government was bound to make a decisive move within a matter of days, whereupon a fight would become inevitable; until then, he said, it would be best to wait. He asked the two couriers to return to Linz at once and to pass on these instructions. Instead of doing so by word of mouth, the two men sent a telegram: 'Ernst and Otto critically ill. Postpone action.'*

On 12 February at nine a.m. the telephone rang.

Oscar Pollak was on the line.

'Take a taxi and come here at once. The comrades in Linz have gone into action.'

To find a taxi in Ober-Sankt Veit was no easy matter. I walked to the tram stop and found to my horror that none of the services had been suspended. All trams and trains were still running. When I reached the Pilgrambrücke, I could see two policemen standing on guard outside the closed doors of party headquarters. A sub-editor of the *Arbeiter-Zeitung* – Karl Hans Sailer, if my memory serves me aright – came up to me. 'Instructions are for everyone to remain in their own districts.' He gave me an address in the Margaretengürtel – 'for emergency use only', and added that someone would always be available in the Café Museum. Back to Hietzing, then!

Ruth was to meet me in a café near Hietzing Bridge, bringing with her all our money, after she had handed over the flat to our household help Rosa. I took a taxi to Hietzing station. Schutzbund men nodded to me as they went past; policemen hurrying in the same direction – the former in as much haste as the latter, each aware that, like themselves, the others were on their way to an assembly point where guns were to be distributed. Sometimes they exchanged a covert glance but mostly they looked awkwardly away. How odd! I thought.

---

*Historians differ as to the exact wording of this telegram. My version derives from Bernaschek's *Brandherd*, p. 279.

Even killing has its conventions. In a couple of hours' time they'll be shooting each other dead. Why put it off? Why not tackle the enemy now, overpower him on the spot? Because both sides are in isolation. The people have made themselves scarce, refused to participate. So if the Schutzbund were to attack a policeman, or the police a Schutzbund man, the result would not be a riot but rather a vacuum. The individual would be guilty of assault if not of murder. Only the collective, the fighting community, can be relieved of responsibility by an order. Killing is then no longer an outrage but the execution of a duty.

Ruth was waiting for me at the café with a few comrades. She told me that, half an hour or so after I had left, Münichreiter had arrived. His wife, he told her, had cried and tried to stop him going, but he had come all the same. 'Tell Ernstl they can count me in!' he said. The assembly point was in the pavilion beside the tennis court, a jerrybuilt place with big windows on every side, providing no cover at all.

Then suddenly the trams weren't running any more. It was after half past ten. We heaved a sigh of relief. So the strike was on! But it wasn't a strike. Franz Schuster and some of his fellow workers at the municipal power station had shut down the plant and dismantled the machinery. This man, who kept his fiery spirit in leash, and whose resolution was as indomitable as it was unobtrusive, had an invalid wife whom he looked after with touching devotion; in order to be adequate to the political struggle he had to strain his every nerve and sinew. After the annexation of Austria he, as an active Communist, was ferreted out by the Gestapo, condemned to death and executed.

This wasn't a strike. While the Schutzbund men were arming, the trains continued to run. And it was not only the railwaymen who reported for work as usual, but virtually all industrial workers. Greater than their fear of death was the fear of losing their jobs. Many a Schutzbund man remained at work, and not till the whistle blew did he pick up his gun to take part in armed resistance during the hours of the evening or the night. By midday it was already quite clear that life would go on as usual, bleary-eyed – a trifle disquieted perhaps, a trifle confused, but still undeterred. At twelve o'clock official notices were being posted up.

'In Vienna a section of Social Democratic workers in the municipal gas and electricity undertakings have stopped work. For this reason martial law will be enforced in Vienna.'

Groups began to congregate in front of each notice. Martial law? Because of a strike? What could be happening? At all events, best lay in a store of food, remembering the 'hoarding', the wartime shortages. Questions were being fired at the crews of the motionless trams: 'What's happened?' 'Don't know. Maybe the electricity's failed, maybe the Nazis, maybe a general strike.' Outside the shops, crowds of housewives. 'Don't push. I was here first. Get back into the queue!' Strike? Insurrection? Revolution? The atmosphere wasn't one of revolution but of uncertainty.

And we, sitting in this café by the Hietzing Bridge, what could we do to help things along with such little strength as we possessed? The left-wing opposition had made no provision for conducting its own armed struggle and had been right not to do so. Two competing commands could only have made confusion worse. Our mistake lay in not having made any provision for an underground political headquarters, although even this would not have enabled us to intervene effectively. The result of our deliberations was that I should draft a leaflet. A comrade undertook to distribute it, but whether this was ever done I do not know.

It now seemed to me imperative to find out what the battle command was planning to do.

I went to the house in the Margaretengürtel, to the address I had been given earlier that morning. There I found Oscar and Marianne Pollak.

'What have you come here for?' Marianne demanded.

'We must be given some general idea of what the party's plans are. Have you proclaimed a general strike?'

'Yes,' said Oscar Pollak. 'The tramway stoppage was the signal. Otto Bauer and Johann Schorsch organized that. Korbel, the commander of the Schutzbund in the western region, has ratted on us. It's made everything far more difficult.'

Eduard Korbel had been in command of the Sixth, Seventh, Thirteenth, Fourteenth, Fifteenth and Sixteenth Districts. Though he had given grounds for suspicion as early as the summer of 1933, the party executive had not relieved him of this most important command. Some days before his open defection he had been arrested along with other Schutzbund commanders, only to be released on

11 February. 'Then,' according to Gustl Deutsch, 'he began ostentatiously seeking out Schutzbund functionaries, but after every such meeting a detective inspector would turn up and arrest the Schutzbund man with whom Korbel had been talking.'*

'Is there a central battle-command?'

'It's somewhere in Favoriten.'

'Are you in contact with it?'

'Not at the moment. All our couriers are out on duty.'

'And what has been planned? What ought we to do?'

'And you actually call yourself a revolutionary?' snorted Marianne. 'A revolutionary doesn't ask what he has to do. He does it!'

'That's all very well. But the Schutzbund men in Hietzing are going to ask me what they are to do – more especially since Hietzing is part of Korbel's region. Has an offensive been planned? Are the workers from the major working-class districts invading the inner city? Is there any point in attacking individual police stations, or should smaller groups try to fight their way through to the main centres of the battle? I can't decide these things off my own bat!'

'In a revolutionary situation?' exclaimed Marianne.

'But it's not a revolutionary situation! Armed detachments are preparing to fight, but the masses are keeping out of it, they're not lifting a finger. So it's essential to know if there's any military plan.'

'It's a reasonable question,' said Oscar Pollak soothingly to his agitated wife and, turning to me: 'To the best of my knowledge, the original idea was not to risk an offensive but to wait until attacked.'

'But that's . . .'

'I may be wrong. But at the moment everything's out of control. Each man must decide for himself. Your left-wing opposition seems no more capable of action than the party leadership.'

What I had heard convinced me that defeat was inevitable. Back once more to Hietzing. There I learnt that the police had attacked and dispersed Münichreiter's as yet inadequately armed group. Gravely wounded, Münichreiter had fallen into the hands of the police. The Schutzbund motorcyclist who had brought us this news offered to take me on his pillion to Speising where a Schutzbund section was awaiting instructions from the battle command. He

* *Der Bürgerkrieg in Österreich*, Carlsbad, 1934, p. 58.

also told us that, according to an unconfirmed rumour, there had already been fighting in Sandleiten as also in the Ottakring Arbeiterheim, and that what the combatants felt most was the lack of contact, the sense of isolation. I went with him to Speising and told the Schutzbund there about my conversation with Oscar and Marianne Pollak, going on to suggest that it would be very unwise to wait any longer since the police were liable to act before any orders could arrive from the battle command which was somewhere in Favoriten. I did not, I said, regard myself as competent to advise in military matters, but thought that the best thing for them to do was to arm themselves and make their way to the working-class districts of Meidling and Favoriten, taking care not to engage in any serious fighting until they had joined forces with a larger formation.

The men found my advice acceptable but it now transpired that they had not got enough ammunition for their machine guns. They gave me an address in the Pensingergasse, the name of somebody who might be able to provide ammunition. I went there in a taxi and found the comrade whose name I had been given. Though he knew me he prevaricated, seemed mistrustful and anxious, but finally gave me two boxes which I loaded into the taxi. The driver, whom I had handsomely tipped, winked an eye, although probably very well aware of what was afoot, and drove me and my peculiar cargo back to Speising. I was keenly aware of the incongruity of the situation, the absurdity of riding through civil war in a taxi; the boxes were duly delivered, however, and were found to contain the required machine gun belts.

In some café or other – which, I no longer recall – I met Ruth and one or two other comrades. It was between four and five in the afternoon. Reports were confused, their gist being that there had been heavy fighting in the Reumannhof and in Sandleiten. The Schutzbund in Sandleiten, who had been ready for action in the morning, had been attacked by the police in the early afternoon but had pushed them back into the Kongresspark. An infantry battalion and an artillery brigade had recently been brought up. The Schutzbund had successfully held the Reumannhof. The Ottakring Arbeiterheim had been the scene of the heaviest fighting. We decided to make our way there. Not far from the building we were stopped by some comrades. 'You'll never get through. The police station in the Panikengasse is under heavy fire. So far police reinforcements haven't been able to do anything. In the Hasnergasse and other streets, the Schutzbund have erected barricades. You won't get through.'

We remembered that the Café Museum was a possible rendezvous. Several times on our way there we had to produce our papers. Police and Heimwehr men, sullen but jumpy, examined our passports. 'Ernst Fischer, assistant editor ... What paper?' '*Neues Wiener Tagblatt.*' 'Is there a Fischer there?' 'Why shouldn't there be? Try ringing up.' 'Where are you going?' 'Home. Before it gets dark. No electricity.' Barbed wire and barriers. Machine guns. Patrols. Police cars. Armoured cars. Artillery. At the Café Museum editors, writers, foreign reporters, crowded together in the dusk. I recounted what I had seen and heard. 'Is the Schutzbund going to attack?' someone asked. 'Let's hope so,' I said. 'Meidling, Favoriten ...' whereupon Ruth: 'Don't talk so loud!' And suddenly a woman's shrill voice: 'Comrades! The *Arbeiter-Zeitung* ...' and Ruth dashing up to her: 'Shut up you fool! There aren't any comrades here, and there's no *Arbeiter-Zeitung*!' And dozens of people with pads scribbling notes, some of them certainly members of the secret police, and somewhere an English or American correspondent, if I remember rightly. 'Just now Schuschnigg was on the air. He spoke at seven o'clock. Told the workers to send the hyenas packing.' Then he read, the beam of a pocket torch picking out his shorthand notes from the candle-lit gloom: 'That there can be no shadow of a doubt as to where the responsibility lies is apparent from the fact that the two men long notorious as ringleaders have taken refuge from that responsibility in flight, leaving others to man the barricades. In addition the majority of those responsible have been arrested.' Bauer? Deutsch? 'Do you believe they've cut and run?' No. I didn't believe it. Schuschnigg was lying in order to undermine the courage of the Schutzbund. Those who had been arrested, we heard, were Renner, Danneberg, Breitner, Weber and Karl Seitz, the latter in the town hall. His reply to the Heimwehr officer had been: 'I am the legally elected Burgomaster of this city. I yield only to force.'

We went out of the café into the darkness. Headlamps of military and police vehicles flitting over the ground and suddenly, in one's face, the hurried beam of a torch, from afar the chatter of machine guns, and now the sound of artillery, they're shelling the workers' flats with artillery. And us? Where to? Where can we find shelter in this blacked-out, devastated city?

Elias Canetti and Veza Magd lived in the Second District, in the Ferdinandstrasse. They let us stay the night.

Veza seemed taken aback but this impression was quickly effaced by her warmth, her cordiality, her evident pleasure at being able to help us. We were more clearly aware of Canetti's surprise, of his disappointment. About a fortnight previously he had asked me to tell him, spontaneously, without prior reflection, how I envisaged myself behaving. Leaping up, I stood against the wall, raised my right hand as if I were speaking, let it sink slowly to my side and then stood motionless, my arms held obliquely, the palms of my hands pressed against the wall. 'Condemned to death!' cried Canetti. 'Put up against the wall, awaiting the fusillade!'

Our arrival at his flat contravened the picture he had kept in his mind's eye; instead of a rebel with his back to the wall I was simply a man in search of a night's lodging.

'I'm glad to see you,' he said, shaking me by the hand and squinting up into my face. 'No, I mean it. I really *am* glad, Ernst! We've been talking about you, wondering where you were, what district you were fighting in.'

'That's not quite how it was!' said Veza in an attempt to hush him up.

'But *of course* that's how it was!' Canetti was intent on making me feel guilty for not being at the scene of the shooting. 'Every time we heard shots . . . And the terrible announcements on the wireless . . . The Government has the situation well in hand . . . sandwiched between Lehar and the *Radetzky March* . . . Any chance of winning the battle?'

'I rather think not. Individual groups are resisting, islands in a sea of inertia. The whole structure of militant labour has been disrupted; it's a battle between a tiny minority and a superior if somewhat muddle-headed opponent. Not one centre of resistance has become the nucleus of a mass.* And as you know better than I do, everything depends on that.'

'And how about you? If anyone can turn people into a mass, it's you!'

*Rendered as 'crowd crystal' in *Crowds and Power*, Elias Canetti, Victor Gollancz, 1962, p. 18 *passim*.

'As a speaker, yes. But now? A really resolute battle command might be able to do it, though even that is doubtful.'

I was in a bad mood. My conscience was beginning to plague me, to reproach me for not being among those who were shooting or being shot. Had I really tried hard enough to get through to one of the centres of the fighting? Hadn't I frittered away the time writing an unnecessary leaflet, transporting ammunition, sitting in cafés? A bad soldier, I couldn't have done much to help. But to be in the thick of it, wasn't that a moral duty? Mightn't it have been a help and an encouragement to others? Or was it not rather incumbent on me to take *political* action? But how? Finally we decided that the next day Ruth should try to establish contact with members of the left-wing opposition and, if possible, find out how to get through the barricades into Favoriten.

'Why didn't you seize the wireless station?' asked Canetti.

'Why didn't we push our way into the inner city? I don't know. Obviously things moved too fast for what was in any case a vacillating party leadership. The police were better informed than the Schutzbund. There seems to have been no centralized plan, or if there was one it has been abandoned. The military defensive action is simply a continuation of the political one.'

The wireless poured out an endless stream of Austrian *Gemütlichkeit*, interrupted only by announcements to the effect that nowhere were there any strikes, that the fighting was confined to a few places only, that, their ringleaders having fled, other prominent Social Democrats and Schutzbund commanders had given themselves up to the police, that complete calm reigned throughout the whole Wiener-Neustadt industrial area.

'Infinitely more deadly than artillery or machine gun fire!' remarked Canetti. Demoralizing and deceptive as these announcements were, perhaps the worst thing about them was that they bore some relation to reality. The defection of the Wiener-Neustadt industrial area, which was largely under the influence of Renner and Helmer, contributed materially to the defeat of the Schutzbund in Vienna. After the February battles Pertinax (Otto Leichter) wrote: 'Had Lower Austria fought, it would have been impossible to suppress the determined resistance, which extended from Vienna to Graz and Leoben.'*

*Pertinax, *Österreich 1934*, Europa-Verlag, Zürich, 1935, p. 260.

And on 27 February the *Berliner Börsenzeitung* stated that the Austrian authorities, lacking the ammunition they required, had urgently requested aid from Hungary. That aid was duly given:

The ammunition was brought across the frontier and into Vienna in uninterrupted convoys of heavy, purpose-built vehicles belonging to the Hirtenberg cartridge factory. Had the Marxist Schutzbund risen in Lower Austria and blocked the roads in the Wiener-Neustadt industrial area, the Government would have found itself in an extremely critical position.*

On the night of 12 February, though not yet in a position to gauge the full implications of the calm that reigned in the Wiener-Neustadt industrial area, we felt deeply depressed.

Veza was restive, constantly going into the next room and returning in a distraught condition. When Elias looked inquiringly at her, she put her finger to her lips. There was something secret, something inexplicable going on.

Perhaps they were both afraid?

Though we thought this improbable, we each of us decided independently to spend no more than that one night with them.

*

A few days after having written this, I happened to meet Canetti who had come to Vienna to give a lecture. After some hesitation I ventured to ask him whether my recollection of what had happened was accurate.

'You've got an astounding memory!' Canetti replied. 'What you've just told me isn't just the gist of what I said, but a literal rendering of it. That's exactly how it was.'

'And how about being afraid?'

'You're right about that, too. Veza was afraid – afraid for *you*, in case the caretaker had noticed you, might denounce you. You're familiar with that caretaker; he comes into my novel *Auto da fé . . .*'

The caretaker Benedikt Pfaff who thrashes his wife and daughter to death; who bores a peephole in the door through which to spy on beggars, who makes his daughter put on a pair of his trousers and pose as a beggar, then fells her to the ground.

*Kerekes, *Abenddämmerung einer Demokratie*, Vienna, 1966, p. 180.

'Because,' he excused himself later, as if this were the first time he had ever hit her, that's the way it has to be, because you're a rat. Shave their heads in prison, they do; cut 'em off would be more like it. A burden on the taxpayer. Eating themselves full in prison. The bleeding State pays. I'll wipe the vermin out. The cat's at home now. The mice can keep in the holes! I'm Ginger the Cat. I'll eat 'em up. A rat, you'll know what crushing means!'*

The caretaker of power, eager to assist the Heimwehr and police in their rat-crushing operations.

'But that was by no means all,' Canetti resumed. 'In the next room Veza's mother was at the point of death. She died a day or two later.'

It was just like Veza. She hadn't wanted to worry us, to worry her dying mother.

*

That night I couldn't sleep.

Tormenting thoughts bored into me like a drill.

What's the good?

What are they dying for?

It's a lost battle. Has anyone the right to summon others to such a battle?

Out of the blood of the martyrs . . .

What will arise?

The honour of the working class?

What is that?

A verbal phantasm.

Anyone who thinks like that has no sense of honour . . .

Why aren't you out there, where men are dying . . . ?

*

At seven o'clock in the morning when the curfew ended Ruth, armed with a number of addresses, went out on her errand.

In spite of the apparent futility of the procedure, I drafted another leaflet. Then I waited, pacing to and fro, up and down.

Out of the blood of the martyrs . . .

A pious cliché!

No one lays down his life for a cliché. Their blood will turn them into . . .

*Elias Canetti, *Auto da fé*, Jonathan Cape, 1946, p. 371.

Truth?

A call, perhaps. Hear the call, O ye peoples . . .

Will they hear it?

Maybe one day. Maybe never.

What lesson can blood teach us? To learn from experience? Has anyone ever learnt anything from the blood, the experience of others?

But dying of cancer, of t.b., in one's bed – is there any more sense in that? Dying is one's own business. To die *of* something, futile, idiotic. To die *for* something, the only justification.

Why aren't you out there, where men are dying?

★

On this same morning the Ottakring Arbeiterheim fell to the enemy.

During the night an assault by armoured cars supported by machine guns and artillery had failed to break the resistance. At one a.m. Fey had arrived at the scene of battle and had ordered the operation to be called off until dawn and the arrival of reinforcements.

Early in the morning the wireless announced:

The Federal Government has the situation completely under control. The general strike planned by the Marxists has failed miserably. The gas, electricity, water supply and telephone services are functioning fully and the public transport system is operating. All that remains to be done is to smoke the red criminals out of the last of their nests.

At seven-thirty a.m. heavy howitzers and mortars began to bombard the Ottakring Arbeiterheim whose defence was being conducted by old Albert Sever. At eight-thirty Fey reappeared again. At nine-thirty the order was given to storm the building. The gates were forced open; with bayonets fixed and sinking hearts the soldiers pressed forward into the shattered building. It was an invasion into silence. The place was empty. In one room they found a dead woman, in the next one another woman, Frau Ida Sever, at the point of death. Slumped over the window sill the body of a man. The Schutzbund defenders had escaped through the sewers. In the cellars the victorious invaders found terrified women and children upon whom they revenged themselves for the men's resistance.

At nine a.m. the bombardment of the Karl-Marx-Hof began.

Schutzbund forces who had assembled in Meidling during the night began to move forward towards the Margaretengürtel. This had been only lightly manned since the storming of the Reumannhof on the evening of 12 February, after which the soldiers and police had been transferred elsewhere. Was the Schutzbund going over to the offensive?

Josef Spanner, commander of the 'Kreta' Schutzbund battalion, was assembling his forces in the Quellenhof in order to go into the attack. But meanwhile a battle command consisting of Otto Bauer, Julius Deutsch and – up till midday 13 February – the municipal councillor Speiser – had been set up in the 'Gartenstadt', a municipal housing estate on the outskirts of the city near the 'Spinnerin am Kreuz'. They ordered the Schutzbund in the Quellenhof to stay where they were and defend the building. The battle command also rejected out of hand a further proposal of Spanner's, namely that an ultimatum be presented to the government forces, then concentrated in police headquarters: either these forces must capitulate and lay down their arms, or the building would be blown up by the Schutzbund's 'Sewer Brigade'.

My brother Walter, now a doctor and living on the Laaerberg, was much respected – indeed loved – by all the inhabitants of Favoriten. He told me that when the electricity was suddenly cut off on 12 February he went to see Draskovich, a spirited and active member of the left-wing opposition who at the time was unemployed. 'I told him the balloon had gone up,' Walter continued, 'and also that, although the battle was pretty well lost in advance, we had to do everything in our power to win. When we rang up the district party office, the district secretary – the municipal councillor Hiess – yelled down the telephone: "Don't bother me with that! It's nothing to do with me. It's the Schutzbund's business." We heard later that the Schutzbund district commander, Sispela, had surrendered the Schutzbund's main arms depot in the Arbeiterheim to the police. Other arms depots had either already been raided by the police or were inaccessible to the Schutzbund because those who held the keys were not to be found. When the police wanted to seize the weapons in the Kennergasse depot, they were forestalled by the Schutzbund under the command of Josef Spanner, whose battalion had assembled in the Quellenhof . . . Draskovich and I tried to mobilize the Laaerberg Schutzbund, at first without success because the battalion commander had not yet returned from work. Meanwhile we transferred the Schutzbund detachments in Oberlaa and Leopoldsdorf to the Laaerberg. The police had been withdrawn from the Laaerberg station as they had from the other stations in Favoriten, and had been concentrated at district headquarters. When the Schutzbund commander came home at midday, arms were issued to the Laaerberg detachment which was composed mainly of unemployed.'

The Schutzbund men in the Quellenhof, demoralized by long and pointless waiting, by wireless announcements about the collapse of the resistance and by news that the battle command in the 'Gartenstadt' had ceased to exist, decided to go home. On the Laaerberg a few dozen Jungfront and Wehrsport members together with a number of Young Socialists had set up barricades of dustbins and other objects. Josef Brüll, the secretary of the industrial employees' trade union, assumed command of this small band and hit on the idea of setting up mock machine guns in the old trenches that still survived from 1866. The 'guns' consisted in sheets of cardboard with stout sticks thrust through the centre.

The Laaerberg with its old trenches and its cardboard machine guns has become a legend, thanks to the revolutionary determination and the cohesive spirit of the workers who manned them. Not until 15 February did the Government dare attack the Laaerberg, sending in seven battalions of infantry, five batteries of artillery, and a number of armoured cars supported by police and Heimwehr, the whole under the command of the Minister of War, Fürst von Schönberg-Hartenstein. Step by step, the troops advanced in extended order. When they finally rushed the Laaerberg, not a single armed man was to be seen; those with jobs had returned to their work, the rest had dispersed across the plain, either singly or in small groups. All that the conquerors were able to lay hands on were a few cardboard machine guns . . .

★

Late one afternoon we met Käthe Leichter and other comrades in a café. 'Has anyone been in touch with Otto Bauer?' we asked. From Käthe Leichter's evasive reply we could only assume that the rumour of the leaders's flight was not mere idle gossip. In actual fact Bauer and Deutsch had gone to ground in Vienna. It was not till the next day that Otto Bauer was smuggled across the Czech frontier in disguise. Julius Deutsch, too, succeeded in getting out of the country and thus escaping trial.

Almost more upsetting than our leaders' defection was the senseless jumble of rumours, hopes and fears. I caught myself in the act of telling an American, or perhaps a British, journalist that things might well take a turn for the better, that Schutzbund men were rallying for an attack on the inner city and that the battle was by no means lost; no sooner had these words been spoken than what had been little more than wishful thinking became a newspaper story.

Even as I told the journalist that all hope was not lost, I was unable to suppress the nagging doubt that I was deluding myself no less than others, that I didn't really believe what I was saying. And all those arguments after the event – *if* there had been a resolute and experienced command, *if* the Schutzbund had occupied the radio station or the Bisamberg transmitter, *if* the demolition squad had blown up police headquarters or the bridges – all these hypotheses were concerned with questions of secondary importance. February 1934 had been lost in March 1933.

'Under Social Democratic leadership victory is not possible,' I said on the evening of 13 February, after we had taken refuge in Mauer outside Vienna, in the house of Herbert von Meyenburg, manager of the Viennese branch of Chlorodont. But hadn't the C.P.A. also failed, as the C.P. in Germany had so disastrously failed before it? And, come to that, had we of the left-wing opposition shown ourselves capable of becoming a leading force at the crucial hour? On the one hand, the gallant fight of a few thousand Schutzbund men, on the other, the political ineptitude of all the groups of the left – such was the state of affairs in February 1934.

Herbert von Meyenburg had been the first red blot on his highly respected family's escutcheon. Ruth was the second. Herbert, whom the October Revolution had converted to Communism, had put his intelligence and labour power at the disposal of the new Soviet state but had later turned away in disillusionment. Now he worked as the Vienna representative of his domineering uncle, owner and managing director of the Chlorodont factory in Dresden.

It was Ruth who thought of asking him to put us up and I agreed on the grounds that outside the Vienna police district I should have greater freedom of movement and a better opportunity to bring together the nucleus of a left-wing opposition. The idea proved mistaken. Kind, cooperative and sympathetic though Herbert von Meyenburg was, he quite manifestly did not wish to become involved. But this was not the worst; on the morning of 14 February the city boundary was being closely watched and all those entering or leaving it, whether on foot or by car, were being subjected to a thorough scrutiny by the police. In the circumstances it was impossible to ask members of the left-wing opposition to come out to Mauer; on top of this Meyenburg said that he couldn't possibly risk sending me into Vienna either in his own car or in one belonging to the firm.

Yet another evening spent beside the wireless, listening to waltzes and marches interspersed with announcements about the collapse of the resistance.

Bruck: the Schutzbund commanded by Koloman Wallisch has been compelled to evacuate the Schlossberg and is retreating across the mountains.

Graz: all firing has ceased. The rebellion is over. Its ringleader, Otto Fischer, is in hospital, gravely wounded. After his leg has been amputated he will be tried before an emergency court.

I left the room, ashamed that others should witness my tears. I thought of my mother, her features rigid with pain when my sister died. And now, all by herself, listening to the news . . .

The news I had heard over the wireless in Meyenburg's house paralysed my powers of resolution. That morning, as already related, Meyenburg had not allowed me to drive into the city. Ruth had gone in on her own, informed my mother that I was safe and returned with the news that my brother Walter had been arrested. She also passed on to me my mother's request that I should not uselessly expose myself to danger.

Uselessly? Wasn't everything useless now, I asked myself. None the less, and despite my mother's plea and Ruth's objection that I was too well-known, too readily recognizable, I wanted to discuss possibilities and consider decisions with members of the left-wing opposition. I wanted to have nothing to do with Social Democracy, however, and was dubious about the usefulness of an alliance with the C.P.A. Would this mean an independent organization? What would its chances be, and what its future?

★

In my hide-out in Mauer I no longer believed in the future. At first I planned to make my way on foot across country to the Laaerberg, but gave up this idea on learning from Ruth about Walter's arrest. (In fact Walter was still at home and was not arrested until 15 February.)

Back to the wireless then, blaring out the *Radetzky March* and little gigolo, my poor gigolo, times have changed since I first saw you, riding down the street, soldierly and neat, didn't all the girls adore you? and in Floridsdorf all resistance has ceased, and play gypsy, play gypsy, songs that I love, and the Schutzbund commander Korbel has ordered all Schutzbund members to refrain from acts of violence and has appealed for clemency on behalf of all those who have been led into regrettable excesses by the party leadership, and all the world is gold and blue, my darling, just for me and you, and don't switch off your sets, the Federal Chancellor is about to make an important speech and what do you do with your knee, little Hans, when you dance? and the red criminals are being cleared out of the last of their nests, and stand by for an important announcement, the Federal Chancellor and just to be, to be, to be head over heels in love, and the pride of the infantry, great is our fame, Hoch- und Deutschmeister our regiment's name, and stand by for the Federal Chancellor, and call, call, Vienna mine, call night and day with your songs divine, and stand by, and at long last, at eleven p.m., eight hours after the first announcement washed up on a tide of waltzes, spewed out by marches, the voice of the Federal Chancellor:

I, the Chancellor, now declare that the Government is prepared to give you one more chance. Anyone who from now, eleven p.m. onwards, refrains completely from all illegal and hostile acts and who tomorrow, Tuesday, between seven a.m. and twelve a.m., surrenders to the organs of the Government, will – with the exception of the leaders responsible – be able to take advantage of an amnesty. After twelve a.m. tomorrow there will be no amnesty for anyone whomsoever.

And a fine amnesty it proved to be!

On 15 February Herbert von Meyenburg brought us the morning newspapers.

The *Neues Wiener Journal* gave a description of Karl Münich-reiter's execution. Gravely wounded, he was carried into court on a stretcher, the police surgeon declared him fit to stand trial – 'despite his injuries not seriously incapacitated in the eyes of the law' – and, after cursory proceedings, he was condemned to death by hanging.

2.41 p.m.: beside the gallows stands the executioner. He wears a black robe, a black hat and black gloves. The court officials have assembled at the scene of execution, Oberlandesgerichtsrat Kreuzhuber, his fellow judges, the lawyer Dr Wachsmann, the police surgeon and a priest. The sentence is read over again. The corners of the man's mouth twitch. As the hangman draws the noose tight around his throat, Münichreiter shouts Marxist slogans. The hangman's assistants who, all this while, have been holding the man upright, pull the ladder from under his twitching feet. At the end of seven and a half minutes the police surgeon pronounces him dead.

'Long live Socialism! Freedom!' Such, we learnt later, were the 'Marxist slogans' shouted by Münichreiter before he died.

On the same day, 14 February, at 9.43 p.m., the chief of the Floridsdorf fire station, thirty-five-year-old Georg Weissel, was condemned to death by hanging.

'After your courageous admissions concerning yourself,' said the judge, 'I shall not press you to incriminate others.'

Weissel's last words were: 'Long live the International!'

★

On 15 February the checkpoints were removed from the city boundary. The battle was over. Under the leadership of Heinz Roscher, a powerful dynamo of a man, sixty-seven members of the Floridsdorf Schutzbund armed with three machine guns escaped across the Marchfeld in a forced march of nearly fifteen hours and fought their way through to the Czech frontier. Ten of their number, who had dropped out exhausted, were taken prisoner by the gendarmerie.

In the Karl-Marx-Hof armed resistance suddenly flared up again. At eleven-thirty the Schutzbund hoisted a white flag in one of the windows and then escaped from the building through the sewers.

Ruth and I drove into the city in a Chlorodont delivery van.

We debated where to go.

To Canetti's in the first place. On the way there, no longer in the van but on foot, walking along the Fernandstrasse, I was twice hailed by name: 'Hallo, Ernst! What are *you* doing here?' These incidents lent substance to the argument that I was ill-suited to illegal activities.

Ruth had devised a plan which she now explained to me. Our presence in his flat was endangering Canetti. There was the possibility to be considered that the police would go hunting for me among my friends. She would therefore ask her old friends Hans Schlesinger and the dancer Cilly Wang to put me up, while she herself went to Prague to obtain a passport for me. Hans Schlesinger came from the same town as Ruth, Teplitz-Schönau. He had been in love with her and had dedicated poems and sundry other writings to her. Now he lived with Cilly Wang, an exceptionally able mimic, whose eccentric humour and caustic wit recalled some elemental spirit, possibly Puck. As I hardly knew them, Ruth thought it unlikely that the police would search for me in their flat. After a short stay with Canetti, I became the guest of Ruth's friends.

★

On 2 March Ruth returned from Prague with a passport belonging to Hans Burger, the film director. Since Burger was dark, Cilly Wang dyed my hair and the moustache I had recently grown. On 3 March we left for Prague.

For many years I continued to reproach myself with cowardice because of this flight.

Was I a coward?

Although today I judge myself more severely than ever I did in the past, I do not believe that the accusation of cowardice is applicable. I was not afraid of death. Nor of imprisonment; my only fear was of torture, and there was little likelihood of that. A rigorous cross-examination of myself would seem to suggest that I was motivated less by fear than by revulsion at the thought of being seized upon, trampled, kicked. Even as a child, when riding in a tram, I had shrunk from all physical contact with strangers, from any kind of throng as the first stage of being squashed. But this revulsion was not the decisive factor.

What drove me into exile was the consciousness of having failed. Against my own wishes, I had found myself at the head of a political movement. I was quite unsuited to the role that had been thrust upon me, having none of the attributes essential to a political leader. I can influence people, rouse them, convince them, but I cannot organize their activities. I knew then that I was not even remotely qualified to build up an illegal organization.

During the early days in Prague we lived in a cheap hotel. Then Ruth went to visit her parents in Teplitz-Schönau and I moved into an unfurnished room in the Verdunska.

Franz Schuster arrived from Vienna and upbraided me for having made off. While admitting that the police were searching for me and that my appearance was too striking for me to remain incognito for any length of time, he insisted that there was much that could not be decided without me.

I made no bones about telling him that I was not cut out to be a political leader and felt unequal to the position allocated to me; hence I intended in future to participate in the anti-Fascist struggle solely in the capacity of writer. He retorted that I had no right to do this, that I had already assumed a role, and that it would be difficult to find a successor for me. Mine was a responsibility that could not be shrugged off. He went on to tell me that the left-wing opposition had begun to organize itself on an illegal basis as the Red Front, of which some members wished to join forces with the C.P. while others expressed a preference for autonomy. Since yet another organization was being set up by the Revolutionary Socialists, as successors to the Social Democrats, a clear decision was now called for.

I asked Schuster whether there was any trend towards a joint organization, a new left-wing Socialist party. Far from it, he replied, for no one in the left-wing opposition desired a return to Social Democracy, and neither the C.P. nor the Revolutionary Socialists showed the slightest inclination to join forces and form a new party. This meant that, unless the Red Front adopted an unequivocal position, its members would either lose interest or leave it for the C.P., or join the Revolutionary Socialists. How about the National Socialists, I asked? That was another point to be considered, Schuster said, for they were attracting an appreciable number of Schutzbund members. I remarked that the existence of three separate parties in the left-wing underground showed a serious lack of unity. Schuster concurred, adding: 'Whatever you decide will point the way for a great many others. You can't simply abdicate.'

I allowed myself to be persuaded.

Together we deliberated: although for the time being the

Revolutionary Socialists appeared to be more radical even than the Communist Party, there still remained at their backs the inert, silent mass of what had once been Social Democracy, a mass which, in the event of a Fascist collapse, would absorb the now activist avant-garde; hence there was very little prospect of a genuine 'new beginning'. And if we were to join forces with the C.P. – join *forces* with, not merely join, it – would there be any hope of overcoming the sectarian spirit, of engendering a new revolutionary mass party? Dimitrov's conduct in the Supreme Court appeared to provide grounds for such a hope. Moreover, in the final analysis, any form of anti-Fascist policy that excluded the Soviet Union was an absurdity. The C.P. then?

Dito Pölzl, a member of the Wagner–Biro factory's works council, who had emigrated from Graz after the February battles, suggested that I should meet the General Secretary of the C.P.A., Johann Koplenig, who had been living in Prague for some weeks.

Still I hesitated. But was there any convincing alternative? Given the circumstances, was not amalgamation with the C.P. the only possible course? And if I were to advocate such a move, would I have the right to stand aside instead of devoting myself wholeheartedly to the policy of a united front?

Fully conscious that I was opting for the cause and against myself, against my capabilities and my inclinations, I joined the Communist Party in April 1934.

III

MOSCOW

15

Crossing the Frontier

Crossing the frontier . . .

Never before, never again was this feeling so quintessential as on 24 April, when we crossed the frontier into the Soviet Union.

The Schutzbund members who had taken refuge in Czechoslovakia had been invited to Moscow by the central council of the Soviet trade unions. A few days before my companions' departure I was informed that the Soviet comrades would welcome my inclusion in the party.

Behind us lay the Polish frontier post, ostentatiously smart, shop windows full of goods for tourists only, haughtiness and hypocrisy: refined Europe, the West, dismisses you, dirty Bolshevists that you are.

Negoreloye, the Soviet frontier post, its dowdiness hardly less ostentatious, its proletarian poverty unconcealed, received us with warmth, cordiality and a brass band playing the *Internationale*.

At the time, I wrote of this arrival:

The archway dividing one world from the other: 'Workers of the world unite!' and on the other side: 'Communism tears down all frontiers!' The first Red Army men, soldiers of the victorious Revolution. Flags over the railway. A sense of elation: here is a country with the *Internationale* for her anthem, a country where all those things are triumphant for which men in the capitalist countries are shot, beaten up and imprisoned. We are here not as guests but as people visiting their homeland.

For all its sentimentality this was genuine, yet it fails to convey the real pathos of the experience. Crossing the frontier, homecoming into the unknown, arriving in one's homeland. Even today as I

write this my emotions, my sense of excitement, are almost as intense as they were then.

Crossing the frontier . . .

Moscow.

The *Internationale* which greets us on the platform has a mightier
ring to it than at Negoreloye.

Then we emerge into the big square in front of the Byelorussian
Station.

Was this Moscow?

Our eyes noted the dingy grey of the dilapidated buildings. And
grey, too, the faces of the ill-dressed, morose-looking people awaiting
us, some of them factory delegates, some of them rubbernecks
curious to see the legendary foreigners who had fought for Socialism
at the barricades. And the flags were grey, grey not red. We saw it
with our eyes. But our hearts replied: you're lying. The flags are
red, the faces aglow with welcome and the buildings are no different
from those in any other station square.

Such was the dichotomy at the very start: the two faces of
reality.

You're coming, I said to myself, from a world you reject to this
other one you have always accepted, to a faraway place obviously
quite unlike anything you've previously experienced. Now, when
you crossed the frontier, it was with the determination to bring
about a radical change in yourself, to renounce all scepticism,
individualism, intellectualism. You couldn't expect perfection of
this counter-world by which you have now been adopted. You came
in the knowledge that it would be immature, uncompleted, an
impoverished, inchoate world. For the first time it confronts you
not as a vision but as reality. But what is reality?

The flags are grey, my eyes do not deceive me. But they *ought* to
be red; perhaps after all my eyes are deceiving me. They *are* red,
though a little faded, a little worn and dusty. The Revolution has
shaken the world, stirring up the dust of centuries which has settled
on the flags, on the drawn, weary faces. It would have been different
had we in Europe not left the Revolution in the lurch, had *we* been
different, shown greater courage, greater selflessness and solidarity.
We are the guilty ones. And instead of seeing the flags as grey,
instead of being disappointed, which you have no right to be, you
should keep your guilt ever before your eyes, your duty to make up

for past errors. Learn to look at things differently, to see them as better than you've been taught to do! In *reality* these flags are red; and the new day you're facing would have been a brighter one had you helped to bring about its dawning.

It was in this twofold light, in this twofold image that I saw Moscow after arriving at the Byelorussian Station.

I had, though I could not have guessed it, come at a time of radical structural change in Soviet society and the Communist Party of the Soviet Union. To me, this party was the party of Lenin, of the Old Bolsheviks, of revolutionary impetus, having all the radiance of major historical achievement – to me, it was all these things in a period when it was ceasing to be so, when under the old name, the old substance was disappearing, when the power of a terroristic apparatus was on the increase. The erstwhile Social Democrat, determined with all his heart and soul to assent, seeing Moscow for the first time, knowing no one, unaware of factions or conflict, was hardly in a position to interpret the transformation and distortion taking place before his eyes. One historical period, that of revolution, had not yet drawn to a close, the new period of absolute domination by the power apparatus was only just beginning. The puritanical heroism of ruthless industrialization still displayed revolutionary features. The saying then current: 'We've not spared our strength!' had yet to become an empty catchphrase. Trotsky was in exile but most of the Old Bolsheviks were still in prominent positions. Bukharin was the chief editor of *Izvestia*, Pyatakov was in charge of the People's Commissariat for Heavy Industry, Zinoviev, Kamenyev and Radek still made their voices heard, appeared in public. We received an invitation to the Old Bolsheviks' club. There was nothing grey about this meeting. We were breathing the very air of the Revolution. The flags were red.

To be sure, the party was no longer the party of Lenin but it was not yet a party that venerated the dead Lenin while devitalizing his work, replacing the dialectic of the Revolution with bureaucratic pragmatism. The party, like the Revolution, had become a myth, not as yet a dogma. But in myth reality is preserved, experience continues to be effective, a living, not hidebound, answer to essential questions, a malleable because living answer. It is only in ritual, only in dogma that what is dead and desiccated lies in state, is placed on display as something sacrosanct, immutable, unassailable. This ritualization and dogmatization, this reduction to the 'Marxist–Leninist' canon of what Marx, Engels and Lenin had thought, had tested in practice, continuously developed, expounded and modified – this process now taking place was something I suspected on occasion but failed entirely to grasp.

Contradiction was eliminated and hence dialectic and hence, too, Marxism. According to the doctrine, the new society had overcome class antagonism; it was no longer developing within a magnetic field of antagonistic forces. In principle it was harmonious, every conflict could be resolved – was not, therefore, tragic. The occasional contradictions that emerged could be overcome by rationality, by the wisdom of the party. The party leadership was historical reason, all-provident Providence. It was infallible.

When today I try to understand, to relate, how it was that, intellectually and emotionally, I succumbed to such undialectical *simplisme*, I am horrified by the self I then became. Nevertheless the distortion was perfectly explicable. Little fault could be found with my determination not to be taken in by appearances – grey, cheerless, overbearing, authoritarian – but rather to discover behind these alienating attributes the revolutionary substance and to identify myself with it. It was impossible for someone arriving in this unknown world to find his way about on his own. He was dependent on the help of others if he was to catch up on what they had experienced together, achieved together – dependent on shrewd instruction, on friendly advice. He came to know people in whom he could have confidence and others whom he found repugnant. Crucial to his attitude was the fact that, even in his very earliest encounters and discussions, he seemed to descry the conflict of two viewpoints: one fanatically upholding the traditional policy of the Communist Parties, the other searching for fresh concepts, striving for renewal . . .

We were accommodated in communal quarters. Allotted to us as 'supervisors' were a few Russians, but most were Germans and Hungarians.

'Well now, Comrade Fischer, what's it like on the other side of the barricades?'

The man who put this question to me in tones of ironic condescension was a German Communist. I cannot recall whether at that time he had already started work with the periodical *Kommunistische*

Internationale. At all events he was later a member of the editorial staff.

Taken aback, I answered: 'What d'you mean on the "other" side? I can't imagine what you're trying . . .'

'You were a Social Democrat until very recently weren't you?'

'There's no secret about that. But why did you mention the other side of the barricades? The ones standing on the other side were the Fascists, not us.'

'But you can't deny that Social Democracy was the mainstay of the bourgeoisie.'

'What was that you said?' shouted one of the Schutzbund men.

'I don't mean you. You realized what had to be done, a bit late, but better late than never. It's the Social Democratic leaders I'm talking about.'

'What we think of those leaders is our own affair. But where were *your* leaders, come to that? Which side of the barricades were *you* on? We took up arms against Dollfuss – too late, admittedly. But you in Germany, what did you do?'

Then the uproar began.

'Why did you people come to Moscow, then?'

'To learn from the Russians, don't you understand, from the Russians, not the Germans.'

The German Communist turned to me. 'And what have you to say to that?'

'I know that after the Reichstag fire you were without leaders and that by then it was perhaps already too late.'

'Only our enemies could have wanted us to send our cadres to senseless slaughter.'

'Agreed. But what was going on before that? To you, we Social Democrats were Social-Fascists – you made no distinction. Was that right? Was that revolutionary policy?'

'Ideologically speaking,' the German Communist said, 'you're still standing on the other side of the barricades.'

That was my first tussle with him. We remained adversaries. To me he embodied the principle of obstinacy, of pig-headed ortho-doxy, a principle with which I took issue as I took issue with Com-munist arrogance, self-delusion and rigidity, turning instead to all that was by contrast not only more reasonable but more friendly, prepared to accept one newly arrived from Social Democracy as a comrade with equal rights.

Once, in the middle of the heated diurnal discussion about the February battles, about political, strategic and tactical mistakes, in the midst of a dispute in which Schutzbund members not only criticized but cursed the Social Democratic leaders, while angrily contesting the right of the German Communists to chip in with uncalled-for advice, there came a shout: 'Comrade Fischer! Is Comrade Fischer here? Comrade Manuilsky wants to see him at once. The car's waiting.'

I drove to the Comintern, to the old, somewhat unimposing building opposite the Manège and flanked by the wall of the Kremlin. Hitherto the Communist International had been something vast, no more than a vague form on the horizon of world politics. That it should have suddenly materialized, become a building, the Comintern, with porters, passes, labyrinthine stairs and corridors, then more porters, more passes, was in no way a disappointment, on the contrary, I had never been so excited in my life. Only a few days ago I had crossed the frontier into the Soviet Union and now I was entering the Comintern – it was the almost physical experience of leaving further and further behind a self to which I had grown accustomed, but had never really felt happy in, a piece of unwanted baggage left to roll away down the steep slope while I, relieved of this burden, climbed upwards, a self not yet formed but already outlined and predetermined by my decision.

Manuilsky came towards me, all amiability and charm, in emphatic contrast to the brusque manner of many Communists.

Everything about him appealed to me: his easy unaffected manner, his shrewd face, his dark, unusually alert eyes, attentive, intelligent, quick and wily and, every now and again, some unfathomable, unexpressed sadness – barely perceptible as a backdrop to a stage on which a rapid succession of ideas, aims, combinations, deliberations, premeditated effects and spontaneous wit executed a ballet that compelled the attention of his interlocutor. Not for one moment did I doubt that Manuilsky *wanted* me to find him agreeable, that it was his intention to win me over, and I was already half won over simply because I knew it to be a game – a game whose object was not to instruct the 'newcomer' pedantically but rather to make him say to himself: here you're among friends.

'I asked you to come on your own and I thank you for coming. Would you be kind enough to answer a few questions without trying to spare anybody at all? Did the Communist Party of Austria fail during the February battles?'

Was it a straightforward question? The shrewd, wide-awake eyes were observing me. A faint twinkle, the hint of a smile: 'Well, *did* it fail?'

'We all failed – apart from those fighting in the Schutzbund. The Social Democrats, the left-wing opposition, the C.P.A. – all of them failed.'

'Did the C.P.A. play a leading role?'

'It couldn't have done. But there were Communists who linked up with the Schutzbund in the fighting.'

'And before that? Was the C.P.A.'s line the correct one?'

'I rather think not.'

'Ought we to disband the C.P.A.? Constitute a new party? Tell me frankly what you think.'

Uncertain what Manuilsky meant by this question, whether it was merely to put me to the test or whether wider considerations were involved, I replied: 'I joined the C.P.A. and I believe our task should be to unite the revolutionary forces of the Austrian working class within the party.'

'Do you really believe that or are you merely saying so out of loyalty? Hasn't it sometimes occurred to you that a *new* party might be better able to gain the confidence of the Austrian workers?'

'Such thoughts did occur to me, perhaps they still do; all the same there are stronger arguments in favour of consolidating, enlarging and, to some extent, renewing the existing C.P.A.'

'What do you mean by that?'

'Previously the C.P.A. had never taken root in the masses; in some respects it was a sect. If there were now to be an influx of revolutionary factory workers and Schutzbund and Jungfront members, the disadvantages inherent in too small a party would soon be overcome. Believe me, Comrade Manuilsky, we'll do everything, everything in our power to make possible the complete fusion of the left-wing opposition with the C.P.A. And when I speak of renewal, please don't misunderstand me: we make no claims whatever to leadership, we don't feel ourselves to be the new men, we're adaptable and our one wish is that the concept of old

Communists and new Communists should be abandoned, that equal rights should receive more than just formal acknowledgement.'

'Is this a complaint? If it is, I – we, are here to give help and advice.'

'It *isn't* a complaint, nor are there any grounds for one. But it *is* a problem and it could turn out to be dangerous.'

Manuilsky observed me thoughtfully, in his shrewd, alert eyes a glimmering of something very like warmth.

'Do you really feel you are a Communist? Forgive the indiscreet question. I'm not asking it because I mistrust you, quite the contrary.'

'I'm determined to become one.'

'To be a Communist is often not easy. Are you hard enough? The dictatorship is hard.'

'I accept that hardness.'

'Even though you yourself aren't hard?'

'It's a question of consciousness.'

'And freedom?'

Startled, I looked at my questioner. His expression was grave and expectant. I wondered why he wasn't smiling.

'Mussolini is fond of saying that he has frequently heard the call for bread, never the call for freedom. In this age of iron we should, we must, hear that call. Freedom and the dictatorship of the proletariat are not irreconcilable.'

'Write about it! Write about dictatorship and freedom! We haven't always been attentive to the call for freedom and sometimes we've misunderstood it. Write about your thoughts in your *own* language!'

At that moment the C.P.A.'s Comintern representative, Oskar Grossmann, was announced.

'Excuse me, Comrade Manuilsky,' he said breathlessly as he came in, 'they didn't let me know . . .'

'I wanted to speak to Comrade Fischer *alone*. But you're not disturbing us. We have no secrets. Comrade Fischer has convinced me that the C.P.A. hasn't made only mistakes.'

This conversation with Manuilsky helped me tremendously in 'restructuring' myself in accordance with the new world, as the elaboration of the self along new lines would now be called. In this new world of building-sites, of ill-dressed, hard-working, undernourished men and women, of *besprizorni** roaming the streets, of patient queues in front of stores, newspaper kiosks and tram stops, of dreary shop windows with their busts of Lenin and Stalin, of blaring loudspeakers, of grandiose hopes, of wooden houses amidst the reinforced concrete, of drink and discipline, of privation and optimism, of misery and learning, in this rubble of the past, in these difficult birth-pangs of the future others, too, were striving to make the correlations clear to us. I am thinking particularly of Jakov Mirov, one of Manuilsky's two political secretaries (the other was Ernö Gerö, a Hungarian of vast intellect but lacking in compassion).

Mirov was one of those Russian Jews whose existence presages a human race that has yet to exist. 'He's a hopeless person,' his wife would occasionally say in some concern but with enormous affection. 'He's always so clever on behalf of others and so stupid when it comes to himself. He'll never go far.' And so it was. Invariably thinking for others, he never had time for himself. He never forgot what he had undertaken to do for others but was self-forgetful, in the radical sense of the word, in all matters concerning his own person. He never did go far, no farther than the friends who loved him, no farther than restarting something that had come to a standstill, one step forward, a tiny step acclaimed by none yet without which the Soviet Union might have collapsed – without the minute steps made by the country's unacknowledged Mirovs. I once found him playing with an alarm clock, shaking his head and every so often bursting into peals of astonished laughter. 'We've begun to manufacture our own alarm clocks – in Leningrad. A man from the Schutzbund gave it to me. How on earth d'you think a person is going to get to work on time? You see, it's not only the hour hand that moves, not a bit of it – the alarm hand moves as well, more slowly than the other, so you see, if he sets the alarm hand at six he'll be woken at eight. That sort of thing could only happen here, that's the sort of people we are. But then again, October 1917 could only have happened here.'

On May Day the Austrians who had been invited to Moscow took part in the parade in the Red Square.

Standing on the reviewing platform were Stalin, Molotov and Kaganovich, together with the leading men of the party, the state

---

*Children, victims of enforced collectivization, who had strayed away from their villages and were parentless and uncared for.

and the army. As we marched past, Molotov pointed at us; Stalin and some of the others laughed. We were too far away to hear, but we could *see* that they were roaring with laughter. As likely as not it had nothing to do with us but nevertheless the incident jarred on me. Above all it was Stalin, his bearing, his movements, that I tried to imprint on my mind. I was determined to identify him with the Revolution, with the Soviet Union, with the future of us all. What displeased me about him I cannot say – perhaps it was just that he had laughed. Yet it may have been this initial movement of recoil on my part which led me, in my own mind, to exaggerate, to magnify his stature. I blamed myself, not him, for the alien quality I discovered in him. Too coarse, I mocked, not refined or spiritual enough for the petit-bourgeois intellectual, the neurotic Bohemian who, in a crucial situation, fails to come up to scratch. Here you have no right to criticize. Your duty is to surpass yourself.

A few years previously, in 1928, I had written an article entitled 'The Trotsky Tragedy':

Lenin is dead. The Revolution is now stabilized. The name of Lenin's successor is not Trotsky but Stalin . . . The Trotsky tragedy is the tragedy of the Revolution, the tragedy of the dictatorship . . . The dictatorship was the armour, the weapon, the apparatus of the Revolution. And now the Revolution is suffocating in this armour, now the weapon is turned against it, now it is being crushed by the apparatus. Stalin is right: Soviet Russia needs the economic policy he advocates, a Trotskyist dictatorship would be disastrous. But can the party forgo everything that Trotsky embodies? Can it reject the spirit of the old guard? Can it dispense with the flame of 1917? Can it really afford Trotsky's exclusion, however imperative that exclusion may be? Is a party which forbids the conflict of opinions, which does not combine in its ranks both Trotsky and Stalin – human names for profound historical antitheses! – is such a party a pledge for a living future? That is the question. Events, not theories, will provide the answer.

This article, written with more verve than knowledge, characterized by polemical over-simplification rather than historical analysis, contained an inkling of the truth, but it was above all an attempt to do justice to two personalities as the representatives of two epochs.

On 1 May 1934 I saw Stalin for the first time. Had I known what we know today I would never have decided to regard him as the incarnation of Socialism; to some extent that decision was subjectively conditioned, as a suppression of the critical, anarchical intellectual in me, as a verdict against a self to whom any form of authority was abhorrent. Since, however, Stalin has become a myth, a symbol for millions, personal motives alone are not enough to account for my attitude.

Man's need to see historical processes not in terms of anonymous forces alone but also in terms of actual personalities is particularly urgent at times of revolutionary upheaval. Thus the development of the French Revolution is seen in terms of personalities – Danton, Robespierre and Napoleon – and their dramatic rivalries; and thus, too, the development of the Russian Revolution which, after Lenin's death, became manifest in the struggle between Stalin and Trotsky, is seen as a tragedy whose protagonists are living people rather than events. Whatever sympathy may have been felt for his defeated rival, in the consciousness of millions of people (with whom I hesitantly associated myself) Stalin's victory was the victory of Socialism in the Soviet Union. This was partly due to the fact that he was a master of simplistic argument so that even today, despite all that we have since learnt, many of his speeches are extraordinarily impressive. And propaganda, too, the systematic glorification and deification of Stalin, did not fail to have its effect. What turned intellectuals such as myself into admirers of Stalin, however, was not the 'personality cult' which tended, indeed, to repel us. Above all we succumbed to this *simplisme* which so greatly facilitated the adoption of a point of view in contradictory situations, for nothing is more difficult than at all times to reconcile the critical reason of the thinker with the *élan*, the all or nothing, of the man of action. The Soviet Union, so the argument ran, whatever her merits or demerits, is the only Socialist country. Every blow that is aimed at her is a blow aimed at Socialism. The Soviet Union is represented by Stalin; every attack on him is an attack on the Soviet Union. It was simple, terribly simple, the total suppression of the critical faculty, but in terms of dynamism it was an asset. I am offering no excuses, for the suppression of the critical faculty is inexcusable; but to learn never to suppress it without a corresponding loss of efficiency is not easy.

The fact that I, like millions of others, succumbed to the Stalin myth was due not only to the complexity of the circumstances but also to my personal weakness. In order to function I had always to overstimulate my nervous system, to exaggerate reality, to outwit myself.

Each time I extolled Stalin it meant silencing a dissentient voice inside myself. I silenced this dissentient voice in order to conserve energy and so concentrate the quota at my disposal on the needs of the day. It was for the sake of the cause and to respond to the demands of the age, in so far as my modest resources allowed, that I crossed the frontier between the capitalist world and the promised land of Socialism, the frontier between reality and hope.

16

Dimitrov

On 27 February 1934 an aircraft landed in Moscow. It had flown from Berlin and on board was a man who, twelve days earlier, had become a Soviet citizen: Georgi Dimitrov.

I saw him for the first time in May 1934 when he addressed the Schutzbund members who had been invited to Moscow. 'Your cause in Austria,' he said on that occasion, 'your armed struggle, would surely have ended in victory had you not lacked two things: a Bolshevik party at your head and a revolutionary orientation among the masses . . .'

It was after this rally that I first spoke to him – of all living persons the one I admired most. This tall man with the dark, luminous eyes beneath an imposing forehead was still suffering from the effects of imprisonment. Nevertheless there was an aura of elemental vitality about him.

'It was a good decision you made. I hope a lot of other Social Democrats will follow your example. The February battles in Vienna and Paris marked the beginning of a new era.'

I would like to have answered: 'As did your behaviour at the Leipzig trial.' But the stature of the man precluded such facile homage.

As an infant Georgi Dimitrov was not destined for greatness; he was no Hercules who kills snakes while yet in the cradle. Nor was he a man whose greatness is the result of slow and steady maturation. He achieved grandeur at one bound, through finding himself in a situation which demanded the utmost in daring, intelligence and consciousness. The eyes of the world were upon him. The German working class had failed to offer armed resistance to Hitler. A

Dutch psychopath, a German Communist deputy and three Bulgarian Communists stood before the Supreme Court in Leipzig on a charge of arson. Everything was admirably stage-managed: the mumbling Van der Lubbe, Ernst Torgler's wary pleading, no sign of anger, of accusation, of rebellion – at this trial the fate of the Weimar Republic, its demoralizing withdrawal in the face of force, was re-enacted once more. And then the unexpected happened. Dimitrov rose to his feet.

The routine questions were asked – 'Name?', 'Date of birth?', 'Nationality?' – only to be dismissed in proud, incisive tones.

I am a proletarian revolutionary. I stress the word 'proletarian' because in these topsy-turvy times even the German Crown Prince proclaims himself a Socialist. I am not that kind of Socialist. I am a revolutionary by conviction, a responsible and leading Communist. But for that very reason I am neither a terroristic adventurer, nor a putschist, nor an incendiary . . .

The interjections of the President of the Court, his nervous, deprecatory gestures, were of no avail. Dimitrov had seized the initiative and he intended to retain it.

'What, actually, do you think you are here for?'

'I am here to defend Communism and myself.'

Dimitrov was not there as an individual but as a representative. He knew it and through the role he assumed, he achieved greatness. A combination of strength, courage and intelligence enabled him to exploit to the utmost the opportunities offered by the situation.

'This Bulgarian seems to have a natural dignity,' *The Times* reported. The greatness of this Bulgarian was self-acquired.

'He's done well,' a leading German Communist said in May 1934. 'The Comintern will take this into consideration, will entrust him with an important job – perhaps make him head of the Central European Department.'

This man, who under a false name had for years represented the Comintern's line in Vienna and Berlin without attracting any particular notice, had at Leipzig become the initiator of a new political strategy. He drew on a forgotten concept to which he gave new life and a richer content. In post-war Bulgaria the Agrarian Federation in alliance with the Communist Party had become the leading force in the country. On 9 June 1923 the Agrarian Government was overthrown by a group of officers with the connivance of the King. Stamboliisky, the Prime Minister, and thousands of his followers were murdered. On that day the Communist Party did not take up arms to defend the democratic Government, nor did it attempt to reinforce its ties with the democratic peasants. Instead it adopted a 'neutral' attitude. It was an attitude that Dimitrov was later to criticize ruthlessly while at the same time accusing himself of sectarian isolationism. When, on 23 September 1923, the Communist Party attempted to redeem its error it was too late. The armed insurrection was crushed. Dimitrov, at the head of one thousand militants, fought his way through to Yugoslavia. Several months after the uprising the Bulgarian authorities condemned him to death.

Now, against his inclinations, he became a man of the apparatus, learning, observing, following the directives of the Comintern. Nevertheless, in the midst of present problems, a warning note was struck by the memory of 9 June 1923, of the disastrous failure of the Communist Party to commit itself in a crucial situation to an alliance with all the forces of democracy. And in the courtroom Dimitrov appealed to the working class over and beyond the heads of the judges: you are on the defensive. The need of the hour is not a frontal attack upon capitalism, but self-defence in the face of the Fascist offensive. What matters is the united front, the rallying of all those whose mortal enemy is Fascism. Goebbels realized what Dimitrov was about and in his evidence he declared: 'My impression is that Dimitrov's intention in this court is to make propaganda for and to defend the Communist and/or Social Democratic Party.' Dimitrov aimed some harsh and well-deserved criticism not only at the Social Democratic leaders but indirectly at those Communists who underrated Fascism and continued to attack the Social Democrats as being the chief enemy. What Dimitrov stressed was the community of interests, and when he spoke of the absolute supremacy of the armaments industry and the Nazi Party, of their war of extermination against popular parties and organizations without exception, he was making a carefully considered statement.

No less significant was Dimitrov's testimony to his fellow countrymen:

Not only have I myself been roundly abused by the press – I am not concerned with that – but, because of me, the Bulgarian nation to which I belong has been described as fanatical and barbaric; I have been referred to as a shady character from the Balkans, as a savage Bulgarian, and that I cannot let pass without comment. It is true that Bulgarian Fascism is fanatical and barbaric in the extreme. But the Bulgarian workers and peasants, their native intelligence, these are not fanatical and barbaric . . . A people that has lived for five hundred years under a foreign yoke without losing either its language or its national identity – a people of that description is not savage and barbaric. The only thing that is savage and barbaric in Bulgaria is Fascism. But I ask you, Mr President, in what country is Fascism not savage and barbaric?

Bünger (the President of the Court): 'You are not, I take it, alluding to conditions in Germany?'

Dimitrov (with a sarcastic smile): 'Of course not, Mr President . . .'

This again struck a new note: the defence of a nation's dignity and its substance against Fascism, the appeal to the working class to rally the nation against its administrators and destroyers.

Dimitrov's overt struggle against the Fascist rulers was simultaneously a covert but unmistakable endeavour to reorientate Communist policy.

Dimitrov won the admiration of many of his political opponents while at the same time arousing the hostility of more than a few Communists.

The King of Bulgaria sent him his greetings but the group then in control of the Communist Party of Bulgaria did their best to consign him to oblivion.

Togliatti, Thorez and others supported Dimitrov in his efforts to bring about a strategic change and wanted to see him at the head of the Comintern, whereas a number of leading German Communists were at most prepared to concede him the directorship of a department.

And when, during the discussions at the Seventh World Congress of the Comintern, Bela Kuhn referred to 'Comrade Zinoviev's speech – I mean Dimitrov's', his slip of the tongue was a sign of the times.

I was too much of a newcomer to be conversant with this subterranean struggle and I knew too little of the ins and outs of the various factions, but even I was aware that a vital decision was at stake. And for me there were no ifs and buts: I was on Dimitrov's side.

The Seventh World Congress of the Comintern, which opened on 25 July 1935 in the Hall of Columns of the Moscow Trade Union Building, revealed this vital decision to the world – the concept of a new revolutionary strategy. The decision was Stalin's. What contributory factors had induced him to accept the new concept, we could only conjecture. That it was in accord with the demands of the world political situation I am as convinced now as I was then. During the world economic crisis the revolutionary forces had been outflanked by the forces of counter-revolution – a circumstance largely attributable to the split in the working class, to Social Democracy's compromise with the capitalist system and to the insularity of the Communists. Fascism was threatening to overrun the continent of Europe; in the U.S.A. the Democratic wing of the bourgeoisie had come to power and embarked on the reformism of the New Deal. The shortsighted tactics of the 'united front from below' which amounted to nothing more than an attempt to erode Social Democracy and incorporate the resulting detritus in the Communist Parties, had not, indeed could not have, been successful. A Fascist Europe would have placed the Soviet Union in mortal peril. To defend democracy was at one and the same time to defend the Soviet Union. Even if Stalin was swayed, in advocating the Popular Front, by the desire to strike out at Trotsky and so pave the way for a purge, such malicious aforethought does nothing to invalidate the new strategy.

In Europe the situation was anything but revolutionary. The postulate that it should change to a revolutionary situation provided a new blueprint for revolution, a carefully studied long-term policy of alliances.

Dimitrov – no mere head of a department but now General Secretary of the Comintern – based his great speech on certain fundamental assumptions:

1. On its own the proletariat cannot achieve victory, an essential prerequisite being an alliance with the agrarian masses and with the intelligentsia; indeed the more advanced the country, the more important the latter alliance.

2. The Communist Party is not the sole representative of the workers; only in exceptional circumstances may it seize and wield power on its

own. [The fact that such absolute rule must in all circumstances be disastrous, though this remained unsaid, had nevertheless become conceivable to Communists.]

3. A policy of alliances is no more to be trifled with than is armed insurrection. An alliance whose purpose is to cheat and deceive one's partner is fundamentally unstable and not particularly effective. The slogan 'Under the leadership of the Communist Party' should be relinquished, and not simply as a slogan. You don't become a leading force by proclaiming yourself as such, but by dint of intelligence, imagination, steadfastness, by your ability to stand the test and by the example that you set.

Dimitrov's speech was followed by a discussion – the more heated for not being publicly conducted – as to whether the change was *strategic* or *tactical*. If tactical it meant winking an eye: let's-change-the-vocabulary-not-the-issue! If strategic, it meant the conviction that something new had started, something with which it was necessary to persevere.

Much of what Dimitrov said at the time has an exciting immediacy:

In our day sectarianism often ceases to be merely a childish complaint, as Lenin put it, and becomes instead a deep-seated vice . . . In the present situation it is *primarily* sectarianism – qualified as *self-complacent* sectarianism in our draft resolution – which is hampering our struggle for the realization of a united front – the kind of sectarianism which rests content with its *doctrinaire narrowness*, with its detachment from the real life of the masses, which rests content with its *simplistic methods*, with ready-made solutions for the labour movement's most complex problems. The kind of sectarianism which lays claim to omniscience, spurning the lessons to be learnt from the masses and from the labour movement. Sectarianism, in short, to which everything is child's play, as the saying goes. In its self-complacency sectarianism *cannot and will not* grasp the fact that the leadership of the working class does not automatically fall to the Communist Party. The leading role of the Communist Party in the struggles of the working class must be earned. This cannot be done by means of proclamations about the leading role of the Communists; it is only daily activity among the masses and a right policy that *will win, will conquer the confidence of the masses of the workers*.

Perhaps it was not possible at the time to follow this thought through to its conclusion, namely that the Communist *Party* is not invariably called upon to assume the leading role, that the very fact of struggle may give rise to a less rigid leadership, that Communists can only lead the masses if they themselves are autonomous and not circumscribed by doctrine or fettered by bureaucratic centralism. As Dimitrov put it:

We are opposed to all schematism. We must take notice of the concrete situation as and where it arises instead of invariably acting in accordance with *one specific formula.* We must not forget that in *varying* circumstances Communists cannot adopt the *same* posture.

It was not for me alone, newly arrived as I was from Social Democracy, that this congress represented almost a *physical* experience of the international working class. At this great gathering the *Internationale* was not merely an anthem, a hope, a concept, it was a presence, visible, palpable reality, continents awakening, masses on the move, hurled back, surging forwards wave upon wave, ever mightier, irresistible. To us, the vanquished of Italy, Germany and Austria, it was as though we were emerging from an abyss into a spaciously unfolding world. And in Paris the masses marched through the city from the Place de la Bastille to the Place de la Nation, the Red Flag and the Tricolor heading the procession of five hundred thousand Communists, Socialists, Radical Socialists, the two trade union federations, all united for the first time, two fallen governments behind them and Laval's as yet to be overthrown, onward to the victory of the Popular Front, the great demonstration of 14 July 1935, only nine Communist deputies in the chamber but outside Parliament the forces of progress for 'we, no less than Léon Blum, the leader of the Socialist Party,' Thorez wrote, 'have worked and planned to make the united front "inevitable" and indeed we have made it inevitable.' And on the other side of the world China's Red Army, having broken through the encircling enemy, the troops of Chiang Kai-shek strategically deployed around it, forced its way from Kiang-si province towards north-west China, the Long March of 2000 miles through nine provinces and across 'high mountain ranges' as Wan Min, the spokesman for the Chinese delegation, put it, without raising the pitch of his voice. 'They crossed trackless wastes and mighty rivers', and he named the rivers: the Wu-kiang, the Yangtze, the Ching-kiang, the Tatu-ho, a note of magic in the matter-of-fact tones of a report. And in Brazil the alliance of workers and students, of peasants and intellectuals, the National Liberation

Alliance, and Luis Carlos Prestes, the legendary 'Knight of Hope', the Communist folk hero, and the struggle of the Asturian miners, the voice of La Pasionaria, restless, flaring, explosive Spain. And behind it all, the Soviet Union, which had evolved from a land of mattocks and wooden ploughs, of illiteracy and indifference, into a major industrial power – and at what cost in sacrifice, deprivation and disruption! Manuilsky spoke of a 'heroic period of Socialist construction', of apparently insuperable difficulties, though not in the form of high mountain ranges, trackless wastes or mighty rivers. 'What we needed,' he said, 'was metal for construction, but there wasn't any,

we needed building materials, but they were in short supply; we needed to move these materials and large numbers of people to new locations but the transport system was inadequate; the building workers and all the other workers had to be provided with food, footwear and clothing; they had to be provided with basic accommodation but there was a shortage of resources and supplies; skilled workers were needed, but where to find all this at such short notice? There were no engineers, no technicians and not even the most elementary technological training was available. From the old régime we had inherited the burden of age-old Russian improvidence, of centuries of indolence, of bureaucratism. And the class enemy took advantage of every mistake made by our young, inexperienced cadres . . . During these years the nerves and muscles of our people were stretched taut like a cable. We were wholly wrapped up in the work of construction. When we thought, we thought in terms of construction figures, when we spoke, we spoke only of construction, when we met together, we discussed it and argued about it, when we slept, we dreamed of nothing else. Everything was subordinated to this one single goal . . .

And the whole was linked with the name of Stalin.
Manuilsky quoted Lenin:

We do not regard Marx's theory as something completed and inviolable; on the contrary, we are convinced that he has only laid the foundation stone of the science which socialists *must* develop in all directions if they wish to keep pace with life.*

And this anti-dogmatic quotation was followed by a panegyric to Stalin, the great and only creative Marxist.

*V. I. Lenin, *Our Programme*, in *Selected Works*, Lawrence & Wishart, 1969, p. 34.

Stalin provides the model for the policy of the proletarian state . . . Stalin elaborates the principles for the policy of the proletarian world party, the Communist International . . . In the light of the experience of the Chinese Revolution Stalin has elaborated the question of how to graft the national-revolutionary movement onto the Soviet Revolution by concrete means. Stalin has raised the teaching of Marx, Engels and Lenin . . . to a new level.

With every spotlight at the congress constantly playing on Stalin, with his name re-echoing from every struggle on every continent, it was virtually impossible to withstand the power of suggestion.

Nevertheless the draft of my speech omitted all reference to Stalin; it was centred entirely round Dimitrov:

At a time when all the leaders of Social Democracy were disseminating a dreadful atmosphere of defeat, when the masses of the German workers were beginning to despair of Socialism, one man stood up . . . His German may have been imperfect but his command of the international language of the proletarian revolution left nothing to be desired. And because of the proud bearing, the boldness and sagacity of this man who, as the victor of tomorrow, confronted the sordid conquerors of today, millions of workers took heart. We shall win, they told themselves, no one can beat us. At that moment one man became the leader of the international working class: Georgi Dimitrov.

The members of the Austrian delegation to whom I showed the draft insisted that a eulogy of Dimitrov without any mention of Stalin was out of the question and indeed might almost be construed as provocation. It would also be desirable, they said, that the speech of one who had come over from Social Democracy should contain some reference to Koplenig, the chairman of the C.P.A. I objected that my spontaneous homage to Dimitrov would thereby be reduced to little more than pious acclaim, but eventually I agreed to include both names.

On 1 December 1934 Kirov, next to Stalin the most popular of the party leaders, had been murdered in Leningrad. It was only after the Twentieth Party Congress of the C.P.S.U. in the summer of 1956 that I discovered that Kirov, not Stalin, had been elected Secretary General of the party by a majority vote of the delegates to the Seventeenth Party Congress. Kirov had requested that the result be reviewed and that Stalin be re-elected. This was done; nevertheless, not only Kirov but the majority of the delegates to the party congress paid with their lives for the outcome of the first secret ballot. Kirov was killed by agents of the N.K.V.D. who were then shot for their pains, since it was vital that no one outside the innermost circle should come to know of the affair. The clutching hand of the N.K.V.D. reached out, now in one direction, now in another, Old Bolsheviks were arrested; the ground was being prepared for the grand trials.

The atmospherics of fear were inaudible to my ears as Manuilsky said:

All those who were cowardly, self-seeking, mean and idle remained by the wayside, hung their heads, whimpered, sowed unbelief, prophesied disaster, allied themselves with world capital in their malicious hatred of the victory of Socialism; a group of mean, disgusting, vile, politically degenerate individuals belonging to the Zinovievite–Trotskyite bloc were responsible for the murder of our friend, the darling of the whole party, the architect of the victories of Baku, Leningrad and Khibini: S. M. Kirov . . .

Stalin's genius, the genius of the working class, was guiding the country . . .

Under the leadership of Comrade Stalin our party was simultaneously schooled to oppose each and every deviation with rigorous, Bolshevik implacability . . . Earlier on, the Trotskyites, no less than the Zinovievite faction and the right-wing opportunists, were trying to destroy the unity of our party. Today the whole of this opposition has been knocked on the head. The Zinovievite–Trotskyite bloc has been reduced to a puny band of Fascist terrorists whose counter-revolutionary nature is now apparent to millions of workers.

Thus the revival of the international revolutionary movement, given added impetus by the departure of the Seventh World Congress from a policy which had resulted in the total failure of the German Communist Party, was calamitously bound up with Stalin's character, his vengefulness, his skill at making others shoulder the responsibility for his own failures (the C.P.G.'s delusions being no less attributable to Stalin than the consequences of his brutal and premature collectivization of agriculture). Dimitrov represented the new and propitious policy of the Communist Parties. Stalin needed him and gave him a free hand. His popularity did not endanger Stalin but was, on the contrary, of assistance to him. At the same time, however, Stalin was seeking to rid himself of all the really able men in the party and the military power apparatuses, with the result that the success of the new policy was increasingly jeopardized. I, a comparative newcomer, had no inkling of this combination of circumstances. I did not see what was happening in the shadows. The man I saw was in the light: Dimitrov. In retrospect I can see no reason to qualify the love and admiration I felt for him. Even his weaknesses were engaging. In his craving for size, the big desk, the big room, the sweeping gesture, in his undisciplined refusal to conform to a medically prescribed diet – he, who in chains had shown such exemplary discipline – in his obliviousness, when deep in conversation with the beautiful Pilar, to the fact that the members of the Praesidium were waiting for him, one could detect the voice which, in the Supreme Court at Leipzig, had addressed the Mrs Grundys: 'I am neither impotent nor homosexual, but in every respect a man!' . . .

'If you're going to write about me,' he said, on my submitting to him the schema for my book *Das Fanal*, 'you ought to stress my intelligence rather than my courage. Obviously courage is necessary but there's no shortage of that among Communists. Most important of all is *this*!' He struck his forehead. 'And *this*!' He grasped his nose. 'Head, heart and nose, those are the tools of a revolutionary politician. He's got to be able to smell what's in the air. For example, I soon realized that Bünger, the President of the Court, was not my enemy – he's an old German Nationalist whom the National Socialists dislike. So I couldn't hurl insults at the court, nor could I bandy Communist phrases about; the greater my respect towards the judges, the more effective my attacks upon the police, the prosecuting counsel, the Nazi press, Goering and Goebbels. After the Reichstag fire there were serious disputes between the German Nationalists and the National Socialists; it couldn't have been otherwise. Hitler had become too powerful for his allies' liking – I had to bear that in mind. Equally in evidence was the conflict between the anti-capitalist forces in the N.S.D.A.P. and the pro-capitalist leadership; and again the conflict between Goering and Goebbels. I believed that Goebbels derived a good deal of malicious pleasure from the spectacle of my clash with Goering, so Goebbels, too, had to be made an object of mockery. My strategy had been thoroughly worked out. But I had to be constantly on the alert so as to exploit every tactical advantage.

'One of my barometers was the behaviour of the guards who escorted me. They were changed each day to prevent any contact being established. When they were friendly I knew that I had been putting my case well; when they were hostile I thought to myself, what mistake did you make? Where did you go wrong? I cast my mind back to the cross-examination and more often than not I discovered the mistake and tried to put it right the next day.

'After my clash with Goering the men were more forthcoming than they had ever been before; one of them gave my shoulder a friendly nudge while the other would have been only too pleased to shake my hand. Well satisfied I lay down in my cell with the feeling that I was going to have a good night . . .

'And then the unexpected happened: noises and heavy footsteps, the door was flung open, the guard sprang to attention and Goering walked in. Was the bull going to gore me with its horns in revenge for the defeat in the courtroom? With his legs astraddle he stood staring at me, then suddenly stretched out his hand: "Pity you're an enemy! It's men like you one needs as one's friends!"

'There was a sort of oafish chivalry about it. But you'd better not write about this for the time being. Later, perhaps.'

After his enemy's acquittal Goering had him taken to Berlin, to a dark, damp dungeon that had at one time been the cellar of the Prussian Academy of Arts. 'The Academy of Arts,' Dimitrov told the French newspaper *Intransigent* in an interview, 'had to make do with a minute house; meanwhile their old building was being converted into a large prison. That shows you the régime in all its glory.'

On 22 December, the day before the verdict was announced, the American Ambassador William E. Dodd wrote in his diary:

A newspaper man, whose information I have found always to be reliable and whose name I dare not mention even in this diary, came to me this morning to say that a high German official – my guess is the secret police chief Rolf Diels – had told him that the German Supreme Court would declare all the Communists except Van der Lubbe, on trial since February for burning the Reichstag, not guilty. But Georgi Dimitrov, the Bulgarian Communist disowned by his own country, was to be murdered before he could get out of the country, by order of the Prussian Prime Minister Goering.*

Dimitrov was released after he had been made a Soviet citizen. Goering invited him to go hunting in the Forest of Dars – Goering, the podgy hunter, the guzzling lecher lusting after pomp and decorations, wild boar and uniforms. In remote and sombre Dars it was his custom to organize the wholesale slaughter of game. Dimitrov declined. 'I know the *Nibelungenlied*,' he said.

Many of the Comintern meetings were simply time-wasting routine. Yet another meeting in 1937, in 'this one thousand nine hundred and thirty-seven times accursed year' as Evgenia Semyonovna Ginzburg put it in her shattering book *Into the Whirlwind*. Here in the Comintern we received the messages tapped out on the walls of every prison cell in the world; the only ones we didn't hear were those tapped out next door, on the walls of the Lyubyanka, the Butirki and many other prisons. Nevertheless, we knew that the terror was going its rounds.

Yet another of those innumerable meetings. A speaker reading from his compendious, vacuous notes. Dimitrov was doodling on a sheet of paper, Manuilsky winked at me.

The German, D., indicated his desire to speak, thus presenting a prospect of further tedium. But then we pricked up our ears. 'Permit me, comrades, to recall the words of the militant German humanist, Ulrich von Hutten: It is a joy to be alive! In the German concentration camps the spirit of the Communist International and the love felt for our beloved, brilliant and wise comrade Stalin, remain invincible, as the encouraging reports we have received go to show...'

★

Klara lay down on her bed, turned over on her stomach and pulled up her skirt. Her calves and buttocks were monstrously scarred, as though wild beasts had clawed at her flesh. Her lips tight in her swarthy face and her grey eyes flashing pale fire, she said hoarsely:

'Zis – Gestapo.' She jerked herself up and held out both hands: 'And zis – NKVD.'

The fingernails were deformed and the fingers blue and swollen.

* William E. and M. Dodds, *Ambassador Dodds' Diary 1933 to 1938*, London, 1941.

'Special apparatus . . . *wie sagt man* . . . to obtain sincere confessions . . . Torture!*

★

'The name of Stalin renders every torture ineffective. It heals the gravest wounds. With this name on their lips, men meet their death with their heads held high. I have here a report from Germany . . .'

★

'Can I speak to you a moment, comrade?' said a pure Russian voice.

Apparently there were some other soviet people besides myself. This was Julia Annenkova, a woman close on forty who had edited a German paper published in Moscow. Though not beautiful, she had a vivid, memorable face with dark, smouldering eyes. She looked like a Hugue-not. Drawing me aside, she whispered confidentially:

'You were quite right not to answer their questions. Who knows which of them is a real enemy and which are victims of a mistake, like you and me? Do go on being very careful, to make sure you don't commit a real crime against the party after all. The best thing is to say nothing.'

'But it's true, I don't know anything. I come from the provinces, I've been in prison for six months. Do *you* know what's happening in the country?'

'Treason! Appalling treason which has worked its way into every link of the party and government apparatus. Secretaries of territorial commit-tees, secretaries of national-minority communist parties have turned out to be traitors – Postyshev, Khatayevich, Eiche, Razumov, Ivanov, Antipov, president of the Soviet Control Board, and any number of army officers . . .'

'But if everybody is supposed to have betrayed one man, isn't it simpler to think that he has betrayed them?'

Julia went pale and after a moment said tersely:

'I'm sorry, I made a mistake.'†

★

D., holding forth before the meeting of the Comintern, looked more like a character actor in some provincial theatre than a Hugue-not. I am positive that he was unaware of what was going on in the

---

*Evgenia S. Ginzburg, *Into the Whirlwind*, Penguin Books, 1968, p. 124.
† *Into the Whirlwind*, p. 124.

cellars of the N.K.V.D. when he spoke of the joy of being alive at that time. But, like all of us, he must have known that people were being arrested, people whose innocence we could not doubt.

His histrionic pathos seemed to be turning into a genuine frenzy. He was indeed in a frenzy, obsessed by an anxiety that was stripping away every vestige of dignity and decorum.

'But now at last there is firm action, a cleansing, a purging. Self-criticism compels us to admit that we had relaxed our vigilance and we give thanks to our Soviet comrades for the liquidation of the enemies of the people. Our defence of Socialist humanism must be implacable . . .'

Up till this moment Dimitrov had continued to doodle. Now he suddenly raised his head.

'What did you say just then?'

D.'s voice was no longer so assured as he answered: 'I was talking about the defence of Socialist humanism . . .'

Dimitrov jumped up, clenched his fist and shouted:

'That word is inappropriate to the times. I don't wish to hear it!' . . .

Dimitrov died on 2 July 1949. I went to the funeral with a delegation of the C.P.A. The corpse had been brought to Sofia from Moscow. I stress the word 'corpse', for the lay figure which was placed upon the bier in front of us had nothing in common with Dimitrov. This stalwart and uncompromising man had resisted death as fiercely as he had resisted his foes. All of that had been touched out, not a line or wrinkle remained of the living man, not a trace of his anger, his tenacity, his passion. From the black, impeccably pressed suit there emerged a smooth, pallid, unreal face. It was as though some deserving people's artist, one of those well-trained sculptors who so fashion statues of Lenin that the revolutionary is turned into an unassuming citizen, had taken over the body and made of it an advertisement for death. The embalming of the dead, whatever the circumstances, borders on obscenity; even the remains of Lenin, which are curiously moving by reason of their grace and gentleness, look wrong in their mausoleum. But the remains of Dimitrov are like a dreadful nullification of the living man.

As long as I live I shall see this living man and hear his voice, the proud, incisive voice.

'That word is inappropriate to the times. I don't wish to hear it!' ...

'Are you by any chance afraid of my questions, Herr Minister-präsident?'

'I admit that my manner of speaking is short and sharp ...'

'I'm used to calling a spade a spade ...'

'What I'm defending is the purpose and content of my life ...'

17

Between Lux and Comintern

After the Seventh World Congress of the Communist International I became, at Dimitrov's suggestion, the representative of the C.P.A. on the Comintern. I accepted on condition that I might leave Moscow at frequent intervals for Prague where I would not be so far away from Austria. Since 1936, therefore, I had been dividing my time between the two capitals.

I found Moscow a difficult place to settle down in. Everything seemed strange to me. I knew no one. Nor could I be aware that every one of the old Communists I encountered, far from being just the man I was looking at, was also and at the same time a cadre report, an indestructible past: right deviationist, left deviationist, appeaser, social revolutionary, Menshevik, Trotskyist, Bukharinist, Brandlerian, etc. Hence every word he spoke contained both an immediate and a hidden meaning, referring not only to the topic currently under discussion but also to past discussions, reprimands, admonitions, defeats, and penances that went by the name of 'self-criticism'. I had plunged into a labyrinth without the scarlet thread by the help of which others hoped to elude the Minotaur, and the fact that I did not even know that I was in a labyrinth gave me a kind of innocence more helpful than the scarlet thread, which was just as liable to mislead as to guide. Although I enjoyed the evident confidence of Dimitrov, Manuilsky and Togliatti, the *apparatchiks* continued to look on me as the 'Social Democrat'.

I lived in the Lux, the old hotel in the Ulitsa Gorkovo, formerly the Tverskaya. My room was on the sixth floor of this building which, under Soviet rule, had been added to, modernized and equipped with comfortable if simple furniture. Next to my room was the communal kitchen with the gas stoves upon which we cooked our breakfasts. Opposite me lived Wan Min, the distantly polite representative of the Chinese Communist Party, with his beautiful wife and equally beautiful sister-in-law. On the ground floor, at the bottom of the stairs and close to the lift so frequently labelled '*Nye rabotayet*' (out of order), was the porter's cubbyhole or *stol propuskov*, an obligatory staging post for all visitors, whence the N.K.V.D. girl would telephone to inquire whether she should issue a *propusk*, or pass. Without a *bumazhka* – a 'chit' – one was not a human being.

The Lux was inhabited by the foreigners who worked at the Comintern. In the same building there was a restaurant where bad food was served by lackadaisical waiters, and entertainment provided by massive *chanteuses* or well-upholstered gypsy women whose wriggling shoulders, I was told by a knowledgeable companion, were supposed to indicate sensuality. The restaurant was frequented by an ambiguous clientèle, some aggressively out to enjoy themselves, others surly and taciturn, yet others giving vent to gross outbursts of merriment. Who these people were, I don't know; most of them looked like commercial travellers or members of the secret police. I avoided the place, which was not an integral part of the Lux Hotel. It was a world with which we had nothing in common.

But in what kind of world did we, the inmates of the Lux Hotel, exist? Day in, day out we travelled or walked to the Comintern where we read and wrote reports, articles and pamphlets, took part in committee meetings, discussed problems of international politics, our thoughts directed towards Austria, Germany, France, Spain, knowing virtually nothing about Moscow. I lived among foreigners, worked among foreigners or among Russians concerned with foreign affairs, and it was not easy to make contact with Russians unconnected with the Comintern; the few whom I got to know at all closely were unbiassed Jews. The full extent to which I was cut off has only become clear to me now, in retrospect.

Our link with day-to-day life in Moscow was through the Schutzbund men. The difficulties of which they complained I at first took to be those of adapting to the working conditions, the deprivations and customs of a people who, emerging from the world of '*nichevo*', untutored, and with no tradition of discipline, were endeavouring to build up a modern industry. By comparison with the average Russian workers the Schutzbund men were privileged; in the factories they were able to make some headway – Heinz Roscher, for example, who had been chief of the Floridsdorf Schutzbund, became a close associate of Likhachev, his manager; they were envied for the way they were housed, and they would 'mutiny' against inadequate work methods and bureaucratic sluggishness. Two Austrians in the Cadre Division of the Comintern were responsible for the routine work connected with the Schutzbund men; I would intervene only in exceptional cases, or where the men concerned appealed directly to myself. In the Cadre Division there was a list which I never saw, although I was the C.P.A.'s official representative. Nor did I ever see my own cadre report, though I did happen to hear that certain matters had been 'rectified' – to my advantage, I gathered, though whether this was so I do not know, nor did it very much interest me at the time. The Schutzbund men fell into two categories, 'good comrades' and 'undesirable elements'. This again I did not learn till later when, upon my inquiring about this or that individual, I would receive the prompt reply: 'A good comrade', or 'An undesirable element'. My actual work was virtually confined to journalism. 'It's not your business to act as consul,' said Togliatti upon my communicating to him my multifarious worries about the Schutzbund men. 'You should concentrate on your political and journalistic work.'

One day resembled another. Writing this sentence, I start back, hesitate, cut myself short. But the words insist upon their validity, maintain that, if unexpected, they are in no way inapplicable even when confronted by the fact that those years in Moscow were filled to overflowing with tragic, overwhelming, cataclysmic events. As a person with his own special attributes and requirements I had been virtually eliminated; I was a being who thought and wrote, but if I tried actively to intervene I was quickly given to understand that I wasn't competent, that no one of my kind was competent, that indeed only the unapproachable, intangible, infallible apparatus was competent, the 'castle' foreshadowed by Franz Kafka. Exciting, confusing, terrible things were going on, but whatever was happening, one day resembled another. Between Lux and Comintern, a pedantically regulated life. The reality of the Comintern manifested itself in a mass of written and oral 'material' which took the form of reports, bulletins, newspapers and journals, discussions and resolutions; we were perpetually engaged in ordering and analysing this material, and abstracting from it recommendations and directives. Under Dimitrov's leadership the Comintern was an amalgam of genuine analysis and peremptory voluntarism, of critical intelligence and bureaucratic red tape, of inter-party consultation and Soviet-determined objectives, a 'General Staff of world revolution' in an epoch of defensive action in which it was becoming increasingly difficult to uphold the postulate of a 'World' Communist Party – but a general staff none the less, whose business it was to coordinate revolutionary resistance to Fascism.

To collaborate in this reality, even in so small a way, was emotionally satisfying. Whatever work I might be doing was no longer mere self-gratification but conscious integration into a whole, a depersonalized anonymity. I had a function, had become a 'functionary', unbureaucratic, sometimes rebellious, not striving after power, but yet a functionary. What was incumbent on me was not to evolve new thoughts, insights, concepts, but to say what it was my job to say as convincingly as I could, while avoiding set patterns wherever possible. Hence I was concerned above all to discover a new 'style', to fight against linguistic convention, to find new ways of expressing what I recognized as new in the Popular Front, the alliance of all anti-Fascists. These efforts, too, evoked mistrust, though they were regarded approvingly by the leading men in the Comintern.

The first political discussion in which I took part was held in the editorial office of the *Kommunistische Internationale*. The theme was 'Trotskyism'. Togliatti was in the chair. The speaker – who it was, I cannot recall – set out to demonstrate that at that particular time the most dangerous form of Trotskyism was a Social Democracy that assumed left-wing airs. Our main task, he said, must be to unmask this enemy, to shatter his arguments, to destroy him without mercy. 'It's not enough to disassociate oneself from this or that thesis of Social Democracy; we have to distinguish here between the so-called left-wing Socialists and right-wing Socialists.'

He looked at me. Everybody looked at me.

'The most dangerous enemy of the revolutionary working class today is Otto Bauer. He must be publicly branded. He's a traitor, a Trotskyist, an agent of the bourgeoisie.'

More than fifty pairs of eyes were turned on me. I signified my desire to speak. Togliatti tried to ignore the fact. But the speaker exclaimed: 'Comrade Fischer wants the floor!'

I began to speak, at first restraining myself with difficulty, then casting caution to the winds, vehemently and in anger. 'Otto Bauer is no traitor. He failed in a crucial situation, admittedly, but he didn't betray us.'

'Objectively, he did! Are you prepared to deny that?'

'Betrayal is always subjective. Otto Bauer is neither objectively nor subjectively a traitor. Neither is he a Trotskyist. These terms lose all meaning if their definitions are blurred. I have shaken off Austro-Marxism, but I'm not prepared to dismiss it as the theory of betrayal.'

I had well and truly laid myself open to attack. Among the company there were supporters as well as opponents of the policy initiated by Dimitrov, fanatical Stalinists as well as haters of Stalin, intelligent Marxists as well as sedulous trouble-makers. Without knowing it, I had helped every one of them to outdo the others, to present himself in the light of a staunch, unswerving Communist, true to the line, methodical, uncompromising.

All spoke against me, for hours on end, some lecturing me without malice, others talking down to me, grown-ups reprimanding a beardless youth, yet others cold and hostile, determined to liquidate the Social Democratic interloper and in so doing strike a blow at Dimitrov, at the new policy, the betrayal of the 'class standpoint'. More venomous than anyone else was D. who, in 1934, had welcomed me with the words: 'Well now, Comrade Fischer, what's it like on the other side of the barricades?' Had I, he now asked, ever by any chance read the classics? Did I by any chance know that there had been a man called Lenin? He could not, he said, bring himself to believe that I was so naïve as to overlook Otto Bauer's class betrayal.

How understand a game in which the devil cuts the cards? How could I have known that D. was about to be arrested and charged with having plotted Stalin's assassination during the Seventh World Congress of the Comintern?

After the discussion in which they had set upon me like a pack of wolves – only Togliatti saying in extenuation that, regrettable though my views might be, too much should not be made of them

– Joszef Revai, the Hungarian *Referent** of the Central European Secretariat, walked back to the Lux with me.

'Tell me, was it very unpleasant?'

'It was instructive.'

'Didn't you notice how Ercoli stood up for you?' Ercoli was the name under which Togliatti worked in the Comintern as head of the Central European Secretariat.

'I noticed nothing of the kind. He described my views as regrettable.'

'So they are. But he also praised you for your exemplary behaviour in going over to the Communist Party and he admitted your sincerity.'

'Thank you. I've learnt now that in Moscow sincerity is not welcome. In future I shall keep my mouth shut.'

'That wouldn't be right. You've got the courage of your convictions, wrong though they may be. We need such courage.'

'How can you be so sure what's wrong and what isn't? Are you people infallible?'

'As individuals no, of course we're not. But as a collective very nearly so.'

'Do you know what G. told me? That I think too much. Not a good thing, he said; what was needed was discipline, not individualism.'

'We do need discipline, but thinking as well. You mustn't be so easily discouraged. And don't be so sensitive.'

Sensitive I very probably was. A sensitive intellectual? It would have been dishonourable not to stand up for Otto Bauer. They had all been against me. Did that mean I was wrong? Isn't it arrogance to insist that one is right and everyone else wrong? To regard oneself, one's own conscience, one's own intellect as the sole arbiter? Otto Bauer felt drawn to Bukharin, not Trotsky. But hadn't he perhaps been influenced by Trotsky very early on? And what if he had? – 'What if he had?' Surely no way for a Communist to argue? Intellectual arrogance! But . . .

'Thinking is essential,' said Revai. 'But you have also to consider the situation.'

The situation: Hitler. The Berlin–Rome–Tokyo axis. The Anti-

*A *Referent* was a specialist in his own country's problems, responsible to the Central European Secretariat.

Comintern Pact. The attempt to bring dissension, sabotage, conspiracy into the Soviet Union. The Popular Front in France, in Spain. And polarization: to oppose Stalin is to oppose the Soviet Union, to oppose the Soviet Union is to oppose the most significant anti-Fascist power. But Otto Bauer was in favour of the Popular Front, in favour of an alliance with Moscow. And D. is opposed to the Popular Front, opposed to Otto Bauer. What utter confusion! Who against whom? And who is playing whose game? When the devil cuts the cards . . .

Another 'situation' was the trial of Zinoviev and Kamenyev. And the indictment of D., who had accused me of 'Trotskyism' because I had stood up for Otto Bauer. Who was it murdered Kirov? Whose is the game that's being played? Isn't *anything* possible if Hitler is possible?

'You'll attend as an observer,' said Revai. 'As a reporter.'

'I loathe the whole business.'

'Are you mad? Don't you realize that there was a plot to murder Stalin? That it's a matter of life and death for the Soviet Union? Are you still incapable of comprehending the revolutionary dialectic?'

'I never cared for Zinoviev and I detested D. He may have detested Stalin still more. But he isn't a murderer.'

'How do you know? You just feel it, as usual, in your bones, your nervous system! You only have to read the history of the French Revolution. One day Danton's a revolutionary, the next he's hand-in-glove with England, with counter-revolution. When fractional struggle begins to impinge on the class struggle, *anything* goes, can't you see that? The most unnatural alliances, any crime you care to name, and no looking back! Which dog eats which? That is the question.'

This kind of dialectic was too much for my nervous system and it rebelled. Revai may have been right, but my nervous system produced an illness and a temperature of 104°. My consciousness was answered by an ague.

I don't know if the thermometer convinced the N.K.V.D. people. Revai knew that my illness was genuine. Togliatti came to see me and stayed for a few minutes. 'The trial's being rottenly conducted,' he said. 'Get well soon!'

'A band of unprincipled conspirators,' Vyshinsky called the

accused. Vyshinsky, the erstwhile Menshevik, the man with eyes as cold as death, the public prosecutor. Togliatti replied in *Pravda*. Vyshinsky, he said, was wrong; seasoned politicians like Zinoviev and Kamenyev were not unprincipled conspirators. Their aim was the overthrow of Soviet power, the integration of Russia into the capitalist system. What must be taken into account was the world situation, the international class struggle with all its complex correlations. Within the Soviet Union, too, the class struggle, far from being over, had entered an extremely acute phase. It was an inauspicious article. Later Togliatti was to denounce the thesis that the struggle had entered an acute phase. In doing so he was denouncing his own past, for at the time he had been convinced that this thesis was true.

It was a conviction I did not at first share. On the other hand, there were the confessions of the accused. And the international class struggle – had that become a struggle between states, between social systems . . . ? Perhaps, I thought, I am too untutored to be able to conceive its outermost possibilities. In politics, the strangest alliances can occur and what, considered in isolation, appears retrogressive may, in the context of world history, appear progressive, and *vice versa*. Perhaps, I thought, Zinoviev, Kamenyev, David and the rest really did believe that the orientation towards the Popular Front alliance was a betrayal of Communism, that 'Socialism in one country' was a betrayal of the world revolution, and that Stalin was a calamity against whom extreme measures were called for. But if such were the case then could the possibility of absurd combinations, of secret agreements be excluded? It was nonsensical to assume that these men had wanted to help Hitler – but supposing they had meant to use him as a trump card in order eventually to over-trump him? To carouse with the devil and ultimately drink him under the table? It seemed to me highly improbable but, having grown up in the temperate climate of a Social Democratic Party, what could I know of the hell's kitchen of international politics? In Austria the classes stood face to face along more or less well-defined fronts, but was that so in the rest of the world? Might not, in certain circumstances, an Arab sheikh or the Emperor of Abyssinia be figures of progress, and honourable democratic statesmen be retrograde factors? Who, and for what reasons, was seeking alliances with whom? And even if the conveyor belt upon which the one was speeding forwards were running backwards, might he not fall behind the other, striding backwards upon a conveyor belt which was speeding forwards? Who was in a position to distinguish, to control movements and counter-movements, actions and reactions, in their totality? And was there in fact any such totality?

Revai was quite ready to argue with me along these lines. I quarrelled with and liked him. There was something boyish, immature, headstrong and unyielding about him. His was a complex character and he was, for that reason perhaps, inclined towards dogmatic over-simplification. Touchy, aggressive, cultivated, boasting himself a disciple of Lukács yet vigorously polemicizing against him, busy with studies of Petöfi and Ady yet wholly subordinating the aesthetic to the sociological, he was one of those intellectuals who fiercely curb, when they do not entirely subjugate, their intellects. He had installed within himself a monitory voice, the voice of the party, with which to override the voice of a latent self at moments of crisis. When he was Minister of Culture of the Hungarian People's Republic, I lunched with him one day during a writers' congress and asked him to disassociate himself from the ideological methods of coercion then being used to combat 'formalism'. Having promised to do this, he surprised me by making a speech like that of a prosecutor in a heresy trial. The inconsistency between the private conversation and the public denunciation was not the result of any intrinsic duplicity but of the deep inner conflict which afflicts a man who thinks it his duty to obey the voice of the party rather than his own individual insights. This dichotomy was to become a mortal sickness which, after the Budapest rising in 1956, was ultimately to destroy Revai. But today I am convinced that it was this same internal dichotomy which originally drew me to him and contributed so much to our prickly friendship.

I felt similarly drawn to Herbert Wehner who, under the pseudonym Kurt Funk, worked as *Referent* for German questions in Ercoli's Secretariat and lived a few doors away from me in the Lux. Ercoli-Togliatti held him in high esteem. His reports on the situation in Germany were accurate, matter-of-fact, convincing and free of all illusion. This brought down upon him the wrath of those – and they were many – whose one desire was to hear that Germany was heading for a crisis, that the German workers were putting up an increasing resistance and that the régime, though inhuman, was not by any means firmly ensconced. Wehner detested such empty vapourings. He also detested most of the leading German Communists. This hatred was the carapace that shielded a highly ambivalent individual who combined in himself anarchic passion and almost pedantic meticulousness, the urge for freedom and the will to power, the desire for warmth and rebarbative taciturnity, and whose tight-lipped self-control would suddenly give way to explosive anger when, in his longing for community, he broke ranting and roaring out of his solitude. Once, when he was in bed with a temperature, I and his wife, a delightful person, went into the kitchen to make coffee. When we returned we found him sitting up on the divan playing his guitar and shouting wild, incoherent songs. He was like a boiler without a safety valve, from time to time finding relief in a tremendous explosion. There was too much for him to stomach. He did not like what was happening in Moscow and felt no affinity for most of his comrades. Of Dimitrov he spoke admiringly, of Togliatti with great respect. I enjoyed his confidence for a time, then he withdrew from me also, retreating into the bitterness of solitude.

The terror, of which I had hitherto perceived nothing, was groping its way towards its first Schutzbund victims. When I approached the Cadre Department for information I was told that the men concerned were notorious as 'undesirable elements', that each case was being scrupulously investigated, that the organs of the revolutionary Soviet Government were experienced and intent on discovering the truth and were, moreover, above all suspicion. Indeed to harbour such suspicion would be to question the Revolution, the party and the latter's infallibility. The terrible doctrine of infallibility began to serve as justification for every arbitrary act, while any stirring of an individual conscience was reprobated as petit-bourgeois or as indicating susceptibility to the class enemy's propaganda. The victory of the October Revolution, the consolidation and stabilization of Soviet rule in spite of all prognostications to the contrary had, it was maintained, finally proved that everyone else was wrong and only the Bolsheviks right, and that the party and Stalin were infallible. Once, in talking to a very experienced and educated Russian woman, I remarked: 'No one's infallible, not even the Pope, except *ex cathedra*.' She started back in alarm and, with a nervous gesture, replied: 'We aren't in a position to judge.' The substance of infallibility permeated the whole party down to the very least of its organs, so that times without number I received the anxious and deprecatory or else malevolently provocative reply: 'In the Soviet Union no innocent people are ever arrested. The N.K.V.D. knows very well whom to seize and when. Revolutionary vigilance isn't blind, like bourgeois justice; it has a thousand eyes and is able to see what many people are incapable of seeing, indeed may not even be *willing* to see.' An arrest, therefore, amounted to a verdict of guilty, and anyone seized by the N.K.V.D. was already convicted.

The first arrests of 'undesirable elements' were soon followed by those of others, among them Schutzbund men whom I knew to be courageous, upright and whole-heartedly devoted to the Socialist cause. I by-passed the Cadre Department and intervened with Dimitrov.

'Are you certain that he can be trusted *in all circumstances*? That he isn't allowing himself to be exploited, perhaps wholly without evil intent, simply out of carelessness or indiscretion?'

This would sometimes give me pause; but not with regard to Josef Brüll, Armand Weiss, Heinz Roscher and a number of others for whom I was prepared to answer unconditionally, *in all circumstances*.

Dimitrov shook his head. 'We haven't the authority to meddle in the affairs of the N.K.V.D. However, in view of your persistence in pleading this particular comrade's case . . . I'll make inquiries. But please understand that I have neither the right nor the power actually to *intervene*, though I might be able to arrange for the inquiry to be speeded up. Of course, mistakes are sometimes made, the wrong people are picked up – but generally speaking you should trust the organs of the Soviet Union.'

I told Dimitrov that my brother Otto had spent a night under arrest. 'What do you know about Franz Maier?' his interrogator had asked. 'Are you in contact with him?' 'It's remarkable,' my brother replied, 'really I ought to know at least a dozen Franz Maiers since it's the most common of names. But extraordinary though it may seem, I don't know a single one.' 'There's no point in your denying it. You must help us with our investigation. Franz Maier's an agent, a spy, and you know him perfectly well.' 'I would gladly help you if I could, but I know neither your particular Franz Maier nor any other.' The interrogation lasted many hours. And my brother had had to wait many hours before he was told he could leave. Why?

'Well then, doesn't that show that there's nothing arbitrary about it but that everything is carefully investigated . . . ?'

'But someone else may be detained because of some such Franz Maier.'

'Then he'll be released.'

Did Dimitrov really think so?

Be that as it may:

The era of accusations, calumnies and arrests had barely begun when the alarm was sounded in the Lenin Institute. It was here that foreign Communists were taught dialectical and historical materialism, political economy, the history of the C.P.S.U., and also, after the Seventh World Congress of the Comintern, the history of their respective countries.

The Institute was directed by Kirsanova, wife of the bewhiskered and complacent Yaroslavsky, whose own speciality was atheistic propaganda and who liked to be apostrophized as the 'party's conscience'. Kirsanova was a very intelligent woman with the imposing airs of a general. I had once asked some small favour of her on behalf of the Austrian teachers and students – just what, I can no longer recall – and she had agreed to do exactly as I wanted. When several months had gone by and nothing had been done, I reminded her of the promise she had failed to keep.

She laughed, not without charm: 'Surely you know the laws of dialectics?'

'What have dialectics got to do with a broken promise?'

'Oh, you're not much of a dialectician, are you? It all depends on time and space. On their interaction. Several months have gone by. At the time, my agreement accorded with the circumstances. Since then, the circumstances have changed. What was right at the time is right no longer. Don't you see?'

'No.'

'I'm afraid you may get into difficulties if you don't understand the dialectical law of interaction.'

Her look was mocking, friendly, disquieting.

The 'Klahr case' was a result of this dialectical law of interaction.

One of the teachers in the Austrian section of the Lenin Institute was a clever and cultivated woman, Genia Lande, whose husband later fell victim to Stalin's terror; the other was Alfred Klahr. Undogmatic, thoughtful, with a flexible mind, he was, if not a typical, at least a very likeable Communist. He did not die at Stalin's hands but at Hitler's. Death changed its uniform and caught up with him in the West, no less brutal there than in Russia. The National Socialists murdered a man who was not only a Jew, but had actually dared to characterize the Austrians as a nation in their own right, an assertion he supported with cogent arguments. At first I had taken the opposite view.

'So you don't feel yourself to be an Austrian?' Dimitrov asked me during a theoretical debate.

'Not really, no.'

'Then you feel wrong!' he said, wagging his head and laughing in the lazy, kindly way he had, a laugh that was never hurtful.

I began to take a serious interest in the ambiguous, twilit, contradictory history of Austria and came increasingly to agree with Alfred Klahr. 'Unwelcome allies', was the verdict given in Austria by the Catholic newspaper-editor Kerschbaum on the studies of the Austrian nation brought out by Klahr and myself. In 1945 Kerschbaum joined me as assistant editor on the newspaper *Neues Österreich*, a welcome ally in the endeavour to build up an Austrian national consciousness from its rudiments. What eventually emerged was a caricature of our intentions, a caricature that gave the lie to the illusions with which I had returned home from Moscow.

The 'Klahr case' bore only an indirect relation to the idea of an Austrian nation. The German Communists, to be sure, took violent exception to that theory, accustomed as they were to having the C.P.A. in leading strings. When Kirsanova engineered the 'Klahr case', however, the Austrian question was involved only in so far as it formed part of the general complex of 'liberalism', 'objectivism', and 'Social Democratism'. For it was with these deviations – if not in fact something worse, namely, 'capitulation to the ideology of the class enemy' – that Klahr was being charged. He was criticized for his analysis of Austro-Marxism, for his attempt to do justice to Otto Bauer's personality, for his critical remarks about the C.P.G.'s policy prior to 1933, and was taxed with insufficient severity towards the false opinions of several of his students, with lack of vigilance, etc. He was not, or so Kirsanova opined, fit to teach in the Lenin Institute.

I did not know then, nor do I know now, why she attacked Klahr. She was probably afraid that she herself would be accused of lack of vigilance if she proved incapable of detecting an 'enemy of the people' in her Institute, of unmasking one of these so suspect foreigners. She may have been acting under pressure, aiming a blow through Klahr at someone else in this impenetrable struggle between cliques. Maybe she was frightened. I couldn't tell. But I was determined to take issue with her.

Teachers and students were assembled in the main hall of the Lenin Institute. I was welcomed by Kirsanova and the assistant director Vladimirov, Dimitrov's brother-in-law.

'Are you going to speak?' Vladimirov asked.

'Yes. After Comrade Kirsanova.'

She spoke, every word carefully weighed, at first with restraint, expressing concern for the party, for every party member, for the common cause, then emotively, in tones of entreaty, of admonition, about the intensification of the class struggle, about how any weakness on the ideological front would be immediately exploited by agents, deviationists and spies, about the greatest danger of all, which, she alleged, was the infiltration of ideas alien to Marxism–Leninism and therefore anti-Marxist, anti-Soviet. When students asked unauthorized questions, the objective error was still distinguishable from the subjective, but when the teacher gave unauthorized answers, what might have been objective at once became subjective. The transition from quantity to quality, in this instance from objective error to subjective guilt, was a law of dialectics. If, in addition, the circumstance of the intensification of the class struggle were taken into account, a teacher's carelessness became sheer irresponsibility – indeed more than that – ideological disarmament. Comrade Klahr was an old Communist, not one who had recently come to us from Social Democracy . . . although she didn't look at me everyone knew whom she meant . . . an old Communist who could not exonerate himself on the grounds of inexperience. Instead of holding aloft the banner of Marxism–Leninism, as we are taught to do by our great, wise, beloved Comrade Stalin, Comrade Klahr had deviated from the class standpoint and had not enlightened his students but sown confusion amongst them. At the very best, at the most lenient, a reprimand was called for; in addition, the Austrian party should be asked to withdraw him from the Lenin Institute.

I was no longer subject to the sudden fits of rage that had some-times used to overwhelm me in childhood. But the cold infamy of Kirsanova's speech sent a hot surge of anger flooding through me. I managed to cool off before I answered, and my voice was cold and cutting.

'I have no intention of talking now about the Klahr case, but about the Kirsanova case.'

It was as though everyone had been struck by lightning. For a moment my interpreter, Genia Lande, hesitated, her eyes flashed, then she translated what I had said into Russian. Vladimirov rose to his feet and hurried across to the exit but did not leave the room. The only person who appeared completely unconcerned was Kir-sanova herself; for a split second she looked at me, then turned an impassive, mask-like face towards those in the main body of the hall.

Comrade Klahr, I continued – myself hardly less surprised than my audience by the almost independent course my extempore speech appeared to be taking – Comrade Klahr had justified the confidence placed in him by the party. In the spirit of the Seventh Congress, he had not taught his students by rote; he had taught them how to think. Instead of wielding the ideological cudgel, he had opposed rational argumentation to the doubts expressed by his students. In appealing to reason and consciousness rather than relying on autho-rity and red tape, he was following the example of Dimitrov. Com-rade Kirsanova, on the other hand, embodied the opposite principle, namely that of command and obedience, of the suppression of all undogmatic thinking. One of her favourite topics was dialectics; but her dialectic consisted in failing to keep promises, in fomenting discord, in creating an atmosphere of mistrust and suspicion. We could have no use for an Institute where eavesdropping, duplicity and intolerance were the order of the day. Hence, instead of asking my party to withdraw Comrade Klahr, I would ask them to lodge a complaint against Comrade Kirsanova.

Kirsanova did not answer.

Vladimirov made a telephone call.

The next morning I went to Dimitrov's office.

'What happened yesterday at the Lenin Institute? I've already had one report, but I'd like you yourself to tell me why you took such an exceptionally strong line. What were your motives?'

He listened attentively and in silence. Then, moving his head from side to side in a slow, deliberate movement, not a shake, he asked:

'Wasn't it – a trifle unconsidered?'

'Possibly, but what she said was infamous!'

'Beware of judging her too hastily! She's a woman of enormous merit. An old Bolshevik. But we shall see . . . we shall see.'

A few weeks later, Kirsanova was removed from her post as head of the Lenin Institute.

Like a fool, I imagined at the time that innocent men could be saved, their powerful prosecutors compelled to give ground – not, of course, by a feeble show of resistance, but by a resolute and daring counter-attack. I was misled by the fact that Kirsanova, not Klahr, had come to grief, for this had given rise to the hope that the forces at work were not wholly arbitrary and that the undeniable abuse of its power by an over-zealous apparatus would be kept within reasonable bounds. Why the 'Klahr case' should have become the 'Kirsanova case' still continues to puzzle me to this day, as does my own survival in the increasingly dense and clinging web of paranoia, treachery, fear, cruelty, vengefulness, greed and folly. I was a sleep-walker, on either side of me a precipice; perhaps it was by reason of my very ingenuousness that I escaped the fate suffered by countless others.

The arrests continued. Members of the Schutzbund, at first only a few at a time, then in their dozens and hundreds, would vanish from their lodgings in the early hours of the morning. Finally things got to such a pitch that the men would sit waiting all night on their luggage and when, in the small hours, the N.K.V.D. came knocking at the door, would greet them with the words: 'So there you are! We were beginning to think you'd forgotten us.'

What else could I do but continue to intervene with Dimitrov? But ever more plainly his features betrayed impatience and un-willingness.

'You shouldn't insist so much. Things must take their course. The whole country's caught up in a web of conspiracy, sabotage and espionage. To uncover all the ramifications of the business is difficult, extremely difficult. There may be isolated instances of wrongful arrest but you must understand that any clue, however tenuous, may provide some sort of information. It would be pointless to intervene in every one of these cases. We can't speed up the proceedings.

We'll just have to be patient. And pin our faith on the Soviet authorities.'

Although I had no idea of the full extent of the terror, I found all this incomprehensible. Was it mistrust of foreigners? Envy, too, perhaps, because they were privileged, well-housed, yet still grumbled because day-to-day life was hard, because conditions of work in the factories often did not conform to acceptable standards? In Austria, many former Schutzbund members had gone over to the Nazis. With the intensification of the class struggle, the spread of Fascist contagion. As before I continued to vouch for the innocence of the majority of the Schutzbund men under arrest in the Soviet Union. But did I really know them all well enough to answer for them just like that? Might not an unconsidered step have unforseeable consequences? Dimitrov had spoken of a 'web'; might one not unwittingly fall into it, maybe in a fit of exacerbation, and suddenly find oneself caught and trapped, the victim of an indiscretion? To the Schutzbund men, Austria's Clerico-Fascism was the mortal enemy against which they had taken up arms. But was every one of them immune to National Socialism? Most of them were, yet mightn't there be one or two exceptions, men who had made contact with the German Embassy – or could all that be dismissed as thoughtless or malevolent gossip?

When I intervened yet again with Dimitrov I met with unmistakable resistance. Dimitrov did not *want* these perpetual reminders. Today I realize that I was overestimating his powers, not understanding that, though he might occasionally be able to obtain the release of one of his closest colleagues, there was nothing more he could do. Moreover he, Togliatti and other proponents of the Popular Front policy, though disturbed by the arrests, put their political views before any doubts or misgivings and were not prepared to jeopardize their positions by indulging in pointless internal struggles. Unlike myself, they were seasoned politicians who carefully weighed up the possibilities and did not fritter away their strength. Were they motivated by the consideration that the apparatus of the N.K.V.D., or sections of it, might have been unleashed against themselves, to gather material with a view to 'liquidating' them as well? I cannot say, but it may be assumed that they had no reason to feel they were safe. And if I ask myself today whether determined opposition on their part would have done anything to abate the N.K.V.D. terror, I cannot but feel convinced that they would themselves have fallen victim to that terror, in spite of the fact that as individuals they enjoyed Stalin's confidence. Yet it would have required no more than a hint from a chief of police to shatter this confidence in men who commanded no power apparatus and had never belonged to an opposition, and an irritable wave of Stalin's hand could have spelt death to those who had hitherto been privileged.

And Manuilsky? In his eyes there was still the golden gleam, the sparkle of an exceptional personality – but at times also something tired, grey and sorrowful. He has often been the target of adverse criticism; there are tales of his intrigues, of his unpredictable changes of front, of the craftiness and ruthlessness with which he carried out the instructions of the central authority, making or breaking politicians. He was, I believe, capable of many things, of ambiguity, of ambivalence, but I made his acquaintance in quite other circumstances and, from the beginning, I returned the sympathy which he extended to me. It was illuminating to watch him when, indulging his pleasure in play-acting, he recounted his experiences as a tourist guide during his exile in Paris. I believe that a delight in assuming a variety of masks, roles and situations, a delight in disguise for its own sake rather than for any particular purpose, was an essential constituent of his character. Inspired ideas fluttered about him like a flock of birds, numbers of them swooping down on him all at the same time, snatching their food and flying off before he could or, indeed, so much as tried to, catch them. 'Why don't you write a major work?' I once asked him, dazzled by the wealth of his ideas. 'I couldn't,' he replied, 'it isn't in me. What I think up others have to elaborate.' But even as he said it his eyes were twinkling as if to tell me not to take his words too seriously. He could never resist telling a joke, even though it might prove fatal either to himself or to others.

Along with Radek, Manuilsky was at the origin of most anti-Soviet jokes. During the period of the arrests he made a speech at a Comintern party meeting, a speech charged with pathos and underlaid with irony, in which he condemned jokes, counter-revolutionary, anti-Soviet jokes, as being out of place in so grave a situation. After the meeting he drew me to one side: 'Have you heard this one . . . ? When Trotsky rode across the Red Square during the 7 November parade, the crowds shouted: "Trotsky! Trotsky!" When Voroshilov rides across the Red Square, they shout: "Look at that horse! What a beautiful horse!" ' Attached though I was to Manuilsky, such cynicism displeased me. Not till much later did I understand that there was a great deal more to it than cynicism; it had been a display of confidence in myself, a gentle hint that his speech had been dictated to him, a commemoration of Trotsky, the rider for whom a horse had been substituted. He did not dare speak openly, even to me, but I recall with respect and gratitude the number of times he came to my rescue. Once during a period of 'thaw' in the Comintern, we foreigners were invited to attend a party meeting where we were to voice our frank criticism of anything that particularly irritated us. Assuming the invitation to be genuine, I vigorously assailed the bureaucratic methods responsible for so much wasted time, so many frayed nerves; the factitious debates in which speakers underlined, concurred and reiterated; the tedium of party life. My outburst was followed by an embarrassing silence. Then Manuilsky leapt into the breach, praising my talents, my loyalty to the ideas of Communism; no one should hold a few exaggerations or unfortunate turns of speech against a speaker and publicist of my quality; such outspokenness was refreshing and should cause the bureaucrats to ask themselves why a man such as Comrade Fischer should not yet feel properly at home in Moscow and should still fail to see things in exactly the light that might be desired. Today I know how much courage was needed to stand up with such eloquence for one who was an outsider.

Once, in the year of the terror 1937, we were sitting in the garden of Manuilsky's *dacha* in Kuntsevo. I was not infrequently the guest of Manuilsky and Varya, the daughter of an aristocratic Petersburg family, gentle, beautiful, ardent, her ardour invariably muffled up in grey scarves and heavy overcoats. She was tubercular but it was not because of this that she always felt so cold; it was from a winter far more harsh and growing steadily more glacial that she was seeking refuge in her wraps. She was a cloud charged with electricity; when a thunderstorm was about to break and the air grew dark there would be a halo round her head, and if anyone touched her hair, it would stand on end and give off little sparks. Though she never said anything at the time, I know now that she was afraid Manuilsky might at any moment be arrested. We were sitting, then, outside the *dacha* when Manuilsky suddenly remarked quite out of the blue: 'Terrible things can happen. Any Communist is liable to find himself in an inconceivable situation. In the kind of situation, let me tell you, where nothing is any help – whether it be faith in something, or moral steadfastness or courage – nothing except . . .', and here he tapped his forehead, 'intellect. For us, it's the ultimate court of appeal, our refuge from madness. This,' and again he tapped his forehead, 'is all we have. We intellectuals have less resistance than those of coarser fibre.'

Varya had approached us on silent feet.

'I believe we women are better able to cope than men. You don't have to worry about us.'

Wasn't the image in Varya's dark, tragic eyes a reflection of what was happening, what was about to happen, all over the country?

Had Manuilsky been warning me?

I did not understand it as a warning but rather as a pronouncement, a reflection concerning the resources upon which an intellectual can draw in an emergency . . .

Meanwhile, something unexpected happened. One of the arrested Schutzbund men, Armand Weiss, was put on trial before a normal Soviet court with lay magistrates, a public prosecutor and a counsel for the defence. I was admitted as a witness. The stuffy room in which the court was sitting might, in its dusty seediness, its depressing shabbiness, have come straight out of Kafka (whom I had not then read and who – perhaps – might have helped me to see things in a clearer light). Everything proceeded in orderly fashion, even if somewhat slowly and haltingly. There were only a few witnesses. The public prosecutor was astonished that I, as Comintern representative of the C.P.A., should vouch for Weiss, for his innocence and integrity. Did I then, he asked, know him very well? Though I did not know him very well, I answered the question in the affirmative and repeated my testimony on his behalf. The public prosecutor spoke, as public prosecutors will, with the cold rhetoric of power, differing from his Western colleagues only in his political phraseology and his liberal use of quotations from Stalin. The N.K.V.D., he said, had thoroughly investigated the case; since this was not an isolated but a typical case selected from the whole complex of anti-Soviet activity, espionage and deviation, there was every reason why much of the evidence should be withheld; he was, however, convinced that the vigilant guardians of Soviet power would receive from the court the confidence that was their due, as also assistance in destroying the agents of the class enemy in the Soviet Union; quite clearly the accused had succeeded by his ingratiating manner in hoodwinking Communist functionaries not sufficiently acquainted with what was happening in the Soviet Union; but revolutionary vigilance should transcend all personal predilections. The defence counsel acclaimed the great leader, Stalin, spoke of the indignation felt by every upright Soviet citizen against saboteurs, spies and deviationists who sought, albeit in vain, to besmirch and disrupt the construction of Socialism, and agreed with the prosecuting counsel that everyone should do his utmost to destroy the class enemy, 'whom we shall indeed destroy!' So far as the accused was concerned, he went on, his class antecedents were impeccable, he had taken part, albeit as a Social Democrat, in the Schutzbund's battle and had become, to judge both by his own words and by the testimony of those acquainted with him, a patriot of the Soviet Union. Undoubtedly, revolutionary vigilance was more important than personal predilections and it was not because the accused was a likeable man or because his assertion of his innocence rang true, but rather and above all for exemplary reasons that he would ask for an acquittal, I repeat, an acquittal. Socialist legality went hand in hand with the interests of the party and of the Soviet Union; the acquittal of a man whose guilt was not proven would give the lie to the enemy's calumnies and provide evidence that vigilance struck out only at the guilty.

Armand Weiss was acquitted – on the grounds that his guilt, which he had strenuously denied, had not been proven, and on the understanding that in future he would exercise greater vigilance and spare no effort in helping to construct Socialism and to defend it against the class enemy. Armand Weiss, a quiet, rather retiring man, was killed in the Spanish Civil War.

There were no more trials of the kind. Why this particular one was staged, what purpose it was supposed to serve and at whose instance it took place, I do not know. Were there forces that were endeavouring to combat the N.K.V.D. terror, upholders of legality against uncontrolled violence? Were there conflicts among the party leaders? Had the trial been an experiment to find out, on a small scale, what might result from a big show trial? But no confession had been extorted from Armand Weiss and there was nothing for him to recant before the court. What, then, had been the intention, and who would have risked assuming responsibility for such a trial, who would have had sufficient influence to have it staged? I can hardly assume that the motive behind the trial was its undoubted effect upon myself and others like me. Utterly bemused as I was, and doubting the rationality and good intentions of the Soviet authorities, I felt a sense of relief on hearing the verdict of not guilty. It seemed to me possible, indeed probable, that in the higher echelons enemies were at work, people who had always been enemies or had lately become so, and that the party leadership was attempting to stamp out the infection, a process involving errors and miscalculations. For by what criteria was it possible to distinguish between well-intentioned if heavy-handed intervention and even more radical forms of intervention whose sole purpose was to distort and confuse? But if a trial like that of Armand Weiss could take place and could result in an acquittal, wasn't it permissible to hope that we would emerge from the horrible half-light, exchange the ill-defined shadows cast across the land by mistrust, rumour and fear for a well-defined reality?

The way in which permanently maintained atmospheric pressure can distort consciousness is truly terrifying. The most absurd statements, the most implausible lies begin to take effect if repeated day in, day out. Arrests and accusations on such a scale *cannot* be the result of pure arbitrariness – and arbitrariness on *whose part*? Of course, once an apparatus is in motion, it is bound by its very nature to gather momentum, and its progress cannot easily be controlled. Vigilance! Are you blind? Can't you see the enemy? Anyone may be an enemy, unless you know him inside out. Vigilance became a matter for competition. Haven't you discovered an enemy yet? You mean to say your organization's the only one without an enemy? How strange, how suspect! The only person who's not a witch is your neighbour? The only person who doesn't deal in black magic lives next door? And then, how is it that *he's* got a flat and I haven't, when flats are so hard to come by? That *he's* got a good job and I haven't? That *he* enjoys the chief's confidence and I don't?

I more than suspected that such things were at work in that horrible half-light. But to carry these thoughts to their logical conclusion was something of which nobody was capable unless he dared to think that Stalin was at the origin of the methodical madness, of the apparatus's gradual encroachment, as it crushed everything that aroused the fear of the paranoiac ruler. It was a thought that was beyond my imagining, nor would I have been able so much as to suspect the full extent and systematic nature of the terror, the destruction of the old Bolsheviks, of all those who at some time had opposed Stalin, who might become his rivals, who represented the spirit of the Revolution, who enjoyed the confidence of the army, of the intellectuals, of non-Russian nationals, and so I groped my way helplessly, clinging to any explanation that was even remotely plausible and, in the great events taking place outside the Soviet Union – in Spain, and in France – I was able to find justification for the Communist policy in favour of which I had decided. I was powerless to help the arrested Schutzbund men. But it was not only on their behalf that I intervened with Dimitrov.

'You don't have to worry about us women!' Varya had said. But I was afraid for Ruth. I was afraid because she was such a daredevil and because she was doubly threatened – by the Gestapo and by the N.K.V.D. She was working in Nazi Germany for Russian intelligence and was friendly with General Hammerstein, Chief of the German General Staff; it was a miracle that she had so long escaped being dragged to the execution block by Nazi hoodlums or shot by a Soviet firing squad. Undoubtedly the Gestapo were keeping a watch on her; in addition I had heard of arrests within the Russian intelligence service.

When in the summer of 1937 Ruth came to Moscow on leave, I begged her to give up her perilous work. Although she herself was somewhat uneasy about it, she refused to listen to me.

'I shall speak to Dimitrov,' I said. 'Then it won't be you who has asked to be relieved. I'm the one who's afraid. All I ask is that you don't do anything behind my back.'

'I won't do anything behind your back. But if they ask me if I want it . . .'

'You can tell them that *I* want it. And that for my sake you're willing . . .'

I told Dimitrov about Ruth, how proud and fearless she was, and asked him to back me up.

'I know about her work. She's very highly thought of. Are you married?'

'We got divorced for the sake of her work. All the same, even a wife from whom I'm divorced is of interest to the Gestapo. I'm afraid for her – and not without reason.'

'Very well. We'll see.'

Dimitrov lived in the Dom Pravitelstva, a tall building beside the Moskva where only the highest party and government officials were lodged. He invited us to tea. Colonel Uritsky, the officer responsible for liaison between military intelligence and the Comintern, was there.

'So you want to take your wife away from us, Comrade Fischer? Georgi Michailovich is on your side. But I want to protest. There are no real grounds for your request.'

'It's an understandable request,' said Dimitrov. 'You can't blame him for it. He's afraid for his wife.'

'Afraid? Rubbish! Ruth's clever and she knows what she's about. She isn't afraid. Or is she?'

'No!' exclaimed Ruth, her cheeks burning. Even to be suspected of being afraid was intolerable to her.

'*Molodyets!*' cried Dimitrov, 'splendid, isn't she?'

I pointed out that it was irresponsible to entrust work of this kind inside Nazi Germany to the wife of a Comintern official.

'Which job is the more important?' Uritsky asked. 'I am sure Georgi Michailovich will forgive me if I say that it is the Red Army, not the Communist Parties, that will decide the issue. The C.P.G. was the largest party in Europe and yet . . .'

'And how about Spain? France? Does that count for nothing?'

'Not in the final count, I'm afraid . . .'

'And how about the Communists in Germany and Austria, in the underground? They may be no more than small groups, but it all contributes towards the future.'

'Don't imagine I don't appreciate that! But in the final count it'll be the Red Army that will decide the issue. It's *we* who'll have to bear the brunt of everything . . . You're right, of course, about your job in the Comintern being detrimental to your wife. But I hope you won't mind my saying that your wife's work is the more important. And as for your own, does it really satisfy a man like you? Wouldn't you be able to achieve more as a freelance writer?'

Unbeknown to me, my expression betrayed my feelings. Encouraged, Uritsky continued:

'With Georgi Michailovich's permission, I shall speak frankly. What would you think of a house on the Riviera? Time and leisure to write books? With only the occasional interruption?'

Uritsky, Dimitrov and Ruth were watching my face. Had they been hatching all this between them? And wasn't it a tempting offer? A freelance writer . . . ? Desertion! I shook my head.

'Without putting too high a value on my work in the Comintern, I think it's more important.'

'So you refuse?'

'I refuse and would again ask you most urgently to relieve Ruth of her duties.'

Dimitrov laughed. 'I don't think we can withhold his wife from him any longer.'

'And what do you say . . . ?' Uritsky turned to look at Ruth.

'Me? You know . . .' abruptly she broke off.

Dimitrov stood up. 'There's nothing for it. A high decoration for the little woman. A worthy farewell celebration . . . And after all, isn't the Comintern also a fighting force . . .?'

We agreed that Ruth should pay her parents a visit in Teplitz-Schönau and then come to live in Moscow.

Ruth left. I heard nothing from her. A fortnight, a month went by without any word. My suspicion that she had again gone to Germany at Uritsky's instigation and without any hint to me later turned out to be right. Meanwhile every man jack of the group for which she was working was arrested. By the N.K.V.D., not the Gestapo. She was the only one to survive.

Uritsky had given me his telephone number. 'Use it only if it's really urgent . . .' It *was* really urgent. I telephoned his number.

'May I speak to Comrade Uritsky?'

A woman's voice answered: 'Uritsky? *Takovo u nas nyet!*'

The tone was casual, almost bored. Then the line was cut.

'*Takovo u nas nyet!*'

'There's no one of that name here!'

Not known in this office.

At Christmas I had news of Ruth.

She was alive.

18

The Trials

'How could you have written such a thing?' Lou said, handing me two pamphlets. She had found them while putting our books in order. 'They're dreadful. I can't understand it.'

I knew that I still possessed these pamphlets. From time to time I had wanted to re-read them but had lacked the courage to do so. One of the horrors was entitled 'Destroy Trotskyism!', the other 'The Murdered Workers of Kemerovo'. I had kept them away from her, hoping somehow to persuade myself of their acceptability. Lou is right: they *are* dreadful. But the question is: how could I have written them?

For practising Catholics it is easy enough; they confess their sins, undergo penance and are absolved. It is as though their sins are simply a piece of luggage which they discard, an extrinsic object which is left behind, not something that becomes rooted in the organism, lingering and harmful. I am concerned not so much with obtaining the relief that invariably results from confessing one's own iniquities, but rather with the endeavour to understand the self I once was. But to understand does not mean to forgive, for neither am I myself competent, nor has anyone else the right, to confer absolution on me.

The confrontation with the self I then was cannot be postponed: not a defence but a critical analysis.

First, however, the plea put forward on my behalf by a number of well-disposed critics does not tally with reality, the plea, namely, that I was under severe pressure, harassed by the fear that I myself would be indicted should I fail to endorse the indictment and publicly avow my allegiance. I was under no pressure, I was not afraid and I had no inkling that I was in fact mistrusted by the organs of the Soviet Government. How, then, did this obfuscation of my consciousness come about?

In an attempt to restore my lost identity with myself, Lou said: 'Your trouble is that you often don't know what's going on round you. You never ask questions, you don't try to find things out and you overlook important details. You're living partly in the real world and partly in one created out of your own imagining and contriving. Because of this and despite your intelligence and powers of imagination you're liable to come to the most improbably crack-pot conclusions. On top of that you're too pigheaded to go back on those conclusions but instead you look for arguments to support them. I knew from the very start that the trials of the old Bolsheviks were the vilest put-up job ever; you never once envisaged that possibility even though you were in Moscow at the time.'

Not *even though* but *because* I was in Moscow at the time.

Togliatti invited me to attend and report on the trial of Radek, Pyatakov, Sokolnikov and other Trotskyists.

The indictment, 'drawn up in Moscow on 19 January 1937', was like some primeval dragon intruding into a world which invoked Marx and Lenin, reason and the rights of man, a monster with the power of speech, spouting the jargon of a demented bureau-cracy. The definition of the charge reads:

The investigating authorities consider it established:

1. That, on the instructions of L. D. Trotsky, there was organized in 1933 a parallel centre consisting of the following accused in the present case: Y. L. Pyatakov, K. B. Radek, G. Y. Sokolnikov and L. P. Serebrya-kov, the object of which was to direct criminal anti-Soviet espionage, sabotaging and terroristic activities for the purpose of undermining the military power of the U.S.S.R., accelerating an armed attack on the U.S.S.R., assisting foreign aggressors to seize territory and to dismember the U.S.S.R., overthrowing the Soviet power and restoring capitalism and the rule of the bourgeoisie in the Soviet Union;

2. That, on the instructions of the aforesaid L. D. Trotsky, this centre, through the accused Sokolnikov and Radek, entered into communication with representatives of certain foreign states for the purpose of organizing a joint struggle against the Soviet Union, in connection with which the Trotskyite centre undertook, in the event of its coming to power, to

grant these states a number of political and economic privileges and territorial concessions;

3. That, moreover, this centre, through its own members and other members of the criminal Trotskyite organization, systematically engaged in espionage on behalf of these states, supplying foreign intelligence services with secret information of the utmost state importance;

4. That, for the purposes of undermining the economic strength and defence capacity of the U.S.S.R., this centre organized and carried out a number of wrecking and sabotaging acts at certain enterprises and on the railways, which caused loss of human life and the destruction of valuable state property;

5. That this centre prepared a number of terroristic acts against the leaders of the Communist Party of the Soviet Union and of the Soviet government, and that attempts were made to carry out these acts . . .

The following passages also appear in the indictment:

In committing sabotaging acts in collaboration with agents of foreign intelligence services, and organizing the wrecking of trains, explosions and fires in mines and industrial enterprises, the accused in the present case did not scruple to resort to the vilest methods of struggle, and deliberately and with aforethought perpetrated such monstrous crimes as poisoning and causing the death of workers for the purpose of provoking discontent among the workers against the Soviet government . . .

Such are the vile, treacherous, anti-Soviet activities of the Trotskyites, the contemptible Fascist hirelings, traitors to their country and enemies of the people . . .

Constituting an isolated and politically doomed group of bandits and spies . . .

Outrageously betrayed the interests of the working class and the peasantry . . .

Betrayed their country . . .

Became espionage, sabotaging and wrecking agents of the German and Japanese Fascist forces . . .*

Reading this now it is beyond my comprehension that I could have believed such lunacy.

But to an observer in the Hall of Columns of the Moscow Trade Union Building, the incredible became each day more credible.

I fell victim to the terrible power of appearances, to the power of

*Indictment in the case of Y. L. Pyatakov, K. B. Radek and others, official English text.

suggestion exercised by the spoken word, a word not as yet dead
and printed, not as yet available for careful autopsy. It was, for all
its unnaturalness, a gruesomely natural performance. The indictment
assumed human shape in the person of the prosecutor himself,
Vyshinsky. He spoke the same brutal, nauseating jargon, while his
face bore the fixed expression of hatred and disgust that was to
become a model for thousands of his ilk. In his pale blue eyes there
was nothing but ice. Death was in charge of the production; the
performers, however, were living people, not to all appearances
playing a part, but simply being their own selves. Their movements
were relaxed and they did not look as though they had been tortured
or had had their confessions extracted from them by other means.
What they said sounded spontaneous, unafraid, articulate. They
were given tea, and frequently the trial assumed the air more of a
discussion than of legal proceedings. Arguments were met with
impulsive counter-arguments followed by general recapitulations.
Only Radek appeared to be acting, his role that of a tragic, equi-
vocal clown, unexpectedly addressing the public in a mixture of
German and English, incomprehensibly supporting the prosecutor.
During his cross-examination Tukhachevsky's name was suddenly
mentioned. Everyone held their breath, amazed and horrified. But
effortlessly bridging the deathly silence, the clown emphatically
affirmed that Tukhachevsky was Stalin's most faithful adherent,
that he had had no part in any conspiracy and that he had indignantly
repudiated any such suggestion.

Next to me sat a small man with a look of thoughtful concentration on his exceptionally intelligent and likeable face: Lion Feuchtwanger. I had not met him before. He turned to me:

'What do you make of it?'

'As a non-Communist you're more impartial than I am. What do
you make of it?'

'I followed the Zinoviev and Kamenyev trial at a distance, in the
West. What I read in the papers seemed highly implausible. One
simply couldn't believe it. But here at close quarters, in the atmosphere of Moscow, where one can see and hear everything . . .'

Feuchtwanger went on thoughtfully: 'The first trial reminded me
of some gruesome play. But this trial . . . the impression it makes
on the senses is wholly convincing. If this is a fabrication, then I
don't know what's genuine . . .'

'So you believe the confessions . . .?'

'To be genuine. I can see no other alternative. The indictment is open to question. But the accused carry conviction. One only has to observe their relaxed movements, their dispassionate, natural way of discussing things. If it were a masquerade it would have needed years of rehearsal and even then it would never have looked as uncontrived as this. What convinces more than anything else is the manner, the intonation, the attitude of the accused. That could never get across in a transcript of the proceedings. I daresay that many of my friends, if they simply read the transcript, will find this trial as abhorrent as the first; I myself, having laid a finger in the wound, know that it isn't an illusion. There is much that is obscure, inexplicable – but the alternative is utterly unthinkable.'

So it was; Feuchtwanger's view does not excuse the obfuscation of my consciousness but for me, too, the alternative was unthinkable. And, indeed, it still is, although we now know that the unthinkable actually happened. At the time I asked myself whether it was conceivable that the Soviet Union should be in a highly critical situation, that her economy should be lagging behind both plans and requirements, that the old Bolsheviks should be sacrificing themselves and taking the blame so as to save what had been achieved in October 1917 and was now in jeopardy. In themselves these things were not, I thought, inconceivable. But then the old Bolsheviks would surely have preserved their dignity, would not have accused themselves of the most infamous crimes, would not have showered accusations on the expatriate Trotsky. This alternative must therefore be excluded. But I did not, dared not, entertain the notion that the trial had been instigated by Stalin, that he was the murderer of Kirov and that it was he who was responsible for the disgrace, the destruction, the annihilation of the old Bolsheviks, of virtually all Lenin's comrades-in-arms. To me that was something utterly unthinkable.

But why was I more disposed to accept as a fact the other unthinkable alternative, the treachery, the criminality and self-abasement of the old Bolsheviks?

What misled me above all were not the interlocking confessions, or Radek's fitful flame, or Muralov's touching presence, but Pyatakov, the strongest personality in this dance of death, brave, intelligent, unemotional. From the way he stood there, more like a professor than a conspirator with his reddish goatee, recounting in even tones the steps he had taken to organize sabotage in the industry of which he had been put in charge, as though he were speaking of the distant past – of Penelope destroying overnight what she had woven during the day – in this matter-of-fact quality of the monstrous, I believed I could perceive for the first time what the struggle for power really was. 'You people carry on just like in Shakespeare!' Charlie Chaplin once said to Hanns Eisler. And of Communists Stalin had said that they were hewn from different wood to other people. What was involved, we learned from Pyatakov, was a life-and-death struggle. He and his friends had regarded Stalin's policy as wrong. They had combated him openly and lost. Not being prepared to accept defeat they had continued the struggle, but with different weapons, had allied themselves with the devil. Now that they had lost this fight also, they would themselves suffer the fate they had intended to mete out to Stalin and his régime. In this attitude I detected the greatness of the fallen Lucifer, and my imagination was stirred.

What could I know, I asked myself, I who had grown up in a small, impotent country and in an atmosphere which, despite Seipel, Dollfuss and the Heimwehr, was relatively democratic, what could I know of power, of political fanaticism, of the extreme consequences which one reared on illegality, revolution and civil war, is determined to draw? For the first time I believed I understood that an age of iron had begun, that the international class struggle, the interplay of classes, countries and systems, was about to assume terrible forms, that Hitler, no longer just an isolated pathological phenomenon, was become a symptom, that no one could predict what tomorrow's alliances would be – the craziest, the most improbable alliances. The period depicted by Shakespeare was one of great social upheaval; yet what were those struggles between aristocratic factions, what the collapse of the feudal order, the rise of capital and centralized power, by comparison with the twentieth century? Richard III, Macbeth the murderer are reduced to the stature of dwarfs beside the monsters of our age of iron.

Though I had little experience of factional struggles, they seemed to me more productive of hatred than any other form of conflict. Many of my friends in the Social Democratic left-wing opposition hated the Social Democratic leaders more than they hated

the class enemy. Orthodox Communists would speak more vitrio-
lically of renegade or expelled Communists than of National
Socialism. In factional strife of this nature, what is at stake is not
only power as such, but also opposing concepts, dogmas or strategic
considerations, so that the struggle for power becomes a struggle
between true believers and heretics, between the infallible party and
its saboteurs. I myself could not envisage any situation in which
I would be prepared to treat with National Socialism, indeed I had
deplored the rapprochement between the Schutzbund and the Nazis
both in the struggle against the Dollfuss régime, and subsequent to
the events of February and of July 1934. But such deliberations, I
told myself, were typical of an intellectual who had never striven
for power and hence was no politician. Richard III is turned into a
'villain' by his deformity, by the hatred felt by the ugly man for the
well-favoured, by the discovery of his power of seduction assayed
beside Henry VI's bier; Macbeth, in order to murder sleep and
become enmeshed in the mechanism of power, requires the witches
and Lady Macbeth; but suppose the incentive is neither deformity nor the art of magic but the conviction that the victor in the
struggle between factions is destroying and betraying the idea of
revolution, and that it is therefore the duty of the vanquished to
overthrow the victor by whatever means? And supposing those
means, having relentlessly supplanted the ends and reached the point
of no return, of all or nothing, proceed to cross the borderline
between historically justifiable destruction and the nihilism of
crime – supposing the mechanism continues to function independently?

I began at this time to appreciate the alarming implications of
power. But why did I turn these reflections only against the vanquished and not against Stalin in whose person all power was vested?
Why, if I was prepared to attribute the incredible to the accused, did
I harbour no suspicions against the power apparatus? No doubt
because I was not only deceived by appearances but also, and without
knowing it, contaminated by power. For such power does not
merely reside in an apparatus; it feeds upon the atmosphere that
engenders it, upon the *ambiance* of ideology, of custom, of convention, of set phrases, and exerts its influence through its uncanny
ordinariness, its inescapable ubiquity, through the layer of dust it
daily deposits on men's minds. The arguments which had been used

by Stalin in the struggle between the factions had become plausible by dint of constant reiteration and had sealed his victories with the stamp of necessity. If, then, Stalin was *right* – and I was fully convinced that he was – if he had at his back the large majority of the party and the people, what did he have to fear from the defeated? At the time we did not know and could not have suspected what we were not in fact to learn until after the Twentieth Party Congress, namely that at the Seventeenth Congress of the C.P.S.U. the majority had voted against him in the hope of putting Kirov in his place. Although my tendency is to side with minorities against power, the concentrated power of Stalin clearly did not fail to make its impression on me. In the atmosphere diffused by that power it was more difficult to escape being impressed than it would have been outside the Soviet Union.

What mainly influenced me, however, was the fact that the men who represented the new political strategy – a strategy which I myself had fervently embraced – the men of the Seventh World Congress, all unconditionally supported Stalin; the fact, too, that without, or in opposition to, Stalin they would never have been able to put across the shift to the Popular Front and its system of anti-Fascist alliances; and, finally, the fact that, in talking to me, they described the accused as advocates of the old policy of disastrous isolationism, of the fanatically reiterated formula that Social Democracy was the chief enemy, the Social-Fascist mainstay of the bourgeoisie. The defendants comprised a number of fanatical opponents of the new policy; it should, of course, have struck me that this aspect was never alluded to publicly, that the public prosecutor never raised the matter against them and that all discussion of it was confined to ourselves. The point never occurred to me; so far as I was concerned, the crucial question was whether a man supported the militant anti-Fascist community or whether he opposed it. The fatally *simpliste* view firstly, that there were only two antagonistic fronts so that the slightest departure from one necessarily entailed a rapprochement with the other and secondly, that the tendency of the age of iron was not towards multiplicity but towards polarization, the concentration of extremes, led me to draw conclusions that were wide of the mark.

As a left-wing Social Democrat I had admired Trotsky and respected Stalin, but had felt no particular affinity for either of the two men. The fact that Trotsky, the brilliant writer, the opinionated political thinker, the great revolutionary, was closer to me than Stalin – an arid, remote personality who had only begun to emerge after the October Revolution – induced me to oppose myself to the man by whom I was fascinated. In my play *Lenin*, written in Vienna in the twenties, I had depicted Trotsky as a brave but vain and ego-centric revolutionary, an 'operatic tenor of the Revolution'. Recognizing his exceptional ability, I now persuaded myself that he was capable of anything and that, where his concept or his power was involved, he would jib at nothing. I should have been put on my guard by the fact that, at a crucial phase in the struggle for power between himself and Stalin, he chose to go hunting, regarding his own intellect, the forcefulness of his personality, as stronger than the apparatus. He was undoubtedly an over-weening, ruthless man with complete faith in his own genius, prepared to play for the highest stakes, to run extreme risks, to perpetrate monstrous deeds, but not to commit degrading crimes such as were attributed to him by Stalin and his apparatus.

Lenin has been criticized for accepting the help of the German General Staff when, in 1917, he was conveyed across Germany to Russia in a sealed railway wagon. Lenin was not afraid of thus temporarily compounding with the foreign class enemy; the military defeat of the Russian Government would, he hoped, bring not only a Russian but a European revolution, and the German General Staff, not the revolution, was to be the loser in this game of dice with the devil. To me, therefore, in 1936 it did not seem beyond the bounds of possibility that Trotsky might have been envisaging temporary cooperation with Hitler, since he regarded Stalin as the chief foe and stumbling-block where revolutionary development was concerned. Trotsky was opposed to the policy of the Popular Front. He spoke of it as a betrayal of the working class since it meant surrendering the dictatorship of the proletariat for which, in France and in Spain, it was essential to fight. I recalled the common strike action by Communists and National Socialists in 1932 and the conversations I had had with German Communists at that time: 'Let Hitler come to power! Willy-nilly, he'll pave the way for the pro-letarian revolution. After Hitler, the dictatorship of the proletariat!' And yet, in spite of the horrifying example of Germany – Hitler in power because there had been no united front, no Popular Front, no alliances anywhere, from the extreme left to the conservative generals – in spite of all this, Trotsky was again daydreaming of a struggle for the dictatorship of the proletariat and denouncing the Popular Front as a betrayal; hence, it seemed to me not improbable that he **might** resort to extremes.

I therefore believed the reproaches that were levelled at Trotsky by the accused men, reproaches which I summed up as follows:

Both in his statements to Pyatakov and in his letters to Radek, Trotsky declared that it would be foolish to expect support from the masses of the Soviet people, this being a Social Democratic fallacy. The masses of the Soviet people were too much 'hypnotized by the construction of Socialism' to be of any use. Policy must be based on the fact that Fascism had triumphed in Germany and certain other countries, and that the whole world was on the threshold of a Fascist era. Hence an alliance with the real forces of Fascism was essential if the goal was to be attained; just as Socialism in one country was a utopian concept, so too it would be utopian to hope to conduct the struggle against the Soviet Government in one country rather than join up with the international anti-Soviet forces. Germany and Japan would inevitably go to war against the Soviet Union; hence it was in the Trotskyists' own interests to accelerate the advent of that war and to do everything in their power to bring about the Soviet Union's downfall. There were two methods of seizing power; the first consisted in engendering panic in the Soviet Union by means of terrorism and sabotage, followed by Trotsky's own assumption of power; this, however, was unrealistic, since the Trotskyist forces in the Soviet Union were not nearly strong enough. The second and only realistic method was war: to come to power through the military defeat of the Soviet Union, to conclude a peace treaty with the major Fascist powers, cede large areas of territory to them and grant them considerable concessions in return for which they would help maintain the new régime. It would, of course, be nonsensical to suppose that the latter could be a democratic régime; after a lost war and the class struggles that would be unleashed between the peasants and the old *kulaks*, between the workers and the interloping capitalists, only a Napoleonic régime would be capable of controlling the situation. It would be equally nonsensical to suppose that this could be a Socialist régime. Russia could only become viable by assimilating herself to the Fascist states and restoring capitalism. An alliance with the victorious Fascist powers would make it possible for Russia to exist; she must, however, be prepared, firstly to give the German Fascists a free hand, not only in the Ukraine, but also in the Balkans and, secondly, to abandon Czechoslovakia and the other countries of the Little

Entente to their fate. Equally she would be obliged to cede the territory beyond the Amur to Japanese imperialism and to support the latter in its penetration of China and its struggle against the United States of America. This would be the only realistic programme. In the meantime, however, it would be necessary to step up terrorism and the work of sabotage in the Soviet Union, not in the hope of overthrowing the Soviet Government, but above all in order to demonstrate to Fascist allies that Trotsky-ism was to be taken seriously and that Trotsky's valuable offer of help to the Fascists was more than just hot air.

That, then, is what I wrote and that is what I believed, while my brain was busy spinning threads between the Spanish Civil War and the Moscow trials and weaving them into a fearsome web. Were not these the two fronts of the Second World War, fronts against Hitler, here no less than there? Must not all combatants necessarily belong either to one front or the other – most, but not all, of them being aware of the fact? It was the mechanistic theory of *two* worlds, *two* camps, *two* fronts, between which there could not be a third, the appalling over-simplification of the international class struggle, that clouded my intellect – a theory that conflicted with the Popular Front policy, based as this was on the assumption that temporary alliances need not involve the sacrifice of one's own views and aims. Hitler, I reasoned, was no less ready to support Trotsky than Franco, both of whom accepted his support although to do so was not without its dangers.

And so I brought myself to believe what I then wrote:

The Fascist adventurers counted on Trotsky as a real force; the destruction of the Trotskyist centre in the Soviet Union, like the heroic resistance of the Spanish people to the interloper, may well give them pause for reflection. And what Radek said in court will not be pleasing to their ears. Radek declared that Trotsky had failed to understand the tremendous changes wrought in the Soviet Union. He (Radek) knew the Soviet Union, he knew the *kolkhozes*, the factories, the transport system, the Red Army, and felt compelled to admit that in recent years the Soviet Union had changed beyond recognition. Only a few years ago, he would have regarded her defeat as a distinct probability, but today the Soviet Union was invincible; he had, therefore, found Trotsky's directive preposterous and had come to feel more and more that he and his companions had entered a cul-de-sac.

Today after thirty years I force myself to read what I wrote then, confronting my recalcitrant memory with the printed word. If I voluntarily subject myself to this torture, it is not for the purpose of self-mortification but in order to demonstrate the lengths to which a man can go who, though neither stupid nor vicious, deliberately ceases to see, to listen, to think *critically*, subordinating his intellect to the '*Credo quia absurdum*' so as not to doubt the cause he serves and, having thus subordinated his intellect, proceeds to abuse it by clothing the resulting nonsense in threadbare syllogisms.

And so I read:

The Confessions.

Why have all the accused confessed? This very justifiable question raised by anti-Soviet propaganda is sometimes foolishly repeated by people who are not in the least ill-intentioned, but merely thoughtless . . .

The diplomats and reporters from capitalist countries who attended the trials were completely convinced of the authenticity of the confessions; one of the diplomats present said: 'If it isn't the truth then I don't know what is.' The diplomats and reporters saw how physically fit the defendants looked, how relaxed were their movements, how free from restraint their speech and their arguments, how politely they were treated . . . And finally they asked themselves: 'For what reason would the Soviet Government accuse people's commissars, leading men in industry and world-famous party members of such crimes, why should they present this terrible spectacle to the public, if the indictment had not been corroborated and substantiated a hundred times over?' What stupidity to suggest that Stalin and the leadership of the party would stage a trial of this kind out of 'sheer vindictiveness'. Too stupid indeed for anyone but the most idiotic reactionary to believe; the diplomats and reporters knew perfectly well that such an idea was pure stupidity.

I pause; does not this piling-on of invective in lieu of argument ('stupidity', 'idiotic reactionary' and again 'stupidity'), this invocation of 'diplomats and reporters' indicate a suppressed suspicion that all was not well, that there was *another* alternative? That must have been the case – yet even now, even mistrusting my memory as I do, I can safely affirm that the idea of Stalin's possible guilt did not at the time remotely occur to me; the thought would have been unimaginable. Hence what the defendants had confessed *had* to be true.

The favourite trick practised by the Trotskyists and their allies lay in convincing well-intentioned people that the defendants had voluntarily confessed to everything of which they had been accused in the indictment, indeed that, mysteriously complaisant, they had insisted upon saying everything they were wanted to say . . .

In reality the defendants denied everything until the very last moment, only admitting their guilt when it could no longer be gainsaid . . .

So they did finally confess? Why didn't at least one of them remain silent to the end? Why didn't one of them at least persist in his denial to the end? Because an accused man has a natural desire to defend himself yet cannot do so if, having been incriminated by witnesses and other defendants, he insists that he has nothing to do with the business and that all the accusations are false? Radek and Pyatakov persisted in their denials for months, but Romm admitted that he had carried letters to and fro between Trotsky and Radek; Bukhartsev admitted that he had been responsible for putting Trotsky in touch with Pyatakov and further stated that, equipped with a German passport, Pyatakov had been flown in a German aircraft to see Trotsky; some of the arrested spies described their collaboration with the Trotskyists, some of the arrested Trotskyists, including Muralov and Boguslavsky, confessed because they realized that Trotskyism had failed – so what else could Radek and Pyatakov do? If they wanted to defend themselves *politically*, they had to admit the *facts* in so far as these were known to the public prosecutor. There is nothing strange about their confessions as such: it would have been strange had they not talked, had they awaited the inescapable verdict without making any attempt to justify themselves politically . . .

Very diverse are the men in the dock at the Soviet assizes, very diverse the paths by which they have come to confess, very diverse the degree of their responsibility – but to most of them, during the final period of their terroristic activities, one thing had become more or less clear: that they were now in a cul-de-sac, that they were sinking ever deeper into a quagmire of infamous crime. This aspect too must be taken into account before the value or otherwise of their confessions can be assessed. If, in a capitalistic country, thirty Communists or Socialists are arrested, there is a distinct probability that not one of them will incriminate the others but that each will proudly confess to his own beliefs. They have at their backs a great and heroic movement with which they keep faith and which keeps faith with them; it is this consciousness, not the relative strength or weakness of an individual, that makes every one of them great and heroic. But what do the Trotskyist counter-revolutionaries have at their backs? The hatred of their own people; the abhorrence of their own class; the Gestapo, Fascist espionage, and capitalism which despises its own tools . . .

The attitude of the accused corresponds exactly to their deeds, corresponds exactly to the situation in which they found themselves . . . In order to defend themselves they had to confess; they defended themselves in so far as it is possible to defend the nameless iniquity of frightful crimes. And that is not easily possible.

'Not at all convincing,' was Lou's comment.

'It may not be so now. At the time its apparent logic did convince me.'

And not me alone.

In his book *Moscow 1937, My visit described for my friends*, Lion Feuchtwanger wrote:

Imagine this man Trotsky, condemned, as he was, to inactivity, compelled to look on idly, whilst the noble experiment which Lenin and he had begun was transformed into a sort of gigantic petit-bourgeois allotment. For to him, who wanted to steep the terrestrial globe in Socialism, the 'Stalin State', as he says in word and writing, appeared a ridiculous caricature of his original idea . . . Trotsky has given expression time and time again to his unbounded hatred and contempt for Stalin. Would he not translate into action what he had expressed in word and writing?[*]

It was not, Feuchtwanger continues, 'inconceivable' that Trotsky, believing himself to be the only fit leader for the Revolution, should go to any lengths to topple the 'false Messiah' from the throne which his petty mendaciousness had enabled him to usurp. And here Feuchtwanger draws a comparison between Trotsky and Coriolanus: 'Shakespeare's Coriolanus, when he goes to Rome's enemies, the Volscians, says, in speaking of the false friends who have all forsaken him:

> . . . suffer'd me by the voice of slaves to be
> Whoop'd out of Rome. Now this extremity
> Hath brought me to thy hearth . . .
> . . . but in mere spite,
> To be full quit of those my banishers,
> Stand I before thee here.

This is Shakespeare's opinion on the likelihood of Trotsky's having come to an arrangement with the Fascists.'[†] Feuchtwanger further comments:

[*]*Moscow 1937* . . ., pp. 136–7.   [†]ibid., p. 138.

I must admit that although the trial has convinced me of the guilt of the prisoners, I can find no completely satisfactory explanation of their behaviour before the court, notwithstanding the arguments of the Soviet people. Immediately after the trial, I summarised my impressions in a commentary for the Soviet Press: 'West Europeans are experiencing some difficulty in arriving at the fundamental causes of the procedure adopted by the accused, and, above all, the ultimate reasons for their behaviour before the court. It may be that the deeds of most of these men deserved death: but invective and outbursts of indignation, understandable though these may be, will not give an explanation of the psychology of these men. It would take a great Soviet poet to make their guilt and their sin comprehensible to Western minds.' That is on no account to be taken as meaning that I want to find fault with the conduct of the trial or with its findings. Were I asked for the quintessence of my opinion, I could perhaps only follow the example of that modest essayist Ernst Bloch, and quote Socrates, who, when questioned regarding certain obscurities in Heraclitus replied: 'What I have understood is excellent. From which I conclude that the rest which I have not understood is also excellent.' *

Why all this? Can the mistakes of another do anything to mitigate one's own failings? Should I invoke Romain Rolland, or Henri Barbusse, or Louis Aragon, or so august and significant a figure as Ernst Bloch? Again, why not Bernard Shaw?

The strength of the case was the incredibility of the accusations against him ... But Trotsky spoils it all by making exactly the same sort of attacks against Stalin. Now I have spent nearly three hours in Stalin's presence and observed him with keen curiosity, and I find it just as hard to believe that he is a vulgar gangster as that Trotsky is an assassin.†

Or yet again Bertolt Brecht:

Even in the opinion of the bitterest enemies of the Soviet Union and of her Government, the trials have clearly demonstrated the existence of active conspiracies against the régime, and the responsibility of these conspiratorial caucuses both for sabotage at home and for certain nego-tiations with Fascist diplomats regarding the attitudes of their govern-ments towards a possible change of régime in the Soviet Union ...

We must try to discern behind the actions of the accused what was to

---

*ibid., pp. 152-3.

†cit. Isaac Deutscher, *The Prophet Outcast. Trotsky: 1929–1940*, Oxford University Press, 1963, p. 369.

them a conceivable political conception – a conception which led them into a quagmire of infamous crimes . . . This false political conception led them into the depths of isolation and deep into infamous crime. All the scum, domestic and foreign, all the vermin, the professional criminals and informers, found lodging here. The goals of all this rabble were identical to the goals of the accused. I am convinced that this is the truth, and I am convinced that it will carry the ring of truth even in Western Europe, even for hostile readers . . .*

I have no intention of trying to hide behind others. My own argument was as follows: it was with good reason that Stalin feared Trotsky's magnetism, his influence upon the old Bolsheviks and, above all, upon the intellectuals. Many of these left-wing intellectuals, just because they found Stalin so alien, so uncouth and unfamiliar, were at pains to depict him on a magnified scale, to exalt him as the great revolutionary practitioner of *Realpolitik*. And many who at that time were convinced of the defendants' guilt, read Shakespeare and Dostoyevsky in the endeavour to understand their attitude, the riddle of their confessions; essentially, however, it all remained inexplicable. In my pamphlet I concluded:

It would serve no purpose to lose oneself in idle speculations and observations about the individual psychology and the underlying motives of the men who pursued the path of betrayal to the very end; undoubtedly there were faults and flaws in their characters, but in a different age and a different world they would probably not have become criminals. The age we live in, the world we live in are those of decaying capitalism; this disease, this process of decay found a breeding-ground in the faults and flaws of their characters, and it is only in the total context of a world out of joint that men like Trotsky, Radek and Pyatakov can be understood. Their deeds are no less credible or incredible than this world of decaying capitalism, a world which destroys grain and bread, which renders barren good arable land, which allows fruit to rot on the branch, which extracts poison gas from the hunger of the peoples, shapes guns from their misery, goes stumbling onward from one mass grave to the next. That the great German people should be ruled by men like Hitler and Goering, that the democratic governments should look on unmoved at Fascism's butchery of the Spanish people, of Spanish democracy, is just as incredible as that Trotsky, Radek and Zinoviev should have betrayed the proletarian

* Bertolt Brecht, *Über die Moskauer Prozesse*, Collected Works 20, Suhrkamp, 1967, p. 111 ff.

revolution and allied themselves with the mortal enemies of the working class. But in the incredible resides the reality by which we are confronted – a reality which it is our historical mission radically to change.

'When you read that today,' said Lou, 'can't you see how easy you made things for yourself? That simplistic, vulgar Marxism, that high-flown superficiality – the process of decay of the capitalist world infecting characters such as those of Trotsky and Pyatakov! The incredibility of reality – that was true enough. But which was the more incredible – that Trotsky, along with Lenin the initiator of the October Revolution, that the Old Bolsheviks, should have become the Gestapo's henchmen, murderers and saboteurs, or that Stalin and his bureaucratic apparatus should need scapegoats in order to justify the misery of the people and the state of economic chaos? Wouldn't it have been rather more credible that Stalin should have gone to any lengths to vilify anyone who might constitute a threat to him, so as to stifle the last remnants of debate within the party and to ensure absolute dictatorship by the party apparatus, headed by a single, infallible leader? Wasn't that obvious? I shall never understand why you should have believed the more improbable alternative.'

'Was it the more improbable alternative?'

'Yes!'

If, then, the person who is nearest and dearest to me is unable to understand my attitude of those days, is there any hope that even the most honest and determined effort will succeed in making others understand an attitude which today I abhor? Can it have been that I, who mistrusted any form of power, unwittingly succumbed to this particular manifestation of it, to its ubiquity, its sway, its anaesthetic atmosphere? In addition, there was the fact of my being in Moscow and involved in the mechanism of the court proceedings so that I heard nothing of what was happening outside, nothing about the disclosure of blatant fabrications – the meeting between Pyatakov and Trotsky, for instance, alleged to have taken place in a Copenhagen hotel which had long since ceased to exist. But why didn't I subsequently check everything carefully, point by point, why didn't I balance improbability against improbability? Did I in fact *want* to be blind? Did the position I had chosen, my unconditional acceptance of the Soviet Union, inhibit me from questioning the Stalin myth? Had I become – as I certainly would not have admitted at the time – such an out and out Stalinist? . . .

From books, from verbal and written accounts and from documents (the latter, alas, still hard to come by since the authorities in Moscow continue to impose an absurd censorship on world history and to rectify this or that situation in accordance with the current demands of propaganda), we now know that it was Stalin's apparatus which murdered Kirov, that it was Stalin, the 'deserving murderer of the people' as Brecht described him in 1956, who was responsible not only for thousands of judicial murders, but for the 'liquidation' of millions of people. We know that, to extract confessions and thereby fulfil the quota demanded by the bureaucratic terror, no form of coercion, deceit or psychological persuasion was shunned, from physical torture to an appeal to party loyalty, from the threat to murder the victim's wife and children should he refuse to sign, to the promise that the confession was a saving formality.

Thus it was then, and thus it was later. After 1948 my old friend I.V. was arrested in Hungary. He was given the usual confession to sign: Gestapo agent, then agent of the American secret service, from birth an enemy of the people, a parasite, a deviationist, under orders to organize sabotage, assassinations, etc. 'And you expect me to sign that?' 'You refuse?' 'You know very well what rubbish it is!' 'So you refuse?' 'Of course!' His wife was brought in, led by two guards. They were armed with steel rods. 'Strip the woman! First her blouse!' Her face was like a mask. She turned away her imploring eyes as they bound and gagged her, naked to the waist. 'Before we beat her up and then rape her in front of your eyes, are you going to sign?' 'I'll sign anything. Just give it me. Anything you like, that I'm the devil, that I've been ordered to convey all the leaders of the party to hell, to drop atom bombs on Budapest – anything else you want?' And so he signed the confession.

My old friend Maria Švermova, sentenced during the Slansky trial. In a quiet, matter-of-fact voice, unemotionally, almost in a monotone, she talks for hours, telling how she finally came to sign: ' "It was you who introduced N.N. into the party and the apparatus?" "Certainly." "He has confessed that he's a spy, an enemy of the party and of the people. Read his confession." "It can't be true." "Read it!" "I don't believe it." "Now read *this* confession. Another of your recruits." Dozens of such confessions, confrontations, confirmations. All of them comrades I had trusted implicitly. A ring of spies, of enemies of the party. For me, the party was my life. And how had I served it? I had not been vigilant enough. I'd been too gullible. Gullible? Something seemed to tear inside me, I was split in half: defendant and prosecutor. Schizophrenia, isn't that what it's called? If everyone was saying the same thing, could I be right and all of them wrong? There's something wrong with me, there must be. How can you justify yourself in the eyes of the party? You'll have to confess. But confess to what? I've committed no crime. Lack of vigilance? Or something more? Was there something more? "You've been a party member from the beginning. You must help the party. Make a confession!" "But what am I to confess?" "You were a member of a conspiracy directed against the party." "That's not true." "Everyone has said so. Are they all lying? Your closest colleagues? Is that what you taught them? To lie? And you're the only one who hasn't erred, who never suspected? The party needs your confession." "Really needs it?" "Yes. If you, an experienced party member of long standing, a comrade in a leading position, surround yourself with agents, and nothing but agents – who's going to believe that's mere coincidence?"'

For months M.S. went on refusing to sign. She stood firm despite the nightly interrogations, the arc lamps, the psychological bullying. But alone in her cell, she put herself on trial. Her doppelgänger accused her: 'Try and remember! Perhaps after all ... Try and remember. The party's always right. It needs your confession.' All around her the world had gone mad and now this madness was assailing her, beginning to get the better of her. 'Objectively I was a saboteur, introducing treachery and espionage into the party. Objectively? Had it been just objective? Who will believe that? Do you believe it yourself, even? Did I believe myself? There was nothing I could believe any longer, nothing at all. More and more confessions came in, leading comrades incriminating themselves and me. The party, my party, said: Confess! And if you don't confess, we'll throw you out. Want to be a reject? Nothing but a confession can reunite you with the party. What I was to sign, to learn to repeat, parrot-fashion, was crazy. But if everything's insane, the whole world is insane, not a handhold anywhere, only the party, and that party demands that I sign the confession, learn it by heart, like a part in a play? Aren't you bound to take on any part – party secretary or defendant, executioner or victim – if the party's directing the play, if this and no other is the part they want to assign to you?'

And in the end it was not an investigating judge, not a torturer, but she herself, Maria Švermova, who brought herself to the point of assuming the incredible, the humiliating and deadly role. The infamy of the pedants who compelled the accused to learn their parts by heart and expressionlessly to recite these enormities aloud turned the Slanksy trial from the very first day into an infernal comedy, into grim self-mockery on the part of the judicial murderers.

Evgenia Ginzburg gives the following account of the confession made by the Communist Evgenia Podolskaya:

When Evgenia had first been summoned by the N.K.V.D., she felt no alarm. She thought, as an old Communist, that they wished to charge her with some important mission. So they did. The interrogator asked her, to begin with, whether she was ready to take on a difficult and dangerous task for the party. She was? Very well. She would have to spend a short time in a cell. It wouldn't be for long. Once she had carried out her mission, she would receive new papers and a new name, and would have to leave Moscow for a while.

The mission was to sign a number of statements about the wicked doings of a certain counter-revolutionary group, to which, for the sake of plausibility, she would confess that she belonged.

'In fact, give evidence of something she knew nothing whatsoever about?'

'Well, she had the N.K.V.D.'s word for it, hadn't she? They said they knew for certain that the group had committed the most monstrous crimes. All they needed her signature for was to give the case a certain legal weight. Besides, there were top-level considerations of the sort an ordinary party member didn't need to know if she was really willing to perform a dangerous task.'

Step by step, she followed them into this maze of duplicity. Finally, they stuck a pen into her hand and she began to sign. She spent her days in the common cell and at night they called her upstairs, gave her a good meal and let her sleep on the sofa. Then one evening, when she came up, she found a different officer who looked at her ironically and said:

'And now, my dear, you're going to be shot.'*

* Evgenia S. Ginzburg, *Into the Whirlwind*, Penguin Books, 1968, p. 148.

Today this is familiar to us from numerous accounts (among them that of Arthur London), and we know by what methods the most nonsensical confessions were extorted, how the murderers set to work – not hired cut-throats as in Shakespeare's tragedies, but respectable civil servants whose sadism, combined with zeal and with fear for their own skins, served to fulfil the plan; we know how the machinery worked – and yet what we witnessed and failed to understand remains inconceivable and, behind our knowledge, there still lingers a trace of uncertainty, a realm of darkness.

'How could you write such a thing?' Lou was right; but difficult though it is to answer that question, it is even more difficult, despite all we have learned since, to understand the bureaucratic terror, the trials, the confessions of the thirties. Here, then, was a dictator, afraid of a rival, afraid of Kirov, whom we all believed to be his favourite, his chosen successor; at this man's behest, Kirov was assassinated, and after him the tools, the accomplices of the murder; at this man's behest, his former opponents and allies, the old Bolsheviks, were accused of that murder and, worse still, of conspiracy against himself, of a plot to murder him, of 'criminal anti-Soviet espionage sabotaging and terroristic activities for the purpose of undermining the military power of the U.S.S.R., accelerating an armed attack on the U.S.S.R., assisting foreign aggressors to seize territory and to dismember the U.S.S.R., overthrowing the Soviet power and restoring capitalism and the rule of the bourgeoisie in the Soviet Union';* at this man's behest, tens of thousands of the most intelligent, most loyal, most trusty Communists were imprisoned, shot or tortured to death, and whole strata of the population were decimated – intellectuals, men and women of non-Russian origin and, finally, the military. What were the motives? When everything has been summed up – on the one hand, fear, persecution mania, hatred of Trotsky, of Lenin's old guard, of the leaders of the October Revolution who had not forgotten the ambiguous and minor role once played by Stalin, on the other, economic difficulties, the search for scapegoats and later Beria's idea of exploiting the far North and the consequent need for millions of slaves – when all this has been taken into consideration and allowance made for the appalling view that anything is permissible where the cause is con-

*Indictment and definition of the charge in the case of Pyatakov, Radek Sokolnikov and fourteen other Trotskyists.

cerned, the question still remains as to whether the cause of Socialism, if not indeed the cause of the man who chose to use such means, was not thereby impaired beyond all measure? And to what ends? The aim was clearly no longer to achieve Socialism as Marx and subsequently Lenin had conceived it, but rather to turn the Soviet Union, already an industrialized monolithic state, into a top-ranking major power, and Stalin himself into an omnipotent Augustus elevated to the status of a god. With the growth of Stalin's power, however, the power of the apparatus also grew until it became an end in itself and, having once been set in motion, proceeded to rationalize the terror in a precipitate flight from reason, lashing out in every direction with methodical madness and thus functioning as a power in itself, crushing for the sake of crushing, destroying for the sake of destruction, in the blind urge to tolerate nothing but itself. Was Stalin, then, still in control of himself while exercising complete control over others? Had not his power grown beyond control? Did not the elimination of her most intelligent, capable, finest citizens, and the establishment of a servile, demoralized apparatus only a few years before the outbreak of war so weaken the Soviet Union that she was exposed to almost certain defeat?

'And it's only now that you realize all this?' asked Lou.

'I couldn't have known it at the time.'

'You attended the trials of Radek and Pyatakov as a reporter. Like Feuchtwanger, you were misled by appearances. But there's another pamphlet of yours, an account of a trial at which you were not present. It's a pamphlet called "The Murdered Workers of Kemerovo": how could you have written it? I know as well as you that we're no more able now than at the time to see how and why all these horrors happened, but surely it should be possible for you to discover what made you act as you did?'

'I'm trying very hard, doing my best to worm it all out of myself. At the trial of Radek and Pyatakov an aggravating circumstance was a pit disaster in the mining district of Kemerovo. The Kemerovo miners worked under appalling conditions. They either pined away or were poisoned by fire-damp or killed in explosions. "We worked as though we were demented," reads the workers' report, "and though we exerted ourselves to the limits of our strength, we could not meet the norm. It was like working in hell and we were completely at our wits' end how to improve things; the greater our efforts the worse the results – and the engineers cursed us for slackers and saboteurs . . ." Nevertheless on their own initiative the workers of the Centralnaya Mine set about trying to rationalize working conditions and to improve the pit. They decided to organize a Stakhanovite ten-day stint – a stint that was scheduled to begin on 23 September 1936. On that day a terrible explosion occurred. The bodies of ten dead and fourteen gravely injured men were brought to the surface. Amongst the dead were some of the best Stakhanovite workers. Before the Moscow assizes the defendant Shestov declared that the explosion had been caused by sabotage and had been organized by the German chief engineer Stickling, the works manager Peshekhonov (who had been sentenced to three years' exile in 1928 for sabotage, but had been reinstated because of his technical qualifications), by the Trotskyist divisional chief Shubin, and other leading employees. According to Shestov's deposition, there had been contacts with German heavy industry, with the Gestapo and with the "Trotskyite centre". Unlike the majority of the accused, Shestov gave the impression of being a criminal adventurer.'

'You don't seem to care for this fellow Shestov,' said Togliatti one day when we were discussing the trials.

'I think he's a common-or-garden criminal – a completely different type from Pyatakov or Muralov. But look here, couldn't I go to Kemerovo, to see what there is to see and hear what there is to hear? It's all pretty mysterious. Engineers hiding away ventilation equipment in an old shaft while men die from the effects of fire-damp and then telling the workers: "You'll get the machinery for ventilation equipment when the Soviet Government can afford it, not before." The engineer Shubin saying, "We'll show 'em how to make merry. They'll die like rats, will these laddies." A young worker being suborned with a bottle of vodka to help engineer the explosion. I'd like to be in the place where international politics and crime actually interlock. The words "sabotage" and "acts of terrorism" somehow have an unreal ring about them, you press a button – but who knows what actually *happens* at the other end? I'd like to witness the incredible not only in the shape of court records, in confessions, and depositions, but in the flesh. People tell you, "There's a struggle for power at the top, that's what it's about";

but it's those at the bottom, how it works out for *them*, that we ought to describe.'

'I entirely agree,' replied Togliatti. 'I'll speak to Dimitrov. You have a word with him, too.'

Dimitrov also approved. I waited for the Soviet authorities' authorization. That it failed to materialize surprised me at the time. 'It's excessive caution where foreigners are concerned,' said Togliatti. He and Dimitrov asked me to write about Kemerovo all the same. My suggestion, they said, was both right and good. I would be provided with the necessary material. Instead of saying no, I consented. The reports of the trial which had taken place in November 1936 were inadequate for my purpose. Many of the details, however, seemed genuine and not to have been tampered with, and even to this day I feel sure, not only that the disaster did take place, but that many of its circumstances had not been faked; what had been faked was the context in which they had been placed, and hence the garish mosaic I assembled was also false. 'An indifferent thriller!' remarked Lou. But that was not its basic fault – for how many indifferent thrillers have since then become chapters in world history! The fault lay in the fact that I had allowed myself to be persuaded to write about Kemorovo without ever having been there. On the other hand, had I been there, I would not have discovered anything that was different from the commentary on the official text. Because I had attended it, the trial of Radek and Pyatakov had convinced me of the authenticity of the indictment and the confessions. Hence I wrote:

The miners of Kemerovo . . . had to die as Kirov the great workers' leader died, they had to die as tens of thousands of workers in Spain have died, because the working class has grown too strong for the enemies of the workers. 'Five hundred thousand Spaniards must die so that we may rule!' said the seditious general Queipo de Llano. 'The best men of the working class must die that we may conquer!' say the German Fascists and their allies. The murder of workers forms part of their programme.

'But how could you depict Old Bolsheviks on the same plane as Fascist generals? And what possible connection could there be between Spain and the ostensible Trotskyist terror in the Soviet Union?'

'The Spanish Civil War ushered in an extremely acute phase

of the international class struggle, it was the prologue to the war between Nazi Germany and the Soviet Union; the unification of all the anti-Soviet forces, and their readiness to resort to extreme measures, was therefore only to be anticipated. In the accounts of Kemerovo which were put at my disposal I believed I could discern how the web came into being and how it grew ever denser. Reading today what I wrote at the time with its indifferent, inflammatory style and its many exclamation marks, I get the impression that I was shouting down my own doubts. And over and over I called attention to the incredibility of what I believed or was determined to believe. "Sometimes it's a detail which, like a tumour, overgrows one's thinking, which blots out reality with the intensity of a nightmare. Before the court Shubin said that he had deliberately turned the pit into a "gas gunpowder cellar" and had, for good measure, added the words, "They'll die like rats, will these laddies!" So reminiscent were those words of the language used by the S.A. that I could almost hear them being said, they seemed to haunt me, and no less shrilly I echoed them: "The workers' murderers are mistaken. The workers will not die like rats. Victoriously they will defend their world, their lives, against Hitler's and Trotsky's bands of assassins. In Spain they have taken up arms to combat the workers' murderers. In the Soviet Union they are fighting with the weapon of class vigilance, the weapon of revolutionary justice, against the workers' murderers.""

I have hesitated before reproducing these atrocious lines, first written thirty years ago, but I cannot evade this confrontation with myself. With whom?

The self that wrote those accounts was not mentally dishonest. But does that self still exist? Is it not someone else with whom I no longer have anything in common? Nobody forced it upon me, the self which it is so difficult, so agonizing to reconstruct. It was a partial, a party-self: the conscious negation of my individualism, that is to say of my earlier, spontaneous, ever-changing self. This new self did not strive for identity with past states but for identity with a voluntarily recognized super-ego: with the cause, with the party, with a collective which has still not become part of my flesh and blood. A party which prides itself on being 'monolithic' demands that the self of each of its members shall also be monolithic, firmly cemented into a whole by a few principles, qualities and modes of behaviour. I did my best to be that kind of self, and the concentration of all my thoughts, efforts and achievements on *one goal only*, the overthrow of Hitler, made this easier for me. In extreme situations it may *seem* right to reduce oneself to a party-self, that is to say to a function, and to cease to be an inconsistent person. I don't believe that it *is* right: the possible momentary advantage thus gained is more than offset by a distortion which steadily increases and finally becomes irremovable. To revert critically to a self which I no longer am is therefore more than moral self-examination (with which I am not concerned); it is indeed in the general interest, since not a few intelligent and capable people have imposed (and still are imposing) upon themselves a similar party-self, and are thus in danger of sacrificing their intelligence and ability, of coming to regard the nonsensical as true and defending it in tones of shrill indignation.

The identity of the personality, the self as a continuum and totality, is still in our day a necessary contrivance. I hope that some time there may be a free society in which the plurality of the self will thrive naturally, in which every man will be able to enjoy the plenitude of his self and will not be obliged to bind himself to one particular aspect of it. In the age of irresponsibility in which we are living, the loss of identity means a total loss of responsibility. Is it permissible to transfer our responsibility to the power apparatuses, to the systems and 'structures', and ourselves take refuge in a condition of being perpetually 'under orders'? In that case each person would only have *practical* responsibility for the execution of his set task, his profession, his speciality: piloting an aeroplane, reducing a village to ashes, mass murder at command. Everything would become the execution of an order, and the order, whether direct or indirect and no matter *who* gave it – whether president, general or computer – would confer freedom from all responsibility. To have a bad conscience is no longer fashionable; but dubious though it may be in a religious-moral context, I would plead the cause of the bad conscience in this age of irresponsibility, and hence I speak of *my own* bad conscience, of the responsibility of my total self for every one of my many disparate selves, the many metamorphoses of my existence.

It was my *function* to report on the trial, and it was my *ambition* to do it better than anyone else, to find some way of explaining the inexplicable. This, too, may have helped me to see events in the light in which their instigators wished them to be seen; not an objective light, that is, but a partial one. My decision to report them, not *sine ira et studio*, but in the interests of the Soviet Union, meant that each time my intellect ought to have said no, the objection raised by reason was thrust aside by brute argument and the incomprehensible occurrence rearranged in accordance with my pre-conceived opinions. It was not *truth* I was striving for but effective propaganda in the service of a cause of whose justice and greatness I was convinced.

'And what else could you have done?' asks the other, a voice that sounds as strangely in my ears as my own voice reproduced on tape, and hence perhaps another who is or was myself, or someone not clearly distinguishable in the obscurity.

'I shouldn't have written the account.'

'Perhaps. Let us assume that you had trusted the man you are today more than the man you were then, and had refused to write the account. What difference would it have made politically?'

'Politically, my silence, my resistance, would have made no difference. But I'm concerned with something more than politics.'

'Yourself, your integrity?'

'I did nothing that contravened the law of the land, but there's a form of guilt that is worse than criminal. If ignorance is no argument before the law, still less is it an argument before one's conscience – a conscience by which that very ignorance stands condemned. In one who sets out to describe something, one who wields the power of the word, ignorance is inadmissible.

'At the time when Hitler was preparing for the Second World War all genuine anti-Fascists were duty-bound to defend the Soviet Union. Of course, Stalin's crimes did more harm to the Soviet Union than did any anti-Soviet propaganda. But whoever was then in power in Moscow, whoever represented the Soviet Union, had to be given support; for in the long run nobody could beat Hitler except the Soviet Union, whatever her prevailing régime. By remaining silent you would not have served the cause, and any indictment of Stalin could only have done it harm. That is another thing to be borne in mind.'

'Wouldn't that mean that even the worst representatives of a cause which, from an historic viewpoint, we affirm, must in all circumstances be accepted and supported? We must rid ourselves of such sophistry, for in the first place we do *not* serve the cause by identifying it with someone whose methods are corrupting it and, in the second place, personal integrity is valuable as such, even if the "no" of the person concerned seems at the time to run counter to the general interest.'

Reading again what I have written, I am impelled to ask what has been omitted.

No one answer suffices.

What is omitted is the quintessence of all I then was: my hatred of Hitler. Though I am not a hater, I detested Hitler more than anything else in the whole world, detested him to the very foundations of my being. He was for me not simply the representative of the most extreme form of imperialism and chauvinism, not the administrator of social decay – there was, indeed, no one social category in which he could be fitted. I loathed everything about him, his voice, his face, his figure, his form of expression, his gestures, the very least of his pronouncements. Although he did not drink, he was the beery smog of all beer cellars made flesh, a toper drinking himself crowd-silly, after every mass-meeting drained, drooping and pallid, seemingly wading through slime. And beforehand, the baying, the bellowing, the screaming of the little man in the throes of hysteria, gone off the rails, the *déclassé* petit-bourgeois turned gangster, an amalgam of pity for himself and vindictiveness towards all those who have made something of their lives – the skilled worker, the noted writer, architect or painter, the senior executive officer – a pariah dog taking his cue from a werewolf, a man gone down in the world, self-commiserating and ruthless, perfidious and attitudinizing, struggling to reach the top by fair means or foul, a sob in his throat, teeth bared, a sham Nero dreaming of ovations, of artistic renown, of holocausts, the rabble-rousing genius of complete dehumanization. I loathed this man as a monster of mediocrity, as immeasurably bloated provincialism, as a pin-headed troglodyte suffering from megalomania and all at once finding at his disposal the whole potential of technology, of verbal and armed coercion, of concentrated power. The effluvium of his speeches, the fixed insanity of his gaze, foreshadowed Auschwitz. The breach-of-promise specialist as an heroic figure of the primeval forest, ludicrousness dressed up as Lohengrin, impotence as the twilight of the gods, and all this, together with the mumbo-jumbo of his isms and ologies, his rabid gentility, his bloody dilettantism, added up to the most terrifying thing that has ever loomed on my horizon. And when he held a baby in his arms it was as though he were inhaling the smell of human flesh, as though he were dandling tomorrow's dinner, sentimentally licking his lips at the thought of the corpse to come. That the world should become Hitler's world was unimaginable, inconceivable. Nothing else mattered when it was a question of preventing that calamity. To contribute my own mite to Hitler's downfall became the whole meaning and content of my life.

I have not written this to justify my blindness. For, indeed, it was not blindness, only that my eyes were fixed on Hitler, looking neither to right nor left, seeing nothing but the face of the abortion that came oozing out of the abyss like the exhalations of a corpse.

If I had known all the rest, if I had not refused to acknowledge its existence – what would have been the consequences?

Either suicide or continuing as before, with diminished fervour and confidence, to work despite everything for a Soviet Union identified with Stalin, to work against Hitler.

But even that realization does not suffice to exonerate me.

19

The Pact

It was a few weeks after the annexation of Austria. Ruth and I were once again on our way to Moscow by air. Since it was not advisable to travel through Poland we were flying by way of Rotterdam, Stockholm and Helsinki. The weather conditions were bad. Suddenly the passengers were informed that the aircraft would be compelled to land in Germany. Ruth and I were carrying legal passports, Austrians without citizenship, non-citizens of a non-existent state, non-persons. Our names were not unknown to the German authorities.

We went forward to speak to the pilot.

'Are we really having to land?'

'Yes.'

'In Germany?'

'I see . . .' said the Czech pilot, looking at us out of the corner of his eye. 'Are you . . . might it be awkward for you?'

'Yes.'

'All right,' he said. 'It's taking a bit of a risk, but I might just be able to reach Holland.'

He did reach it. We landed in Rotterdam.

'Thank you!'

'What for? After all, I'm human and I'm a Czech. I hope we'll all of us get through this.'

'May we smoke?' we asked in the waiting-room where we had been kept back.

'This isn't Germany!' replied the Dutch official, smiling. 'Things aren't *verboten* here.'

Nevertheless it was under police escort that we drove to our hotel and it was under police escort that we drove back to the airport. We were not honest-to-God emigrants but Communists, in transit to the Soviet Union.

★

Dimitrov suggested I take over the editorship of the periodical *Kommunistische Internationale*. I was aghast. The paper's first editor-in-chief, the erstwhile Menshevik Martynov, had died of natural causes. Every one of his successors had been arrested, the last being a Pole named Valecki.

'Do I have to?' I asked. 'The seat's too hot!'

'Then you'll have to try and cool it down.'

I did my best to render readable a journal which had hitherto been couched in party jargon. The paper in effect became more readable, I worked doggedly, wrestling with my colleagues over every phrase and sentence and deriving from the result a real sense of achievement. I asked to be relieved of the editorship of the Russian edition, how-ever, for I could make no headway with it. The assistant editors of this edition were intelligent and they were devoted to me; but as they were answerable to their party and any appeal to my authority could have done them nothing but harm (Does your vigilance amount to no more than that? You actually defer to a foreigner?), they were afraid of any departure from the usual routine. An article of mine about the nature and position of the petit bourgeoisie met with their delighted though not unqualified approval, for I had failed, apparently, to adorn it with the requisite quotations, an offence even more heinous than walking naked down the street. An article on this scale, they averred, should have roughly two Marx, one Engels, three Lenin and six Stalin quotations, and they set about making good the deficiency. I scored my greatest triumph in their eyes when they discovered quotations that were wholly apposite and fitted my article like a glove. Thenceforward they regarded me as a creative Marxist.

Dimitrov praised my efforts. Others were rather more critical. Reading again, after an interval of three decades, the many articles and polemical commentaries I wrote at the time, some anony-mously, others under my real name or the pseudonyms 'Peter Wieden' or 'Pierre Vidal', I blush for shame. Though here and there in all this mass an original argument may occasionally be found, though much of it is effective and pertinent journalism, how crass the remainder, how banal the language and triumphant the cliché which I had striven so fervently to avoid. Nor is my feeling of discomfort any the less for the realization that it would have been virtually impossible to banish clichés from the journal of a 'monolithic' party let alone from that of a world centre of an international apparatus.

What then, ought I to have done, what *could* I have done?

I had assumed a *function*, I was not a freelance writer but an instrument and I was writing, not for unbiassed readers, but for Communist functionaries. I saw the world through the eyes of the Comintern rather than through my own, though this was not to do violence to myself since on the whole I agreed with the views of that organization. I didn't want to be a stranger in this monstrous building with its innumerable porters, passes, corridors, back-stairs; but how easy it was to take a wrong turning, to lose yourself there! And, on finding yourself again, were you still the same as before, had you not become a photograph in one of the interchangeable passes of the apparatus, a photograph in someone else's pass? But in that world of lowering catastrophe, what was our real concern? The preservation of individuality? Was it not rather to serve the *cause*, in other words, the Soviet Union, the only power capable of stemming Hitler's advance?

On 29 September 1938 Hitler, Mussolini, Chamberlain and Daladier met in Munich and agreed to the partition of Czechoslovakia. The 'Sudetenland' was ceded to Germany. Poland and Hungary took part in the great division of spoils. I was not the only one to feel convinced that this marked the actual beginning of the war against the Soviet Union.

At the time Manuilsky remarked to me: 'The German working class failed to rise up against Hitler, and though in 1934 the Austrian Schutzbund did put up a fight, Austria in 1938 surrendered without a struggle. As Czechoslovakia is surrendering now. The war in Spain is nearing its end, the Popular Front is on the verge of collapse. The Soviet Union will stand alone. Alone and unaided she will have to wage war against Hitler – against Hitler who has the support of every government in Europe – a desperate war whose outcome cannot be predicted. The Soviet people, alone in the hour of decision, always sacrificing themselves for everyone else, always paying for everyone else in blood and suffering, always alone, without effective international solidarity; the Red Army, and the Red Army alone, will pit its strength against Hitler. To save our country from this war, I would be prepared to treat with the devil – but even the devil is hobnobbing with the others.'

On 27 January 1939 Barcelona fell. On 8 February Franco reached the Pyrennean frontier; the remnants of the International Brigade withdrew into France where they were interned. On 28 March Madrid was occupied. There was no organized armed resistance. Two weeks earlier, on 14 March, Slovakia had, by the grace of Hitler, been declared a 'sovereign' state; on 15 March Bohemia and Moravia were incorporated into the German Reich as a 'Protectorate'. Today no more than an historical chronology, this spate of events kept us at the time in a state of permanent turmoil. The epoch of the Popular Front was at an end. War could no longer be avoided.

Manuilsky's sombre prognosis seemed incontrovertible. But after the trials of the Old Bolsheviks, after the truncation of the army and in the midst of a profound internal crisis, how could the Soviet Union stem the tide *by herself*? Surely no effort ought to be spared to earn goodwill, to activate potential allies?

What contribution, I asked myself, could I make to that end? I was putting heart and soul into the production of a paper whose readership probably consisted in no more than a handful of functionaries. To be able to exist I had to postulate, against my better judgement, that my words did not fall on deaf ears and that, even if indirectly, they would somehow, somewhere evoke an echo. I was therefore disposed to overrate each little success as providing proof that I was working to some avail, thus justifying my insignificant existence in this gigantic mechanism of power, of public and secret decision-making.

We were all of us sensible to the economic recovery of the Soviet Union. Food was more plentiful, the queues outside the shops were fewer, faces less drawn, less anxious. On 21 January 1939 Yezhov made his last appearance. It was said that he had been felled by a blow from Kaganovich's fist. Swathed in bandages, the executioner's head disappeared from view, soon afterwards to be followed by his torso. Yezhov's place was taken by Beria. We heaved a sigh of relief. At last, we thought, a modicum of reason, a modicum of security. No longer will a black cloud blot out Stalin's sun.

At the Eighteenth Congress of the C.P.S.U. the Kasakh bard, Djambul, recited the following lines:

> The lapping waves of the lake are singing the praises of Stalin,
> The dazzling snowy peaks are singing the praises of Stalin,
> The millions of blooming flowers are thanking, thanking you,
> The well-laden tables are thanking, thanking you . . .

And so the chorus swelled, turgid with honey and roses, oceans and mountain peaks, 'the heavens declare the glory of God, And the firmament showeth his handiwork', but HE, far from being intimidated by his likeness to the Almighty, delivered a perfectly sensible speech. Stalin accused the Western powers of inciting the Germans to push farther and farther eastwards. Czechoslovakia had been a sop thrown to Germany to induce her to make war on the Soviet Union. 'All I can say is that this dangerous game upon which the advocates of non-intervention have embarked may well end up badly for them.' What was essential now, he went on, was to continue to pursue a policy of peace and economic cooperation with all countries, while taking all possible care not to become embroiled in armed conflict as a result of the machinations of provocateurs. Meanwhile the newspapers were proclaiming the invincibility of the Red Army which, they said, would meet aggression, from whatever quarter, with overwhelming force. 'The great Stalin will lead us on from victory to victory.'

On 1 August the Agricultural Exhibition was opened. 'With this exhibition we celebrate a glorious victory of Socialism,' *Pravda* wrote. 'We are celebrating the tenth anniversary of the *kolkhoz* system, the balance-sheet of success.' With its gigantic statues of Lenin and Stalin, its abundant display of agricultural produce, its gaily attired peasants who might have stepped straight out of some operetta, its extravagantly decorated pavilions, its pointed towers and turrets, its luxuriant gardens, pools and fountains, a pastry-cook architecture striving after monumentality, this exhibition, depicting agriculture as an oriental fairy-tale, as a triumphant antithesis to the 'progressive pauperization of Germany', seemed to be a distillation of Soviet contradictions: achievement and rodomontade, rationality and mystification, science and idolatry. We sat in the Usbek pavilion drinking green tea out of beautiful bowls and argued about Vera Mukhina's vast silvered sculpture adorning the main entrance. This portrayed a worker, a hammer in his upraised hand, and a peasant girl with a sickle, thus constituting the emblem of the Soviet Union. Both were bounding impetuously forwards with a kind of pathetic coquettishness, colossal figures from a traditional ballet, fashioned not without skill and yet utterly false, trite and yet impressive, only that the advance was not being made in silver sandals but laboriously in heavy felt boots. And so, as we drank our green tea out of beautiful bowls, we could not help succumbing to the general mood of optimism; everything was getting better, the worst was over – but with it all a presentiment of ineluctable disaster. It was not a dance into the future, but . . .

'Ever heard the name Drax?' Manuilsky asked me, 'or Doumenc, Demain, Demjan? This Admiral Nobody and this Général Inconnu, this Drax and this Doumenc, you see, are the heads of the Anglo-French Military Mission. Been keeping us waiting for weeks and now at last they've been kind enough to turn up in Moscow. Mr Chamberlain and M. Daladier went to Munich – *j'aime Berlin, mal-à-dieu*, all *frères* and *cochons* together in Munich. But who do we get in Moscow? Drax and Doumenc! Plenary powers? *Pardon, messieurs*, we shall have to refer back. Agreements? Sorry, we are not empowered. Mutual assistance pact? We'll need fresh instructions. Our negotiators proposed a cut-and-dried military alliance. Drax and Doumenc telephoned London and Paris. We regret, deeply regret, that Poland refuses either to allow a single Russian soldier to set foot on Polish soil, or to place a single Polish airfield at the disposal of Russian aircraft. I ask you! How are we supposed to help in that case? Since our frontiers don't adjoin Germany's we are to have a mutual assistance pact – sit back and wait till Hitler occupies Poland and attacks us, what? And in the West they say "Go ahead Herr Hitler, help yourself, and *bon appétit*!" A dirty business!'

It was indeed a dirty business. The Military Mission arrived in Moscow on 12 August. The first meeting was held on 13 August, the second on the fourteenth. I quote from the protocol:

VOROSHILOV: Yesterday I asked General Doumenc the following question: How do the missions or general staffs of Britain and France, here represented, envisage the Soviet Union's participation in a war against an aggressor should that aggressor attack France or Britain, or should that aggressor attack Poland or Romania, or Poland as well as Romania, or should that aggressor attack Turkey?

DOUMENC: ... These countries will defend their own territories, but we shall go to their assistance if requested to do so.

VOROSHILOV: But supposing they do not ask for assistance?

DOUMENC: We know that they will require such assistance.

VOROSHILOV: Then suppose they fail to ask for assistance in good time, doesn't that mean that they will put their hands up, that they'll surrender?

DOUMENC: That would be exceedingly unfortunate.

VOROSHILOV: What does the French Army propose to do in such an event?

DOUMENC: In such an event France will maintain such forces along her borders as she deems fit ...

Voroshilov asked whether, in the event of German aggression, the transit of Soviet troops across Poland or Romania was envisaged.

Prolonged consultations between Admiral Drax and General Doumenc.

DOUMENC: I believe that Poland and Romania will ask you, Marshal, to come to their assistance.

VOROSHILOV: But they might not do so. No such thing has ever been known to happen before ...

After a further lengthy exchange of views with General Doumenc, Admiral Drax replied:

Should Poland and Romania fail to ask the U.S.S.R. for help they would, within a short space of time, become German provinces, and then it would be for the U.S.S.R. to decide what should become of them ... If the U.S.S.R., France and Great Britain were to form an alliance, there could, in my personal opinion, be no doubt whatever that Poland and Romania would ask for help. But that is my personal opinion, and to obtain an exact answer which leaves no possible room for doubt, it will be necessary to put the question to Poland.

VOROSHILOV: It is a matter for great regret that the Anglo-French Military Mission should have failed to put that question already and cannot therefore give an unequivocal answer.

Further exchange of views between Admiral Drax and General Doumenc.

And so it dragged on, exchanges of views, interruptions, telephone calls, until finally General Heywood, in the name of the Anglo-French Military Mission, read out the following statement:

We have already given a sufficiently clear idea of our opinions and we have taken note of the substance of all that the Marshal has said. It should not, however, be forgotten that Poland and Romania are sovereign states and that, should the circumstance arise, permission for the passage of Soviet armed forces across their territories will have to be obtained from their respective Governments. This question thus becomes a political question, and it is for the U.S.S.R. to put it to the Governments of Poland and Romania. This is quite obviously the simplest and most direct procedure.

But it was not as obvious as all that. For upon reference being made to the Polish Government, it transpired that Poland categorically refused to allow either the passage of Soviet troops or the use of Polish airfields by Soviet aircraft. Drax and Doumenc informed their Governments that the Soviet Union earnestly desired a military agreement but only on condition that military intervention should in fact be feasible both in the North and in the South. Then they awaited instructions. By 18 August there was still no sign of any fresh credentials. The meetings were postponed until 21 August when it again transpired that further instructions had not arrived.

On 21 August *Pravda* published a leader on the signing of the trade and credit agreement with Germany. The article declared that the agreement might prove to be 'a turning point in the economic relations between the two countries . . . an important advance in the direction not only of improved economic relations, but also of improved political relations between the U.S.S.R. and Germany.'

I was on my way back to talk to Manuilsky when, in the corridor of the Comintern, I saw Gottwald beckoning to me. He drew me into his office, asked me to sit down, and gave me a sly, knowing, non-committal smile.

Gottwald, the leader of the Czech Communists, the apprentice joiner from Vienna, a man of sound common sense, with an instinct for politics and great experience in the tactical tricks of the trade, used to enjoy talking to me. Unconventional opinions amused him when they originated outside rather than inside his party and came, moreover, from so innocuous a person as myself. Confidential discussions with me could never do any harm and could be helpful – when, for instance, I unexpectedly provided arguments that could be put to use in some future discussion. I was no Kopecky – that schemer with his shifty, boot-button eyes, nervous gestures and hysterical impatience, Gottwald was afraid of this unpleasant creature, why I don't know; perhaps there was some skeleton in the cupboard, some form of unspoken blackmail, for Gottwald, who periodically indulged in bouts of heavy drinking, lost all self-control when in his cups. Whatever the reason, when he talked to Kopecky his expression grew shifty and his voice uncertain. I was glad that as a Communist I had neither a past nor, being averse to all power, any future; talking to me could involve no unpleasant consequences.

'What would you say . . .' he screwed up his eyes, pulled a wry face . . . 'but not a word to anyone, you understand? I'd just like you to tell me your opinion, between ourselves. Well, what would you say if a bandit had been paid to kill you and that bandit suddenly offered you terms? Let's suppose that he's got suspicious of the men whose pay he's in, or that he wants to get more money out of them without doing you in – you follow me? Quite the opposite, in fact; he wants to come to an arrangement with you, a temporary one, at any rate, for once a bandit always a bandit; what I mean is this: if Nazi Germany was to offer to enter into a pact with the Soviet Union, what would you say?'

He observed me narrowly and gave a disagreeable laugh, a laugh that was ferocious and at the same time embarrassed, a player not quite sure of his game who slaps his card down on the table.

'Taken your breath away, has it? Don't believe me, eh? Think it's impossible, outrageous, don't you? And how about Munich – forgotten it, eh? There were the four of 'em in the conference room, Hitler, Mussolini, Chamberlain, Daladier, and us Czechs in the anteroom, lackeys. Then our people were summoned into the conference room. Read that aloud, Dr Mastny! The rogues' pact. Chamberlain yawns, not so much as puts a hand in front of his mouth. And Daladier a bundle of nerves, the four statesmen are pushed for time. Want to wait for a reply? From Prague? No time for that. It's all been worked out to perfection, not another word. Send your representatives to Berlin without delay to arrange the details of the evacuation. Here's a new map of Czechoslovakia, you may go. The French sounded angry and hostile, and Chamberlain, the tired man with the umbrella, went on yawning. That's how it was; Beneš told us. They've chucked *him* out as well. And then in they all came, Germans, Poles, Hungarians, everyone, wanting to grab a hunk, hurling themselves on the prey. They're never satisfied, are the Hungarians, Poles and Germans.'

Gottwald had talked himself into a rage: 'And that was less than a year ago, see? And when they'd finished tearing Czechoslovakia to pieces, Herr von Ribbentrop goes to Paris, in December '38, to be assured by M. Bonnet that France is completely uninterested in eastern Europe, Germany can do what she likes there. And the new project was – the Greater Ukraine. Pray help yourself, Herr Hitler, do! In Paris and London, the press was all for it. And Danzig, Herr Hitler – Danzig wasn't a powder barrel then – pray help yourself to Danzig, help yourself to the Ukraine, the Greater Ukraine, rearrange eastern Europe to your own liking. Czechoslovakia was simply an advance payment for the bandit; but now he's to ride against the East, against the subhuman Slavs; Paris has no objection, Chamberlain waves him on with his umbrella. But the bandit – supposing he thinks it's too risky a business and supposing he drops a hint to the other man, the one he's being paid to do in, supposing he says, "Twenty years ago they tore a big chunk off you, a big chunk of the Ukraine and Byelorussia – grabbed by the Poles in 1920, see? – and suppose you want to take it back now and suppose I don't attack you, but my much-respected employers, what'd you say to that, eh?"'

'A partition of Poland . . .?'

'Horrorstruck, eh? Strikes you dumb? It may not be pretty but, you know, every man's his own best friend, particularly in politics. The noble democrats! Sold us Czechs, they did, they threw us to the Fascist wolves! And take the Poles now, call that a democratic state? Hand in glove with Hitler against us, but where are they at present, those upright, respectable citizens? In Paris, in London, ready to die for Danzig. It's a kick in the teeth for us, eh? But it's blood and sweat to save the gentry of Poland. Honour among thieves, eh? So what would you say to a pact with Germany?'

'Unspeakable!'

'It's a matter of life and death for the Soviet Union, you know. Can we afford to be squeamish? Think it over. But don't talk about it.'

I thought it over.

On 24 August *Pravda* carried a picture on the front page: Stalin, Molotov and Ribbentrop in the Kremlin, their faces wreathed in smiles, and below it the comment that conversations had taken place between Molotov and Ribbentrop 'in the presence of Comrade

Stalin and the German Ambassador, Count von Schulenburg. They lasted about three hours. Then the conversations were broken off and resumed at ten o'clock. They concluded with the signature of a Non-Aggression Pact of which the text is as follows . . .'

In the Comintern the first person to ask me what I thought of it was Grete Lohde. She had been a German working girl and was the daughter-in-law of the leader of the C.P.G., Wilhelm Pieck. Intelligent, conscientious and hard-working, she had a job in the editorial office of the *Kommunistische Internationale*. I was fond of her and tactfully abetted her efforts to improve her general knowledge and to learn how to argue a point, how to express herself. She was tubercular and sweet-natured. Her eyes betrayed perplexity.

I had been thinking things over. Forewarned by my conversation with Gottwald, I was none the less appalled. But I considered the pact to be right.

'Oh, it's . . . it's . . .' stammered Grete.

'A betrayal? No! Ghastly? Yes.'

'We German comrades will never be able to understand. Even my father can't understand it!' This from the editorial department's secretary Elly, who was Wilhelm Pieck's daughter.

I tried to put the result of my reflections into words, to demonstrate the unavoidability of the pact.

An hour later Wilhelm Pieck rang me up to ask whether I'd be prepared to go out to his *dacha* in Kuntsevo that evening, to take part in a discussion with himself and other German comrades.

Assembled in the *dacha* I found Wilhelm Pieck and his family together with Wilhelm Florin, Philipp Dengel and a number of others whose names I cannot recall. Again I said that it would be scandalous to welcome the pact with joyous acclaim. Hitler's Germany was still what it had always been, a state of concentration camps, of mass murder, of pogroms, of terroristic dictatorship. The fact that Hitler had come to a temporary agreement with Moscow had not in any way altered either himself or his system. The pact wouldn't last, but it was imperative for the Soviet Union to gain time; she must use every possible means to avoid becoming involved; it was, I said, a race against death. As things were, it would be France and Britain, not the Soviet Union, that would have to bear the first blow from the German military machine. The state of the Red Army could not at this juncture be particularly good; if

Tukhachevsky, Yegorov, Blücher and all the other marshals and generals who had been executed had in fact been traitors engaged in preparing a military coup against Stalin – and unless this was so, no one in their senses would have condemned them to death, thus robbing the army of its experienced leaders – time would be needed to reorganize the army so that it could hold its own against the German Wehrmacht.

Those who had constantly harped on appeasement, I went on, had in fact desired war, had been fomenting war – not the present one, of course, but an onslaught upon the Soviet Union. Why had Hitler not attacked? Because the risk had been too great. Let France and Britain do the fighting! They had betrayed democratic Czechoslovakia, and now they were calling for a war of liberation, a war on behalf of Fascist-minded Poland which had so manfully taken part in the partition of Czechoslovakia; now they had a war, but it was *their* war, not ours. . . . The German Wehrmacht is more powerful you say? Maybe it is, but when it marched into Austria it met with all sorts of mechanical difficulties. Large numbers of tanks broke down, the road to Linz was blocked, and Hitler failed to keep to his schedule. With all due respect to German technology and military expertise, not even the Wehrmacht is invincible. They won't have much trouble with Poland, but there'll be no *Blitzkrieg* so far as Britain and France are concerned. And sooner or later America's going to intervene because she can't tolerate a Nazi-dominated Europe. America'll mark time as long as she can so as to let the Soviet Union get in first; it remains to be seen which of them can hold out longest. Let the others fight their own war. Maybe in the end the Soviet Union will be a power for peace, the power which, together with the workers of all lands, will dictate the peace. It's not a war against Fascism, since Chamberlain, Colonel Beck and Marshal Smigly-Rydz aren't anti-Fascists, but it could conceivably be an anti-Fascist peace, and perhaps even put paid to capitalism.

While I pursued this argument, I began to experience an inexplicable feeling of unease which grew in proportion as I convinced my listeners. In its vanity my intellect congratulated itself for being able to keep its bearings in so delicate a situation – but there was something else besides. What? A suppressed doppelgänger, moral scruples, a conscience in revolt? Was I or was I not a politician? A Communist for whom the end, the victory of the Soviet Union and hence of Socialism, justified the means? Or merely a petit-bourgeois intellectual, afraid of dirtying his hands? The man who does nothing can keep his hands clean; the man who acts will probably dirty them. I regarded this pact as iniquitous in terms of morality and as essential in terms of politics and world history; was it not therefore my duty to convince others as well as myself? Why in God's name this conflict between conscience and consciousness?

I was not then in a position to understand, let alone resolve, that conflict; the conviction I conveyed to the others eventually began to affect me as well, until finally I succeeded in convincing myself. But had I in fact succeeded? Did not the question still remain? If not an anti-Fascist war, if not a war of liberation – then what? According to the textbook, an imperialist war. But was there nothing in between? Must everything be categorized? For an imperialist war meant one in which the working class in every belligerent country had to work for the overthrow of its own government, thus changing the war into civil war. In that case were not the odds too heavily weighted against us?

'You imply then that the struggle against Hitler remains the most crucial task for German Communists?'

'Now as always.'

'But what about the pact?'

'Makes no difference. Of course we here in Moscow can't call for a revolutionary struggle. But we must make it quite plain that it is not the working class who have signed an agreement with Hitler.'

'And how about the Polish, French and British workers?'

I hesitated. The defeat of one's own country? No – the overthrow of one's own government. The war turned into a war of liberation. But Moscow can't say that. Therefore . . .

At the time the crux of the matter eluded me – namely, the faulty construction of the Communist International, the Communist world party directed from Moscow. Today I can see that even in 1921 its structure was faulty and that it should have been revised no later than 1923. In a Communist world party with its headquarters in Moscow, the Russian party was bound to have an overwhelming preponderance; thus it was inevitable that the political interests of the Soviet Union would come to be equated with the overall interests of the international working class and hence that individual parties would not be allowed to make such decisions as they saw fit, but would be obliged to subscribe to the general line laid down by Moscow. If Stalin concluded a pact with Hitler, therefore, it meant that to him the Communist International was no more than an instrument with which to bolster up the pact and, consequently, Hitler himself.

Weighing up the pros and cons today in the perspective of the thirty years that have since elapsed, I can see no other way out of the dilemma than the Non-Aggression Pact. It is, I believe, just arguable that the Soviet Union was entitled to recover the Ukrainian and Byelorussian territories conquered by the Poles in 1920. What exceeded the measure of the permissible was the secret protocol in which Hitler, by recognizing Esthonia, Latvia and Bessarabia as Soviet 'spheres of influence', condoned their incorporation into the Soviet Union. The *moral* problem of that agreement is inextricably linked with the question of the survival of Socialism. If Socialism is coupled with the partition of the world into 'spheres of influence', if it is equated with the extension, the expansion of Soviet power, if, instead of the peoples themselves, it is armoured divisions that decide which countries are to become Socialist and in what way, then the very essence of Socialism is put at risk. Every revolution leads up to the question of power. But if power takes precedence and discards revolution in favour of armed conquest and the establishment of a power apparatus, Socialism will die by the very power apparatus that enacts it. Self-determination is an elemental prerequisite for Socialism; if military occupation is substituted for it the result, dubbed Socialism, will become infected by the imperialist mode.

As bad if not worse than the occupation of the Baltic states and Bessarabia was the Communist Parties' alignment with the pact between Germany and the Soviet Union. The catchword 'imperialist war' which at the time I thought appropriate, played its part in bringing about that alignment.

On 25 August Britain and Poland signed a Mutual Assistance Pact.

On 31 August Molotov declared in a speech before the Supreme Soviet:

Indeed until recently, in the realm of foreign policy, the Soviet Union and Germany were enemies. The situation has now changed and we have ceased to be enemies . . . History has shown that enmity and war between Russia and Germany have never led to any good. These two countries suffered more as a result of the last World War than any others.

On 1 September the Germans marched into Poland. On 3 September Britain and France declared, but omitted to wage, war on Germany. They were biding their time. The pace of the German offensive was disturbingly rapid; equally disturbing was the inactivity of the Western powers. Why were they not attacking? Why not war on two fronts? What game were they playing? 'And suppose there's another pact,' I asked Manuilsky, 'not just the one between Germany and the Soviet Union?' 'Rubbish!' he replied. But he, too, was worried. 'The Poles aren't fighting well!'

On 17 September the Germans reached Brest-Litovsk. On the same day Molotov declared that two weeks of war had demonstrated the spinelessness of Poland. That country, he said, had lost all her industrial centres. Warsaw could no longer be regarded as the capital. The Soviet Government had therefore informed the Polish Ambassador that the Red Army had been ordered to take over the defence of the population of Western Byelorussia and the Western Ukraine. Defence against whom? At this time only the Non-Aggression Pact was public knowledge, but not the secret protocol concerning 'spheres of influence'. No one knew about Ribbentrop's telegram of 3 September:

Definitely expect Polish army to be decisively beaten in a matter of weeks. We shall then remain in military occupation of the area designated in Moscow as a German sphere of influence. Military reasons will obviously compel us to advance even further against such Polish forces as still remain in Polish territory belonging to the Russian sphere of influence. Please discuss this matter immediately with Molotov and find out whether the Soviet Union might not consider it expedient when the time comes to send in Russian troops against the Polish forces inside the Russian sphere of influence so that they for their part can take possession of this area. In our view this would not only lighten our burden but it would also accord with the spirit of the Moscow agreements as well as with the interests of the Soviet Union.

No one knew about Molotov's temporizing reply of 3 September, nor of his assent given on 9 September, nor of the telegram sent by the German Ambassador Schulenburg to Ribbentrop on 10 September:

In today's conversation at 1600 hours, Molotov qualified yesterday's statement, saying that the Soviet Government had been taken completely by surprise by the unexpectedly rapid succession of German victories. Our first communication gave the Red Army reason to suppose several weeks available for preparation, now only a few days. Soviet forces therefore in difficult position since in hitherto prevailing conditions, preparations would require two/three weeks. Informed that over a million men already mobilized.

On 19 September a joint Soviet–German communiqué declared that the task of the German and Soviet forces was 'to restore peace and order which had been disturbed by the disintegration of the Polish state, and to help the population of Poland to reorganize the conditions of its political existence'.

On 29 September *Pravda* carried yet another front-page picture of Molotov, this time signing the German-Soviet Friendship Pact and the agreement in respect of the frontier between the two countries. I had both countenanced and defended the Non-Aggression Pact – but a Friendship Pact? Did not the use of the word 'friendship' in such a setting degrade that word for ever? Was this really necessary? As my own doubts grew, so the reverse process was observable in a large number of the German Communists. Their horror at the Non-Aggression Pact became overlaid by the consideration that if Stalin was prepared to be friends with Hitler, then the nature of Nazi Germany must somehow have changed and some mysterious transubstantiation be taking place. They were fortified in these deliberations by Molotov's speech before the Supreme Soviet on 31 October. That Poland, 'an abortion produced by the Treaty of Versailles', had ceased to exist was, he said, a matter for satisfaction. Now the word 'aggression' could no longer be used in the same sense as it had been used three or four months earlier. At present Germany stood for peace, while England and France proclaimed their determination to continue the war. 'As you can see, the roles have been reversed!' But Molotov did not confine his remarks to this preposterous 'reversal of roles'; the Soviet Union, he continued, was negotiating with Finland, the latter country having been asked to set back the frontier 'a few dozen kilometres' to ensure the safety of Leningrad.

How find one's way about in all this welter of contradictions? If Hitler represented the dominion of the most reactionary section of monopoly capitalism, of the most extreme form of imperialism and chauvinism – and hitherto this had been the undisputed definition – how and with whom could he change roles? The rulers of Britain and France could by no stretch of the imagination be called progressive, but why all at once ascribe to them the role of the most heinous malefactors while assuring Hitler that he had become the guardian of peace? What lay behind this *quid pro quo*?

'What do you think of it?' I asked Manuilsky.

'In such situations there's always a great deal that seems incomprehensible. We have got to trust Stalin and not jump to conclusions. But what's your own opinion?'

'I'm afraid that Hitler's trying to come to an agreement with France and Britain behind the Soviet Union's back, and that the concern shown for Leningrad's safety is a sign that we're preparing for war.'

'By whom against whom?'

'Germany against us – with the whole of capitalist Europe at her back.'

'You're not the only one who fears that,' said Manuilsky. 'We must be prepared for anything.'

'We've got to gain time,' said Mirov, 'whatever the cost. Friendship with Germany – it's bad, very bad. But if Stalin has concluded a pact of that nature, it's because he knew it was the only way. Stalin knows what he's doing.'

Whenever I discussed the subject with the Russians I came up against this unassailable argument: Stalin knows what he's doing.

Stalin knows what he's doing! That's what the German Communists were also saying. Grete Lohde and others said it, just like the Russians. There can be no such thing as friendship with Hitler, they maintained, but the brute's got to be placated so as to gain time . . . To gain time! Many people put it somewhat differently: we have, perhaps, they would say, overlooked the fact that National Socialism is not just an extreme form of capitalism, but also contains within it the possibility of a transition to Socialism. Hitler is our mortal enemy – but the pact says nothing about friendship with Hitler, it says friendship with Germany. The German working class, so the argument ran, is the most advanced in Europe. Millions voted for Hitler because they hoped he would create a Socialist Germany.

Even in the N.S.D.A.P. there are sincere if somewhat muddle-headed Socialists. These elements will experience a renewal of confidence as a result of the alliance with the Socialist Soviet Union. Stalin knows what he's doing. And how about the prisoners in the German concentration camps? Stalin hasn't forgotten them. Undoubtedly there will be secret agreements of some sort. There were. We knew nothing about them, nor could we have guessed that a number of German Jews imprisoned in the Russian concentration camps – German Jewish Communists – were to be transferred to German concentration camps, martyrs to the outbreak of friendship between Germany and the Soviet Union. Thälmann, on the other hand, was not set free; the Soviet Union's new friends merely alleviated the conditions of his confinement, that was all.

I argued with the German Communists, who were dreaming of Socialist developments in Germany, of the possibility of a 'Socialist bloc' which, after the defeat of capitalist Europe, would form the basis of a Socialist world – a world whose Communism, however, would be hard rather than benign. As an Austrian, they said, I was biassed, a separatist with a mind closed to higher interests and unable to appreciate the tremendous potential power of Socialism within the German people.

'The whole of that potential power will be pitted against the Soviet Union when the German people launch their attack.'

If Stalin makes friends with Germany, came the retort, he knows what he's doing. That friendship must be our guideline. 'Socialism will be defended on the Rhine.' I don't know if Walter Ulbricht was the first man to say it, but say it he did. For tactical reasons – to justify the Friendship Pact? I believe it was more than that, even in the mouth of this consummate tactician. It was a concept of Socialism whose essence is *power*; in the textbook, the 'power of the working class'; in reality, the power of the apparatus, an N.S.D.A.P. refashioned into a C.P.G., a power apparatus guaranteeing increased production and productivity, providing the working people with an ever more abundant supply of consumer goods and guarding them against all freedom of thought, producing a perfectly functioning society with an unproblematical ideology to match, a power apparatus speaking Russian and German, mainly Russian at first, then ever more German, all honour to Moscow, but Berlin the future metropolis. 'Socialism will be defended on the Rhine.' It will extend beyond the Rhine, forge Europe into a unity. The Holy Russian Empire of the German nation.

I could foresee the day when the Neva, not the Rhine, would be the frontier on which Socialism would have to be defended: the day of Leningrad.

Negotiations with Finland continued for two months. Towards the end of November the Russians alleged that the Finns had violated the frontier, killing several Russian soldiers; they demanded that the Finnish troops be withdrawn some twenty miles behind the frontier. The Finnish Government denied the incident and refused to comply with the demand. On 29 November Molotov declared in a note that the Finns had violated the Non-Aggression Pact, thus releasing the Soviet Union from all her undertakings. The war against Finland began. The Finns put up a successful defence against superior Soviet forces. The Red Army had failed to keep up with the demands of modern warfare. It was not until 11 February 1940 that the Soviet Union was able to launch a major attack on the Mannerheim Line, and even then it took ten days for the troops to break through the chain of fortifications. Losses were exceptionally high. Both from the military point of view and from that of morale it was a depressing war. On 4 March Field Marshal Mannerheim, the Finnish Chief of Staff, informed his Government that the army could hold out no longer. The peace treaty was signed in Moscow on 12 March. Finland was compelled to agree to the Soviet Union's territorial demands. The territory gained by the Soviet Union did not compensate for her loss of prestige. Hitler was no longer afraid of the Red Army. Russia could be disposed of quickly enough. Like Poland, in a *Blitzkrieg*.

In that year, 1939, I sought refuge in work as never before. It was as though it enabled me to crowd out, not only the confusion of my thoughts, not only my premonitions of disaster, but also my sense of guilt – for what, I do not know, unless it was the guilt of a man who, finding himself in so uncongenial an epoch of wars, revolutions and counter-revolutions, of humiliations, mutilations and assassinations, had nevertheless got off scot-free: the shame of surviving, untortured, unwounded, without ever having been arrested by the political police, or thrown into gaol, or dragged away to a concentration camp. I was not only working for the periodical – ever more frequently arraigned for 'liberalism' and for deviating from officially approved phraseology – but I was also writing brochures, pamphlets, broadsheets.

In the summer of 1939 I had submitted for publication the manuscript of a short book entitled *The Fascist Theory of Race*. Besides a review of fundamentals it contained a chapter on 'The Jewish Question' and another on 'The Negro Question'. It was due to go to press at the time when Molotov signed the Non-Aggression Pact. Permission to publish it was therefore withdrawn. At first I refused to delete 'The Jewish Question', but then realized that, even without the offending chapter, here was an opportunity of launching an onslaught upon racism in such a way that the object of my attack would be perfectly clear to any reader. On the eve of the book's publication, now renamed *The Reactionary Theory of Race*, the pact disintegrated; Hitler invaded the Soviet Union, the Western 'aggressors' turned into allies and all of a sudden it was 'The Negro Question' to which Glavlit, the censorship department, took exception. In this chapter I had endeavoured to show that the demand for the integration of Negroes into American society was an unreal one which could only serve as a palliative, and that the aim must be to set up Negro states, in other words a Negro government, within the U.S.A. But to say so was no longer permissible; finally the booklet appeared in 1941 under its first title, *The Fascist Theory of Race*. 'The Jewish Question' was included, 'The Negro Question' not.

Still, it meant something to me to see in print sentences such as these:

What is paramount is the shape of a skull, not its contents . . . Human beings are reduced to the status of cattle . . . You have to be an officially certified pedigree animal . . . You have gone to the trouble of being born German, a performance upon which you can never hope to improve. This means that from the start you are predestined to kick, beat and spit upon other nationals . . . To compensate for your being a servant you are to impose an even worse servitude on other nations. Instead of rising up against your own tyrants, you are to deprive of their rights and generally maltreat the Jews, Poles, Czechs and Serbs and, in so doing, rejoice in your own racial superiority.

The degree of a society's culture can be measured against its attitude towards the Jews. All forms of anti-Semitism are evidence of a reversion to barbarism. Any system which persecutes the Jews, on whatever pretext, has forfeited all right to be regarded as progressive. Of this I was as convinced then as I am today.

My book on the theory of race was a by-product of a larger work on *Dialectical Materialism in a Global Context*. I had begun to catch up on what I had missed and in the study of biology and ethnology, but more especially of physics, had found myself inhabiting a world that was purer and better ordered than the world which the highly developed nations had polluted and tainted. The manuscript, like so many others, has been lost.

On 9 April the Germans had marched into Denmark and Norway: on 10 May the invasion of Holland, Belgium and Luxemburg began. And Chamberlain fell, making way for Churchill. On 14 March the Dutch army capitulated. The Wehrmacht invaded France.

What did we care about the pact? We were on the side of France – we, the majority of the Comintern, Dimitrov, Manuilsky, Togliatti – and with us the Russian people. It was not just the hope that, on the distant front in the West, the war would bog down, stick fast, grind to a halt; it was also the sympathy we felt for France, for her culture, her history, her traditions. England we disliked; it was only later that her pilots, who defended London with such bravery and skill, won Russia's approval and finally her admiration.

But now our concern was for France. Would she hold up the German advance? Would she stand firm? And for how long? How many months? 'Months?' growled André Marty, 'Four weeks at the most!' We thought him mad. He *was* mad, the old mutineer of the French fleet which, in 1919, had entered the Black Sea to intervene against Soviet Russia; tall and proud, this stiff-necked man was a de Gaulle translated into the plebean idiom. Possessing the attributes of an imposing personality, he suffered increasingly from persecution mania. As editor of the *Kommunistische Internationale* I had once had the temerity to make a few small emendations to a brilliant article of his on Indo-China. He sent a message requesting me to go and see him in his office. As I came in he stood up without a word, strode past me, locked the door, took out the key, sat down again at his desk and yelled: 'What are you thinking?' I had no idea what I should say in reply.

'I know just what you're thinking. You're thinking I'm a madman who's capable of anything. Putting you up against that wall, for instance. Haven't I read your thoughts aright? Admit that you think I'm mad.'

I admitted it. His tone became more amicable.

'In this building, everyone thinks I'm mad. But it's the building that's mad. I use my own brains, that's all.'

After using his own brains for a moment he said:

'France'll capitulate in four weeks at the most. The Government's corrupt, the army's rotten, the people are leaderless.'

It was 15 May when Marty said this.

Four weeks went by. On the evening of 14 June Ruth and I and several other comrades were sitting in our room in the Lux. Our mood was depressed. We discussed France, the evacuation of Dunkirk, the solitary counter-attack made by one French armoured division commanded by de Gaulle, the inexorability of the defeat. Suddenly the door flew open and a German Communist rushed in:

'We've taken Paris!'

Immediately after the German attack on Denmark and Norway I asked Dimitrov for an interview. Could our attitude to the war, I asked, continue as before? Hadn't its character changed? Could there be any doubt about Germany's aggression? And if the German people, the German working class did not – perhaps could not – organize a resistance movement against the war criminals, could we responsibly continue to call on the French and English workers to combat the war? Was it not rather their duty to complain of their Governments' hesitant, if not reluctant, conduct of the war? Should not the Communists become a resolute and consistent war party? Admittedly the Governments of Britain and France had done everything in their power to induce Germany to wage war on Russia; but now that the German army was attacking the peoples of the West, should not the working class in those countries become their nation's backbone in defence of its independence? I realized, I went on, that a periodical appearing in Moscow could not make a direct appeal for the united action of all forces against a country with which the Soviet Union had a pact; none the less we should seek some means of making this new attitude known.

Dimitrov had been listening attentively, as always swaying his head to and fro in a thoughtful manner. His look was friendly as he said: 'You must write that down! Be very careful how you phrase it, just making it clear enough for the penny to drop but not so plainly as to raise the alarm in Berlin. I agree with you, but it's a complex situation and something I can't decide off my own bat.'

In the Comintern there were rumours of differences between Dimitrov and Molotov; the latter was believed to be pro-German, the former anti-German. It is impossible to say how close such rumours came to the truth but it was also my impression that Dimitrov hated Nazi Germany with an unswerving hatred, that he had appreciated the necessity for the Non-Aggression Pact and had silently reprobated the Friendship Pact.

Though I can recall situations as such with great clarity, my memory tends to confuse the sequence of events. I can remember the pitch of a voice, the flicker of an eyelid; but unless I have written material to hand I am apt to be mistaken about when things happened.

The most violent clash I ever had with the leadership of the C.P.G. may have taken place at an earlier date; but I rather think it was in the following context.

Dimitrov had called for a discussion and he himself was in the chair. There were a great many people present, including Manuilsky, Togliatti, Gottwald and the leading German Communists. I was sitting opposite the Germans. The first to speak was Wilhelm Pieck. He raised the complaint that the German Communist Party had still not been allotted the position in the International that was its due. As a consequence of the Spanish Civil War and the Popular Front policy, other parties had taken pride of place. But now the Friendship Pact between the Soviet Union and Germany had fundamentally altered the situation. Molotov had stated plainly and unequivocally that it was no longer Germany that was the aggressor but that the roles had now been reversed. The present aggressors were Britain and France. If even the Communists in German concentration camps were prepared to take this fact into consideration, it was outrageous that others should refuse to fight British imperialism as the principal enemy. Though Pieck did not mention Harry Pollitt by name, everyone knew that his remark was aimed above all at the courageous leader of the small British Communist Party who had, from the beginning, looked upon Hitler as the principal enemy. In the case of many Communists, he continued, anti-Fascism had taken on an anti-German character and every now and then the wish was expressed that France might beat Germany. It was the duty of the Comintern to take a vigorous stand against such states of mind. That the glorious C.P.S.U., the party of the great Comrade Stalin, was the leading force of the Communist world movement went without saying. But its most loyal aide was the C.P.G., now more than ever entitled to act as guide and mentor to the other Communist Parties. He therefore requested Comrade Dimitrov, who had such close links with the C.P.G., to make an unequivocal statement on this score.

As a child I was very prone to sudden fits of rage, but I have learnt to dam back, to damp down my seething anger. Yet the cold fury that rose up in me then was beyond my control. Nevertheless I waited for a moment before indicating that I wished to speak. Dimitrov waved me aside and asked if there was anyone else among the German comrades who had anything to add to Pieck's remarks, or any different views to express. Walter Ulbricht had no different views to express but underlined, reiterated, emphasized, added; the question, he said, must be posed unequivocally but discussed in comradely fashion. The word 'comradely', the tone of voice in which it was said, infuriated me still more. For by 'comradely' he meant, don't contradict us! Admit that we're right. We are always right. If we take you to task, it's fraternal aid. If you criticize us, it's uncomradely, a breach of proletarian internationalism.

And that's precisely what my answer was – uncomradely. I was, I said, one of the Communists who hoped that Germany would be defeated. I had condemned British imperialism, too much so perhaps, had drawn too little distinction between it and the Nazi German ghastliness, I had spoken of the infamy of the French Government – but my most ardent hope was to see Germany defeated. Unfortunately this was unlikely to happen in the foreseeable future; nevertheless it should never be forgotten that what was being defended was not Socialism on the right bank of the Rhine but European culture on its left bank. If, under the aegis of the Friendship Pact, the C.P.G. was suddenly going to espouse the cause of Germany, which meant in effect advocating Hitler's victory, the question must be asked: what did you do to impede the rise of Hitler? What sort of example did you set to the peoples, to the international working class? It was Dimitrov who set an example, by his conduct before the Supreme Court, not you by your policy. It was the Popular Front in Spain and in France, betrayed by the bourgeoisie, yet still resisting Fascism and pointing the way to the future, that should be the lode-star of the Communist Parties – not the leadership of the C.P.G. Unfortunately just now Hitler is militarily the stronger and unfortunately he won't be overthrown by the German people. He'll have to be overthrown from without, and what that means is only too clear to each and every one of us. Or do you imagine that the pact with the Soviet Union is going to reform the murderers? Do you believe it is possible to share the world with Hitler? Of him more than of anyone else before him it may be said, *écrasez l'infâme*! And that is why our eyes are turned, not towards Berlin, but towards Paris. Could we but pray, we would pray for Paris.

Cold fury had waxed hot. As so often, I had become overheated, had indulged in hyperbole and thereby defeated my own eloquence. All the same, in Dimitrov's immobile features, in the almost imperceptible way Manuilsky was screwing up his eyes, in Togliatti's impassive, abstracted expression, I could sense, not repudiation, but cautious sympathy. The German reply exceeded all expectations. Not only had my speech been anti-German, it had been anti-Communist, a barely veiled criticism of the German–Soviet Friendship Pact and hence of the Soviet Union herself. In his usual sweeping way Comrade Fischer had disregarded both facts and principles. He had revealed himself to be what he had always been and still remained, an unrepentant Social Democrat. He had, to put it no higher, fallen under the influence of imperialist propaganda. An agent of Western imperialism would have spoken in no other terms than had this editor of the *Kommunistische Internationale*.

With the palm of his hand Dimitrov struck the table: 'Enough of that! I will not tolerate such calumnies. Comrade Fischer may not have pondered every word – but he is a thoughtful and sincere Communist and much of what he has said is true.'

'The German comrades,' Manuilsky put in, 'do not seem to appreciate that an embattled France is defending, not only herself, but us. The sooner the Germans win the war in the West, the less time shall we be able to gain. Are the German comrades incapable of seeing this?'

'The situations we are about to encounter are so serious,' said

Togliatti, 'that we should reflect quietly rather than indulge in noisy strife. What Comrade Fischer says is right, not his manner of saying it. And the German comrades must understand that though the pact is a fact, it is not one to be indefinitely invoked. Let us not lose our heads but concentrate on gaining as much time as possible.'

Such was the gist of what was said, not its literal rendering.

On 14 June, then, Paris fell. France had capitulated after four weeks of war. German headquarters issued a communiqué: 'The whole campaign has cost the German army no more than 27,000 killed, 18,000 missing, 111,000 wounded. 1,900,000 Frenchmen have been taken prisoner.'

In the bus a Russian comrade said to me: 'I beg you not to speak German. I can't stand the sound of it!'

I stopped speaking German. I could understand how he felt.

Between 17 and 23 June, the Red Army occupied the Baltic states of Esthonia, Latvia and Lithuania. The occupation of Bessarabia and northern Bukovina took place between 27 and 30 June.

On 23 August *Pravda* celebrated the anniversary of the Non-Aggression Pact.

The signature of the pact put an end to the enmity between Germany and the Soviet Union, an enmity that had been artificially engendered by the warmongers . . . After the fall of Poland, Germany proposed to Britain and France that the war should be brought to an end and the Soviet Union supported the proposal. But they refused to listen . . . We are neutral, and this pact has made things easier for us; it has also been of great advantage to Germany who can now be wholly assured of peace on her eastern frontiers.

On 7 September came the news of the first big air raid on London.

On 7 October the Germans seized the Romanian oilfields. Hitler had made over a large part of Transylvania to Hungary; what remained of Romania was 'guaranteed' by Germany and Italy.

Molotov was in Berlin from 12 to 14 November. We considered the press photograph with repugnance: Molotov staring straight at the camera, Hitler with a histrionic gesture, half embrace, half lunge, the saccharine smile of the man-eater. Little Jack Horner exclaiming, 'What a good boy am I!' as he pulls out the plum. What they talked about we were never told, but today we know that Molotov not only asked Hitler searching questions about his intentions in dispatching troops to Finland and his machinations in Romania, Bulgaria and Turkey, but also asserted that the guarantee given to Romania was obviously directed against the Soviet Union. Hitler twice broke off the talks and did not appear at the official banquet. A British air attack drove the guests down into the air-raid shelter where Ribbentrop proposed to his Russian visitor that they carve up the British Empire between them. Of all this we knew nothing.

But we did prick up our ears and roar with laughter when Eisenstein showed his version of *The Valkyries* in the Bolshoi Theatre. The première took place on 22 November: a wild parody of Wagner's opera, the view-halloo of the Valkyries like ululations of *Heil Hitler*, every kind of cinematic trick and flashback exploited so as to make the transition from the sublime to the ridiculous as precisely as possible – monumental hysteria, bridling heroism and all. We recalled Eisenstein's film *Alexander Nevsky*, the downfall of the knights of the Teutonic Order on Lake Peipus, swallowed up by the breaking ice, a black cross on a white cloak, distorted by the folds into a swastika; it had aroused in us the same hatred of the Teutonic conquerors as did this version of the *Valkyries*. The great director's interpretation of the Friendship Pact failed to tally with the views of some of the German Communists, and their discomfiture, no less than the German attachés' protest against Eisenstein's 'Jewish insolence' in thus 'desecrating' Richard Wagner, gave added spice to our pleasure. The fact that in March 1941 Eisenstein was awarded the Stalin prize for this film was regarded as a portent.

'The Soviet people,' wrote *Pravda* on 31 December 1940, 'looks gladly and confidently into the future'; 1941 would bring a colossal expansion of the Soviet economy. On 11 January 1941 *Pravda* recounted yet 'another triumph for Soviet foreign policy': the signing of a frontier settlement with Germany and additional economic agreements. We were later to learn that between 1 January 1940 and 21 June 1941 Germany had imported from the Soviet Union 1·5 million tons of grain, 100,000 tons of cotton, 2 million tons of petroleum products, 1·5 million tons of timber, 140,000 tons of manganese, and 26,000 tons of chromium.

What Eisenstein had dared to do on a grand scale, I endeavoured to imitate with the small means at my command, namely, to indicate the provisional nature of the pact. One way of doing this was publicly to reaffirm my allegiance to Austria. On 15 January 1941

Nazi Germany celebrated with *éclat* the hundred-and-fiftieth anniversary of the Austrian poet Franz Grillparzer. Amongst many others, the literary historian Nadler acclaimed the 'German-ness' of this Austrian. I replied with a polemical essay in which I stressed all that was peculiarly Austrian about Grillparzer. 'He was,' I wrote, 'Austrian with every fibre of his being' . . .

And it was not only the Austrian landscape, but the whole of the magnificent historical and cultural structure that was Austria with all its attendant contradictions, to which he professed such passionate allegiance. He was not a German, he once said, but an Austrian, a Lower Austrian to be more exact and, all things considered, a Viennese. That was far more than a mere expression of narrow parochialism, it was the result of an unremitting struggle with the Austrian complex of problems . . .

This essay appeared in the April number of the periodical *Internationale Literatur*. The editor-in-chief of the paper, Johannes R. Becher, who indignantly repudiated my Austrian 'separatism', had agreed albeit reluctantly to the essay's publication.

In honour of Becher's fiftieth birthday on 22 May 1941, I wrote, without his knowledge, an article in which I paid homage to his talent and achievements. I gave special emphasis to his anti-Fascist poems, as also to those lamenting what had happened in Germany, and from these I quoted appropriate passages. The article appeared in the May volume of the magazine.

The following day Becher came to my room in the Lux. He was distraught. 'What have you done? It's an onslaught on the policy of the Soviet Union. It's a death sentence! How could you do such a thing?'

'I don't run you down. I sing your praises!'

'That's just it. Nobody'll believe that I hadn't read the article beforehand. You've done for me.'

'Not at all! Can't you see that Hitler's preparing to make war on the Soviet Union? In a few months' time we'll be at war. The Germans have called off the attack on Britain. They're concentrating all their forces in the East. On 5 April Russia signed a pact with Yugoslavia, on 6 April Hitler attacked Greece and Yugoslavia. Against whom was that directed, do you suppose?'

★

We neither of us knew, as Becher heaped reproaches on my head and prognosticated our arrest, that some days previously Stalin had rung up Ilya Ehrenburg to tell him that his novel *The Fall of Paris* could now be printed. From this Ehrenburg concluded that Stalin regarded war with Germany as inevitable.

On 6 May Stalin assumed the office of Prime Minister, Chairman of the Council of People's Commissars.

On 12 May the Soviet telegraph agency, Tass, released the news that Rudolf Hess, Hitler's deputy, had flown to England and that, in the German view, he 'had gone mad'. Was it an attempt to come to an understanding against the Soviet Union?

Dimitrov sent me a message, saying he had something urgent to say to me.

20

War

'It's a long time since you had any leave,' said Dimitrov. 'You'd better go at once, or it will be too late.'

It was the end of May when Ruth and I went down to the Crimea to spend our leave in a Central Committee sanatorium at Mishor.

We were lodged in a small building to one side of the former palace. For neighbours we had a young Moscow couple, a tram-driver and his wife. In spite of our very indifferent Russian we made friends with them. They were warm-hearted, simple, talked no jargon. 'Surely there isn't going to be a war?' they said. 'Stalin wants peace. What a good thing we've got Stalin!'

On 14 June Tass issued a communiqué which stated that in London rumours of war between Germany and the Soviet Union were rife. The whole thing, the communiqué went on, was no more than clumsy propaganda hatched up by the enemies of Germany and the Soviet Union. According to Soviet sources, Germany was adhering to the terms of the Soviet–German Non-Aggression Pact no less strictly than the Soviet Union. Hence the rumour that Germany intended to violate the pact by attacking the Soviet Union was, in the opinion of Soviet circles, totally unfounded.

Our neighbours were worried. People stood about in groups, arguing. Self-important officials reassured questioners: the pact stands firm, Stalin knows what he's doing. Stalin will ensure peace.

During the night of 21 June we were woken by a thunderstorm. There was something unusual about the sound of the thunder. We went back to sleep again.

The following morning we asked our neighbours: 'Did you hear the thunderstorm?'

They avoided our eyes, seemed distraught, unfriendly. 'It wasn't a storm,' they said. 'It was a German air raid on Sebastopol.'

'War?'

'Yes.'

'It'll be the end of Hitler!'

'But the beginning of a terrible time. Years and years, countless dead . . . Why does it always have to be us?'

Any answer we could have given would have rung hollow. We said nothing and felt guilty. The Russians shook hands with us.

'You're not to blame. We're friends. But why does it always have to be us?'

At first all was confusion in the sanatorium. Then a meeting was called. The speeches were not convincing: out of the loudspeakers came all the hollow phrases we had not trusted ourselves to say to our neighbours. It wasn't the speakers' fault. They themselves had no idea what was happening. We had not heard Molotov's stammerings and stutterings over the wireless, the words he had spoken in Stalin's name, but what we heard now from the lips of the speakers was no more than a repetition of those words: glorious Bolshevik party, defence of the mother country, rally round the Soviet Government and your great leader, Stalin. Ours is a righteous cause. We shall destroy the enemy. Victory will be ours. And the inaudible echo: fear, sorrow, horror. Why does it always have to be us. Mayn't we ever be happy?

A telegram arrived from Moscow instructing the party committee to book seats for Ruth and me on an aeroplane, to arrange for our immediate return to Moscow. We waited, from time to time consulted a grumpy official, waited, a whole day, a whole night, and were finally told that all air traffic had been suspended, *nichevo*, comrades, be patient, you'll have to go by train; hope it'll be possible to reserve seats for you, there's a terrific rush, you see, but since Moscow's asking for you, be patient, one thing at a time, we don't know whether we're coming or going; just sit on your luggage and wait.

Finally we were put onto an overcrowded train. Two seats had been reserved for us in the corner of a compartment, on a narrow wooden bench. We were very tired and sat back, resting our heads against our luggage. Many of those who were forced to stand did not conceal their resentment. We were sun-tanned, well-dressed, and foreigners. As the journey proceeded the train grew even fuller, peasants, both men and women, came piling in, a mass of sweating flesh, bodies wedged against bodies, and, constantly reiterated, puncturing our drowsiness, 'So it's war! After all . . . The Germans!' Another swarm of growling, cursing peasants, but there was no more room, they were pushed off the footboard, in spite of which some managed to force their way in. 'Them there, what are they?' Fingers were pointing in our direction, all around a murmuring, a muttering, the hiss: 'Foreigners!' 'They're none of ours. Spies, Germans, maybe, English, to hell with them either way. They're none of ours, for sure. Go on, ask 'em!' We did not reply since our bad Russian would have done nothing to improve matters. A burly peasant with a hard, evil face suggested throwing us off the moving train. Others concurred: 'The Germans are bombing our country and here's foreigners taking our seats! Spies, that's what they are! Chuck 'em out!' One woman objected: 'Just look how tired they are! Who knows what they've been through?' 'Throw 'em off, I say!' 'Don't lay your hands on innocent people. We're not Fascists!' '*They* might be. Chuck 'em out!' 'Leave them in peace!' 'War!' 'Peace!' It was a lengthy argument and one in which our lives were at stake. Strangers in the midst of the Russian people, we experienced their conflicting attributes, brutality and magnanimity, surliness and amiability, brutish spontaneity and wise deliberation, mistrustfulness and a sense of kinship with all mankind. The Germans were dropping bombs on these people, we were in their midst, reduced to helpless silence; one single German word and we might have been dead. The long argument came to an end when some of the peasants reached their destination; dawn was breaking and I, now feeling a little rested, offered my seat to an old woman. It was the saving of us. A peasant who had been shaking his fist under our noses was placated by some of the women.

Having arrived in Moscow I went straight to see Dimitrov.

'A suggestion's been made,' he said. 'They want you to act as a German radio commentator. Are you prepared to take it on?'

'Did the suggestion come from the German party?'

'It is, as it happens, a Russian suggestion.'

'Shall I be able to say what *I* believe to be right, or . . ?'

'You mean – without censorship? The situation's a very grave one.'

'Quite so!'

'Your commentaries will be submitted to the Foreign Office.'

'In other words, censorship?'

'I hardly think so; they trust you.'

'Shall I broadcast under the name of Peter Wieden?'

'Under the name Ernst Fischer.'

'My mother's in Vienna.'

'There's no such thing as private life now. Only a front line, you understand?'

Suddenly and with painful intensity I became aware of how she must be living – an old woman, alone in a Vienna at war, knowing nothing about the fate of her sons, alone among enemies, waiting for the end – the end of the war, of Hitler, or of the world. I knew the strength of this physically frail old woman, her unerring conviction that whichever side her sons were on was right and would ultimately prevail, but *when*? If I were to broadcast she might perhaps hear my voice, would know that I was alive, that I was convinced – and this would convince her, too – that Hitler had passed the point where power begins to decline, that his march on Moscow was a march into nothingness. And even if she herself was unable to listen to me talking to her from Moscow, someone would be bound to tell her about it. But suppose that someone were the Gestapo? Suppose my words were to kill her?

Dimitrov stood up and placed his hands on my shoulders.

'Don't be afraid of broadcasting,' he said, 'the Gestapo are not unaware that Peter Wieden and Ernst Fischer are one and the same person. What name you use makes no difference, and you have already decided for the cause, whatever the consequences. If your mother was here in this room she would tell you to go ahead.'

And so, indeed, she would have done. But did I have the right, far removed from the firing line, to sacrifice the lives of *others*, of someone who was defenceless, whom I loved, to whom I owed my being? I agreed to Dimitrov's suggestion and broadcast my commentaries from Moscow Radio.

But what could a commentary from Moscow achieve? To whom was I speaking? And how?

At the front, Soviet loudspeakers apostrophized the German troops as 'comrades', inviting them to go over to the Soviet army, to point their weapons the other way, in the cause of a Socialist Germany. 'German soldiers,' I told my Russian friends, 'won't listen to the Russian comrades. They'll obey the orders they are given by the German generals, they'll follow their Führer.' For a long time the Russians refused to believe this. The Hitler régime, they had been told, was merely the dictatorship of a criminal minority; the great majority of the German people, more especially the German working class, was only waiting for the day of liberation. The pact with Hitler had refurbished this picture, conjured up by wishful thinking, with fresh tints of hope and self-delusion. The German people had, indeed, welcomed the pact with relief since there was nothing they feared so much as war against the Soviet Union; this mood was interpreted as denoting sympathy towards Russia, Socialist fellow-feeling and solidarity. 'The German working class, the most advanced in Europe!' It was with very good reason that I had asked Dimitrov for exemption from censorship – not only by the Germans, but also by the Russians.

My first commentary went out uncensored. The second had been subjected to cuts. I refused to broadcast. 'But it's mutiny!' wailed Sepp Schwab, the head of the German section in Moscow Radio. 'We're under martial law!' Nevertheless I still refused. Dimitrov sent for me and reprimanded me for being so obdurate. But not a single word of my commentaries was ever changed thereafter.

I had devoted meticulous care to the tone and structure of my talks. Alone in a cell, speaking into a void – for whom, I wondered? – I had to persuade myself that someone was listening to me, to imagine a man or a woman actually sitting beside their wireless. At first it was for my mother I spoke, for all those who were longing for our victory and who, in their solitude, needed comfort and encouragement. In addition, I had to provide the small groups brave enough to tune in to 'enemy propaganda' with factual arguments with which to counter the Führer's trumpet blasts; arguments not only *ad rationem* but also *ad hominem*, arguments that lent themselves to dissemination. Finally, I had to address, not an anonymous mass, but now this, now that living individual. 'Calling Frau Lotte X, her address is such and such. Calling Frau Lotte X. Here is some news for her. Will anyone who hears this please pass on to her the following information. It's a letter you wrote to him. Your last letter. Stained with blood. It was found on his body. The lace from Brussels suited you admirably, you wrote, the stockings from Paris were gorgeous. Now all that was missing was a fur from Russia. What your husband found, Frau Lotte, was not the missing fur, but his death.' Years later I was to read a poem by Bertolt Brecht which, like my broadcast, was addressed to one such Frau Lotte.

And then there was the theme of Russia, not a country like France or Germany, but a land without frontiers, a continent more vast than any other continent. Beyond every river, another river to cross, behind every defeated army, yet another army. Here the German soldier has for his enemy, not only a nation, but the whole of nature. Remember Napoleon! The further you push forward the longer the road back, and then one day there'll be no road back. The summer will come to an end, the winter awaits you. You'll conquer yourselves to death. Every step forward is a step into nothingness.

Nor did I confine myself to the terrors of nature, the vast open spaces and unattainable horizons, but I spoke, too, of the national character, of the giant slowly rising to his feet, and when you cry 'He's finished!' that's just when he's beginning to stand up. And when he has risen, you'll realize how big he is, but it will be too late. What do you know of this giant's patience? You take this patience, this unwieldiness, for weakness, pin your faith on your *Blitzkrieg*, all unaware of the anger that is incubating under cover of that patience, an anger too immense for you to conceive.

Socialist *émigrés* in England have reproached me with not having talked about Socialism in my commentaries, but rather about Russia and her willingness, in alliance with other nations at risk, to break the dominion of Hitler. It would (as my critics in London very well knew) have been wrong to propagate Socialism from Moscow while the allies were engaged in fighting Nazi Germany – wrong not only because it would have failed in its effect on German listeners, but also because it would have been irreconcilable with the anti-Fascist alliance. How the world would look after the collapse of Hitler's empire (which, even when things were at their worst, I knew to be inevitable) could not be foreseen; everyone wanted peace and freedom. But Socialism? Perhaps, in one form or another, so long as it guaranteed peace and freedom. After Hitler's defeat in 1945 I spoke of the possibility of 'fluid transitions' (and was violently attacked for such 'revisionist' deviations), and even in 1941 I had dared to hope for something of the kind. What a hope! What an illusion!

In February 1947 when I was in London for talks concerning the Austrian peace treaty, I visited the B.B.C. where I met some of the commentators who had broadcast on the German Service during the war. They told me that they had always carefully analysed my commentaries in an attempt to discover my ulterior motives. What's Fischer up to with this or that propaganda ploy? Is it just his own idea? Should we play ball over this one and send it back to our opposite number in Moscow, or should we slap it down, refute it indirectly? I told them that I had studied their commentaries with equal thoroughness, making use of a certain amount of their material and carefully eschewing the rest, for latent in this war and over-shadowed by the great interest shared in common, was the struggle between antagonistic social systems. Freedom? Agreed. But how much, in what form, what kind of social structure? The fall of Hitler was good, less so what rose from the ashes. Fortunately at the time this could not have been prognosticated.

In 1941 it was not with the *post-war* world that I was concerned. The immediate problem was the war itself, the unexpectedly rapid and apparently irresistible advance of the German armies, the absence of any Soviet counter-offensive, of all effective resistance. We had attributed the collapse of Poland and later that of France to the incapacity and decay of an outworn ruling caste – but to what could this be attributed? The Germans were pushing forward against Kiev, Moscow and Leningrad no less rapidly than once against Warsaw and Paris. On 28 June, six days after their initial attack, they had already reached Minsk, the capital of Byelorussia, and had penetrated deep into Lithuania, Latvia and the Western Ukraine. Betrayal? Lack of foresight? Unpreparedness? But after all, Dimitrov, Manuilsky, Togliatti, nearly everyone in the Comintern, had *known* that the pact was little more than a breathing space, and that war would inevitably come. *Had Stalin not known?* It was suggested at the time, as it still is sometimes suggested, that Stalin, suspicious, paranoid dictator though he was, did in fact trust his *confrère* Hitler, that the man who considered himself the greatest personality in world history expected from the other, so infinitely his inferior but none the less sole ruler of a large dominion, both admiration for himself as the ruler of a yet larger dominion, and loyalty to the pact between Caesars. The occasional dirty trick was all in the nature of things: let one seize Lithuania in contravention of the agreed distribution of spheres of influence, let the other establish himself in Romania and steal the Romanian oil fields – but total breach, or a war of extermination? Surely Hitler couldn't be intent on suicide? For myself, I believe it not unlikely that Stalin was subject to this passing delusion, but in November 1940, after Molotov's return from Berlin, he must have known that war was on the way.

I am writing memoirs, not a history; yet I cannot leave out of account what we have learnt since the Twentieth Party Congress of the C.P.S.U., and the revelations made by Khrushchev about Stalin's responsibility for the defeats and the enormous losses in 1941. The historian Nekrich and many other military experts have largely supplied the answer to the question we were asking ourselves in 1941.

In his standard work *1941: 22 June*, A. M. Nekrich points out that in the thirties 'Soviet military science provided a source of advanced ideas for military science throughout the world', that 'in 1932 the Red Army became the first in the world to possess a mechanized corps, the mechanized units being upgraded to an independent arm of the service in 1934–5', and that the Soviet Union 'was the home of parachuting and of the airborne forces created on that basis'. Germany began to borrow these ideas from the Russians in 1932–4. In 1941 the Soviet Union rejected the theory of encirclement, the theory of mobile warfare, of an armoured spearhead leading the advance while airborne troops land in the enemy's rear, and reverted to the out-moded concept of static warfare. The former incumbent of the Chair at the General Staff Military Academy, G. Issersov, was arrested on account of his book *New Modes of Warfare?* and not released until after the Twentieth Party Congress. In this book he pointed out the misleading nature of the experiences in the Spanish Civil War and demonstrated that the era of mobile warfare had begun. What had been crucial in Poland, he suggested, had not been the Polish Government's state of decay but the German mode of attack. The defeat of an active opponent could only be achieved by means of an active counter-operation.

The pioneers of this modern strategical thinking, the army commanders Tukhachevsky, Uborevich and Yakir, were executed on Stalin's orders. The majority of the officers who had taken part in the Revolution and the Civil War were arrested. Those dismissed from the army included *all* the corps commanders, almost all the divisional, brigade and regimental commanders, almost all the members of the military councils as also the heads of the political administration departments in the military districts, more than half of the corps, divisional and brigade commissars and about a third of the regimental commissars. A 'bold advance' into the command posts now began. Those given pride of place were the 'good comrades', the yes-men, the lickspittles. When 225 of the new regimental commanders were examined for their professional competence, it was found that only twenty-five had passed out from a military college; the rest had simply completed a course for second lieutenants.

Moreover the land forces, as Marshal R. J. Malinovsky has pointed out in the *Journal of Military History*,*

were being trained as though in peacetime. The artillery units attached to the rifle divisions were located either in their own camps or in the training areas, the anti-aircraft units in the training areas, the engineer units in the technical services' camps and the unsupported divisional rifle regiments likewise in their own camps. With the danger of war so close at hand, these appallingly crude blunders verged on criminal negligence.

In addition there had been the decision made before the war by that infallible dilettante, Stalin, to suspend production of the 76-mm. multi-purpose gun; the builders of this outstanding weapon were arrested. Stalin gave orders for the development of a 107-mm. anti-tank gun; nothing came of this weapon but the 76-mm. was revived in the course of the war. The 45-mm. anti-tank gun and the anti-tank rifle were withdrawn immediately prior to the outbreak of hostilities, again on Stalin's instructions. Hence the troops manning the border possessed only hand grenades and bottles of petrol.

In the *Journal of Military History*† the Soviet Marshal A. A. Grechko points out that the Soviet First Army Group (approximately 32 per cent of the total combat forces) was too weak and the distance between the First and Second Army Groups (between 200 and 300 miles) too great. In his First Army Group Hitler had at his disposal over 65 per cent of all units on the eastern front, with the result that the Germans were able 'to deliver a powerful initial blow with a greatly superior force, to seize the initiative and to attack piecemeal not only the forces of our military districts manning the border, but also the units moving up from the rear'.

At first light on 22 June, all three German air fleets crossed the Soviet frontier simultaneously and delivered a powerful attack against *every*

---

*No. 6, 1961.   †No. 6, 1966.

airfield in our western military districts . . . In the course of the first three to five days we lost 90 per cent of our air force. When the Fascist ground troops crossed the frontier at first light, they encountered only insignificant forces of infantry which were unsupported by tank, artillery, anti-aircraft or engineer units, these being far behind the lines at the time, either in their own camps or in the training areas. The infantry, moreover, was unprepared for battle. No Soviet reinforcements appeared. The enemy sent in his Second Army Group and further reinforcements and, after the destruction of Russia's air power, his air-force units. The Russians engaged the tanks with rifles, aiming at the observation slits, or with bunches of hand grenades and bottles of petrol which they threw on the radiator casings, an act which cost them their lives. This display of soldierly initiative gave birth to the idea of the anti-tank grenade and the petrol or kerosene bottle as an anti-tank weapon.

The order to move off at once was received by the artillery units in their special camps or in the training areas on the morning of 22 June. All requests that departure be postponed until nightfall were refused. Many of the guns were horse-drawn; if the horses were killed the gunners themselves hauled the guns or fetched tractors and horses from the collective farms; they also captured towing vehicles, guns and mortars from the enemy, fighting to the last bullet, the last shell, the last cartridge. As they moved up along the narrow roads many of the artillery regiments were destroyed by German aircraft. Several of the officers commanding such regiments put a bullet through their brains.

Between 22 June and 1 August the German Army Group Centre took more than 755,000 men and officers prisoner and captured over 6,000 tanks and over 5,000 guns.* Marshal A. A. Grechko has stated that over the entire front 'the enemy, in three weeks of war, put 78 of our divisions out of action while more than 70 divisions lost 50 per cent of their strength in men and material.'†

In the first two days Army Group Centre advanced 140 miles. Towards the end of the third week German units were outside Smolensk and had once again encircled a sizeable Soviet force. In the twenty-four days up to 16 July the Germans had covered some five hundred miles as the crow flies.

The remodelling of the outmoded Soviet army, an army that had

*K. Teppelskirch, *Geschichte des Zweiten Weltkriegs*, 1956, p. 178 ff.
†*Journal of Military History*, no. 6, 1966.

been robbed of its leaders, had begun shortly before the German attack, not, however, as common sense should have dictated, in an area somewhere beyond the Urals but in the western military districts. Several of the hastily reformed mechanized corps had still to be provided with the necessary equipment, in particular up-to-date tanks.

At the time we knew nothing of all this, could not have known, yet the failure of the supreme leadership was at once so patent and so incomprehensible that it left us perplexed. Had the period of the pact been used to such little purpose? Why had there been no preparations for meeting an offensive with a counter-offensive? How could the surprise have been so complete, since even we laymen were familiar with German strategy? Such was the power of the myth that our thoughts did not turn to Stalin first but to betrayal – an explanation that was painstakingly disseminated.

But 'betrayal' on every front? That was unthinkable. In a long conversation I had with Togliatti he put forward the hypothesis that perhaps it had been necessary to make the whole population realize that the Soviet Union had been surprised in her sleep, that she had not wanted the war, had never, indeed, even so much as contemplated it. Stalin knew how deeply the people desired peace, how phlegmatic they were, how small their inclination to *hate* the enemy. But this war could not be won unless the people had been schooled in hatred, unless their traditional respect for the Germans were turned into deadly enmity. It was a hypothesis Stalin himself endorsed. In his Order of February 1942 he said:

> The Germans no longer have the military advantage which they gained in the early months of the war by their sudden and treacherous attack . . . The history of the war is now no longer determined by such transient things as the element of surprise but by permanently operative factors.

In a letter to Colonel Razin, Stalin, recalling the Parthians of antiquity and also Kutuzov, described the reversals as a planned and deliberate withdrawal intended to lure a superior adversary deep into Russian territory and there deal him a decisive blow. In his speech on the twenty-seventh anniversary of the October Revolution, he said that the severe defeats in the first year of the war should not be regarded as merely fortuitous . . .

What is involved here is not a question of personal qualities, but rather the fact that aggressive nations interested in war ... have to be better equipped for the purpose than peace-loving nations ... this being, if you like, a matter of historical necessity.

Each time something went wrong, it was a 'matter of historical necessity', every defeat was ascribed to fate or betrayal, every victory to 'Stalin's genius'. In fact I myself, in my radio commentaries, anticipated these subsequent fabrications in which failures were dressed up as prescience, for otherwise it would not have been possible either to talk to the victors or to induce in them a sense of foreboding in the face of their all-too-rapid victories. It was not simply propaganda, for strange as it may seem, I never had a moment's doubt as to the inevitability of Hitler's defeat. There is no denying that Stalin's speech of 3 July 1941 and those that followed helped to foster this personal conviction. His speech of 3 July, delivered in unruffled tones, slowly, evenly and unemotionally, opened with the unusual form of address: 'Comrades, brothers and sisters, fighters in our army and our fleet! I am speaking to you, my friends!' It was an appeal to the people to help the Red Army, to raise production, to act ruthlessly against deserters and panic-mongers, to leave nothing behind for the enemy, not a machine, not a vehicle, not a loaf of bread, not a can of petrol. The moderation of the tone in which Stalin analysed the situation and issued his directives as though discussing production tasks rather than a catastrophic war, instilled strength and confidence into everyone. 'He's pulled us to our feet,' was a frequent comment. 'We can hold up our heads again.'

This is no place for a history of the war. Rather I shall confine myself to outlining situations and indicating the nature of our thoughts and experiences. One thing, however, I should like to record: this war, which began with the total failure of the leadership, was won by the heroism, the spirit of self-sacrifice, the steadfastness and patience of the Russian people. It was a *people's war* in the most profound sense of the word; nevertheless, not only did this people's war bring Stalin – a man responsible for millions of dead – unprecedented fame and adulation, but it also, paradoxically enough, fostered the emergence of a caste system. Stalin invoked the irrational factor, the great national traditions, the patriotic mystique with all its customs, insignia and uniforms. The army was seen less and less as a child of the Revolution and more and more as the grandchild of the Tsarist armies which had defended 'Holy' Russia, and it was with words such as 'holy' and 'glorious', etc., that the old epaulettes and privileges were reintroduced for the officers. After the summer of 1942 certain military decorations were created for 'officers only', the Order of Suvorov, the Order of Kutuzov, the Order of Alexander Nevsky. At the battle of Stalingrad, gold braid and broad epaulettes suddenly made their appearance and the great flame of the people's war served to forge not only the unity of the nation but also the 'officer's honour', the officer's caste-consciousness and his isolation from the 'common soldier'. Russian officers were intended to outdo in splendour their British and American counterparts. Competition with the West degenerated into emulation in respect of ranks, privileges, national pride and Great Power Ideology. The close cor-relation between the Soviet people's unique achievement – the liberation of Europe at the cost of twenty million dead – and a privileged caste system, a power apparatus claiming the credit for that victory, makes this distortion exceedingly difficult to combat. Whenever the Soviet power apparatus is attacked, whenever it resorts to terror, the achievements it invokes are not its own but those of the people. 'Have you forgotten already what *we* did for you, what you have *us* to thank for? It was *we* who saved you and now it's *us* you dare to criticize instead of recognizing us as an exemplar for all other nations.' It therefore seems necessary to recall the deeds and sacrifices of the Soviet people with profound emotion, albeit without ever losing sight of the fact that Stalin's régime and Stalin's ap-paratus were borne aloft on this floodtide of suffering, blood and heroism, which is why those who freed Europe failed to bring about the victory of freedom . . .

On the night of 21 July German aircraft dropped bombs on Moscow for the first time. The organization of the defences was highly efficient. Dozens of searchlights were in action while the anti-aircraft fire was heavy and extremely accurate. Every rooftop was patrolled by young people who, with the utmost daring, snatched up incendiary bombs and flung them away, often burning hands or feet in the process. In the courtyard of the Lux Hotel Togliatti, with his customary composure and thoroughness, took charge of the fire-fighting arrangements and other air-raid precautions. During the night of 23 July we had another air-raid warning; unforgettable the voice of the radio announcer who gave notice of the attack in such mellifluous tones that he might have been inviting us to join in some exquisite pleasure. So effective were the defences round the city and in Moscow itself that from then on the Germans refrained from making large-scale raids.

Moscow was a city of contrasts; on the one hand life went its even course as though at bottom nothing had changed, on the other the whole city was engaged in a spy hunt, and this hysteria gripped us all. After the first air raid we saw a light flash on and off in a window in the Ulitsa Gorkovo, then flash on again, and at once we were all sure that a 'saboteur' was signalling to German aircraft. Evidently this hysteria, this spy hunt, acted as a safety valve for our emotions so that we accepted everything else with astonishing equanimity. During the first few weeks food supplies in Moscow were no less abundant than in peacetime. All at once this came to an end. Rationing of foodstuffs was introduced on 18 July and it was only in the larger hotels that substantial meals were still obtainable. The population was divided into three categories: rations for the first category were ample, those for the third by no means so. And the German advance seemed to be irresistible.

In the middle of August, however, the German offensive was halted for the first time at Yelnia, south-west of Smolensk. Over the radio I spoke to my listeners (Did I have any listeners? Did they in fact exist? It was only much later that I discovered from prisoners of war that they did). 'Today, you are hearing the names Konev and Sokolovsky for the first time but not, I venture to prophesy, the last . . .' General Konev and his Chief of Staff General Sokolovsky had defeated a German army for the first time. 'We saw them running – Germans running!' Strategically the victory had not been decisive, but Sokolovsky was able to report that several German armies had suffered severe casualties, and that hundreds of German aircraft had been shot down. 'The *Blitzkreig* is at an end.' It was not yet at an end; what had ended was the aura of German invincibility.

On 6 October the Germans broke through the Rzhev–Viazma line and advanced on Moscow. On 13 October the hitherto tranquil city was overcome by panic. At a meeting of the Moscow party organization Shcherbakov, the secretary of the Central Committee, said: 'We must not shut our eyes to the fact that Moscow is in danger!' While impressing on the workers of the metropolis the need for a substantial increase in the production of arms and ammunition, he also called on them to send all possible reserves to the front and to volunteer for duty in defensive lines both inside and outside the city. It was decided to evacuate a large number of government departments, including many of the People's Commissariats, to Kuybyshev and other cities in the east; the Comintern's destination was Ufa, the Bashkir capital. All scientific and cultural institutions were likewise to be evacuated within the shortest possible time. The rumour went round that Stalin had left Moscow; not until 17 October did Shcherbakov announce on the radio that the head of the party and Government was in the city. Whether the rumour was true, whether Stalin had in fact lost his head and not returned until a few days later (of which many experts on Soviet history are now convinced) I do not know. Nevertheless I can recall the mood of panic, the massed flight, the chaotic confusion of those days. On their way to report to the 'Communist brigades' defending the city, the workers met large numbers of saloon cars carrying senior party and state functionaries who were fleeing eastwards, some with a genuine pass, some with a pass fraudulently acquired, others with no pass at all. Hence most of these workers, convinced that Moscow had been given up for lost, saw little point in defending the city with makeshift battalions since it was in the east, not beside the Moskva, that the war was now going to be fought. On 16 October the word went round that two German tanks had entered Khimki, one of Moscow's northern suburbs, and had been destroyed by the *opolcheniye*, the home-guard. This, again, was a rumour and could not be verified.

Through Dimitrov I had managed to obtain permission to remain in Moscow so that I need no longer broadcast my radio commentaries from a distance but would be able to do so at really close range. While all the other occupants of the Lux Hotel were packing their bags, I sat at my desk preparing the text of my next broadcast. I had worked continuously through two days and nights and my brain was functioning with that extreme lucidity which results from over-exhaustion.

Suddenly the door was flung open.

'Where are your bags?' the hotel manager shouted. 'Why are you still busy writing? The transport is just about to leave.'

'I'm staying behind in Moscow.'

'What's that? You're staying behind in Moscow? You've got to move out of your room at once!'

'I've been given special permission . . .'

'You've what?'

'From Dimitrov. Here it is.'

'That's just a scrap of paper, don't you understand?' the manager shouted. 'Everyone has got to leave and you're no exception. You've fifteen minutes in which to get ready.'

'Why not ask Dimitrov or Manuilsky?'

'In fifteen minutes. With or without your bags.'

I discovered that Togliatti's permission to remain had also been withdrawn at the last moment. Ruth and I quickly threw what we needed most into a suitcase and made up a bundle. Our old cleaner helped us. 'So you're leaving after all? What a shame.'

And the manuscript of my book? I was convinced that Moscow would hold out and that we should soon be back. The drawer of my desk seemed to me safer than the turmoil of evacuation. And so it would have been but for the fact that the hysterical manager burnt every book and paper, fearing that they might contain secret information for the Germans.

We asked the cleaner to look after our Siberian cat. She promised to do so; but when the door flew open for the second time, again admitting the yelling manager, panic overcame the cat, which fled into the corridor and was instantly swallowed up in the confusion.

Zhdanov has reproached the poetess Akhmatova for dedicating a poem to her cats during the Patriotic War, thereby revealing her petit-bourgeois, anti-Soviet nature. I do not intend to dedicate a poem to the beautiful, silver-grey, Siberian cat which remained behind in Moscow.

Be that as it may: a few months later we returned to the cold desolation of the Lux; that evening we were sitting in our room eating our *payok* [ration] of hard bread when we heard, issuing from somewhere, a low, almost inaudible whimper.

'That can't be . . . ?'

'Nonsense. There's not a cat left in the Lux.'

And again the low whimper, tremulous and unreal as though from beyond the grave.

I went into the kitchen. The cat crept towards me, a skeleton with a covering of singed fur. Too weak to run or jump, she crept towards me and rubbed her head against my shoe, purring. It was almost a death rattle; purring, she was carried into the living-room. We gave her some of our hard bread dipped in water, which she bolted with such eagerness that she nearly choked. For hours on end she ate and swallowed and purred.

She was the only cat in the Lux that had survived; to us she was the symbol of victory.

When we arrived in Ufa there was plenty of bread – the best, most fragrant, most wonderful bread I have ever eaten in my life. Three days later there was none left, the foreigners had eaten it all. The weather was very cold. Some machinery, evacuated from Moscow, arrived under the guard of workers and students. The machinery took precedence where shelter was concerned. The people operating it worked day and night and to start with they slept in the open, under awnings made of tarpaulins; they never had a square meal and they worked with a savage, stubborn determination more powerful than the cold, than hunger, than exhaustion. The simple message 'Everything for the front' had become a heart, a heart that beat in all our breasts.

We slept in the main hall of a school. The town's only hotel was reserved for Category I. Ruth and I were later given a single room, not in the hotel but nevertheless a room. We were Category II. I slept on a plank bed, she on a peculiar sofa that sloped down steeply on all sides. Ernö Gerö (Category I) presented her with a polar-bear skin; we were astounded, for never previously had he shown the slightest sign of amicability or helpfulness, nor was he ever to do so again.

Each night Ruth worked as a radio announcer. In still air the temperature of minus 50° and less was bearable; but even a light wind, however muffled up one might be, was like a knife cutting through one's body. Our offices were so cold that we could only work in greatcoats, fur hats and gloves. The electricity supply was not equal to the new demand, the lights kept going out and dim candles illuminated our typewriters. 'UFA lighting effects' was the name we gave to this alternation of obstinate darkness and flickering shreds of light. Travelling in a sledge at night was marvellous: the small, sure-footed Siberian ponies, their coats a glittering fabric of ice, their nostrils bristling with icicles and, beneath the runners, the singing snow, singing not crunching, music so sweet and tenuous that it might have drifted down from the distant stars, the ghostly purity of a choir of angels.

I had been put in charge of the German station, a post in which I was responsible, not to the C.P.G., but directly to Togliatti. We were posing as an illegal transmitter operating in Germany. Even then this struck me as being an absurd device and the broadcasts themselves – unlike the commentaries on Moscow Radio – a waste of time and trouble. But perhaps I was wrong; though no one listened to us we learnt to make the best use of the sparse information available in an intelligent and imaginative manner and to discuss it from every angle. Togliatti was a stern and attentive listener. 'Too much propaganda and too little advice about how to organize things,' he sometimes said in criticism. But how, from Ufa, were we expected to organize illegal activities in Germany?

On 6 November Stalin spoke at the Mayakovsky metro station. The figures he quoted were fantastic: in four months of war, so he said, the Germans had suffered losses of over four and a half million men either killed, wounded or taken prisoner; the Red Army, on the other hand, could complain of no more than 350,000 dead, 178,000 missing and 1,030,000 wounded. We did not believe it; but even thoughtful people may be prepared to draw strength from such juggling with figures. 'The German invaders want to wage a war of extermination against the Soviet Union. Very well! If they want a war of extermination, they shall have one.' The next task, he said, 'is to destroy, down to the last man, every single German who has come to occupy our country. No mercy for the German invaders! Death to the German invaders!'

That the traditional military parade should have been held in the Red Square on the following day – almost, as it were, under the noses of the Germans – and that Stalin should have been present to deliver his traditional speech, was extremely impressive, despite his deplorable habit of foisting off his own mistakes onto others: 'The enemy is not as strong as many a frightened little intellectual imagines . . .' Words that stick in one's mind: 'Without doubt Germany is approaching a catastrophe . . . In a few months, perhaps in six months, perhaps in a little year (*godok*) Hitler's Germany must collapse under the burden of its own crimes . . .' We knew that it would last more than a 'little year', nevertheless the diminutive did not fail to make an impression. On the crutches of this 'little year', the year dragged on towards its turn.

And there were other words that touched the heart – the words of the *politruk* [political commissar] Klochkov. Thirty-eight soldiers of Panfilov's unit, armed with anti-tank rifles, hand grenades and petrol bottles, were defending the Volokolamsk highway against an attack by twenty German tanks. With these modest weapons they destroyed fourteen tanks and caused the remaining six to withdraw. The few survivors, most of them severely wounded, were then attacked by thirty more tanks. Klochkov shouted to his men: 'Russia is big, but there'll be no retreat because Moscow is behind us!' There was no retreat; they died at the behest not of any 'law', but of the cause, the common cause. Klochkov, already wounded, threw himself under a tank with a bunch of hand grenades and blew it up. The Germans lost eighteen tanks and the advance was halted. Hitler stood on the Lenin Hills and looked down on Moscow. His Wehrmacht failed to break through. It was not 'General Winter' that repulsed them. They came to grief when they met the defenders of the Volokolamsk highway and thousands of others like them.

In November a reporter called Lidin discovered the frozen body of a young woman in the village of Ostrishchevo near Moscow. Round her neck was a rope and the body bore the marks of extensive torture. When she had been on the point of death they had hanged her. She was Zoya Kosmodèmianskaya, an eighteen-year-old schoolteacher who, after joining the partisans, had set fire to a German stable. The girl who had been tortured to death became a legend. German propaganda inveighed against 'these gunwomen'.

On 5 and 6 October the Russians launched their counter-offensive along the Moscow front from Kalinin in the north to Yelets in the south. The Germans, freezing, exhausted and dispirited, were put to flight. During the 1940 campaign in the west their casualties had amounted to 30,000 dead and 156,000 wounded. According to Halder's diary, German losses in Russia up to 16 November totalled 743,000 men, including 200,000 dead. The pursuit of the fleeing Wehrmacht had to be broken off not only because the Russians pursuing them were short of transport (in Moscow no more than 8,000 trucks were available) but also because the exhausted troops possessed insufficient arms and ammunition. Nevertheless the German march on Moscow had ended in a resounding defeat.

The Russians' consciousness of their strength began to take on an armour of hatred. Reports of the first atrocities were coming in. In the last week of December 1941 the Soviet army had succeeded in landing 40,000 men on the Kerch Peninsula (Crimea) and establishing a bridgehead. Here the Russians found the mass graves of several thousand Jews who had been seized and murdered by Himmler's *Einsatzgruppen*. At first the Soviet people refused to credit the reports of German atrocities, the mass murders, the tortures, the deportations. But with time detailed information began to accumulate, leaving no more room for doubt, and the people learned how to hate. Hatred, for the most part, is an indifferent counsellor. The world, viewed through inflamed and gloomy eyes, is distorted and disfigured. Yet in extreme situations this distortion, this disfigurement may do no more than justice to reality – may, even, sometimes fall short of it. As yet we knew nothing of Babyi Yar, of Maidanek or Auschwitz; as yet I knew nothing of the hospital for children who had been tortured by the Germans, some having had their hands hacked off, others a swastika branded deep into their thin bodies, but I heard of incidents to which, if only out of psychological self-defence, there could be no reaction other than hatred.

By March 1942 we were back in Moscow. Our hearts, however, were in Leningrad, starving, freezing, besieged by the Germans. Hitler had ordered that Leningrad was to be 'wiped off the map'. Those seeking to escape were to be shot down and the city was to be razed to the ground. The attempt to seize it by storm had failed. Bombers and artillery carried on their work of destruction. Three million of the population were encircled; two million survived, the others died, mainly of starvation. Small quantities of arms, ammunition and foodstuffs were transported across the frozen surface of Lake Ladoga. While the ice was still comparatively thin, horses were used to bring in the supplies but they were so weak and undernourished that many collapsed and died on the way, whereupon they, whose task had been to bring in nourishment, became nourishment themselves. On 22 November 1941 a hazardous enterprise began – the use of mechanized transport. The ice was still too thin to bear the heavy trucks. Few of them got through. In the period 23 November to 1 December only 800 tons of flour reached the city. Eventually the Russians succeeded in delivering 1,000 tons of foodstuffs daily, as well as petrol and ammunition. But if the frost provided bread it withheld water. The water mains froze solid, pipes burst; in the ice of the Neva and the canals the Leningraders cut holes through which to draw up the muddy, filthy water. December 1941 and January

1942 were the worst months. The city was slowly dying of starvation and typhoid, but the workers kept on working until the time came to give notice: 'It'll be all over for me tomorrow, Comrade Manager. I must ask you for a coffin. My family haven't the strength to go and get one.'

The blockade was not lifted until January 1943. The first Leningraders I spoke to were skeletons loosely enfolded in dry, wrinkled skin; their necks seemed barely capable of supporting their skull-like heads. Nevertheless they were alive.

'I was saved by my wife,' an Austrian employee of Leningrad Radio related. His wife was Russian. One morning he had told her: 'I can't go on any longer.' 'But you've got to!' 'I can't stand up!' 'You've got to! Think of the Kirov workers!' The Kirov workers, members of the former Putilov works, set an example to everyone; they were the pride of the city. 'I can't!' 'Then you'll die.' She shook him. 'Let me die.' She kept hitting him until he stood up. 'She not only thrashed me back to work, she saved my life.'

'Leningrad will fall when we let ourselves fall.' 'Leningrad is where the heart of the Soviet Union beats. There was none of the panic here that there was in Moscow.' Though by no means the main incentive for the resistance, the rivalry between Leningrad and Moscow was certainly a contributory factor. When Lou and I were last in Moscow in the summer of 1962 we were given as escort a young graduate of the Party College. He showed exemplary zeal in teaching me about the nature of imperialism and the need for a monolithic party. In the Pushkin Museum he pointedly turned his back on the works of the French Impressionists and other products of 'decadence'. And one day he suddenly remarked: 'I don't like Leningrad. It's a European city. Moscow now – that's Russia!' It was a grotesque over-simplification of the old antithesis. Leningrad was the city of the Revolution, of the revolutionary workers, of the progressive intellectuals. Moscow, in the Tsarist Empire a city of merchants and *nouveaux riches*, became, in the Soviet Union, the metropolis of the bureaucracy. Leningrad, not so ponderous, leaner, more resilient, more intellectual, vindicated its traditions during the war. Both in major and minor matters the party organization functioned more efficiently, its distribution of the little to be had was more rational, the tasks it set were concrete ones and it encouraged individual responsibility and initiative. Lenin's city never quite became Stalin's city. Many who hated Stalin played an exemplary part in the defence of Leningrad. The Leningrad party organization was too independent, too self-assertive. The Defence of Leningrad Museum was closed down in 1949. Voznesensky, along with Stalingrad's defenders – Kuznetsov, Popkov and others – was executed on Stalin's orders. In short: 'I don't like Leningrad.'

And then came Stalingrad.

Like Leningrad in the north, Sebastopol had stood firm in the south. A few days before the latter town fell, on 28 June 1942, a new German offensive had been launched in the Kursk–Voronezh sector. Voroshilovgrad fell on 19 July. 'The Voronezh–Stalingrad–Rostov triangle will be held,' they told us in the Comintern. Yet on 28 July Rostov was given up without serious resistance. What had happened? Why had Sebastopol defended itself with such stubbornness? Why had Rostov surrendered overnight? Once again the cry of 'Betrayal!' rang out. And it was not only the press but the man in the street who demanded: 'Pull yourselves together! No mercy for the guilty! Iron discipline!' Rostov had been intended to bar the Germans' way into the Caucasus. The way now was clear.

'Perhaps it was panic rather than betrayal,' Togliatti suggested. 'A misfortune, certainly. But our misfortune will be the Germans' undoing. By going for Stalingrad and the Caucasus simultaneously Hitler is splitting his forces. And in doing that he's lost the war – definitively.'

After the fall of Rostov, officers were given unrestricted powers of command. The political commissar, who had hitherto been the officer's counterpart, was done away with. The Red Army became the Patriotic Army.

The Wehrmacht was advancing on Stalingrad. Hitler had given orders that this sprawling city by the banks of the Volga was to be taken on 25 August. On 23 August the Germans broke through to the Volga. Six hundred German aircraft subjected the northern part of the city to continuous attack. All was smoke and flames, a hell which consumed 40,000 dead.

The Soviet Army guarding Stalingrad, the 62nd, was cut off from the rest of the Russian forces on 12 September and on the same day General Chuikov took over as its commander. In his book *The Beginning of the Road** he tells of the troops' despair: 'When I asked

*Moscow, 1959.

them: "Where are you going? What are you looking at?" they gave senseless answers; they all seemed to be looking for somebody on the other side of the Volga, or in the Saratov region.' Chuikov's predecessor, General Lopatin, thought it futile, indeed impossible, to hold Stalingrad. The War Council of the Stalingrad front, whose members included Khrushchev and Yeremenko, issued the order: 'The enemy will be destroyed at Stalingrad.' The words uttered by Klochkov a year previously during the defence of the Volokolamsk highway were given a new rendering: 'Behind us is the Volga, nothing else. There's no land beyond.'

Chuikov put new heart into the army and made plans to go over to the offensive. However, a column of German tanks and motorized infantry broke through to the city centre and attacked the Central Station. During the night of 14–15 September the celebrated Rodimtsev division, ten thousand strong, began to cross the Volga. The artillery remained behind on the left bank. It was from this side that the rockets were launched from the 'Stalin organs'. 'Shoot me if you like,' a German staff officer said after the surrender, 'but first let me see one of your Stalin organs, your new weapon.'

On 1 October Colonel Guriev's division crossed the Volga; many of his men were Siberians, the toughest troops the Russians possessed. In the north of the city small groups forced their way into houses and cellars, fighting with knives and daggers from staircase to staircase and floor to floor. They fought and they died crying: 'For country and Stalin! We shall never surrender!'

On 14 October the decisive battle began. The German air force flew 3,000 sorties in a series of non-stop attacks. By midnight the Germans had surrounded the Stalingrad tractor factory; at a cost of 3,000 dead and forty tanks they had gained a mile and a half. Chuikov records that between 14 and 23 October 'both the Germans' strength and our strength were on the wane. In these last ten days the Germans had again cut our army in two and inflicted very serious losses.' And then: 'By 30 October we began to feel we were winning the battle.'

So much has been written about the battle of Stalingrad that I am unable to add anything new. Most of the transcripts of the broadcasts I made at the time have been lost. One of them, dated 25 October, has been traced. I shall quote from it because it seems to preserve something of the fiery breath of the battle.

Three months ago a name gripped the imagination of the world, a name that has not let go since then: Stalingrad. Do you know what Stalingrad is? Twenty-five years ago it was a sleepy Russian provincial town. From over the water, from across the steppe came the melancholy song of the Volga boatmen. The town was then called Tsaritsyn. In 1918 Tsaritsyn was the bulwark of the youthful Soviet state. Stalin took charge of its defence. Tsaritsyn became Stalingrad, the city of Stalin. It became commensurate with its name during the early years of the construction of Soviet industry. It was here that the first gigantic tractor factory in the Soviet Union was built. Young workers, women as well as men, with unpractised hands but fierce determination, arrived from all parts of the country. The German newspapers wrote mockingly: 'Have these Volga boatmen gone mad? After a lifetime spent dragging salt upstream in their barges, what have they to do with the technology of the twentieth century?' But on 17 June 1930 the first tractor to be built in the gigantic works rolled off the production line and into the Soviet countryside, decorated with leafy branches and red flags. In the first three years of its existence the Stalingrad tractor factory provided Russian farmers with 66,000 tractors; in time the number grew to many hundreds of thousands. The ploughshare of a new era – that's what Stalingrad was. The city stretched its limbs, expanded along the banks of the Volga, mile upon mile, a living production line between river and steppe; housing estates among gardens and hedges alternating with blast-furnaces, factories and tall blocks of flats; 600,000 inhabitants and year by year new schools, theatres, libraries, nurseries. Perpetual growth – that's what Stalingrad was.

That, dear listeners, is what Stalingrad *was*. But what is Stalingrad today? Today it is something worse than hell, something indescribably frightful. German soldiers call it the Stalingrad deathtrap. It is a hell that has swallowed up 400,000 of their comrades. After the hundredth attack, a German lieutenant by the name of Weinar wrote in his diary: 'My God, my God, why hast thou forsaken us?' Fourteen days were spent in a battle for one single house, with mortars, machine guns, hand grenades and bayonets for weapons. Already by the third day fifty-four German men and officers were lying dead in the cellar, on the landings and on the stairs. The corridors between the gutted rooms, the thin ceilings between one floor and the next – this was the front. By fire escapes, over smoking rooftops, help arrived from the courtyard or from the neighbouring house. Detonations, curtains of flame, dust-clouds, blood, plaster, the shredded remnants of what had once been a mattress or a man, smoke-blackened faces, hand grenades hurled from landing to landing, a day-long carnage in one single house. Ask any soldier what half-an-hour's hand-to-hand fighting is like in this war! But eighty days and eighty nights of hand-to-hand fighting – that is Stalingrad. The length of a street isn't reckoned in yards but in numbers of dead. One small sector, about a mile wide and two miles in depth, was bombed by 3,000 aircraft and subjected to a concentrated barrage from thousands of guns and mortars. Every stone was pulverized, every single square yard ploughed up. Then two German infantry divisions, led by a hundred tanks, went into the attack, into the smoking heap of rubble. Not a building remained standing, not a tree or a house beam, but the *living* Stalingrad still stands. Out of the torn, scorched earth men climbed, men who describe themselves simply as 'We Stalingraders'. And 1,500 German dead and seventy-five crippled German tanks remained in this sector of the front. That is Stalingrad, a city no longer. By day an incandescent cloud, by night a sea of flames. And the cloud is devouring the army of Hitler. And the flame flies in the van of the nations. That is Stalingrad.

It was nearly evening, one of those eighty burning, bellowing, bloody evenings, when the dogs rushed howling and whimpering down to the Volga. Animals flee this inferno and not even the hardest stone is proof against it, but the people of Stalingrad stand firm. For them the Volga has but one bank.

What sort of people are these? There was old Ivan Valikov, a man of sixty. He should have left the city with the elderly and sick, the women and children, ten thousand of them, who had been ferried across the Volga in barges. 'I'm staying,' old Valikov said. He went to the City Commandant. 'I'm staying here. It's my city. I defended Tsaritsyn. I helped to build Stalingrad. I watched the first tractor leave the factory. It's my city. It's my life.' The old man stayed. He stood outside the gates of his factory, armed with a rifle. He watched his house burn and collapse. He did not budge from his post. He stayed outside his factory. When the Germans attacked they were thrown back by the workers' battalions. Old Valikov died outside the gates of his factory. Then there was Olga Kovalyova, a steel-casting operative. She was strong and beautiful and the darling of Stalingrad's steelworkers. She wanted to stay alive; she was happy to be there, to love, to bear children, to construct. When the Germans came she took up arms. She joined a workers' battalion. She fought and she died. These are the people of Stalingrad. The workers in the factories who, amid ruins and explosions, restore salvaged tanks to battle-worthiness, working up to seventy-two hours on end without looking up and without sleep. The farmers who plough their fields close to the front, who are cultivating a larger acreage than ever before. The Germans won't be harvesting here, they say. The seeds of corn are germinating for Stalingrad. And across the Volga come bread and ammunition and newspapers and reinforcements for burning Stalingrad.

Stalingrad is a city no longer, only a flame. The Germans dropped leaflets with the message: 'Surrender!' At 3,000 feet the leaflets turned to ashes. Stalingrad will never surrender, the pyre of Hitler's army, the flame of hope for the peoples of the world: Stalingrad.

On 7 November Stalin said: 'In our alleyway, too, the sun will shine.' On 9 November we heard of the Allied landing in North Africa. On 19 and 20 November the Soviet counter-offensive at Stalingrad began. The three Soviet fronts, the Don Army Group under Rokossovsky, the South-West Army Group under Vatutin and the Stalingrad Army Group under Yeremenko, comprised more than 1,050,000 men against an almost equal number of enemy troops, more than 900 hundred tanks against 700, 13,000 guns against 10,000, 1,100 aircraft against 1,200. The Germans were encircled. On 12 November Manstein's army moved up from the Caucasus, advancing rapidly until they were able to 'see the glow in the sky above Stalingrad'. They got no further for they were unable to break through. On 24 December, Christmas Eve, all hope of relieving the city was abandoned. Later, in conversation with me after he had been taken prisoner, Lieutenant-Colonel von Hanstein, one of Field-Marshal Paulus's officers, trotted out the idiotic jingle: 'Manstein comes to Hanstein! Manstein comes to Hanstein! Funny, what?' But Manstein had not come.

In my broadcast on 17 January 1943 I said:

My dear listeners, as I speak to you the remnants of the German Sixth Army are dying in Stalingrad. Hitler gave the order to fight to the last man. He alone is responsible for the death of the German Sixth Army. More than 200,000 German soldiers and officers – that's what it *used* to be, but no longer is. A few days ago only 80,000 were left, now only the last, starving, despairing remnants of twenty-two divisions . . .

On 8 January the Red Army offered the encircled German troops capitulation on honourable terms. Here is the offer made by the Soviet commander to the German Army: life and safety guaranteed to all officers and soldiers and, upon the termination of the war, their return to Germany or to any other country the prisoners of war may choose. They were assured that they might retain their uniforms, insignia, decorations and personal belongings and valuables. All soldiers and officers were guaranteed proper rations, the sick and wounded hospitalization and medical care.

And now imagine the situation in which the German Sixth Army has found itself for many weeks past: herded together in a restricted space, amidst the ruins of the city, all around them the cold, bare steppe. Their bread ration, four to five ounces a day, supplemented by the flesh of dead horses, dogs, cats and rats. No fuel, no winter clothing; starvation, epidemics. Every day 500 soldiers die of exposure, or typhoid, 'flu and pneumonia, while 1,500 are killed by artillery fire or in close combat . . .

But the German troops were told: only a few more days and relief will come. At the same time they were given the order: 'It is the right and duty of every German soldier and officer to shoot on the spot any comrade whom he suspects of intending to give himself up to the Russians.' But finally the truth stared everyone in the face: they saw it in their utter dereliction, in the few remaining dead horses, in the hollow cheeks of the starving, heard it in the death rattle of the dying – the undeniable truth. And then came the Russian ultimatum, the voice of reason, of salvation. And Hitler's answer, out of the far distance, out of the safety of the Führer's headquarters: A crown of oak leaves for General Paulus's Knight's Cross; for his troops, a crown of thorns on a cross of birchwood. Now listen to Hitler's special message, his sentence of death on twenty-two divisions: 'If the German soldier takes the view that it is pointless to continue to hold out, let him remember one thing: the Führer is better informed . . . He must remember that it is the Führer himself who is leading him. His duty is not to ask questions. His duty is blind obedience.' Yes, my dear listeners, it was the Führer himself who led the German troops into the deathtrap of Stalingrad and, being so much better informed, this Führer turned a deaf ear to all admonitions and nominated himself conqueror of Stalingrad. For after all was he not, in his megalomania and irresponsibility, better informed? . . .

Think that right through to its logical conclusion, my dear listeners. Had a small car carrying a white flag been at a given point in a given street at a given time, the life of an entire army would have been saved. The car was not there, and that is why your sons and husbands are dying in Stalingrad . . . Think that through to its logical conclusion! A few months ago the Nazi leaders said: 'Stalingrad is the symbol of the European war of liberation.' And that is absolutely true, as every one of you can plainly see: Stalingrad, the symbol of the European war of liberation. The defeat suffered by Hitler, the supreme commander, is unparalleled in the history of German warfare, and this is only a beginning. I tell you this now with the same urgency as, months ago, I told you: not one German division, not one German company will return from Stalingrad. Is the whole of Germany to suffer the same fate as the German Army that is dying in Stalingrad? . . .

As he broadcasts his words into the void, the speaker believes in the power of the word. Yet the mouths of cannon, the power of command and the habit of obedience speak a language more forceful than the mouth of man. The speaker searches for the word that will find its mark, the word that will tell.

In view of the explicit purpose of my broadcasts I did wrong in appealing to the conscience of the German soldier, in talking about the problem of collective guilt. The Nazi leaders deliberately involved as many Germans as possible in their guilt, not only indirectly but also directly, so that the fear of reprisals should compel them to remain steadfast. During a conversation I was told by a captured German officer: 'You see, the first time you're given the order to destroy a village along with all its inhabitants, you only have two alternatives – either put a bullet through your brain or become an habitual criminal. The most ghastly thing is habituation.' However I was not capable of considering only the effects of propaganda; I went beyond its limits, endeavouring not merely to 'sap the morale' of the German soldier in his capacity as a 'murderous machine', but rather and also to see him as an exploited human being. For at some time some word would surely have impact enough to pierce the surface, to penetrate into regions that had been covered over and buried. 'You believe in the magic of the word,' said Dimitrov one day. I did indeed believe in it.

On 31 January Paulus capitulated.

In the same year, 1943, I assumed another duty besides that of radio commentator, the duty of talking to German and Austrian prisoners and convincing them of the lunacy of Hitler's war, of the inevitability of defeat, of their future responsibility for the fate of Germany.

'An order's an order.'

The young subaltern, his features rigid, his eyes expressionless and evasive as he replied to my question, was not unprepossessing. Yet, as I knew, he had given the order to set a village on fire and to slaughter all its inhabitants and had, moreover, according to one of his men, flung a child into the flames.

'I'm not a commissar, nor am I interrogating you. This conversation won't have any untoward consequences. All I want is to understand . . .'

'An order is an order.'

'You've told me about your home, your wife and two children . . .'

'Here's a photograph of them.'

'Do you think your wife would understand . . . ? You burnt down a village, women and children . . .'

'An order is an order.'

'Would you obey any order?'

He looked me straight in the face.

'Yes!'

'You really mean *any* order . . .'

'Yes.'

'Now take this woman, these children, here in this photograph – suppose they were standing there, against that wall, and your Führer gave you the order to shoot them, your wife and your children – would you obey that order?'

His face turned white. He did not answer.

'Would you obey that order?'

And instead of a no or a yes, came the terrible answer:

'Give me three minutes to think it over.'

And at the end of three minutes: 'I would obey the order. And I'd reserve the last bullet for myself.'

Command and obedience. Command and obedience.

'You're a lawyer, aren't you, major?'

'Yes, I'm a lawyer.'

'And you maintain that, to the best of your knowledge, nothing irregular has ever happened in the Third Reich? You did say – "irregular"?'

'To the best of my knowledge – but how much did we in fact know?'

'*Everything* was in order? Really everything?'

'Yes – but listen, I've just remembered. There *was* something that wasn't quite in order. It was, there's no other word for it, irregular. There was to be a plebiscite – what about I can't remember – and I was sent for by the *Gauleiter*. I was to be in charge of the plebiscite committee. But this time the poll had got to be a hundred per cent! – I didn't know what to make of it. There wasn't to be a single no. You understand? And after all, that's . . . well, er . . . I didn't like it at all, thought it very . . . But it went off more easily than I had feared. Nobody kept a check on me, it just so happened that nobody voted no, or if they did, their papers had vanished. I heaved a sigh of relief. But prematurely, as it turned out. The most embarassing thing was still to come – if embarrassing is a strong enough term. I was asked to sign a document to the effect that the voting procedure had been in order. I, a German university graduate, a lawyer, asked to participate in a fraud, to append my signature to it, something tantamount to perjury! Just imagine asking this of me, a German university man! But I *didn't* sign! No, I did not! Instead of signing myself "Doktor Mayer", I wrote just plain "Mayer".'

The honour of the German university graduate remained untarnished; it was not the doctor who was sullied, but Mayer.

The Battle of Kursk had begun on 5 July 1943. The Russian communiqué after the first day's fighting reported the destruction of 586 German tanks and 203 German aircraft. On the second day: 433 tanks and 111 aircraft. On the third day: 520 tanks and 111 aircraft. Never before had there been such losses. On 24 July Stalin issued an order of the day to Generals Rokossovsky, Vatutin and Popov announcing the 'final liquidation of the German summer offensive and the recovery of all territory lost since 5 July'.

On 5 July the fall of Rome was announced and on 7 June came the Allied landings in Normandy.

On 23 and 28 June four Russian fronts broke through the German positions and surrounded strong German forces at Vitebsk and Bobruisk. In these two pockets alone 20,000 Germans were taken prisoner. On 3 July, east of Minsk, another 100,000 Germans were surrounded; 40,000 were killed or wounded and the remainder surrendered.

How much earth to bury a man?

How many strawberries to feed a general?

This latter question was pensively posed by a general who had held a command on the front that had collapsed.

The Staff had suddenly lost its army. Orders were sent out even though there were no troops to execute them. 'A curious feeling,' remarked the general. Groping their way through a void, the generals went wandering about in the woods.

'How many strawberries?' That was the question. It was answered with Teutonic thoroughness. 'Fifty strawberries are a starvation diet, eighty are moderately satisfying, a hundred and twenty are fully satisfying.'

Hunting, not for their lost army, but for strawberries with which to satisfy their hunger, the German generals went into the bag.

Austrian *Gemütlichkeit* was hardly less hair-raising than this Teutonic exactitude.

On 5 August 1943 Moscow experienced its first salutes and fireworks. The order of the day on the occasion of the liberation of Orel and Belgorod contained the following passage: 'Tonight, 5 August, at 2400 hours, the capital of our country will salute our valiant troops, the liberators of Orel and Belgorod, with twelve artillery salvoes from 120 guns.' Soon things had reached such a pitch that Moscow daily began to anticipate a victory salute. And one evening a captive Austrian medical officer, standing beside a window with his Russian escort, asked: 'Well, what's up today? No victory?'

But other noteworthy and momentous things were also happening.

On 12 and 13 July there was a conference in Moscow attended by German officers and other ranks, writers and former Reichstag deputies; the result was the Komitee Freies Deutschland. Its president was the poet Erich Weinert, one of the finest and most charming people I have ever met; its vice-presidents were Major Karl Hetz and Lieutenant Graf von Einsiedel.

I had just returned with a group of officer P.O.W.s from a camp where, for the past fortnight, I had been holding discussions. We were sitting round a large table eating our lunch. For a time of acute shortage it was a very ample meal. We started off with cheese.

'Odd,' remarked one of the officers, 'very odd! In civilized countries cheese is served at the *end* of the meal.'

A silent, abstracted colonel who had hitherto scarcely said a word, now stood up and, opening his thin, colourless lips, remarked: 'You should be thankful that you're getting cheese at all, whether before the meal or after it!'

'What do you mean?'

'What I mean,' replied the colonel in a low, firm voice, 'is that what we really deserve is to be put up against a wall.'

'What's that you say?'

'Shot as murderers.'

'Outrageous! A German officer! What do you think you're saying? We've the right . . .'

'We have no rights of any kind. Remember Kharkov. You were there. November 1941, at Gestapo headquarters. The inhabitants were all herded together, a proclamation was read. Prisoners were hounded up onto the balconies, remember? A rope tied round their necks, the other end fastened to the railings – have you forgotten, gentlemen? Corpses hanging from balustrades, balconies, windows. For days and days they were left hanging there, until the whole town stank of rotten flesh. Forgotten it already? I shall *never* be able to forget!'

Chairs went toppling as everyone leapt to their feet amid a general hubbub of oaths and imprecations, and in the middle of it all the quiet colonel, with his thin lips, his pallid face, and his low, firm voice.

In civilized countries cheese is served at the end of the meal . . .

An 'Association of German Officers' had been proposed. The scheme had been considered, though inconclusively, by three senior officers – Lieutenant-General Korfes, a military historian, the young Panzer General Lattmann and, last but not least, General von Seyd-litz – the officer who, on 17 January at Stalingrad, had urged Paulus to accept the Russian ultimatum so that the remaining survivors might be saved. These men asked to have a word with me in private. I was taken to see them in a country house outside Moscow.

General von Seydlitz, a member of a famous Prussian army family was, like many of his kind, more than just a military man. An introvert and a mystic, he consorted with the spirit world. Of such material were made, not only cavalry generals, but also men like Kleist and Novalis.

We went out of the house into the park.

'You're the son of an officer,' said von Seydlitz. 'I'd like you to answer two questions – as the man of honour we consider you to be. If we decide to head an association of German officers, to appeal to the army and to the people, and do whatever lies in our power to curtail an insane war which has already been lost – shall we be betraying our country?'

'Austrian law draws a distinction between high treason and betrayal of one's country. What you are contemplating is high treason.'

'So from that point of view we shall be traitors?'

'In the eyes of the law, yes. The law of the land overrides pro-vincial law, and the laws of humanity must override all other forms of legality.'

'Thank you. Now for my second question . . . I have a wife and two daughters . . . Do you think their lives will be in danger if I decide to go ahead?'

'Yes.'

'Thank you for being so forthright. I will do what is my duty. You have convinced me . . . And now, gentlemen, how about you?'

'We shall go along with you . . .'

And that is how the Association of German Officers came into being.

That, too, is Germany.

From my point of view there was a snag about this continual intercourse with German officers. I was an Austrian, a fact which I invariably stressed in the course of conversation and which tended to alienate those to whom I talked. 'Why not give up your Austrian hobbyhorse?' said Manuilsky. 'It's Germany that really counts. And anyhow – what good will a minor state be to you? You need a wider stage for your activities.'

I did not give up my 'hobbyhorse'. There was at the time a tough, underground struggle for Austria – and not only with the German Communists. Molotov was 'pan-German' and opposed to an independent Austria. Dimitrov was on the side of us Austrians and so was Togliatti. To Manuilsky the question was not of fundamental importance; he argued that the cadres of the C.P.A. exerted a wholesome influence on the C.P.G. which, in turn, would give them a favourable opportunity for expansion.

On 19 October the Foreign Ministers of the Soviet Union, the United States and Great Britain met in Moscow. The restoration of Austria as an independent state was announced. The Austrians were warned against cooperating with Germany to the bitter end, and were asked to make their own contribution to the country's liberation.

In a prisoner-of-war camp outside Moscow we hoisted the first red, white and red flag.

One is never so close to home as when one is in exile. Again and again a stretch of the Mur Valley between Graz and Bruck insinuated itself into my sleep. A smell of cool leaves, of wood and of resin. It was dream country. I wrote a paper, 'The Origins of the Austrian National Character', in which I summed up all that was most appealing about Austria. 'You can say what you like,' my Russian driver once remarked in the course of an argument, 'but Austrians are Germans! You're a good sort, but this is one thing you're wrong about . . .' I had long since forgotten this argument, but as he drove me to the office on 17 July 1944 the driver said over his shoulder: 'You're right after all, Comrade Fischer.' 'How do you mean, right?' 'About the Austrians. When you say they're not Germans. I could see that today.' I was not altogether delighted by this change of opinion.

For on 17 July 1944 57,000 German prisoners of war had marched right across Moscow, starting from the Byelorussian Station and dispersing to various other stations. A dense crowd of Muscovites lined the streets. There were no shouted imprecations or other remarks; the general mood was one of wondering reserve. These, then, were the Germans!

The procession was headed by more than a dozen generals and a large number of Staff officers, their eyes staring into nothingness, their faces stony, as they marched with stiff and jerky gait, uniformed marionettes. They had been promised a parade through Moscow by the Führer. The time had now come.

In his book *Russia at War*, Alexander Werth records much the same kind of remarks as I myself heard among the spectators: 'Not all that different from our own lads . . .' 'What's that you say? They're murderers!' . . . 'But not all of them . . .' '*All* of them! . . .' 'Human beings like us, the poor wretches . . .'

Interspersed among the ranks of stiffly marching men with dead-pan expressions there had been small untidy groups, demonstratively good-humoured, their eyes roving curiously about them. Some waved to the Russians. One shouted: '*Kaputt!*' His comrades laughed. They were Austrians. It was they who had finally convinced my driver.

During the last year of war, from 1944 to 1945, it was only in the physical sense that I was living in Moscow, having already flown to Austria ahead of myself – constantly conferring with Austrian prisoners of war and engaged in the study of Austrian history and specifically Austrian problems. I existed not here but there, in the future, in the as yet non-existent. Even as a septuagenarian I feel some reluctance to write memoirs, my face turned rather towards the future than towards the past, waiting as once in childhood for the mysterious postman, the bearer of the wonderful, the all-important letter. That this postman is death frightens me not at all.

Ever since my earliest childhood the death I outwitted has vindictively withdrawn into my dreams. The scene of all my fears, persecutions, tortures, is invariably an hotel. Often the building is decaying, neglected: a dark vestibule, a stuffed bear holding a plate in his right paw, a porter with a long white beard, motionless in his cubby-hole. He doesn't answer, stares with unseeing eyes, for he is dead, a corpse in a blue uniform with gold epaulettes. In all the corners vast spiders' webs crammed full of flies; they remain uneaten for the spiders, too, are dead. Suddenly something alive, a child, an old woman dressed up as a chambermaid, curtseying, beckoning us mysteriously. We follow her up marble stairs, fragments of steps, rubble, an abyss. The creature we have followed opens a side door. A winding stair leads upwards, but this staircase, too, ends in rubble and débris. A ladder is leaning against the cracked and crumbling wall. We climb up it. We can hardly breathe. The air is curdled milk, oozing thickly into our mouths, tasting of carrion. At this point, if I'm lucky, I fall, down into the pit of my stomach, my heart thumping, knocking, pounding, a heavy fall into wakefulness.

I seldom am lucky. More often we find ourselves, Lou and I, in a corridor with satin curtains, sumptuous vases and lots of doors. A severe woman sitting at a table asks to see our papers, puts on a pair of spectacles and makes sure that we are ourselves, not intruders in disguise. Then she leafs through a book, finds our names, nods in silent contempt, indicates a room. Several men are walking up and down the corridor. We are disagreeably struck by their seedy black suits, their expressionless faces, their thin lips. We are also disagreeably struck by our room. It is crammed with pillars, lamps, plush-covered furniture. No light comes from the lamps. The plush-covered furniture has notices on it: 'Not to be used!' Even in the absence of such notices we wouldn't dare entrust our persons to these monsters.

One of the black-suited men has followed us in. Taking no notice of us he goes across to a window, turns his back on us, drums on the panes with his fingers.

'Who are you?'

No answer.

'What do you want?'

No answer.

A second black-suited man comes in, goes across to the other window, drums his fingers on the panes.

'This is *our* room!'

No answer.

'Police!' screams Lou, running out of the room. The word goes echoing down the corridor.

On the threshold a massive police officer, wearing a whole breast-plate of medals.

'Fallen into the trap nicely!' he says with a self-satisfied air. The three black-suited men laugh.

'Are *you* the police?'

The three black-suited men are no longer laughing. They stare at me. The medals tinkle. The police officer shows me his clenched fists, improbable lumps of muscle bristling with black hair.

'Is that enough?'

'I want the *other* police.'

'No such thing.'

I hurry out – no one tries to stop me – and shout down the corridor: 'Police! Police!'

'They're already here!' says the lady at the table.

'I want the others!'

'I *beg* your pardon . . . ?'

I go running down the street. Lou is coming towards me. 'On that corner over there,' she says. 'The police station.'

In a bare room with whitewashed walls, three policemen are standing behind a balustrade.

'Are you the proper police?'

No answer.

'I mean – the *others*?'

They exchange anxious glances.

Then one of them says: 'It's not something we are competent to decide.'

The second: 'We're just subordinates.'

The third: 'To know that, one has to be a superior.'

The superior comes in, a massive police officer wearing a whole breastplate of medals.

'Are you the other police?'

The medals tinkle.

'What – *other?*'

The police officer appears to be reflecting, somewhat uneasily. 'It's not quite certain. One never knows exactly. Of course we're not the same. We're another country, but somewhere the threads connect, you see, so that we aren't in fact the same and yet sometimes we are the same, one never knows exactly.'

'But it's quite clear that you're the other police,' I cajole him, 'the proper ones.'

'You're right,' says the police officer. 'Our culture is, of course, infinitely higher.'

'Then please help us. Come with us to the hotel.'

The police officer is taken aback. His face betrays perplexity. Suddenly he thumps himself on the chest. His medals chime merrily. 'Come along! All the same . . . if by any chance . . . otherwise it might cost us our heads . . . if the highest authority does happen to be interested in you. So we'll have to take you there under escort. I'll go ahead, with drawn sword. You follow behind me, and my men'll march behind you . . .'

In the portico of the hotel the other is already waiting among the marble pillars.

Dumbly our man stops and salutes. The other acknowledges his salute. And then absorbs our man into his person. A quadruped with two heads, then only one, then none; between his shoulders a fist, bristling with black hair.

'To start with, you will survey the instruments of torture.'

Surely – I think – that's a quotation? Galileo Galilei.

The fist opens, the monster's maw: 'We're humane. Aggressive humanists. Resourceful discoverers of new ways of dying. We kill for the welfare of mankind, not for fun . . .'

Dreams of death – a pale reflection of reality.

In the summer of 1943 the Soviet press carried reports about the *mobile gas chambers* that followed in the wake of the German armies. The descriptions of Jewish women and children being herded onto these trucks must, we believed, be atrocity stories. Even the detailed drawings showing how the wagons were constructed failed to convince us. But prisoners of war subsequently confirmed that these mobile gas chambers (*dushe-gubka*, or soul-killers as the Russians called them) were the invention, not of propagandists, but of German engineers.

And again, after the liberation of Lublin in the summer of 1944, when the Russians discovered the extermination camp at Maidanek and Konstantin Simonov described it in *Pravda*, we did not at first have the courage to believe it was true.

A collection of huts in the midst of the luxuriant green of the countryside. Luscious green cabbages with a powdering of white dust. No better fertilizer than that white dust – the ashes of Jews. The S.S. men prized this fertilizer which they used on their vegetable gardens, happily eating the juicy vegetables and even feeding them to the prisoners before these, in their turn, became ashes for the fertilization of German cabbages.

When they arrived the Jews were politely asked to step into a building marked *Bad und Desinfektion II*. In simulation of a normal arrival, their luggage was taken from them and they were asked to have a wash after their long journey. The place was built of concrete, all round it benches on which to put down clothes. The murderers were polite – in no other camp, only at Maidanek. 'Leave your clothes here please. Kindly step this way.' The next room they were invited to enter consisted of a number of square concrete structures, each about one quarter the size of the bath-house but without any windows. Naked, the people were now herded into the dark concrete boxes, 200 to 250 in each, the men first, then the women and finally the children, all decently segregated. Above their heads light filtered in through a small slit in the roof, in the steel door a round spy-hole protected by heavy meshwire. Around it the maker's name, 'Auert, Berlin'. From the roof hot air was pumped into the boxes, followed by a shower of pretty, light-blue crystals which vaporized in the heat: poison gas. Through the spy-hole the staring eye of the S.S. man, sole witness of the gassing. The process of mass dying took from two to ten minutes. The corpses were loaded onto lorries, covered with tarpaulins and conveyed to the far end of the camp to be burnt in the crematorium. The resulting ashes were added to an enormous white mound in which could be discerned the remains of skeletons, finger bones, femurs, one or two small skulls. It was this mound that provided the fertilizer.

The average output of corpses was 2,000 a day. On 3 November, after the Warsaw ghetto rising, it rose to 20,000. The gas chambers being unable to cope with so much raw material, the majority were shot, 10,000 of them outside the camp perimeter. No time was wasted in removing their clothes, only handbags being taken from the women and toys from the children; the dead and all they had on them were saturated with petrol and burnt, forming pyres which continued to smoulder for weeks. The normal process was more economical, the yield – 850,000 pairs of boots and shoes – being stored in a vast barn. In Chopin Street, in the 'Chopin Store', the warehouse of mass murder, men's and women's shoes, overcoats, outerwear and underwear were carefully sorted and packed for dispatch to Germany – with love from Himmler who twice visited Maidanek. About 1,500,000 people were done to death here.

More terrible than any nightmare, the nightmare of reality, inconceivable, the apocalyptic cornucopia of *power* – boundless, uncontrolled power, bloated with dictatorial megalomania. What we had at first refused to believe now confronted us as irrefutable if still inconceivable fact. How could we, unable to attribute the inconceivable to our mortal foe, have dared suspect that in the Soviet Union millions of innocent people had been, not gassed, it is true, but maltreated, tortured, deported to labour camps that were only too much like death camps? How could those who doubted Maidanek assume Kolyma to be possible? It was none the less imperative that we think of everything, do everything that might help to forestall the emergence of a form of power that was boundless and uncontrolled, and thus pave the way for a free society, free from the domination of capital, but also free from any kind of authoritarian, repressive régime. But in the case of people distorted by a Fascist indoctrination and experience, how were we to guarantee and prepare for a free society, and how discover the forms for a modern and effective democracy? How could a humane Europe emerge from this most ghastly of all wars, and what contribution could we make towards it, we who were helping to shape the little Austria of the future?

The dissolution of the Comintern on 22 May 1943 was a concession made by Stalin to his Western allies. The explanation given by the Praesidium of the Executive Committee was more than mere prevarication. It declared the Comintern to be 'out of date' and 'an obstacle in the way of the national workers' parties which were growing ever stronger', a line of reasoning which was perfectly sound. That Stalin had contemptuously dismissed the Comintern as 'moribund' we did not know at the time, but many of us regarded the parties' liberation from Moscow's tutelage as an essential pre-requisite for a Socialist and democratic post-war world.

The dissolution of the Comintern seemed to me to be the logical consequence of the realization that world revolution is a long, laborious process fraught with contradictions and one which cannot be directed from a single centre by a dictatorial 'general staff'. It has taken decades for me to understand that the old concept of world revolution had in fact been superseded by a new concept – that of a Russian world empire. Socialism was reduced to its crudest model: the socialization of the means of production plus government by the Communist Party, the hegemony of the party apparatus, of a new privileged caste. In such circumstances the socialization of the means of production (the fundamental principle of Socialism) does not proceed beyond the stage of nationalization. Not the producers, but the bureaucrats, dispose of the means of production. The monopoly of information, the lack of democratic co-determination, the perversity of the rulers, all serve to inhibit the free development of the individual and of society. Abroad, the Socialist idea is coming to be less and less effective, its place being increasingly usurped by armed forces, rockets, space exploration, landings on the moon and military and economic aid to backward countries. Autonomous revolutionary movements and parties are not regarded with favour. The apparatus requires apparatuses which recognize and endorse as Socialist every move made by the Soviet Union in the game of power politics.

Limestone may swallow up rivers; but the rivers are still there, under the ground, and come gushing forth again mightier than before. So, too, in the Soviet Union Socialism may again gush forth and when it does so it will be invincible.

Will Austria, will Europe, be free, democratic and Socialist?

A final conversation with Dimitrov.

'We in Austria should try, I believe, not to be too precipitate. We shall have to assume that many Austrians have been corrupted by Nazi rule. They will have to be educated for democracy, not from the outside, by inadequate teachers, but in actual practice and from below. Neither Parliament nor the parties can be dispensed with, but they are not enough. I envisage a system of councils, not just workers' councils in the factories, but rather a system of people's councils or people's committees, or whatever they may be called.'

'How would that be done?' Dimitrov inquired.

'It would be done by secret ballot, at the earliest possible date, and in all localities. But a beginning would have to be made by a nucleus of anti-Fascists, of Austrians who have preserved their integrity. These will take the initiative, get things going, prepare for elections – not to Parliament at this stage, but to local people's councils which in turn will send representatives to a central council.'

'And do you hope to find a nucleus of anti-Fascists in every locality?'

I was certain of it, not knowing that in the villages and smaller towns the most active and alert of the young were Nazis and that, though certain groups – Communists, Socialists, progressive and conservative Catholics – had resisted Nazi rule, the large majority of the people, weary of war, were not in the least anxious either to be 'liberated' or to play any part in their own liberation.

Hence, people's councils, a central council, an endeavour to eliminate divisive factors, to agree a programme of reconstruction involving the whole of Austria. First a programme, then parliamentary elections, with parties having their own platform but determined to cooperate on the basis of a common programme of reconstruction.

'That's fine,' said Dimitrov, 'but how about the class struggle?'

'That won't be over. But we have to remember firstly, that in Austria there won't be any *grande bourgeoisie* to speak of and, secondly, that the international balance of power as well as the experiences the people have been through will facilitate the achievement of radical social change without bloodshed.'

'Can the C.P.A. be a leading force?'

'We haven't got a Lenin. Nor are we Bolsheviks. But I believe not only that the courage of the Communists in the resistance will receive due recognition, but that we shall also be able to win people over by a show of intelligence, unselfishness and moral stamina. We shall not be the strongest party, Comrade Dimitrov, and all the problems of the transition to Socialism must be considered in the context of a constellation in which we, as a minority, will be able by degrees to impose our own ideas.'

'Without renouncing revolution?'

'Without renouncing revolution – and doing everything in our power to ensure that, when it comes, it is neither bloody nor violent.'

'The logic of revolutionary situations is unpredictable.'

'And that's precisely why it is possible that new forms and methods may emerge.'

'Fine!' said Dimitrov. 'I think the concept is both reasonable and feasible.'

It was, I believe, reasonable. But things turned out quite differently.

I didn't tell Dimitrov about my higher flights of fancy. Might it not be possible to attempt the bold experiment of making this small country, this small world, into a proving-ground for a larger world? Might not a small nation be able to achieve the dignity of a larger one, and graciousness, geniality, urbanity as well? Be able to steer clear of the insanity of power, to devise and create an enclave of the spirit? Might not Vienna once again become the '*salon* of the nations', the city of symposia, of meetings, of reconciliation? And all the old castles become repositories for the art, the literature, the sciences of the East and the West, of the North and the South? At the heart of Europe a country without soldiers, disarmed of its own free will, allied to no one and the ally of all? Was that not feasible? That this not very stable nation should by its own efforts achieve national self-assurance but without nationalism, without noise or fuss? That there should be an association of workers and intellectuals, progressive – not tight-lipped, but light of heart, humorous, cheerful? Production not for production's sake, not with the product in view but the man? Its criterion not his performance but his abilities as a whole? Was it not feasible, especially with a small country like Austria, to construct a model, a jumping-off place for the future? After all the self-mortification practised by mankind, the dawning of mankind's self-esteem? Halcyon dream of happiness! The dream of a fool, not that of a politician.

'Don't you think rather too highly of Prince Eugene of Savoy?' asked Otto Kuusinen, the astute and very cultivated head of the Finnish Communists. He had been reading my paper on Austria's chequered history and thought my eulogies of Prince Eugene excessive. I had been greatly moved by the fate of this man who was physically both weak and unattractive, if not downright ugly. Louis XIV, disliking the little fellow, had refused him the command of the regiment he coveted, whereupon this young adventurer of Italian extraction and French upbringing set off for Vienna on horseback. The Emperor was in distress, in need of military talent, and the little prince entered the service of Austria, then more of a phantom than a reality, ambiguous of tradition, dubious of future. And this expatriate who was unable to write Italian or French or German correctly, this presumptuous cosmopolitan, became the inventor of Austria. His strategic genius, consisting in the ability to move fast and concentrate all his forces at vital points, the brilliance of his feats of arms which liberated central Europe from the Turkish threat – these things brought him riches and renown. He wanted more: the adventurer, now become a statesman, sought to weld a heterogeneous monarchy into a significant whole and, having left the arena of war behind him, became a patron of the arts and sciences, a promoter of humanism. The young warrior had been very powerful, the ageing man, matured into a humanist, was shipwrecked on the power of the nobility and the court. The inventor of Austria left behind an incomplete structure whose development went hand in hand with decay.

Could Austria be reinvented?

On 13 February 1945 Budapest capitulated.

Hitler ordered that Vienna was to be held at all costs.

On 29 March the Russians crossed the Austrian border.

I was working at an essay on Georg Lukács in honour of his sixtieth birthday which fell on 13 April. It was through Joszef Revai that I got to know this significant man, a man whose powerful intellect was matched only by his lack of physical substance. It was as though his mind had constructed this tough and delicate frame with the utmost economy so that only the minimum worldly provision would have to be made for it, and all else could be requisitioned for thought. His existence is lived thought. 'You know, this is tremendously interesting!' are the words with which he often opens a conversation. After which he will be capable of embroidering a philosophical, political or literary theme for hours on end, with even greater vivacity, colour and brilliance than in his writing. He is one of the most significant Marxists of our age, and his character has great nobility. I revere him as a teacher, love him as a man, and quarrel with many of his aesthetic opinions. But this quarrel, which forms the essence of our relationship, only came later, with my increasing mistrust of all classical, doctrinaire aesthetics, with my gradual realization that an earlier period of art had grown outmoded, was come to an end, and that a new one was in process of taking over. In March 1945 I was still an unquestioning, not yet a refractory, pupil.

It was past midnight. I had just completed the draft of my notes on *History and Class-Consciousness*.

I was interrupted by the ringing of the telephone.

'Who's that speaking?'

'Are you ready to fly to Austria? We'll fetch you tomorrow morning at eight o'clock.'

On 10 April 1945 I was in Vienna.

Historical Note

At the turn of the century Vienna, the hub of a polyglot Empire, was intellectually one of the liveliest capitals in Europe. But politically the Habsburg Empire was crumbling. Split into two after its defeat by Prussia in 1866, it had become the 'imperial and royal' dual monarchy of Austria–Hungary.

In 1908 Austria–Hungary formally annexed the still nominally Turkish province of Bosnia. This stirred up Slav sentiment, already strong in the Balkans, Serbia's attitude being especially belligerent. The Serbs' hostility was more than reciprocated by the powerful anti-Serb faction in Vienna and when the Austrian heir-apparent was murdered by a Bosnian terrorist in 1914, the Serbian Government was accused of having instigated the crime. The resulting conflict was to lead to the 1914–18 War.

Halfway through that war Karl, the last Habsburg Emperor, acceded to the throne. He abdicated in 1918 after a bloodless revolution. Austria, defeated and a mere rump of her former self, with a population of only six-and-a-half million as compared with fifty million before the war, was now in desperate economic straits. Nevertheless, the achievements of the Social Democratic municipal government of Vienna in the field of social welfare, health and education during the difficult years that ensued were such as to receive world-wide acclaim.

The Government consisted of a coalition of the two major parties which had emerged earlier in the century – the Christian Socials, whose Catholic, anti-Semitic views found support among the more conservative elements of the population, and the Social Democrats with a large following of manual workers and intellectuals. Both these parties now saw a possible solution to their country's problems in an Anschluss with Germany, also then under Socialist rule. But the victorious Allies were not prepared to countenance such a move which would not only make Germany potentially more powerful than before, but open up the way to the Balkans and the Mediterranean. They therefore deemed it expedient to help Austria to her feet. To that end the League of Nations set up a committee, one of whose members was the Austrian Chancellor, Seipel.

Financial stabilization went hand in hand with growing political unrest which reached a climax on 15 July 1927, after some rightists had been wrongfully acquitted of murders committed during a clash with the left. But with the Wall Street crash the economic situation deteriorated. The Chancellor, Johannes Schober, a fanatical Pan-German, once again looked to Germany for a solution, and once again the Western powers intervened. A series of bank failures, culminating in the collapse of the Creditanstalt in 1931, brought the country to the brink of bankruptcy and gave added impetus to the world economic crisis which eventually helped to carry the Nazis to power in Germany.

Meanwhile both right and left had been mustering their forces in the shape of para-military organizations – the Heimwehr under the leadership of Prince Starhemberg, and the Republican Schutzbund under Julius Deutsch. Both had been greatly strengthened after the incidents of July 1927 and civil war loomed menacingly on the horizon. The leaders of the left, however, could not bring themselves to implement the decision, reached at the 1926 Linz Social Democratic Congress, to meet counter-revolutionary measures with force, while the right was split by dissension between Nazis and Clericals. The latter gained the upper hand in 1932 with the appointment of Dollfuss as Chancellor.

The new Chancellor incurred the odium of the Nazis, both Austrian and German, by accepting financial aid from the Western Powers on terms that precluded any closer rapprochement with Germany. At home he relied for support on the Heimwehr, abroad on Mussolini who encouraged him in his decision to crush the Socialists. In Parliament the Government had a majority of only one vote over the Opposition, consisting incongruously of Social Democrats and Pan-Germans (a term by now almost synonymous with Nazi). So unworkable was this state of affairs that, on 4 March 1933, Parliament suspended itself. At almost the same time Hitler came to power in Germany.

Meanwhile a wave of Nazi terrorism was unleashed in Austria which led the Government to close down Nazi 'Brown Houses' all over the country. Habicht, whom Hitler had appointed 'Inspector-General of Austria', and a number of other leading Nazis were arrested, and in June the Nazi Party was banned. On 11 September, at a public rally, Dollfuss announced the definitive 'death of Parliament' and nine days later he resigned, only to return to office invested with dictatorial powers. The year 1934 opened with increased Nazi violence and more stringent anti-Socialist measures.

Though the authorities were later to claim that they had saved the country from a left-wing revolution, the fighting that broke out on 12 February in fact marked the culmination of a carefully planned anti-Socialist campaign, and was sparked off by a deliberate act of provocation against the Schutzbund in Linz. Almost simultaneously large numbers of Schutzbund leaders were arrested in Vienna, thus completely disrupting that organization. Nevertheless, the Socialists put up so fierce a resistance that, to subdue them, the Government felt impelled to bring up armoured vehicles and artillery. Those Schutzbund leaders arrested before, during and after the fighting were for the most part kept under lock and key and handed over to the Nazis after the Anschluss in 1936. However, Julius Deutsch, commander-in-chief of the Schutzbund, and Dr Bauer, leader of the Social Democratic Party, both of whom had remained in Vienna to take part in the battle, succeeded in making their escape to Prague. But, undeterred by brutal repression, new leaders took the place of the old and continued the struggle underground.

Germany had been giving ever more blatant support to the Austrian Nazis whom, however, she disowned after the failure of their premature putsch in July 1934 when Dollfuss had been brutally murdered. Hitler's temporary withdrawal of support was also influenced by the fact that Mussolini, on learning of the attempted coup, had rushed troops to the Austrian border.

Fortified by the Italian dictator's gesture, the new Chancellor, Kurt von Schuschnigg, continued to pursue the anti-Socialist policy of his predecessors. He also sought to purge the Heimwehr of its more undesirable leaders, notably Prince Starhemberg and Major Fey. But unwittingly the Chancellor was knocking away his few remaining anti-Nazi supports, and he could not now count on Mussolini either. For the latter, having embroiled himself, first in his Abyssinian campaign, and then in the Spanish Civil War, could no longer afford to defend the cause of Austrian independence at the expense of his alliance with Hitler. The latter took advantage of this situation to force through an Austro-German agreement in July 1936 whereby Austria virtually surrendered her sovereignty, though this did not immediately become apparent. During the next eighteen months notorious Nazi sympathizers infiltrated the Austrian Government, while in France, Blum, and in Britain, Chamberlain, acceded to power, both of them equally determined to preserve 'peace at any price', even if that price was the hitherto so much dreaded Anschluss. In February 1938 Schuschnigg was summoned to Berchtesgaden where, almost literally at pistol-point, he was forced to make further humiliating concessions. In a final gesture of defiance on 9 March 1938 the Chancellor announced a plebiscite which was to give those over the age of twenty-four the opportunity to vote for a 'free and German, independent and social, Christian and united Austria'. Under Italo-German pressure the plebiscite was called off; nevertheless the Germans marched in on 12 March, the day it was to have been held. Schuschnigg was arrested and remained in detention until his release from Dachau by the Allies in 1945.

Almost a year to the day after the Anschluss the Germans – again with impunity – set up their 'Protectorate' in Czechoslovakia; within six months they had concluded a pact with that country's former ally, Soviet Russia, providing for the partition of Poland – who had herself so recently taken part in the dismemberment of Czechoslovakia. Ten days later, on 1 September 1939, the German invasion of Poland began, and by 3 September Britain and France were at war with Germany.

Peter and Betty Ross

Index

Works by Ernst Fischer appear under their titles. Other works appear under the name of the author.